WOMEN

Sex and Sexuality

WOMEN

Sex and Sexuality

Edited by Catharine R. Stimpson and Ethel Spector Person

The University of Chicago Press
Chicago and London

The essays in this volume appeared previously in the summer and autumn 1980 issues of *Signs: Journal of Women in Culture and Society* (volume 5, number 4, and volume 6, number 1).

The University of Chicago Press, Chicago 60637
The University of Chicago Press, Ltd., London

Library of Congress Cataloging in Publication Data
Main entry under title:

Women—sex and sexuality.

  Essays first published in Signs, journal of
women in culture and society, v. 5, no. 4, and v. 6, no. 1,
1980.
  Includes bibliographical references and index.
  1. Women—Sexual behavior—Addresses, essays,
lectures. 2. Femininity (Psychology)—Addresses,
essays, lectures. I. Stimpson, Catharine R.,
1936–   II. Person, Ethel Spector.
HQ29.W667   306.7'088042   80-51587
ISBN 0-226-77476-7
ISBN 0-226-77477-5 (pbk.)

Contents

REVIEWS OF CURRENT LITERATURE

Introduction

The rational scrutiny of human sexuality is a modern phenomenon and preoccupies members of many disciplines today. Often accompanying their studies is an anxiety that they, as sexual beings, might reveal an embarrassing naiveté or violate a hidden code, be it moral or physical. Investigations about female sexuality, in particular, have also suffered from the contrasting vices of garish sensationalism and rigid conventionality. Moreover, just as we have put behind us any consensus of what women ought to do, or be, so too have we lost any common concept of what female sexuality is and how it might express itself.

Obviously, the women's movement and, more ambiguously, the sexual liberation movement, have enhanced that expressiveness. A greater degree of freedom has provoked a complex, perhaps unanswerable, question: Is female sexuality like male sexuality, or does it obey laws of its own? Many researchers have an egalitarian bias that, shunning difference, prefers to see the sexualities as essentially identical. People so inclined have found support in the discovery of Masters and Johnson that female and male sexual response cycles are similar, even in such details as the timing of orgasmic contractions and in the evidence that androgen is the "libidinal" hormone in both sexes. Unfortunately, such a belief can be only apparently feminist. Too often, egalitarians masculinize the model of sexuality. They believe that male sexuality most accurately embodies a human sexuality that neither cultural nor psychological constraints have corrupted. They also tend to esteem a pure, an unfettered, sexuality as an invariant key to self-validation and autonomy.

We distrust any theory of female sexuality that burnishes it as the mirror image of the male, that universalizes it, or that reifies it. We suggest instead that sexuality is a biological process that both follows certain development patterns and that responds to the mediation of culture. Biology may set the outer boundaries of sexual possibility, but cultures work effectively within them. Paradoxically, a common consequence of cultural toil has been to reduce the female to her sexuality, her

1

active being to her flesh. No mere reflex arc, human sexuality, like the process of birth with which it is so entwined, is embedded with meaning. To understand female sexuality, then, is to explore the power of social constructions of reality and symbolic transformations of what seem to be matters of natural fact. Moreover, as feminists rightly warn us, sexuality cannot be assigned only to the domains of psychology and of our private lives. Public production and reproduction, social structures and sexuality, are linked as irrevocably as the brain and our five senses.

Since female sexuality exists within specific contexts, within matrices of the body and the world, no single perspective, no single discipline, can do intellectual justice to it. We have chosen to bring together a suggestively wide range of methodologies, frames of reference, and values to deal with this compelling, confounding question—with erotic desire and gratification, motherhood, the relationship of self-actualization and sexuality, the mutual transformations of sex into metaphor and metaphors into behavior. Our authors are American, but we want them to speak to other countries as well.[1] Our book begins with a forum that assesses the loss of significant paradigms and potential replacements for them. Alix Kates Shulman writes about the deconstructive and reconstructive impulses within the radical feminism of the late 1960s and early 1970s; Elizabeth Janeway about shifts in the ideological and metaphorical legacy that ascribed the characteristics of Eve, or Mary, to all women; and Ethel Spector Person about alternatives to instinct theory and about connections between sexuality and identity.

Adrienne Rich then treats the theory and practice of compulsory heterosexuality, which seeks to constrain women within one mold. Rosalind Petchesky analyzes the tensions between liberal and radical theories of reproductive freedom. Irene Diamond, discussing pornography, and Ann Snitow, novels written by women in the last decade, together contribute to our understanding of the contradictory cultural representations of sexuality and some of their political implications. Describing menstruation rituals among some American Indians, Marla N. Powers also offers a parable about Western misinterpretations of the interpretation of sexuality in cultures other than its own. Examining current books about prostitution, Judith R. Walkowitz warns us against other error: controlling female sexuality in the name of helping females.

1. The articles in this book were originally published in *Signs: Journal of Women in Culture and Society* (either in vol. 5, no. 4 [Summer 1980], or vol. 6, no. 1 [Autumn 1980]). The autumn issue also contains essays that have not been published in this book. They include: Luce Irigaray, "When Our Lips Speak Together," translated and introduced by Carolyn Burke; Kaveh Safa-Isfahani, "Female-centered World Views in Iranian Culture: Symbolic Representations of Sexuality in Dramatic Games"; Nancy Schrom Dye, "Review Essay: The History of Childbirth in America"; Allan Johnson, "On the Prevalence of Rape in the United States"; and Judith W. Leavitt, "Birthing and Anesthesia: The Debate over Twilight Sleep."

In a special Archives section, Martin Duberman edits a set of letters from a young working-class woman to a psychiatrist; and his notes on her case are included. Eli Zaretksy presents the response of a Polish priest to the women who talked to him in the seclusion of the confessional. The documents reveal some responses of powerful, male-dominated institutions—the established Catholic Church, and the growing profession of psychiatry—to female sexuality during the process of change and modernization during the early twentieth century. Finally, several essays survey literature about female sexuality in the social, natural, and medical sciences, and in contemporary mass culture. Succinctly, often skeptically, these review essays present some current thinking that we may, or may not, find acceptable.

We trust that this book will demonstrate the folly of an obsessive insistence upon one normative pattern of female sexuality, and the inadequacy of making simple-minded linkages between an atomistic sexual expressiveness and political autonomy. We believe that our real subject is not female sexuality but female sexualities. We hope, too, that this book will provide material for and provoke theories generous enough to encompass public and private behavior; spacious political structures and individual strength, action, and desire.

We are very grateful to Lilly Endowment, Inc. for a grant to *Signs Journal of Women in Culture and Society* that helped the University of Chicago Press publish the original journal issues.

Catharine R. Stimpson
Douglass College/Rutgers University
Founding Editor, *Signs: Journal of Women in Culture and Society*

Ethel Spector Person
Department of Psychiatry and
Columbia Psychoanalytic Center for Training and Research
Columbia University

Who Is Sylvia?
On the Loss of Sexual Paradigms

Elizabeth Janeway

When Thomas Kuhn, whose work on *The Structure of Scientific Revolutions* gave the word "paradigm" a new currency, was taken to task for employing the term ambiguously, he undertook to rethink its usage. In a postscript to a new edition of his book, he sorted out four major connotations of the term. They can serve equally well as guidelines to the present inquiry. To wit:

As an overall descriptive equivalent of "paradigm" Kuhn chose the phrase "a disciplinary matrix." One component he labeled "symbolic generalizations." These offer a basis for communication and shared judgment. To analogize, a society expects that in normal times sexual relations will follow some pattern or patterns which may differ individually but will fit comprehensibly into the accepted structure of behavior.

Kuhn's second component is a shared commitment to known beliefs which provide a source of "preferred or permissible analogies and metaphors. By doing so, they help to determine what will be accepted as an explanation" of the puzzles that the physical world sets the scientist. Emotional relationships are puzzling too. Privately, sexual paradigms allow an individual to explain to her- or himself the attitudes and conduct of the beloved. Publicly, they lay down the gender attributes which define masculinity and femininity.

Third on Kuhn's list are shared values. These assign weight and priority to the agreed-on beliefs that underlie scientific speculation and communication. We can extend this process of discrimination to ask how well sexual paradigms fit other standards of social behavior, or agree with the sort of identity structure that is reckoned to be normal in any particular context of life. Are they part of a relatively seamless web of cultural connections and directives, or do they force contradictions upon one's sense of self? Do they encourage active engagement with the world around, or are they binding and limiting?

Kuhn's fourth element in the disciplinary matrix brings us back to the adjective, for it is the paradigm as "exemplar." These he describes as "the concrete problem-solutions that students encounter from the start of their scientific education," practical illustrations of theory, such as "the inclined plane, the conical pendulum, and Keplerian orbits." Sexual paradigms are learned in part from the anonymous pressure of prescriptive social mythology, but of course they are also taught intentionally. Exemplars of good, proper behavior and the rewards that it brings, plus horrible examples of disastrous impropriety, have been rehearsed to more or less patient listeners from the time that time began. The very fact that so few exemplars of female sexuality are now dinned into the ears of young girls is clear proof that old paradigms are losing their vitality.[1] One more text from the gospel according to Kuhn. Paradigms fade when their usefulness diminishes. An obsolescent disciplinary matrix not only stops answering questions adequately, it also ceases to generate good new ones. Meanwhile, accumulated data that do not fit easily into old theoretical patterns pile up. These amorphous observations can be assimilated only with difficulty, forcing makeshift, patchwork additions to and emendations of orthodox theory, as if the scientific mind had fallen back to the primitive level of "bricolage," à la Lévi-Strauss.[2] Things fall apart, and if the center holds, it is only because of outside pressure. No longer does this disciplinary matrix find its purpose to be coping efficiently with everyday events in the world of reality. Paradigms cease to be recipes for managing processes and getting on comfortably with one's life. Instead they are preached as ideals to which a life should be dedicated.

Female sexuality, I think, has always been used by society as a sort of glue to hold structures together; we shall come to this. Attempts are still made to enlist its aid in preserving order within family and social relationships, but more and more they take on the air of desperate bricolage. The power of sexuality is being invoked in semimagical fashion, to support outworn paradigms that no longer explain and predict events in the world. The salt has lost its savor, the glue its glueyness.

So much for the word. It is time now to consider its use in the context of sexuality. What is it exactly that we are losing as our images of femaleness shift? What are the exemplars that our culture's definitions of women's sexuality have presented to the young? Western society has long offered two pictures of woman as sexual being. They are not simply contradictory; they have existed in a balanced polarity of good and bad, sacred and profane. In one the female symbolizes chastity; in the other she embodies insatiate, nymphomaniac greed: Pasiphaë, Lilith, woman as whore. In Christian legend, she is Eve the temptress, eternally confronting Mary, virgin and mother.

1. Thomas Kuhn, *The Structure of Scientific Revolutions,* 2d ed. (Chicago: University of Chicago Press, 1970), pp. 181–87, passim.
2. Ibid., pp. 82–83.

This bipolar split is in itself evidence of the external origin of our paradigms of female sexuality. There is no central core here, no kernel of feeling from which puzzled emotions could have diverged to become opponents in confrontation with each other. Eve and Mary are products of divided minds, but they are minds divided by masculine emotions at work in a male-dominated society. So, in Kuhn's terms, the shared beliefs and values expressed in our paradigms of female sexuality are not, in fact, shared fully by the women who have had to take them as models. They do not grow out of the interior emotional reality of the female self. Because they are learned as a means of surviving from the surrounding context of life (or have thus been learned in the past) and are also taught as exemplars, they are of course incorporated into the personality in varying degrees. But coming out of alien understanding as they do, they are never really satisfactory even when they seem to be accepted and absorbed quite thoroughly. This lack of "fit" is surely one source of the sense of "otherness" which Simone de Beauvoir elucidated a generation ago.

All this is well known. The new disciplinary matrix of feminist studies has begun to generate a shared critique of patriarchal thinking. "Otherness," in its social aspect, sets women apart from mainstream ideals and norms of behavior. Feminine goals are deviant even when they are prescribed by the social structure, for they always differ from the true peaks of aspiration, which are reserved for males. Males who forswear such ambitions are unmanly, that is, they act like women. Women who try to attain these normally desirable ends, however, exhibit unfitness for their proper role. It is thus impossible to be both a normal woman and a normal human being, surely a catch much older than "catch-22"—catch number one, perhaps.

Beyond its direct social stigmata, the impact of otherness is psychologically disorienting. Intuitive perceptions of the world cannot be trusted if they are made by an interior self which has learned that it is not considered primary. Its judgments always have to be adapted to those based on male experience. Female a priori knowledge, then, cannot be taken as valid by the female self who is required by the laws of otherness to live as a displaced person not only in man's world but also within herself. As a result, her primary impulses to action are always caught and held on a frustrating brink. Even if the delay is only momentary, the need to overcome it by an act of conscious will changes the quality of female activity by robbing it of the full, playful freedom of spontaneity.

We cannot evaluate the effect this hesitation has had on female sexuality until we have gotten rid of it. We must assume that the impact of otherness on women varies with the weight and extent of the patriarchal belief system in any society. No doubt where a fair area of free action falls within woman's place, the effect is less inhibiting. In Western society, however, we also have to consider the result of a polar split in our vision of female sexuality. Eve and Mary have presided over our existence, offering that meanest of options, an either/or choice. This adds an element of ambiguity to a female identity that already feels itself a bit untrustworthy. Eve is always at work to undermine Mary's dedication to good. Mary is never going to let Eve enjoy herself without waking up to a guilty morning after. The practical effect is to weaken still further the capacity of any woman to act in her own interest: she cannot be sure what her interest is. Eve cannot trust Mary, nor Mary Eve. A state of civil war becomes endemic.

The disciplinary matrix of feminist studies allows us to understand that this war is not a product of female being but of male psychology reacting to male experience of the world. The nineteenth century offers a fully developed exemplar from the great Victorian era of sadistic sentimentality. Having spawned its tens of thousands of prostitutes (Walter Houghton estimates 50,000 "known to the police" in England and Scotland in 1850),[3] the Victorian age simultaneously created a compensatory legend of "the angel in the house," whose dazzling purity was able to counter the lure of license in the dark streets. Love, married love, was exalted as a means of saving men from "the sensuality that threatens society." It was seen as "a great ethical force which can protect men from lust and even strengthen and purify the moral will."[4] The angel was a kind of moral muse, whose duty was to inspire male virtue. Were she to try to act independently, she would mistake her proper role.

We direct our attention today to the negative side of the paradigm, to the condemnation of freedom of action and choice which acting the part of moral muse laid on our foremothers. But we would be wrong to underestimate the positive attraction exerted by the angel in her own time, a time when the either/or choice between Eve and Mary was threatening and extreme. Mary was not only the guardian of a place supported by Victorian social values, she offered the only accepted role in which sexual activity could be undertaken by women at all. In addition, the legitimate outlet which the role offered to male sexuality could (it did not always) make her the object of devotion. Virginia Woolf remembered her own struggle to slay the angel, and well she might. Before her parents married, Leslie Stephen wrote to Julia Duckworth in true Victorian exaltation: "You must let me tell you that I do and always shall feel for you something which I can only call reverence as well as love. . . . You see, I have not got any saints and you must not be angry if I put you in the place where my saints ought to be."[5]

What is being romanticized—or rather sentimentalized—here is a male vision of the ideal mother. There is a mythic attraction to the

3. Walter Houghton, *The Victorian Frame of Mind, 1830–1870* (New Haven, Conn.: Yale University Press, 1957), p. 366.

4. Ibid., p. 375.

5. Noel Annan, *Leslie Stephen* (Cambridge, Mass.: Harvard University Press, 1952), p. 75.

figure. She is imagined as a moral force which works by inspiration, persuasion, charm, enchantment, but never by threat or force. Male fears of the powerful first parent, who later turns out to be female, are undergoing denial by sublimation. The angel in the house is exalted in order to give her sufficient power to order her children (including her husband, whose original identity was learned as a son) in the way they should go. Her duty is to socialize them to norms of affection and restraint, natural for daughters, difficult for sons, who require repeated "exemplars." It becomes an easier task, however, if some supernatural agent can be invoked. If one can just believe in magic, morality becomes easy, the superego is a source of pleasure, and we choose to do what we must do. It is a vulgarized, Bowdlerized version of Dante's vision: Mary, Queen of Heaven, ruling a happy family of six sisters and seven brothers, enshrined in a plush and mahogany parlor. She must stay there, however. The Mary half of the feminine image is invested with moral authority at the cost of giving up any active intervention in the world of events. The angel in the house must not leave the house unchaperoned.

Is Mary wife or mother? She is both; hence the oedipal conflict. The Victorian view of "wife"—and let us not imagine that it has vanished—is of a domesticated mother. The duty of the angel in the house is to accept and sublimate the male sex drive by transforming it into procreation. She allows her husband to fulfill God's commandment to be fruitful and multiply. She will then raise her children according to the norms of male society, and in the process her sons will acquire the double vision of women to which the angel owes her existence. They will experience the classic fears invoked by the myth Freud formulated in the name of Oedipus, whose purpose is the structuring of the psyche into id, ego, and the internalized social-parental deterrent of superego. Meanwhile her husband, also once a son, has the opportunity to assuage his own early fears by the control, in maturity, of a tamed mother-figure. If she can be contained within a mythic structure, playing out her family role of inspiration and muse but forced to limit her power to this sphere, his primal struggle and its accompanying guilt can be resolved where it began. Mother and wife are aspects of the same image of female sexuality. If they compete with each other in real life, it is for the same position of moral authority: the role of saint for those who have no saints but still feel the need for a domestic shrine.

The real opponent to Mary the pure mother figure is Eve. While Mary's ascendance both derives from and is limited by her long investment with moral authority, Eve's power arises in the invitation she offers to unlimited sexuality, that is, immoral authority. For Eve is a goddess too. Her representatives, the whores in the street, can be bought and the serving girl debauched. They yield to male demands and vanish. But Eve symbolizes the temptation to which men yield in seeking them out. In this aspect she is very clearly a projection of male desire. That is why she is dangerous to men, why she can gain the upper hand, catch True Thomas within the fairy ring and transport him to Elfland. She is a dream figure who commands the power of "primary process" feeling because she comes out of the internal realm where it rises. Her power can subvert society, and the superego too, for it is rooted in the unacceptable yearnings which antedate the oedipal drama lived out by children being socialized to patriarchy. To stay for a moment longer with the Victorian confrontation, turning away from the angel in the house and giving oneself to Eve invited damnation even for those who had no saints, damnation via a choice of intemperate pleasure over the challenges of achievement and position in social life.

During the deep Christian centuries it meant damnation in a more vivid sense, and so Eve's lure had to be offset and the perils of yielding to her spelled out by underlining the dangers inherent in female sexuality. Eve the temptress was pictured not only as impure but as filthy. Her needs were declared to be excessive and disgusting, thus sparing the pride of any man who might not be able to satisfy her flesh-and-blood surrogate. Beware of her! say the legends, and not only the legends. Henry Kraus, in *The Living Theatre of Medieval Art,* describes a sculptured relief over the door of a monk's cell in the Chartreuse-du-Val-de-Benediction near Avignon, "a warning against woman's bestiality, meant to rally the monk's resistance at faltering moments. . . . The subject . . . is wild and obscene, representing a recumbent woman in a scabrous position with a goat. 'The old hag is letting the goat do to her,' the concierge commented disgustedly."[6] And when Lady Alice Kyteler was tried for heresy in 1324 at Kilkenny in Ireland, the accusations included copulation with her private demon named Robin who "appeared sometimes in the guise of a cat, sometimes of a shaggy black dog, and sometimes in the guise of a Negro." Robin was, he said, one of the "poorer demons in Hell," but his influence persuaded Lady Alice and her friends to anathematize their husbands, or so said the charge. Copulation with demons (and Robin once appeared in triplicate as three Negroes "bearing iron rods in their hands")[7] thus carries the message that female sexuality stamps women as being not just out of control but inhuman in their desires, more demanding, less fastidious than men. It is not only rape that they really want, but rape by goats and cats and shaggy black dogs and three men carrying iron rods.

All these masculine visions of female sexuality, embodied in the paradigms we know, are attempts to manipulate woman's vision of herself. Historically the purpose has held firm while the image has been touched up to conform to contemporary reality. When the power of the

6. Henry Kraus, *The Living Theatre of Medieval Art* (Bloomington: Indiana University Press, 1967), p. 41.

7. Norman Cohn, *Europe's Inner Demons* (New York: Basic Books, 1975), pp. 199–200.

Church was great, as in these instances from earlier stages of our culture, chastity was enforced by relating it to the sacred authority of the Mother of God, while the unchaste were condemned for consorting with demons. Protestant, bourgeois Victorian England found Mary a niche in the parlor as the angel in the house. At the same time a new element was added. The dogma of women's excessive sexuality began to give way to a quite opposite view: women were, on the contrary, passionless, "less carnal and lustful than men." Nancy F. Cott's analysis of this reversal, in a recent issue of *Signs,* ties it to "the rise of evangelical religion between the 1790s and the 1830s." As women became a majority in the Protestant churches, and as the bourgeois revolution proceeded, moral authority was increasingly assigned to women. But this superiority needed a rationale. It was found in a conviction that the female sex was by nature modest and virtuous. "Passionlessness was on the other side of the coin which paid, so to speak, for women's admission to moral equality."[8]

Cott's views are convincing. The glueyness of women, it would seem, is being called on to promote order in society as an age of change begins. I suspect that the concept of female passionlessness found further support in the Victorian fascination with new, and frequently pseudo, scientific theories. Now the old idea of female chastity can be connected to physiology, and any deviation be declared not just immoral but abnormal. We see here how a shift in the rationale of a continuing social mythology enlists a novel causality as a means for sustaining a desired behavior pattern. As the threat of scientific challenge clouded simple religious belief, chastity acquired an up-to-date reason for being. So two centuries ago the Protestant churches, shaken by the Great Awakening, found female chastity and morality to be a valuable resource in their work. A century ago, it was still important enough to be shored up by some clever pseudoscientific bricolage.

Why, then, is that not the case today? We seem to be looking at a major change in the structure of our shared beliefs. How has this come about? The question lies at the heart of our current paradigm shift in female sexuality. Let me say at once that I do not believe it can be answered solely on psychological grounds. It is due, rather, to a remarkable alteration in the dynamics of our society. The male fears that produced our images of female sexual being cannot be dismissed or glossed over, but the male experience of life which shaped those fears has somehow been changed. Chastity in women is no longer important to individual men because it no longer serves a necessary social function. Either that function has ceased to be necessary, or it can be serviced by other means. We are not wrong to say that definitions of women's proper behavior are the product of masculine psychology, but we must add that

8. Nancy F. Cott, "Passionlessness," *Signs: Journal of Women in Culture and Society* 4, no. 2 (Winter 1978): 227–28.

male ideas come out of lived experience in the real world of events, even though they are shaped by mythic desires.

   Historically speaking, the function of chastity, once great, has now declined sharply. Let us consider the glueyness of women, which in fact antedates history. The exchange of women among groups and individuals, wrote Lévi-Strauss, establishes basic kinship systems, which are elementary social structures. "Kinship systems, marriage rules, and descent groups constitute a coordinated whole, the function of which is to insure the permanence of the social group by means of intertwining consanguineous and affinal ties. They may be considered as the blueprint of a machine which 'pumps' women out of their consanguineous families to redistribute them in affinal groups, the result of this process being to create new consanguineous groups, and so on."[9] The matter of chastity enters the picture obliquely. Obviously the children of one woman form a kinship group whether they have the same father or not, and matrilineal descent is a feature of many social systems. Chastity became important only when society began to worry about legitimate male descent. That concern appears to be linked to the ownership of individual property, as Engels remarked a century ago; or, more specifically, to the inheritance of property or status, or rights to both, by children of one father, as opposed to clan or extended-family rights in the use of territory and prerogatives. The peaceful passage of inheritable property from father to son, from brother to brother, from uncle to nephew, demanded that the legitimacy of the heir be accepted within the social unit; and the chastity of the wife-mother thus became a prerequisite to maintenance of social order in a patrilineal descent system.

   All this sounds very ancient and prehistorical. In fact, shifts in inheritance customs were taking place in Western Europe at the time that our own society was being formed, and their effects are easily traced. True, inheritance customs play something of the same role for medieval historians that kinship systems do for anthropologists, and the lay person had better walk warily among questions of partible versus impartible inheritance, precipit, the joining of conjugal property, and the like, just as with cross-cousin marriage and its rules. But certain general observations can be made. The exchange of women in order to form new families is now explicitly linked to the passage of property no matter what rules may guide the division or validate the entitlement to property. David Sabean, discussing "the ways in which households regulate their holding of property and the passing of property to the next generation" in rural Western Europe in late medieval and early modern times, begins just as did Lévi-Strauss with the need "to insure the permanence of the social group by means of intertwining consanguineous and affinal ties." It is now inheritance of property which conveys permanence. "In

9. Claude Lévi-Strauss, *Structural Anthropology* (New York: Basic Books, 1963).

this context (i.e., inheritance) establishing a new household is itself a fundamental aspect of the process. In passing wealth on to the next generation the parents ensure continuity of social arrangements and provide for their old age. Passing wealth on to the next generation must always be seen in the light of setting up new households or the establishing of new conjugal funds."[10]

Legitimate descent was particularly vital in the case of land. Goods and chattels, like the second-best bed that Shakespeare left to his daughter, could be and were disposed of by will, at will; but the pattern of land inheritance was controlled by custom. Customs did indeed differ, and under the manorial system, minor variations could be sanctioned on payment of a fee to the lord in return for his consent.[11] But, though traditions could be modified to meet particular circumstances, they were the norms. They assumed—indeed, they validated—the existence of the legitimate heirs, whose peaceful right to take over property was unlikely to be challenged.

In addition, a good deal of property tended to be passed from older to younger generations while one or both parents were still living. Elders would hand over active operation and management of family land to an heir, who would in return (by custom and/or agreement) provide the former possessors with a living. Parents thus had a continuing stake in the legitimacy of the passage of property. Reinforcing their concern was that of the lord of the manor, who desired continuity of tenure and service among those who worked his land.

I bring in these mundane matters to illustrate the grounding in daily living of the patterns of female sexuality which Western society recognized and prescribed. Masculine psychology certainly elaborated and fantasized these patterns, and women's lives were indeed distorted by them. But the statics of social structure and the dynamics of social change both come out of customary reality. That is what we expect to put up with whether we like it or not. But when the old customs shift a bit, some of those who have been disadvantaged will try to improve their lot, seizing on opportunities offered by such changes. How far they can get depends on an underpinning of support in the world of events, and perceptions of that support can be slow in coming and, indeed, resisted. Socially speaking, accepted inheritance patterns are desirable precisely because they are accepted and do not demand time, money, and energy to enforce them. Shared beliefs and values will tend to keep them in place, for once a paradigm of governance has been established, it will not be changed by psychological divagations alone. Changes in paradigms

10. David Sabean, "Aspects of Kinship Behavior and Property in Rural Western Europe before 1800," in *Family and Inheritance,* ed. Jack Goody, Joan Thirsk, and E. P. Thompson (Cambridge: Cambridge University Press, 1976), p. 103.
11. Eleanor Searle, "Merchet in Medieval England," *Past and Present* 82 (February 1979): 3–43, see esp. p. 7.

become necessary, says Thomas Kuhn, only when existing rules fail to operate, when anomalies can no longer be evaded, when the real world of everyday experience challenges accepted causality.

The accepted causality enshrined in the customs which directed patterns of inheritance began to be challenged in medieval England by the extension of royal power. The king's law, his courts and their rulings, impinged on daily life and the "custom of the manor," and in so doing they offered an alternate system of causality. Some of the disadvantaged at once rushed to seize on these new opportunities. Among them were younger brothers, denied equal inheritance with the firstborn, who applied for writs of bastardy claiming that their elder siblings had been born or conceived prior to the rite of marriage.

These challenges clearly cast doubt on the chastity of the mother, but noninheriting younger sons seemed unconcerned about morality as long as a writ of bastardy against an older brother gave them title to the land in question. In the event, female purity was regarded as just a fulcrum on which the passage of property turned. Chastity, it appears, ties into the economic substratum of daily life by way of inheritance patterns. It is the glueyness of women, linking generations in the interest of the peaceful passage of property, that matters more than their morals or than filial respect. Lady Alice Kyteler did not face a charge of heresy because of spiritual outrage. Her stepsons and daughters objected to the disposition she made of the property that came to her from their several fathers, for, not content with demons, dogs, and Negroes, Lady Alice had married (and survived) four husbands.[12]

Our sexual paradigms were shaped by the daily existence of our ancestors as that experience filtered through the belief structure of the male power elite. But existence changes, and as it does, beliefs adjust themselves to what is becoming customary. In Western society, property can still be inherited. What has changed is the *importance* of inheriting it. Customary reality, in medieval Europe, did not include a cash economy. Today most of us can sell our labor for enough cash to keep ourselves in reasonable comfort; in the normal course of events, we live on the wages and salaries we earn, independent of inherited wealth and therefore indifferent to it. It is true that this normal course does not apply to everyone in our society. The fact of a self-perpetuating class of disadvantaged poor, an internal Third World, still shames us. But the existence and extent of such a class in the past was exactly the "normal course of events" that forced our ancestors to clutch so frantically at any chance to inherit the goods of this world. The landless and the rootless were a majority and likely to remain in that position, as were their children after them. In such a world the question of who had a legitimate right to inherit a claim on ownership worked out as meaning, who can

12. Cohn, p. 200.

expect to live with some barrier against the worst of hunger, disease, drudgery, and disaster? It was not only property that was inherited, it was the circumstances of life and, quite possibly, life itself.

Even when external disaster broke up inheritance patterns and offered a chance for the redistribution of land, few of the rootless were able to profit from the opportunity. Cicely Howell has undertaken a study of landholding in one English village, Kibworth Harcourt, over a stretch of four centuries, using court rolls and periodic lists of rentals. There was, she writes, a "remarkable continuity of tenure between 1280 [her starting point] and ... 1340; everyone of the 1280 surnames is featured on the 1340 rental without exception." Only five new names were added over sixty years. Even this modest increase was remarkable for, Howell notes, "in other parts of England village populations were already in decline." Then in 1348–49 came the Black Death. Out of fifty-odd names on the rental rolls, forty-four died. And yet by the end of 1349, 80 percent of these holdings had passed within the accepted pattern to sons or brothers or nephews. It took another sixty years, during which the plague returned every decade or so, to bring about real changes, and the end result was not to broaden tenure but to narrow it. Smaller households each held more land. It would seem that the rich got richer, whatever happened to the poor.[13]

My point is this: the chastity of women is an ideal enforced, not simply by a patriarchal social structure, but also by a society in which legitimate inheritance of property is a matter of enormous economic importance. It is the latter factor whose significance has waned. Patriarchy is still with us, but the economic function of chastity is vanishing. A century ago, the linkage between financial comfort and inherited property was still strong enough to ensure that the paradigm of female sexual purity was kept in being as a guarantee that legitimate heirs would not find their claims disputed. When fifty years ago Virginia Woolf declared that, for independence, a woman needed an income of £500 a year on which to get on with her life and her work, she could not imagine that such a sum could be routinely earned in the marketplace, and posited an inheritance from an aunt. Only in the recent past has earning capacity, even for women, risen to make wages or salary the chief component of income. Adding to the lessened significance of property, inheritance taxes have joined in from the other side to whittle away the value of family holdings. With it has gone a major reason for the emphasis our forefathers placed on the chastity of our foremothers. Thus a deepening shadow of unconcern has fallen across the image of Mary, for the female virtue that she symbolizes, the purity which guaranteed peaceful passage of male-held property from one generation to the next, has become of

---

13. Cicely Howell, "Peasant Inheritance Customs in the Midlands, 1280–1700," in Goody et al., eds., p. 123.

small account in our lives—so small, in fact, that curiously little resentment accompanies the loss of what was once a potent and influential paradigm.

That would seem to offer women much greater freedom to imagine a new paradigm, out of authentic female experience. I believe that such opportunities exist; but in working toward them, we have to take into account not only the fading ideal of the angel in the house, but also the opposing image of Eve the temptress, insatiable, multiorgasmed, bound to no continuing relationships, at large in the male psyche as a threatening mythic figure, uncontrolled and inviting the loss of self-control and of command. Eve is still with us. Tricked out in polyester, her doll-sized simulacrum presents herself as the *Cosmopolitan* girl. Other diminished versions appear in popular novels, movies, and of course on television, Charlie's fallen angels. It would be pleasant to think that these superficial puppets could operate as a kind of killed vaccine which would immunize patriarchal society against the mythic terror of Eve and the revenge it invites, but I am afraid that is overly optimistic. Since Eve is the projection of masculine emotions onto the outside world, her influence is not easily affected. She is a figure of patriarchal myth, and only a drastic change in the world, comparable to that which dethroned her polar counterpart, can serve to keep a superficial image from growing into a dream ogress. Eve existed and endured in a balance with Mary, who limited her power. Now the balance has ended. Between Mary and Eve there was a polarity. Within Eve, there can exist only unresolved ambiguity, dread and desire in the same figure.

She is also more private, more emotional, and closer to the inner world of fantasy. Mary, pure mother and wife, served a significant social function, pumped out of her consanguineous group to form affinal ties with the family into which she was married. Her presence was public, legal, and an essential part of a system of kinship and governance. Eve, on the other hand, is subversive and disruptive to social man. She represents passion and forgetfulness of duty, place, and public obligation. She is the body, she is physical nature, she is the darkness where the proudly erect penis satisfies uncontrollable desire and collapses, "spent," in the vivid Victorian word. She is the fatal woman, and her legend is still alive, carried over from the Christian centuries with little change of feeling tone. It was she who seduced Adam, from whose body she had been taken, and so set in motion primal sin and the fall of man, with which it was punished. Not until Mary's son was sent to offer the hope of salvation could Eve's act be redressed.

These teachings shaped the sacred myths in which our western culture took form. As the Mary myth dims, the Eve figure loses the opposing force from which were derived the social limits that controlled her attraction and her menace. What does this shift in the weight of our paradigms of sexuality mean for women? Is it good news or bad? Certainly Eve represents freedom, an explicit denial of the shackling lessons of chastity which forced us to reject the reality of our own feelings. Eve is undomesticated; the doll figures of the media are just attempts to draw a tamed version. She invites us to enjoy our own pleasure. Freedom, delight, wildness, a dionysian testing of edge experience—all this is alluring to those who were not permitted them in the past. With that attraction goes justified anger against a society that denied us autonomy and action. Women feel that change is "right," both personally and politically. We want to stretch ourselves to extremes, and we deeply want to overthrow the social structure and challenge the social myth which bound us to positions defined and enforced by others, for others. For us Eve stands not just as a trickster, but as a heroine too, challenging the gods and disrupting propriety and social controls. Where Mary embodied the superego, Eve represents the force of id.

But that is not all the news there is. We must also take account, first of masculine myth and the weight it carries, and second of the fact that woman does not live by id alone. Instinctive revolt will not do away with patriarchy or create a human society based on other values. The strength of the Eve figure, in the world as it is, still carries its legendary meaning. In that legend, Eve introduced Adam to sexual pleasure, but in the course of doing so she made a fool of him and then brought down on his head the wrath of a righteous God. To the extent that the legend still persists in male imaginings, Eve stands as the source of trouble and the root of desire, and therefore as a cause of guilt. Should she not be punished for provoking sin and muddle-headedness and pain and humiliating need? And the pleasure she offers, is it not unlimited, and therefore excessive, and therefore dangerous? Can a man satisfy her? Somewhere on the edge of that last speculation lurks Robin the demon, a shaggy black dog, and three Negroes bearing iron rods. And for this too should she not be punished? For the fury and fear she provokes? In patriarchal myth Eve the temptress is guilty of inviting the very pornographic violence and sadism that punishes her, of forcing men to yield to the filth of their emotions. A patriarchal social system cannot accept her without seeking to offset the threat that she represents, a threat of dissolution, anarchy, and antisocial disorder. If Mary cannot balance her, more direct means will be sought.

Beyond this, and more important to women's own inner reality, is the fact that Eve is not our own creation. We find license for pleasure within this paradigm, but that cannot disguise the clear evidence that *our* pleasure is not primary there. In the Eve image of female sexuality there is no true sense of internal experience, no vision of a female self choosing, enjoying, directing, and controlling her own pleasure. Eve's sexuality is not related to other female interests and activities, it is not part of a complex individuality, it is most immediately the door to a loss of self, not by transcendence, but by the destruction of coherence. Eve does not serve women, but patriarchy. The media representations of her image do not show us woman as sexual being, but as sexual object. They are intended to teach us how to behave in a "sexy" new way not because that will be liberating or rewarding, or even just fun, but because with Mary gone, men are now free to forget about chastity.

Such a vulgar distortion of women's potential for joyous and free interaction in sex can be seen as another patchwork emendation of the old paradigms. It reverses the attribution of "passionlessness" with the same purpose in mind. Sexual activity is being offered as an up-to-date opiate of the female masses. It is designed to buttress old patterns of male dominance: somewhere in the background of the *Cosmopolitan* girl there exists job continuity, at times elevated to the status of career. But her real status derives from her ability to attract males even though she must combine this with work for pay (the most important males, of course, being those who buy advertising space). A tamed Eve pleases men, a wild one frightens them, but in neither aspect does she serve the needs of women. The message she conveys is, Keep your sexual needs and pleasure at modest levels, where they will flatter your male partners. Passionate or passionless, you are still an object. Become something more and mythic terrors will rise like smoke around you.

This is not only divisive to a felt identity, it is extremely isolating. The Eve figure can never stand level with Adam. In her wild condition she is his nemesis; tamed she becomes a convenience. Needless to say, many heterosexual relationships grow past this dilemma into true human sharing. But to achieve that, the paradigm must be first denied and then overcome, and that is a barrier, even if it is one that affectionate intimacy breaks down in daily life. In addition, Eve presides over a world in which sexual coupling between male and female stands as an isolated peak of pleasure; and affection is not a normal, expected accompaniment of intimacy, but something to be won. That not only devalues female/female relationships, it also devalues any bonds of warmth and affection that are not specifically sexual. The effect is to assign primary significance to a relationship in which a male is necessarily present and which he can control.

In the past, kin connections, local friendships, and shared experience of place and labor were usually a large part of the human environment in which people lived. Urbanization, geographic mobility, and job shifts now combine to make such connections matter for conscious effort. They do not happen by themselves. The female self is thus placed in a more precarious position than in earlier times. This is, of course, part of the decreasing glueyness of women represented by the Mary role, whose chastity legitimized male descent lines; Mary's diminuendo is a psychological reflection of the loosening of social ties. The freedom we gain is accompanied by the loss of social support, and if we want the first we must prepare to cope with the second. Freedom to invent new roles does not just allow innovation, it demands it. The failure of old paradigms forces the search for the creation of new ones.

How are we to do that? As yet no specific answers are possible. We have not had time to live as free people in shared authenticity, though beginnings are being made. But we shall need time, not just to experiment, but in which experience can accumulate and form the basis for judgment so that we shall be able to assess the value of our experiments. There is a process here that must be lived out—judgment of emotional values, the transfer of these values to the human environment, the growth of new sorts of connections which will inevitably affect the grounding of the self and bring about changed relationships developed among changed selves, with other human beings of various ages and sexes and conditions of life. Sexual connections are never only personal. They are always shaped and used by other social imperatives at the same time that they influence the form these imperatives take. The freedom we now feel for the creation of new paradigms of female sexuality is not total freedom. If it were great enough to allow us complete control over sexual relations, we should simply be inventing anew the kind of dominance that has crippled human beings of both sexes during the long reign of patriarchy.

In such circumstances the old paradigms can be used best as guidelines to what we do not want to do. We do not want to remake a Mary figure that has simply been updated to suit current male mythology. We do not want to reglue ourselves into a social structure that is still patriarchal. We do not want to accept the mothering function as central to our true identity, and we should certainly be wary of the attempts now being made to make us chief, if not sole, child raisers, attempts which in the fifties enjoyed a relative success. Mary was revived as nurse instead of legitimizer, with poor results all around, for the important task of raising the next generation is a social duty that cannot possibly be carried by one adult alone. Nor do we want to agree to current efforts to frighten us back into the domesticated version of the Mary role as supportive wife or live-in partner. The proliferation of novels and films featuring deserted husbands, aghast at having to manage personal lives, stunned with self-pity, has this as an end. We certainly do not want to find ourselves split in two between polar roles. Nor do we want to succumb to the lure of patriarchal myth which appears to honor female being but does no more than set up mirrors for projected images of male desires. The myth of matriarchy, in which female authority replaces male, is simply the flip side of one-sex dominance, and it is attractive in bad times to a male power elite that faces problems it cannot solve by its own old paradigms. The re-creation of mother goddesses would condemn us to a continuing displacement of self in favor of some version of the Mary role. And, while the freedom and daring that are part of the Eve image are surely needed in a new paradigm, in Eve they are pushed past intensity to excess.

We are indeed in a situation that differs from the realm of science where Kuhn's analysis of revolutionary process took place. His investigation is useful as regards the past, but he assumes that new paradigms will have begun to take shape as old ones lose their ability to explain relevant problems and suggest means for testing them. Independent scientists have a longer history than free women, it seems. We are not in a position where we have been able to imagine new structures of belief and behavior. We have to invent not only new paradigms but new selves, selves capable of working out the significant generalizations that will make our existence coherent and structure our purposes. It is not my task to consider the creation of new paradigms of female sexuality. But as the Mary image fades, like the smile of the Cheshire cat, it is clear that her loss can influence our vision of the future. The patriarchal grounding of the Eve figure marks her as dangerous, even though she can offer valuable strains of daring, of freedom, and of enjoyment; but she is insufficient for our needs. And yet we would do ourselves great harm if we were to try to cure this insufficiency by dreaming up a replacement for Mary. Any polarity is dangerous to creative thought. Thesis and antithesis claim to sum up the world and resolve our puzzles by merging into a synthesis, but what, we should ask, has got left out because it did not figure in either thesis or antithesis?

We do not know; or rather, we know some elements but surely not all, and we cannot yet be sure of relating them properly (functionally) to each other or even of weighing their importance sensibly. We need a period for self-analysis without pressure. That is rather unlikely, but we must try for it. It will take time to reach the deep layers of repressed and denied mind and feeling, and the shadow of ages of patriarchy still influences our perceptions and our standards. What we could use best would be a time for experiment and play in which alternatives could be tried out in a spirit of lighthearted joy and in which elements from other cultural traditions, newly available, would have a place. Unfortunately the emphasis that our male-oriented society places on sex as achievement or feat is not conducive to an atmosphere of affectionate play. It is easy enough to register a vote for alternatives and options, but not at all easy to assume that we shall have time and space to weigh and judge the value of these alternatives without being frozen into some of them before they have been sufficiently explored.

Let me say tentatively that I think our best chance of finding our way toward new paradigms of female sexuality would be to widen the range of personal connection, from which we draw the values we use in assessing interpersonal relations, beyond the strictly and narrowly sexual. For women, heterosexual coupling has been held to outweigh any other affection by far; even mother-child love has been seen darkly as crippling to children while it is still offered women as a valuable reward. Male friendship is taken seriously, that between women is regarded either as trivial or as abnormal by our social definitions; antilesbianism is certainly the popular anti-Semitism of our day. But taking lesbianism to be an instant cure for male sexual dominance seems to me dangerously reactive and therefore superficial. Can woman-to-woman affection be free, as yet, of the distortions forced on us by patriarchy? So much combat and contest has gone on in our experience of sex, and so much pain has resulted from it; so much denigration of women has been absorbed into our sense of ourselves, and yet so many of us, over time, have been able to approach reciprocal affectionate valuation with men; none of this experience can be ignored or denied or solved in one equation. Merely to reverse our old paradigms leaves us still bound to them.

The "casual" sex of today is much deplored, but it seems to be that if we could be *truly* casual about it—enjoying self and other, noting trauma, rejecting it, and choosing pleasure—we might be on the road to getting over both the binding chastity of Mary and the excesses of Eve. Then the female self, the ego-person who has never figured in past paradigms, might be able to find her way to a valid sexuality that would grow from herself and her own needs and urges.

What will she be like, this uncreated demiurge with "eyes at the back of [her] head," this diver into the wreck, this sleeping fury, this "Psyche, the butterfly out of the cocoon . . . whose attention is undivided . . . [whose] book is our book; written or unwritten"? Our poets are feeling and thinking ahead for us, but a new Eve will have to be tested in reality. Her myth will grow out of dailyness, finding there both the common experience and the deep significance which will shape itself into symbolic generalizations that express shared beliefs and values. Who is Sylvia, whose name carries an edge of wildness and a hint of unexplored memory? We do not know, but we will surely recognize her when she comes.

New York City

Sex and Power: Sexual Bases of Radical Feminism

Alix Kates Shulman

I

Thirteen years have passed since a handful of radical feminists began organizing for women's liberation and analyzing every aspect of the relations between the sexes, including the sexual. Not that the subject of women's sexuality was ignored before then. Sex had long been a "hot," salable subject. Men were studying it in laboratories, in books, in bedrooms, in offices; after several repressive decades, changes called the "sexual revolution" and "sexual liberation" were being widely discussed and promoted all through the sixties; skirts were up, prudery was down. Nor was the sudden feminist attention to the political aspects of sexuality in the late sixties without precedent, as it appeared at the time; for feminists have always understood that institutions regulating relations between the sexes were their concern.[1] But by the 1960s feminism itself had long been in eclipse, and, far from being viewed as a political relation, sex was considered a strictly biological, psychological, personal, or religious matter. Until the radical feminists boldly declared that "the personal is political," opening for political analysis the most intimate aspects of male-female relations, women's sexuality had not for decades been viewed squarely in its political dimension as an aspect of the power relations between the sexes.

In the nineteenth and early twentieth centuries, such sex-related institutions as family, motherhood, chastity, prostitution, birth control, and the double standard of morality had been subjected to feminist

1. Linda Gordon traces the development of feminist ideas about sexuality in the United States, especially as they pertain to birth control, in her important book, *Woman's Body, Woman's Right: A Social History of Birth Control* in America (New York: Penguin Books, 1977).

analysis by the "first wave" of feminists. Sexual repression had been privately acknowledged as a primary problem by the older Elizabeth Cady Stanton when she wrote in her confidential diary, begun at the age of sixty-five, "The first great work to be accomplished for woman is to revolutionize the dogma that sex is a crime."[2] But the suffragists and women's rights advocates mostly shied away from publicly discussing women's sexuality. Though first-wave feminists did focus on the connection between the subjugation of women and *male* sexuality,[3] for the most part they did not make women's sexuality central to their analysis of woman's social condition, except as it affected other institutions, like motherhood.[4]

It was Simone de Beauvoir who reopened the subject of sex and power to feminist analysis in 1949 with the publication of *The Second Sex* in France. A year earlier, Ruth Herschberger, biologist and poet, had published the witty feminist analysis of female sexuality, *Adam's Rib*, in this country; but her ideas seemed too eccentric to postwar America to gain the audience they deserved.[5] A larger feminist context was needed—like that provided in Europe by Beauvoir's work and in this country by Betty Friedan's 1963 *The Feminine Mystique*, which signaled a second round of organized feminism.[6] In her book, Friedan discussed the use of sexual exploitation in advertising, the effect of sex roles on sexual fulfillment, and women's sexual discontents; but NOW, the organization Friedan founded to fight sex discrimination, did not at first concentrate on exposing injustice in the sexual sphere; indeed, that organization's early homophobia may even have exacerbated it. It remained for the radical wing of the new feminism—those mostly young women of the New Left whose discontent with their subordination by male radicals led them in the late sixties to form the women's liberation movement (WLM to the FBI)—to make sexuality a central part of their

2. Miriam Schneir, ed., *Feminism: The Essential Historical Writings* (New York: Random House, 1972), p. 145.

3. In her chapter, "Social Purity," Linda Gordon shows that "feminists believed that men had developed excessive sexual drives which contributed to the subjection of women and hence limited the development of the whole civilization. From this they drew the inference that excessive sex drive had to be *eliminated,* not merely checked or sublimated, in order to create a pure and sexually equal society" (pp. 118–19).

4. Outstanding among exceptions were the free-love advocates, notably the notorious Claflin sisters, Victoria Woodhull and Tennessee Claflin, who wrote frequently on the connection between sexuality and oppression in their publication of the 1870s, *Woodhull and Claflin's Weekly.* Dora Marsdon is quoted by Elaine Showalter in *A Literature of Their Own* (Princeton, N.J.: Princeton University Press, 1977) as proposing in 1913 that frigidity is the result of repression and economic dependence. The anarchist Emma Goldman spoke on injury to woman's sexuality resulting from male domination and publicly defended homosexual rights in the first decades of this century [see Alix Kates Shulman, ed., *Red Emma Speaks* [New York: Random House, 1972]).

5. Ruth Herschberger, *Adam's Rib* (New York: Peligrini & Cudahy, 1948).

6. Betty Friedan, *The Feminine Mystique* (New York: W. W. Norton & Co., 1963).

analysis of sexism. Applying the tools of analysis and organization they learned in the civil rights movement and the New Left to their own situation, and drawing on the works of both Beauvoir and Friedan (as they would later draw on their earlier feminist predecessors), they used their sexual discontents to help them understand the power relations between men and women.[7]

By late 1967 small groups of women were meeting regularly to discuss the effects of male supremecy not only on women's professions, education, and public life, as the women in NOW were doing, but on their "private" lives as well. I was a fortunate participant. Those early discussions (which soon evolved into the technique called consciousness raising, later abbreviated CR) produced a great emotional outpouring of feelings against the way women had been used sexually and revelations of sexual shames and terrors we had all lugged through our lives. I was surprised to hear so many women who had come of age in the sixties talk resentfully about their sexual experience, for I had believed the media version of the great sexual revolution among the young. But far from having felt freed by the so-called sexual revolution of the sixties, those young, dedicated women—many of whom had been politicized in the New Left—actually felt victimized by it. They complained that they were expected not only to type the speeches, stuff the envelopes, and prepare the food and coffee for the radical men they worked with, but to sleep with them besides, without making any demands in return. Their own feelings, their needs for affection, recognition, consideration, or commitment, did not count. If they did not comply, they were often made to feel like unattractive, unhip prudes who could readily be replaced. Sexual favors were often the price of political favor. Naturally, these women resented being used sexually, as they resented performing political labors without appreciation, and resented being relegated to doing what they called movement "shitwork"—all by so-called radicals whose proclaimed purpose in life was to end oppression. And these women saw an intimate connection between the way men treated them in their organizations and the way they treated them sexually; they were two sides of a single demeaning attitude toward women—one that would not take them seriously.

As soon as the earliest radical feminist groups were organized many women without prior political experience began joining them and voic-

7. Sara Evans recounts the emergence of radical feminism from the civil rights movement and the New Left in her valuable history, *Personal Politics: The Roots of Women's Liberation in the Civil Rights Movement and the New Left* (New York: Alfred A. Knopf, Inc., 1979). Although Evans does not discuss radical feminist analyses of sexuality, she does document the sexual insults and exploitation of women within the New Left and the persistent refusal of the male radicals to take the complaints of the women seriously. For a firsthand account of the sexual resentments of New Left women, see Marge Piercy's essay, "The Grand Coolie Damn," in *Sisterhood Is Powerful*, ed. Robin Morgan (New York: Random House, 1970).

ing other resentments. Some said they felt sexually rejected by their partners, others complained that their husbands never left them alone sexually. Some said they were afraid to tell their lovers what pleased them sexually, others said their partners resented being told. Some told about passes they had to submit to at work and on the street, others were bereft because men were intimidated by them and they, the women, were forbidden to make advances themselves. Some spoke about re-prisals they feared or suffered as lesbians, others spoke of their fear of lesbians. Some shamefully confessed to having masturbated all their lives, others declared in anguish that they could not masturbate. Many complained bitterly that their men never took responsibility for birth control, for children, for the progress of their relationships.

The stories poured out. In those days, few of the women had had the opportunity to talk honestly about sex with anyone; it had been a taboo subject in the fifties and was still suspect in the sixties. Certainly, women had not felt free to talk about the intimate physical details, for not only were sexual topics embarrassing, but sexual problems had long been taken as signs of personal failings or illness and as such were shameful, and talk about sexual secrets was considered a betrayal of your man and thus dangerous. I remember the excitement generated when the women in my group in 1967 first admitted to each other that they had been faking orgasm—and for various "reasons." Once the truth was out, we tried to analyze why so many of us had all felt the need to fake. Instead of feeling guilty about it, we saw faking as a response to pres-sures that had been put upon *us* by men.[8]

Still, no matter how liberating and exhilarating our discussions of such intimate matters may have felt, our purpose was not simply to improve our sex lives or to find some personal solution to our problems. We wanted nothing less than to understand the social basis for our discontents, including the sexual, and then to do something to change it—for everyone.

This is a very important point. Consciousness raising was not simply a technique to make people feel better about themselves or to cure their personal problems. It was not therapy.[9] It was conceived as a political tool, modeled on the Chinese practice called Speaking Bitterness. The idea was this: The so-called experts on women had traditionally been men who, as part of the male-supremacist power structure, benefited

8. This attitude is explored in the article, "When Women Rap about Sex," evidently the transcript of a meeting edited by Shulamith Firestone, in one of the first publications of the women's liberation movement, *Notes from the First Year* (New York: New York Radical Women, 1968).

9. In "The Personal Is Political," an article by Carole Hanisch in *Notes from the Second Year: Women's Liberation, Major Writings of the Radical Feminists,* ed. Shulamith Firestone (New York: New York Radical Feminists, 1970), Hanisch discusses the differences between therapy and CR groups.

from perpetuating certain ideas, and therefore what they said was suspect. If we were truly to understand the situation of women in our society, we had to base our analysis on information we could trust, information that was *not* suspect, and for this we had to gather it ourselves. We had to question all the generalizations that had been made in the past about women and question the interests they served, substituting knowledge based on the experience and feelings of women, starting with ourselves. Those early CR sessions were really fact-gathering sessions, research sessions on our feelings. We wanted to get at the truth about how women felt, how we viewed our lives, what was done to us, and how we functioned in the world. Not how we were *supposed* to feel but how we really did feel. This knowledge, gained through honest examination of our own personal experience, we would pool to help us figure out how to change the situation of women. Those early meetings felt like life-transforming discussions because our object was justice for all women.[10] We *had* to tell the truth; so much depended on it. We were going to change the world.

What made the discussions so powerful was the sense we had that a great floodlight had been turned onto the world, lighting up *all* our experience; it was as though all the murky and scary shadows we had been living with all our lives were suddenly wiped away by the powerful new light. Sex was a central and explosive subject to which we continually returned; but as we talked of our most intimate feelings we began to see how interconnected were all our experiences and our seemingly disparate lives.

Since everything we discussed was connected, we felt we could start anywhere in our analysis of women's lives: sex, class, work, marriage, motherhood, sex roles, housework, health, education, images, language—all these aspects of women's lives were riddled with sexism. The movement we envisioned would change them all.

A review of the major actions of those earliest years of WLM—actions initiated by a mere handful of ardent women, at first maybe 100 in 1967, then, by 1970, many thousands—reveals how central was the new feminist analysis of sexuality to our collective struggle for justice. In 1967 the first small groups began organizing and doing CR. By September 1968 the fledgling movement considered itself ready for its first national demonstration: about sixty feminists, mostly from New York, went to Atlantic City to picket the Miss America Pageant, using that event to demonstrate how women are (degradingly) judged as sex objects. Inside Convention Hall women unfurled a huge banner in the

10. In her widely disseminated "A Program for Feminist Consciousness Raising," in *Notes from the Second Year*, Kathie Sarachild, a founding member of Redstockings and a vitally important theoretician of consciousness raising, repeatedly emphasized the importance of connecting personal testimony with testimony of other women, now and in the past, and with political organizing.

balcony that read, simply, Women's Liberation. Outside on the boardwalk, demonstrators mockingly crowned a live sheep "Miss America," filled a "freedom trash can" with items of female "torture" like curlers, bras, girdles, and high-heeled shoes; spoke only to female reporters; and paraded with leaflets and posters. One of the most powerful posters was a replica of a display ad for a popular steak house depicting a woman's naked body charted with the names of beef cuts. The pageant seemed a perfect symbol of the exploitation of women as sex objects, but the ideas of WLM were then so unthinkable that the demonstration was not well understood. Many onlookers and reporters were incensed; it was at that demonstration that feminists became known as "crazy bra burners," though no bra was burned. So acceptable was the practice of valuing women for their sexual attractiveness that many people genuinely believed the demonstrators must be ugly women, motivated by simple jealousy of the contestants, proclaiming a politics of sour grapes.

The following spring the newly formed Redstockings held their first abortion speak-out, at which women gave public testimony describing in heart-rending detail what they had to go through to get abortions. This testimony broke a very deep taboo and started a passionate public debate that is still going on. It is hard to believe how stunned the country was by this action. At the heart of the prohibition against abortion (and birth control) is the deeply held feeling that female sex outside of procreation must be punished. As a national columnist wrote at the time, "She had the fun, now let her pay." (In the same way, the early speak-outs on rape emphasized not only the brutality and hatred in the act of rape but the way in which, by society's "blaming the victim," women's sexuality was held responsible for rape—as reflected in laws, police procedures, and relevance of the victim's sexual history.) What was new at the abortion speak-out was that the women, speaking of their feelings and experience and pain, tied abortion to the question of women's freedom, which had not been done publicly since the birth control debates of an earlier time.[11] Indeed, what prompted the Redstockings speak-out was a legislative hearing on abortion at which the "experts" testifying were fourteen men and one woman, a nun. The Redstockings thought it time to hear from the "real experts": women.

Those earliest years witnessed a proliferation of actions, from a Whistle-In in Wall Street, in which feminists made sexual passes at men on the street at lunchtime, to a protest at the National Bridal Fair by WITCH (Women's International Terrorist Conspiracy from Hell), to a takeover by New York Radical Feminists of legislative hearings on prostitution—all intended to raise public consciousness of sexism. The insults

11. The other source of the abortion movement was the population-control movement, which in some ways promotes the opposite of women's freedom. For the relation between the feminist and population-control movements as they apply to birth control, see Gordon.

flung at demonstrators by angry observers at these demonstrations were predominantly sexual: we were called dykes, whores, and beasts, as well as commies, bitches, and nuts.

In 1969 a coalition of feminist groups staged a sit-in at the *Ladies Home Journal* offices until we were granted twenty pages in which to present feminist ideas to the *Journal*'s vast female audience. I joined the committee that wrote the article on sex. Many of the articles the *Journal* editors could stomach, but the sex piece scandalized them—in part because it briefly discussed lesbianism but also, I think, because it so clearly brought together the private and public, the personal and political. Late in 1969 the first Congress to Unite Women was held in New York City, attended by more than 500 women. That same year, 1969, Barbara Seaman's *The Doctor's Case against the Pill* was published. Then, in 1970, came Kate Millett's *Sexual Politics,* Shulamith Firestone's *Dialectic of Sex,* and the first of the large publishers' anthologies of articles and pamphlets that had been circulated earlier in movement journals: Robin Morgan's *Sisterhood Is Powerful,* Leslie Tanner's *Voices from Women's Liberation,* Sookie Stambler's *Women's Liberation: A Blueprint for the Future,* and, the next year, Vivian Gornick and B. K. Moran's *Woman in Sexist Society* and others—all including important articles on sexuality. There was a great outpouring of articles, stories, books, conferences, demonstrations, debates. Lesbian feminists began forming separate groups and exploring the connections between lesbianism and feminism; at the Second Congress to Unite Women (1970), a radical lesbian group calling themselves the Lavender Menace forced the movement to examine its attitude toward lesbianism. The women's self-help movement encouraged women to examine their own and each other's bodies, inside and out, not only to overcome ignorance and shame, but to free us from the bias and control of the male medical establishment. New York Radical Feminists and other groups outside New York organized speak-outs, frequently modeled after those early Redstockings abortion speak-outs, on such volatile topics as rape, prostitution, marriage, motherhood. Feminist ideas were spreading everywhere as we made new connections and more women joined the movement. It seemed to us then that we could not be stopped.

II

What were the early radical feminist ideas about sex? Naturally, as WLM was a political movement the new attention directed by radical feminists to our sexuality had to do with power; with taking for ourselves the control of our lives and our bodies that men—through the laws, customs, and other institutions of a male-ruled society—had appropriated. The feminist movement for reproductive freedom, the women's self-help movement from California, the broader women's health movement—of which the Boston collective's best-selling *Our Bodies, Ourselves* was a product and a source—all organized around the idea of reclaiming for ourselves control over our very bodies. So with the new feminist analysis of sexuality.[12] Perceiving sexual relations as but one aspect of the power relations between men and women, early radical feminists questioned traditional definitions of women's sexuality, of women's "nature," of sexual satisfaction and health (conceived as heterosexual) on the grounds that such definitions, as propounded by men, tended to justify the sexual exploitation of women by men. "If sexual relations were not programmed to support political ends—that is, male oppression of the female—then the way would be clear for individuals to enter into physical relations not defined by roles, nor involving exploitation. Physical relations (heterosexual and homosexual) would be an extension of communication between individuals and would not necessarily have a genital emphasis," read a 1969 position paper put out by "The Feminists: A Political Organization to Annihilate Sex Roles."[13]

"We must begin to demand that if certain sexual positions now defined as 'standard' are not mutually conducive to orgasm, they no longer be defined as standard. New techniques must be used or devised which transform this particular aspect of our current sexual exploitation,"[14] proclaimed Anne Koedt in her famous essay, "The Myth of the Vaginal Orgasm," published in 1968 in *Notes from the First Year* and expanded the following year. Though Koedt focused on technique, the point of her article was clearly political. She was concerned not only with the true facts about female orgasm, then under scrutiny by sexologists, but with exposing the distortion of those facts into the "myth" of the vaginal orgasm:

> Today, with extensive knowledge of anatomy . . . there is no ignorance on the subject [of female orgasm]. There are, however, social reasons why this knowledge has not been popularized. We are living in a male society which has not sought change in women's role. . . .

12. Important pre-WLM feminist analyses of female sexuality included Herschberger's *Adam's Rib* (see n. 5 above) and Mary Jane Sherfey's 1966 paper for the *Journal of the American Psychoanalytic Association,* "The Evolution and Nature of Female Sexuality," based on her studies of multiple orgasm in women. After WLM was launched, *Adam's Rib* was reissued in paperback by Harper and Row, and Sherfey's essay was published in *Sisterhood Is Powerful* as "A Theory of Female Sexuality" and later expanded into a book.

13. *Notes from the Second Year,* p. 114.

14. Anne Koedt, "The Myth of the Vaginal Orgasm," reprinted in *Voices from Women's Liberation,* ed. Leslie Tanner (New York: New American Library/Mentor Books, 1970), p. 159.

The establishment of clitoral orgasm as fact would threaten the heterosexual institution. For it would indicate that sexual pleasure was obtainable from either men *or* women, thus making heterosexuality not an absolute, but an option. It would thus open up the whole questions of *human* sexual relationships beyond the confines of the present male-female role system.[15]

This analysis was continued by Ti-Grace Atkinson, a founder of The Feminists, the early antimarriage group which limited to one-third of its membership those women who lived with men. In "The Institution of Sexual Intercourse," in *Notes from the Second Year,* Atkinson analyzed sexual intercourse itself as a "political institution," analogous to the institution of marriage, which serves the needs of reproduction and often the sexual desires of men but not necessarily those of women. Atkinson coolly proposed that we try to "discover what the nature of the human sensual characteristics are from the point of view of the good of each individual instead of what we have now, which is a sort of psychological draft system of our sexualities." Never reducing sexual relations to mere technique, Atkinson elaborated the insight that orgasm is not everything by observing that what lovers add to the sexual experience "cannot be a technique or physical improvement on that same auto-experience" but "must be a psychological component."[16]

Carrying the feminist rebellion against the sexual exploitation of women a step further still, Dana Densmore of Boston's Cell 16 proposed a reordering of women's priorities away from the sexual altogether. After all, the belief that sexual love of man is the core of woman's aspirations—or is even necessary for fulfillment—justifies woman's exploitation and keeps her enthralled. In her powerful 1969 essay, "On Celibacy," which appeared in the first issue of *No More Fun and Games,* the journal associated with Cell 16, Densmore wrote:

> We must come to realize that we don't need sex, that celibacy . . .
> could be desirable, in many cases preferable to sex. How repugnant
> it is, after all, to make love to a man who despises you, who fears you
> and wants to hold you down! Doesn't screwing in an atmosphere
> devoid of respect get pretty grim? Why bother? You don't need it.
> . . . This is a call not for celibacy but for an acceptance of celibacy as
> an honorable alternative, one preferable to the degradation of most
> male-female relationships. . . . Unless you accept the idea that you
> don't need [men], don't need sex from them, it will be utterly im-
> possible for you to carry through, it will be absolutely necessary for
> you to lead a double life, pretending with men to be something
> other than what you know you are. . . . If we are going to be liber-

15. Ibid., pp. 161 and 166.
16. Ti-Grace Atkinson, "The Institution of Sexual Intercourse," in *Notes from the Second Year,* pp. 45–46.

ated we must reject the false image that makes men love us, and this
will make men cease to love us. . . . An end to this constant remaking
of ourselves according to what the male ego demands! Let us be
ourselves and good riddance to those who are then repulsed by us![17]

Writing on "Lesbianism and the Women's Liberation Movement,"
Martha Shelly, an early Radicalesbian, pursued Densmore's argument
down another path:

> To me, lesbianism is not an oddity of a few women to be hidden in
> the background of the Movement. In a way, it is the heart of the
> Women's Liberation Movement. In order to throw off the oppres-
> sion of the male caste, women must unite—we must learn to love
> ourselves and each other, we must grow strong and independent of
> men so that we can deal with them from a position of strength. The
> idea that women must teach men how to love, that we must not
> become manhaters is, at this point in history, like preaching pacifism
> to the Vietcong. Women are . . . told to be weak, dependent and
> loving. That kind of love is masochism. Love can only exist between
> equals, not between the oppressed and the oppressor.[18]

Thus, the price of maintaining sexual relations with men in a sexist
society sometimes seemed too high to pay for many radical feminists, just
as the price of motherhood in a sexist society has made many women
reasonably decide to forgo that experience as well. But most radical
feminists, rather than renounce heterosexuality, advocated struggle to
change its basis. (Many considered separatism a cop-out.) In *The Dialectic
of Sex,* Shulamith Firestone, shrewdly analyzing prevailing heterosexual
relations, tried to specify the price women pay for male love. In the
chapter on "Love," she describes love as requiring "mutual vulnerability
or it turns destructive: the destructive effects of love occur only in a
context of inequality." But because men and women are not equal, love is
destructive for women. While "a man must idealize one woman over the
rest in order to justify his descent to a lower caste,"[19] it is different for
women:

> In their precarious political situation, women cannot afford the lux-
> ury of spontaneous love. It is much too dangerous. The love and
> approval of men is all-important. To love thoughtlessly, before one
> has ensured return commitment, would endanger that approval. . . .

17. Tanner, pp. 264–68.
18. Martha Shelly, "Lesbianism and the Women's Liberation Movement," in *Women's
Liberation: Blueprint for the Future,* ed. Sookie Stambler (New York: Ace Books, 1970), p.
127.
19. Shulamith Firestone, *The Dialectic of Sex: The Case for Feminist Revolution* (New
York: Bantam Books, 1970), pp. 130–31.

In a male-run society that defines women as an inferior and parasitical class, a woman who does not achieve male approval in some form is doomed. . . . But because the woman is rarely allowed to realize herself through activity in the larger (male) society—and when she is, she is seldom granted the recognition she deserves—it becomes easier to try for the recognition of one man than of many; and in fact this is exactly the choice most women make. Thus once more the phenomenon of love, good in itself, is corrupted by its class context: women must have love not only for healthy reasons but actually to validate their existence.[20]

To this end, women must subordinate their true feelings, cultivate sex appeal, aspire to meet beauty standards, inhibit sexual spontaneity, and even fake orgasms—anything to catch a man. It is less this behavior many radical feminists deplored than the condition of unequal power and vulnerability between the sexes that makes such behavior seem necessary for survival. As Jennifer Gardner wrote in the essay "False Consciousness" that was published in the California journal, *Tooth and Nail,* "Our oppression is not in our heads. We will not become unoppressed by 'acting unoppressed.' Try it—if you have the economic independence to survive the consequences. The result will not be respect and support. Men will either not like you—you are a bitch, a castrator, a nag, a hag, a witch; or they will accuse you of not liking them."[21] As Kathie Sarachild wrote, observing the double nature of sex and power, "For most of history sex was, in fact, both our undoing and our only possible weapon of self-defense and self-assertion (aggression)."[22]

That some women seem to be able to have satisfactory sexual relations with men is as much beside the point, given sexism, as that some manage to gain economic security: sexual (and economic) injustices nevertheless prevail. From the point of view of radical feminism, which addresses the problems of the many, not of the privileged few, even the best "individual solutions" will be chancy, for unless a woman is strong and independent her solution can disintegrate when she alienates her male protector, which happens to many women simply by aging. (The early feminist group, OWL, Older Women's Liberation, defined "older" as thirty and up—by prevailing sexist standards a ridiculous cut-off age for men but a realistic one for women considered as sex objects.) Irene Peslikis placed at the head of her list of "Resistances to Consciousness": "Thinking that our man is the exception and, therefore, we are the exceptions among women. . . . Thinking that individual solutions are possible, that we don't need solidarity and a revolution for our libera-

20. Ibid., p. 138.
21. Jennifer Gardner, "False Consciousness," reprinted in *Notes from the Second Year,* p. 82.
22. Sarachild, p. 78.

tion."[23] As for those "personal solutions" which do not depend on male protection but involve withdrawal from men, women who choose them are subject to all the sanctions, reprisals, and punishments traditionally dealt to women without men under male supremecy. "Until we have a movement strong enough to force change," wrote Firestone in *Notes from the Second Year,* "we will have to accommodate ourselves as best we can to whichever . . . adjustment each of us can best live with," never forgetting, however, as Anne Koedt wrote in *Notes from the First Year,* "to go to the root of the problem rather than become engaged in solving secondary problems arising *out* of [woman's] condition." Just as women without control over reproduction will feel sexual anxiety, so women without control over conditions for their survival will also suffer sexual anxiety. From the beginning, radical feminists had differing analyses of sexuality, but all agreed that sexual relations were deeply affected by the general power relations prevailing between the sexes, that the way to change sexual relations was through solidarity and struggle to change the power relations, and that the way to discover how these relations oppressed women was through consciousness raising.

III

Like many other radical feminists at that time, impressed by how quickly our ideas were spreading and how much activity they generated among ourselves, I was optimistic about the effect of our movement. Our intense examination of our personal experience for its social and political significance even helped me to develop as a writer. It was hardly an accident that the first article I wrote for publication in 1969, called "Organs and Orgasms," was on sex.[24] In it I cited case after case of the injustice done to women by bias in the very terminology of sex and suggested that a solution to our sexual problems might be advanced by reexamining our assumptions, definitions, and beliefs about sexuality from a woman's point of view. It was not that I discounted the importance of political struggle, but I believed we would have to change the way we *think* before we could change the way we live. The ideas of the movement were spreading so fast that it seemed to many of us in those days that it would not be difficult to organize masses of women to revolt. (Firestone thought it would take "several more years" to build a strong enough movement to "force change.") When the first mass August 26 Woman's March was held in large cities all over the country in 1970 to commemorate the fiftieth anniversary of the women's suffrage ammendment and to demonstrate our power—as thousands and thousands

23. Morgan, p. 337.
24. Alix Kates Shulman, "Organs and Orgasms," in *Woman in Sexist Society,* ed. Vivian Gornick and B. K. Moran (New York: Basic Books, 1970), p. 198.

of women marched to demand their rights—it looked as if we might win with ease. And in the years immediately following, our hopes rose as the ERA passed through Congress for the first time since its introduction fifty years before; as the Supreme Court ruled that abortion, at least in the first trimester, was a woman's right; as suits for equal pay were launched against large corporations; as prestigious all-male colleges, professions, and institutions considered admitting women.

However, even then a powerful resistance was organizing. After a few years had passed, almost everything remained to be done. People spoke differently but acted pretty much as they always had. Following our initial success came a certain foreboding. Alice Paul, the veteran suffragist who had witnessed the defeat of feminism once, warned against allowing a time limit to be attached to the ERA; but, heedless of history as Americans—especially the young—tend to be, too ready to project our own changed consciousness onto the world, feminists failed to heed her. In time it became clear that our expectations, like my own sex article, were too optimistic; we had changed only the surface of what was wrong. Even if every woman acknowledged the injustice of sexism and every man understood about the role of the clitoris in female orgasm, sexual strife would continue, for the sexual arrangements of the world were still based on unequal power. Organized antifeminism followed each of the movement's successes in changing public consciousness. Movement or no movement, feminist feelings were not given public expression, our testimony was not considered "expert," our power in the world of public decisions remained miniscule. The heart of our sexual dissatisfaction with men was still that without power women were forced to sell it or forgo it, and we were still powerless. Even if we objected to Miss America standards we still had to be judged by them in our daily lives and then be tossed on the junk heap when we no longer measured up. Reexamining everything, even achieving *perfect understanding*, was not going to be enough to enable us to change the relations between the sexes, because sex had to do with power and those with power were not about to smile sweetly and give it up. A long, difficult struggle would have to follow understanding.

This is not to discount the considerable political gains we did make during the seventies in the fight for sexual justice. Of all the movements that emerged in the sixties, the WLM was the one that most securely became a mass movement in the seventies. Out of those early efforts grew changed attitudes and laws regarding women's work, reproductive freedom, physical abuse, and vast changes in notions of family. But many of the changes are extremely vulnerable to the growing antifeminist backlash, and if we stop far short of our original goals we may lose the gains we have won. It happened to the women in the first wave—they gained certain important but only partial victories, and they were defeated and silenced for decades. It could happen to us if we let up the pressure or lose sight of our original goals. If consciousness can be changed once, twice, it can be changed again. We are experiencing a strong move to the right. Sterilization abuse, hormone abuse are on the *rise*. The gap between average male and female income is *larger* than it was a decade ago. If abortions were outlawed again, if women were pushed back out of the work force, if we returned to viewing sex as an exclusively private matter affecting each person in isolation rather than a political matter affecting all of us, it could happen again. Just as frightening as the organized political backlash, which at least we know how to fight, is the backsliding of consciousness, the erosion of radical feminist ideals. The radical feminist critiques of sexuality and sexual repression, originally presented as aspects, or examples, of a much larger male domination of women but hardly as leading by themselves to solutions, have been diverted into concern with mere sexual technique or increased activity. Co-optation and tokenism have made it easier for people to deny that anything is still drastically wrong between the sexes. Again and again it is claimed that women have won sexual equality because the family is in a state of flux and chaos; that since the pill there is no longer any double standard—as if fear of pregnancy (which persists in any case) were the sole source of women's sexual anxiety. People say we are equal because a relatively small number of women are in positions of token power. (As with all "individual solutions," token power is different from real power, because as soon as the women who have it refuse to play the game they will lose their positions; knowing this, they are mostly supporters of the men to whom they owe their power.) But these facts only disguise the true situation of women's continued powerlessness.

A new generation does not know that ten years ago what are now our basic demands were unspoken, many even unmentionable. The ideas of women's liberation that were so recently shocking, thrilling, and liberating are already put down by many of the young as old hat and boring and by the old as a fad that is passe, obliterated in the swing of the pendulum. The presentation of feminism in the mass media has trivialized the movement's goals; in the name of "liberation" courses for women too frequently teach self-promotion instead of understanding and changing sexism in society; books on sexuality too often focus on technique and, worse, on how women may make themselves more sexually appealing to men, teaching us to blame the victim rather than on how to end victimization. The renewed search for personal solutions to collective problems is as arid today as it was a decade ago. Personal solutions to sexual problems center on finding the right partner or the right attitude or the right technique—at best chancy, at worst harmful, since they obscure the power relations inherent in sexual relations.

Several years back some of the women from the earliest movement days got together to discuss the changes that had occurred in their own sex lives since the movement began. All agreed that sex had changed for them, but very few thought it had really improved. True, some of them were now able to specify what they wanted their sex partners to do, but in some relationships the man resented the woman's desires. Several women who had changed from nonorgasmic to regularly orgasmic were sorry to find that nevertheless they were unhappy in love. Some of the women who had become lesbians found themselves facing a whole new set of problems and anxieties in a world that punishes homosexuality.[25] One woman grieved that since she no longer "played the game" she was no longer interested in sex at all and another that no one wanted her.

Not even the most ardent feminist can claim to be "liberated" in a sexist society. "Sexual liberation" can mean nothing unless it includes the freedom to reject or enter into sexual relationships fearing neither exploitation nor punishment. But sexual exploitation and punishment still threaten every woman. The denial of complete reproductive freedom, the total responsibility for child rearing, the psychological intimidation of rape victims are all punishments for the sexually active woman. The threat of job loss, ridicule, rejection, isolation, and even rape are punishments threatening the woman who refuses sex.

As the radical ideas of feminism, developed under the powerful insight that the personal is political, are absorbed by institutions adept at deflecting change through co-optation, and as our radical programs come under direct attack by an increasingly vocal conservative backlash, our awareness of the political dimension of sexual relations, with its powerful potential for change, is in danger of being lost. Conceiving sexual liberation apart from feminist liberation can land us where women have too often landed—not with more real freedom but with new pressures to put out or to withhold. Our only recourse is to deepen our radical insights about the connections between sex and power and build a political movement which can put insight into action.

New York City

25. Sydney Abbott and Barbara Love observe that lesbians "suffer the oppression of all women but are not eligible for any of the rewards. . . . Fear of punishment creates tremendous anxiety, even though punishment may not occur" ("Is Women's Liberation a Lesbian Plot?" in Gornick and Moran, pp. 443 and 445.)

Sexuality as the Mainstay of Identity: Psychoanalytic Perspectives

Ethel Spector Person

It has long been recognized that certain conventions—the double standard, the cult of virginity, and the requirement that female sexuality find expression solely within monogamous heterosexual marriages—control and inhibit female sexuality. Whatever their origins might be, these conventions are major supports for male dominance and patriarchy. Consequently, various feminist critiques have proposed one or another new prescriptions for sexuality as a part of a general restructuring of society.

However, it is difficult to formulate such prescriptions without a large theory of sexuality. The aim of this paper is to evaluate psychoanalytic paradigms, themselves in transition, in order to see what they imply for a contextual theory of female sexuality. Two popular assumptions will be challenged: (1) that sexuality is an innate force that achieves its ideal expression when free from cultural inhibitions; and (2) that female sexuality is inhibited (hyposexual), while male sexuality represents the norm. On the contrary, individuals do internalize their culture, which shapes both their experience of desire and expression of sexuality. If female sexuality is now inhibited, male sexuality is driven and cannot serve as a model. Sexuality must be understood, not only in terms of its source, but also in its relationship to the maintenance of identity.

Theories about the Nature of Sexual Motivation

While the terms "sex" and "sexual" appear to be self-explanatory, they are difficult to define because sexual life in humans has so evolved that sex is not identical to the mechanism of reproduction. Sex refers to four separate, but related, physical-psychological sets of data: (1) biological sex, defined by six anatomical and physiological characteristics: chromosomes, gonads, internal genitalia, external genitalia, hormones, and secondary sexual characteristics; (2) gender, composed of core gender identity (the sense, "I am female," "I am male"), gender role identity (the sense, "I am feminine," "I am masculine"), and gender role behavior; (3) sexual behavior, overt and fantasied, expressed both in choice of object and nature of activity; and (4) reproduction.[1] However, the term "sexual," as used in everyday speech, refers almost exclusively to sexual behavior, expressed by pleasurable genital activity and its associated fantasies, or by any sensual experience that has erotic meaning for the individual.

Theories about the nature of sexuality are, in general, theories of sexual motivation, why people initiate or respond to erotic activity. They address the question of the source of sexual desire and arousal. Beach states the problem, "Since no animal mates in order to reproduce, but animals must mate in the service of species survival, we are faced with the problem of identifying the source of reward or positive reinforcement which impels individuals to copulate."[2] Sexual arousal may occur with direct genital stimulation, but arousal also occurs many times without its benefit. The reasons an individual becomes aroused or initiates sexual activity may appear, at first glance, to be self-evident, because sex is so integral to life and so highly valued in contemporary culture. Yet there is little agreement concerning the source of sexual motivation.

An adequate theory of sexual motivation must offer explanations for the following aspects of sexuality: (1) the motor force behind the desire to initiate sexual behavior; (2) the immense strength of the sexual impulse as it is sometimes subjectively experienced; (3) the absence, avoidance, or inhibition of sexuality and the variable intensity of sexual desires; (4) the diversity of erotic stimuli and situations that trigger sexual arousal in different individuals (e.g., heterosexual, homosexual, or inanimate objects); (5) the existence of a "sex print," that is, the restriction of an individual's erotic responses to limited stimuli (e.g., being "turned on" to only one thing, say, a shoe); (6) the confluence of sexual

1. John Money, Joan G. Hampson, and John L. Hampson: "Hermaphroditism: Recommendations concerning Assignment of Sex, Change of Sex, and Psychologic Management," *Johns Hopkins Hospital Bulletin* 97 (1955): 284–300, and "Sexual Incongruities and Psychopathology: The Evidence of Human Hermaphroditism," *Johns Hopkins Hospital Bulletin* 98 (1956): 43–57; Joan G. Hampson, "Hermaphroditic Genital Appearance, Rearing and Eroticism in Hyperadrenocorticism," *Johns Hopkins Hospital Bulletin* 96 (1955): 265–73; Robert J. Stoller, *Sex and Gender* (New York: Science House, 1968); Lionel Ovesey and Ethel Person, "Gender Identity and Sexual Psychopathology in Men: A Psychodynamic Analysis of Homosexuality, Transsexualism, and Transvestism," *Journal of the American Academy of Psychoanalysis* 1, no. 1 (1973): 53–72.

2. Frank A. Beach, "Cross-Species Comparisons and the Human Heritage," in *Human Sexuality in Four Perspectives,* ed. Frank A. Beach (Baltimore: Johns Hopkins University Press, 1976), p. 299.

and nonsexual meanings in both sexual and nonsexual behavior; and (7) the cultural preoccupation with sexuality. In sum, a sexual theory must account for both the power and the plasticity of sex.

There are now two major paradigms for the source of sexual motivation in humans. Dominant for some fifty years is Freud's libido theory, essentially a biological theory that postulates a fixed sexual drive. However, some theorists follow Beach's lead. They postulate an appetitional theory of sexual motivation, which stands in opposition to the libidinal or drive theory. While the second paradigm acknowledges a neural reflex for orgasmic release, the occasion for sexual arousal is viewed as learned or conditioned rather than biological.

Profoundly different implications attach to the two paradigms. The drive or libidinal model describes a tension which must be discharged or converted via sublimation, neurosis, or perversion. The appetitional model posits the pursuit of pleasure as the motive force for sexuality. This difference in focus reflects a current dichotomy in theories of behavior. Although there is a formal consensus that a mind-body dichotomy is untenable, interpretations of behavior are increasingly polarized in the direction of either biological determinism or cultural contingency, so much so that the belief in the existential self as the locus of choice has almost vanished. In libido theory sexuality is both a motor force in culture and an innate force with which culture must contend. In appetitional theory the content of sexuality is formed by culture. The dichotomy posed is whether sexuality is creator of culture or itself created by culture.

Each of these paradigms has significant limitations. While less fully articulated, a third paradigm exists that remedies some of the problems inherent in the first two. An amalgam of Freud's psychological theory of sexuality and object-relations theory, it places the appetitional component in a developmental motivational context. Rather than view libido as controlling interpersonal relations, it emphasizes the way in which early object relations shape the experience of desire. Each of the three paradigms must be judged in terms of its usefulness in explaining the different aspects of sexuality described previously. In addition, each paradigm has different implications for the way we view both female and male sexuality.

The Libido Theory of Sexual Motivation[3]

"Libido" is a term which is rarely defined in the psychoanalytic literature. Freud suggests it is "that force by which the sexual instinct is

---

3. Sigmund Freud, *Three Contributions to the Theory of Sex*, trans. A. A. Brill (1908; reprint ed., New York: E. P. Dutton, 1962), and *A General Introduction to Psychoanalysis*, trans. Joan Riviere (1920; reprint ed., New York: Washington Square Press, 1960), chaps. 20, 21.

represented in the mind. . . . "[4] He considered it the equivalent of sexual longing. At times, he uses it synonymously with sexual excitation, which led him to speculate that many different organs contributed sexual tension to sexual instinct. In Freud's theory, drive is generated within the body and propels itself toward discharge; as such, it is outside the realm of consciousness, though it acts as a stimulus upon consciousness, which is transformed into a wish. The fulfillment of the wish leads to reduction of tensions and thereby to pleasure. Freud's notion of instinct both implies a tension to be discharged and suggests the mode by which this discharge takes place. Libido is considered an energy that has direction (some specific aim to accomplish), object (the instrument by which the aim is to be fulfilled), different intensities, and the capacity for transformation into equivalences, such as neurotic symptoms. Psychosexual development unfolds in accordance with maturation. All psychic development derives from a biologically scheduled unfolding of libido. From the polymorphous condition of infancy, libido moves through a series of preordained orderly stages (oral, anal, phallic, oedipal), each attached to an erotogenic zone and, after latency, subsumed into genital sexuality. Sexuality, then, is distinguished from genitality. It refers to sensual, pleasurable gratification from specific body zones, using thumb sucking as a prototype. Freud's theory is both a physical energic theory, because libido is viewed as an energy, and a biological theory, because each stage of sexuality is intrinsically connected to a stage of biological development.

However, a psychological theory is superimposed upon the biophysical theory. Freud describes two purely psychological events that interact with the deployment of libido and are crucial to development: first, the child's discovery of anatomic distinction with her or his subsequent reaction to that discovery; and second, the entrance into the oedipal stage. The psychological aspects of his theory will be amplified later when we turn to the third paradigm of sexual motivation. In this theory, there is only one kind of libido: masculine. Perhaps because of constitutional endowment, or because the path of libidinal development in women is so circuitous, the relative attenuation of sexuality in women is considered a foregone conclusion.[5]

Critique of Libido Theory

Despite its enormous heuristic value, particularly for understanding the apparent centrality of sexuality to mental life and for collating a vast

4. Sigmund Freud quoted by Ernest Jones, *The Life Work of Sigmund Freud,* 3 vols. (New York: Basic Books, 1955), 2:282.

5. Sigmund Freud, "'Civilized' Sexual Morality and Modern Nervousness" (1908), *Collected Papers,* vol. 2, trans. Joan Riviere (New York: Basic Books, 1959); Sigmund Freud, "Femininity" (1933), in *The Standard Edition of the Complete Psychological Works of Sigmund Freud,* ed. James Strachey (London: Hogarth Press, 1953), vol. 22.

array of clinical data, the concept of libido has been critically evaluated in a number of disciplines. Feminist critiques point out the masculine bias implicit in any theory that takes male development as the norm and female development as a deficit model of male development. Psychoanalysts have argued that Freud's concept of instinct is based on a pre-Mendelian model. Some analysts claim that Freud uses the concept of instinct to mean just drive (or motivational source) and not inherited patterns for discharge since he uses the word *Trieb* (drive) rather than "Instinct." While these two meanings may appear blurred, Ernest Jones suggests that "on the whole the word *Trieb* in Freud's writings more often means 'instinct' in our sense . . . which definitely implies an inborn and inherited character."[6] But there are serious objections even to the narrower concept of instinct.

One of the earliest, most comprehensive and forceful critiques was that of Kardiner, Karush, and Ovesey.[7] They point out that libido has two different sets of connotations: an appetitive component and an energic component. With regard to the first, Kardiner et al. regard sex as a physiologic need, like that for food, water, oxygen, and warmth. Their quarrel with Freud is that he not only postulates libido as the subjective perception of the sexual need, but also that the "behavior which brings gratification is also held to be instinctual."[8] In their view, regarding the array of needs (for food, sex, etc.), "The goals of such needs are not learned and one may, if he wishes, call them 'instinctual.'"[9] But, the authors maintain, the route to satisfaction of those needs is learned. Insofar as the infant needs the breast (mother) to satisfy its hunger, that need is a learned association. Kardiner et al. are unable to concede that there is an "inborn need either for a sexual object in general or for a sexual object of a particular gender."[10]

As for the energic connotation of libido theory, Freud holds that libido is a transmutable energy, which can be moved from one body zone to another and from one sexual object to another, and which can be transformed into anxiety, symptoms, and so forth. However, as Kardiner et al. have pointed out, libido is a hypothetical construct, derived from nineteenth-century physics as a model. Libido cannot be observed; it is used to "explain" different intensities of behavior and as such is tautological. The assumption of libido as the life force is totally unproved.

Kubie, among others, raises questions about the one point that Kardiner et al. are willing to concede to Freud's theory of libido, that is, the equivalence of sex and hunger.[11] The need for water and for metabolites

6. Jones, p. 317.

7. Abram Kardiner, Aaron Karush, and Lionel Ovesey, "A Methodological Study of Freudian Theory," *International Journal of Psychiatry* 2, no. 5 (1966): 489–542 (originally published in *Journal of Nervous and Mental Disease,* vol. 129, no. 1 [July 1959]).

8. Ibid., p. 502.

9. Ibid., p. 503.

10. Ibid., p. 507.

11. Lawrence S. Kubie, "Instincts and Homeostasis," *Psychosomatic Medicine* 10 (1948):

is manifest through the subjective experience of thirst and hunger and is mediated through a demonstrable disequilibrium in homeostatic processes. Therefore, in the case of thirst and hunger, one is able to formulate the mediating link between body process, on one hand, and "felt" need, on the other. Freud's organic sexual excitation, the biological substratum of libido, has yet to be established.

There have been several attempts to identify some homeostatic disequilibrium that might account for sexual need and that is analogous to the mechanisms which account for the need for food and water. If one considers male sexuality, pressure on the seminal vesicles has been proposed at various times as the motor force of sexual desire. However, this model of male sexuality, what we might term the "elimination" model, has been discredited as too limited:[12] it cannot account for childhood sexuality, continued desire in castrates, or a number of other special cases. Nor has it been possible to correlate arousal with specific hormone levels.[13] There is some evidence, however, that arousability, if not arousal, is dependent on hormone level.[14] Hormones act on sexuality in at least two ways: indirectly through their role in dimorphic development (and, some say, in the genesis of the male or female brain), as well as directly on arousability.

Attempts to locate the source of some homeostatic disequilibrium to account for sexual need have thus far failed. In part, Freud's analogy of sexual need to hunger is intrinsically poor, based on the individual's subjective sense of need, often experienced as peremptory. But in hunger and thirst, arousal occurs at fairly regular intervals and is relatively predictable and autonomous. Furthermore, only the satisfaction of the appetite is socially prescribed, not the need itself. Contrast this with sexuality, in which arousal itself is prohibited in many circumstances, for example, if arousal is attached to an incestuous object. Thus, one might guess that the biological and psychological mechanisms that underlie the regulation of sexuality differ from the regulatory mechanisms of those other appetites with which sexuality is compared.

In sum, the concept of instinct applied to human sexuality is outdated. Even in animal studies the concept of instinct has been replaced by the concept of "innate" behavior conceptualized in terms of the release and inhibition of specific physiological mechanisms. In the lower

15–29, and "Influence of Symbolic Processes on the Role of Instincts in Human Behavior," *Psychosomatic Medicine* 18 (1956): 189–208.

12. Frank A. Beach, "Characteristics of Masculine 'Sex Drive,'" in *Nebraska Symposium on Motivation*, ed. M. R. Jones (Lincoln: University of Nebraska Press, 1956).

13. Kenneth R. Hardy, "An Appetitional Theory of Sexual Motivation," *Psychological Review* 71, no. 1 (January 1964): 1–18 (reprinted in *Human Sexual Behavior*, ed. Bernhardt Lieberman [New York: John Wiley & Sons, 1971], pp. 61–77).

14. Richard E. Whalen, "Sexual Motivation," *Psychological Review* 73, no. 2 (1966): 151–63.

mammals sex is considered "stereotypic" rather than "instinctive." As one moves up the evolutionary scale, sex is no longer predominantly controlled by reflex and endocrine mechanisms. In humans, sexual behavior appears to depend more on learning and experience and less on hormonal and genetic contributions. As Ford and Beach put it, " . . . the human male does not have to learn how to fill his penis with blood so that it becomes erect and rigid, but he may have to learn how to copulate. . . ."[15] Such a revised concept of instinctive behavior does not deny the importance of biological factors in the organization and expression of sexual behavior; it does suggest that sexuality is subject to great variability and even disruption on the basis of experience. With the current spate of biological research being conducted, it is still possible to speculate that the biological basis for sexual drive will be revealed.[16] But the burden of proof must fall on proponents of instinct theory since several viable alternate theories can account for sexual appetite and sexual motivation.

The Appetitional Theory of Sexual Motivation

This theory, too, is biological insofar as it acknowledges the individual's innate or biological capacity for physiological sexual arousal and discharge. However, it emphasizes different origins for the motivation for sexuality than libido theory does. As proposed by Hardy, sexual motivation represents one special case of principles common to motives generally.[17] In summary, a motive derives from a learned expectation of affective change (e.g., pleasure or the avoidance of pain or fear). Because local stimulation of the genitals and genital climax are pleasurable, the quest for sexual discharge will become a motive force. Many stimuli, in and of themselves neutral, become associated with the pleasure of genital stimulation and serve as cues for sexual arousal even in the absence of direct stimulation. Hardy further postulates that various stimuli become linked to sexual arousal or avoidance based on cultural prescriptions and sanctions. Female hyposexuality would be viewed as a product of cultural inhibition. This schema for sexual motivation,

15. Clellan S. Ford and Frank A. Beach, *Patterns of Sexual Behavior* (New York: Harper & Bros., 1951), pp. 178–79.

16. No one doubts that there are neurophysiologic and neuropharmacologic underpinnings in sexuality. The question in dispute is the initiating event for arousal. Current works that focus on the biology of sexuality are: R. A. Gorski, "The Neuroendocrine Regulation of Sexual Behavior," in *Advances in Psychobiology,* vol. 2, ed. G. Newton and A. H. Riesen (New York: John Wiley & Sons, 1974); R. G. Heath, "Pleasure and Brain Activity in Man: Deep and Surface Electroencephalograms during Orgasm," *Journal of Nervous and Mental Disease* 154 (1972): 3–18; P. D. MacLean, "Brain Mechanisms of Primal Sexual Functions and Related Behavior," in *Sexual Behavior: Pharmacology and Biochemistry,* ed. M. Sander and G. L. Gessa (New York: Raven Press, 1975).

17. Hardy, pp. 4–6.

whether explicitly labeled an appetitional theory or not, provides the theoretical base for those formulations that focus on historical contingency and culture in the genesis of sexual fantasy, patterns of arousal, and behavior. These latter theories focus on the social sources of sexuality, whereas in libido theory, sexuality is viewed as biophysical in source.

The most forceful argument for the social origins of sexual motivation is presented by Gagnon and Simon in their classic work, *Sexual Conduct: The Social Origins of Sexual Development.*[18] They argue that Freud, like other post-Romantic innovators, transferred the image of the individual against the state to the arena of sexuality with a contest between the instinctual aims of the individual and his repressive culture or parents. They view the "unproven assumption . . . of the 'power' of the psychosexual drive"[19] as the major obstacle to understanding sexuality. According to Freud, sexual arousal is natural; according to Gagnon and Simon, the physiological concomitants of excitement are not necessarily recognized as such until they are appropriately identified. The latter idea dovetails with Schacter and Singer's demonstration that external events influence the individual's interpretation of physiological change.[20] In other words, the conscious interpretation of a biologic event is subject to variation, depending on cultural input. More and more analyses of sexuality emphasize historical contingency. Take, for example, Foucault's *History of Sexuality,*[21] in which the title itself throws down the gauntlet to the biological determinists. "Sexuality must not be thought of as a kind of natural given which power tries to hold in check, or as an obscure domain which knowledge tries to uncover. It is the name that can be given to a historical construct. . . ."[22] Foucault focuses on the relationship of power and social control to the construction of sexuality, which took on its modern form in the eighteenth century. Such a construction renders the content of sexuality.

Critique of the Appetitional Theory of Motivation

While the appetitional theory is adequate to explain arousal, diversity of sexual stimuli, and even sexual inhibition, it offers no basis whatsoever for understanding either the peremptory nature of sexuality or its symbolic valences. Those theories that emphasize social origins are extremely useful in pointing to cross-cultural and historical variations in

18. John H. Gagnon and William Simon, *Sexual Conduct: The Social Sources of Human Sexuality* (Chicago: Aldine Publishing Co., 1973).

19. Ibid., p. 15.

20. Stanley Schacter and Jerome E. Singer, "Cognitive, Social and Physiological Determinants of Emotional State," *Psychological Review* 69 (1962): 379–99.

21. Michel Foucault, *The History of Sexuality,* vol. 1, *An Introduction* (New York: Random House, 1978).

22. Ibid., p. 105.

the deployment of sexuality and in challenging the concept of sexuality as instinctive and biologically mandated. However, within the terms of their own assumption, they do not offer adequate insight into those mechanisms that mediate between culture and the individual's subjectivity. This is, of course, the same objection raised against the interpersonal school of psychoanalysis, in which the oversimplistic assumption is so often made that subjectivity simply mirrors what is exterior. What is required is a theoretical formulation that can address the problem of how family, society, and culture are reflected in individual psychological development. Such a task was first undertaken in adaptational theory, particularly in the work of Kardiner and Rado, and more recently in object-relations theory.[23]

Toward a New Paradigm: Freud's Psychological Theory and Object-Relations Theory

Despite the shortcomings of libido theory, it will not be readily replaced until an alternate paradigm emerges which can "explain" the same data. Such a paradigm does in fact exist within psychoanalysis. It is in large part a distillate of Freud's work, omitting the emphasis on sex as instinct but postulating a developmental sequence by which sex comes to have central significance in personality with particular focus on the interrelationship between the capacity for sensuality and the development of object relations. It offers great flexibility and coherence in integrating biology and social reality.

As George Klein makes clear in an essay, "Freud's Two Theories of Sexuality," it is more than plausible to preserve the importance of sexuality in the etiology of neurosis and in motivation in general without adhering to a drive-discharge or libido theory.[24] He elaborates this position in a closely reasoned argument in which he suggests that Freud really proposed two theories of sexuality: the libido theory and what he calls Freud's clinical theory. I prefer to call this Freud's psychological theory to distinguish it from his biological theory. Klein finds it unlikely that Freud himself believed he had formulated two different theories. Some Freud scholars may have the same difficulty. The suspicion does emerge, as one reads Klein's paper, that he may be introducing new twists to Freud and attributing them to Freud in the hopes of avoiding controversy.

23. Abram Kardiner, *The Individual and His Society* (New York: Columbia University Press, 1939); Sandor Rado, "An Adaptational View of Sexual Behavior," rev., in *Psychoanalysis of Behavior* (New York: Grune & Stratton, 1956).

24. George S. Klein, "Freud's Two Theories of Sexuality," *Psychological Issues* 9, no. 4, monograph 36 (New York: International Universities Press, 1976): 14–70; first published in *Clinical-Cognitive Psychology: Models and Integrations*, ed. L. Breger (Englewood Cliffs, N.J.: Prentice-Hall, Inc., 1969), pp. 136–81.

Yet there is within the body of Freud's work a theory of sexual behavior which does not depend on accepting libido as a necessary construct. It allows the correlation of insights from psychoanalytic theory with those from cognitive theory and affective theory (on which the appetitional theory is based). Klein states, "In the clinical theory, sexuality is viewed as appetitive activity within a reticulum of motivational meanings rather than the manifestations of linear force impelling itself against a barrier."[25] He points out that Freud correctly identified sensual pleasure as the shared factor in different sexual experiences, both infantile and adult, nongenital and genital. This pleasure is different from the removal of unpleasure; it is primary because it comes from the direct stimulation of dermal surfaces.[26] (The argument is congruent with Hardy's.) From Klein's point of view, Freud's major contribution to the theory of sexuality was his discovery that nongenital, infantile sexuality was in emotional continuity with genital sexuality. Both the capacity for sensual pleasure and the means of eliciting it undergo serial development. In clinical (or psychological) theory, this "is a guided process, one in which societal sanctions, values, and encouragement are vital."[27] "From this premise . . . Freud evolved a conception of how this development is affected by a person's symbolized record of interpersonal encounters through which he has been sensually aroused."[28]

In object-relations theory, the close interrelationship between infantile sexuality and early object relations is definitive for mental life. The earliest bonding between mother (or surrogate) and child takes place in the experiential context of the tactile-sensual modality. In fact, it has been demonstrated that physical skin contact between the infant and caretaker is critical to the infant's emotional and cognitive development.[29] Lichtenstein has raised the question of the evolutionary purpose of pregenital sexuality (nonprocreative sexuality);[30] it may be precisely to promote bonding between the infant and significant others. Thus,

25. Ibid., p. 41.
26. It is this aspect of sensuality which accounts for the pleasure in foreplay. In drive theory with its emphasis on pleasure as the outcome of tension reduction, there is no adequate explanation for forepleasure, a problem that Wilhelm Reich tried ingeniously to solve.
27. Klein, p. 21.
28. Ibid.
29. These conclusions are demonstrated in the work of Renee Spitz, "Hospitalism: An Inquiry into the Genesis of Psychiatric Conditions in Early Childhood," *The Psychoanalytic Study of the Child* (New York: International Universities Press, 1945), 1:53–74, and "Hospitalism: A Follow-Up Report," ibid. (1946), 2:111–13; see also I. Dowling, *Attachment and Love* (New York: Basic Books, 1969). For a speculative essay on these issues, see Nathaniel Ross, "On the Significance of Infantile Sexuality," in *On Sexuality: Psychoanalytic Observations*, ed. Toksoz Karasu and Charles Socarides (New York: International Universities Press, 1979).
30. Heinz Lichtenstein, "Identity and Sexuality," *The Dilemma of Human Identity* (New York: Jason Aronson, 1977).

sexuality will always carry the affective connotations of early object relations. "As development occurs, the conceptual scope or sensual experience comes to include representations of the actions and relationships
through which the pleasure is won or thwarted, of restraint and controls,
and of self-related meanings."[31] Because sensual pleasure is the vehicle
of object relationships in the real world, sexuality expresses an enormous
variety of motives, predominantly dependent or hostile.[32] Or sexuality
may be used in the service of stabilizing one's sense of self, assuaging
anxiety, or restoring self-esteem.

Furthermore, because sensuality arises directly from body surfaces
which have other functions as well, sensual experience will by its very
nature be symbolically interlocked with nonsensual activities or aims.
The force of sexuality exists precisely because sexuality is linked with
other motives. Klein suggests that it is neither the need nor the wish for
sensual experience that motivates an individual toward sexual behavior
but, rather, "manifestations of the cognitive schemata in a state of continued or repetitive activation."[33] The clearest expression of this union
of sexual and nonsexual motives is found in those clinical instances in
which an individual feels driven by sexual desire (e.g., any bout of compulsive sexuality such as episodic fetishism). Don Juan is not just in
search of sex.

In sum, object-relations theory attempts to formulate those ways in
which the experience of the external world is internalized, not just in the
organization of perception and affective relationships but in the very
creation of subjectivity. While all psychoanalytic theory acknowledges
the internalization of external values and prohibitions in the formation
of ego ideal and superego, there is more emphasis in object-relations
theory on the way subjectivity (fantasies, wishes) is influenced by the
experiential. More than an amalgam of object need tied to pleasure,
sexuality reflects desire, which depends on fantasy. The substance of
fantasy itself draws on experience.

Critique of Psychological and Object-Relations Theory of Sexuality

This theory, too, has its limitations. It is useful in unraveling certain
clinical phenomena, but because of all the special conditions that
mediate the shape of internalizations (affect, perception, maturational
stage, conflict, etc.), the theory is not predictive. So, for example, object-
relations theory *alone* cannot account for the division of the world into

31. Klein, p. 27.
32. The psychoanalytic formulation of nonsexual motives in sexual behavior was
made in the mid-1950s in a significant series of papers by Lionel Ovesey; see particularly,
"The Pseudohomosexual Anxiety," *Psychiatry* 18 (1955): 17–25, and "Masculine Aspirations in Women," *Psychiatry* 19 (1956): 341–51.
33. Klein, p. 28.

two genders, a division that has such profound consequences for the shape of individual desire.

Once we establish the possibility that the shape of sexuality owes more to culture than to biology, it is difficult to justify the claim that sexual inhibition, by definition, does violence to the individual. If we are to sustain our conviction that the expression of sexuality is crucial to autonomous personality development, we must make explicit those mechanisms (in distinction to drive discharge) that account for the central importance of sexuality in psychological life. We must consider its function in personality development, its meaning and value to the individual, and, above all, the relationship between sexuality and the consolidation of identity. It is in these contexts that we may be better able to understand the implications of inhibited sexuality for women.

The Function and Value of Sexuality

At the simplest level, the function of sexuality is to obtain sexual discharge or pleasure or experience ecstasy.[34] Orgasm has been described as a biological opiate, offering the relief of pregenital as well as genital tension, strengthening the ego, regressive in the service of the ego, and so forth.[35] But the function of sexuality extends beyond either the pursuit of pleasure or the remediation of discomfort. First, self-stimulation in infancy provides sensual pleasure independent of reliance on external objects. The ability to produce orgasm at will, through masturbation, lends itself to a sense of self-sufficiency and power in the adolescent. Consequently, the development of a sense of autonomy (characterized by the ability to function independent of external objects) may be developmentally linked to masturbation. Second, sexuality may symbolize union with the loved object; it may be the primary vehicle for the expression of intimacy in a culture in which so many other expressions of physicality are proscribed. One analyst has gone so far as to suggest that the primary aim of the sex "drive" is object seeking rather than pleasure seeking.[36] At the very least, sexuality is intertwined with object relations and may become the vehicle of the expression of love, hostility, or dependency.

But while the "beneficent effects of orgastic experiences"[37] are

34. Heinz Lichtenstein, "The Changing Concept of Psychosexual Development," *The Dilemma of Human Identity* (first published in *Journal of the American Psychoanalytic Association* 18, no. 2 [April 1970]: 300–318).

35. Nathaniel Ross, "The Primacy of Genitality in the Light of Ego Psychology," *Journal of the American Psychoanalytic Association* 18, no. 2 (April 1970): 267–84.

36. W. R. D. Fairbairn, *An Object-Relations Theory of Personality* (New York: Basic Books, 1952).

37. Ross, p. 267.

widely documented, the primacy of sexual development in personality is no longer taken for granted. This is the case even among analysts who subscribe to the libido theory of sexuality. It has been found impossible to correlate genitality and orgasmic competence with overall personality maturation; there is even less correlation among women than among men.[38] Based on Hartmann's work, sexuality is considered no more than one variable among three to five variables in personality development. Given the findings of ego psychology, it is not possible to see personality maturation as the dependent variable, sexuality as the independent one.[39] In the case of "perversions," the "perverse" symptom represents sexuality as it has been filtered through a distortion in object relations, rather than a sexual fixation that disturbs object relations.[40]

Even though analysts have downgraded the theoretical importance of sexuality, they still believe that sex maintains a unique position in psychic development. If sexual development is not the independent variable in psychosexual development, what is the justification in claiming it is the leading variable? There is an assumption in psychoanalysis, sometimes tacit, sometimes explicit, that sexuality is linked to identity. Many individuals corroborate this psychoanalytic assumption and report that they experience their sexuality as self-defining. If sexuality does not have a "nature" as libido theory suggests, one is left with the task of explaining the experiential testimony that sex is the "core."

Sexuality and Identity

Eissler and Lichtenstein explicitly suggest a direct link between sexuality and identity.[41] Eissler says that "orgasm (aside from the biological aspects) when viewed in its relationship to the ego must contain a meaning and function beyond the attainment of physical pleasure and the reduction of tension."[42] He suggests that orgasm serves the ego function of the affirmation of personal existence. But the capacity for orgasm

38. Ibid.; Helene Deutsch, cited by Burness Moore, Panel Report, "Frigidity in Women," *Journal of the American Psychoanalytic Association* (1964), pp. 571–84; Lichtenstein, "The Changing Concept of Psychosexual Development."

39. Ross, p. 281; Lichtenstein, "The Changing Concept of Psychosexual Development," p. 269.

40. Ethel Person and Lionel Ovesey, "The Transsexual Syndrome in Males, Part I," *American Journal of Psychotherapy* 28, no. 1 (January 1974): 4–21, "Transvestism: New Perspectives," *Journal of the American Academy of Psychiatry* 6, no. 3 (1978): 301–23, and "The Transsexual Syndrome in Males, Part II," *American Journal of Psychotherapy* 28, no. 1 (April 1974): 174–93.

41. Kurt Eissler, "Notes on Problems of Technique in the Psychoanalytic Treatment of Adolescents: With Some Remarks on Perversions," *Psychoanalytic Study of the Child* 13 (1958): 223–54, also "Problems of Identity," *Journal of the American Psychoanalytic Association* 6 (1958): 131–42, abstract; Lichtenstein, "Identity and Sexuality."

42. Eissler, "Notes on Problems of Technique in the Psychoanalytic Treatment of Adolescents," p. 237.

appears relatively late in development. Consequently, Lichtenstein suggests that all libidinal gratification serves the same function early in development that orgasm does later and that "the very core of a person's being fully himself profoundly depends on the affirmation of the conviction of his existence as incontrovertible truth."[43] He believes that non-procreative sexuality serves the evolutionary purpose of establishing a "primary identity." While psychoanalytic theory customarily derives the emergence of identity from early object relations (the separation-individuation phase) and from the infant's development of body image, Lichtenstein proposes that both identity and sexual theme are two transformations of the infant's perception of its instrumental use by mother. He conceives of this process as a version of "imprinting."

Against the proposition that sexuality is a cornerstone of identity, we have the historian's contention that self-identification in the modern sense of a conscious sense of self may not apply to earlier historical epochs at all, let alone a self-identification based on sexual practice. In contrast to Lichtenstein's position, and in view of the historical variability of the sense of self as separate, it seems that in contemporary culture, sexuality is nearly always, but not invariably, linked to identity. That the linkage is not invariable is a salient point, particularly in reference to the difference between female sexuality and male sexuality. When sexuality does play a large role in identity it is through the mediating structure of gender and "sex prints."

Gender

There is contemporary agreement (with the significant exception of one major study) that gender differentiation is prephallic, observable by the end of the first year of life and immutable by the third year.[44] The first and crucial step in psychosexual development and gender differentiation arises in the early years of life, most often in agreement with the parental designation of the child's sex. This self-designation, defined by the term "core gender," may have unconscious as well as conscious components. Gender plays an organizing role in psychic structure similar to other modalities of cognition such as space, time, causation, and self-object differentiation. Why core gender is of such crucial importance in organizing personality is still an open question. Put another way, the question is why only two gender possibilities exist. This question has been pointedly raised by Fineman, who suggests that the fixity of *two*

43. Lichtenstein, "Identity and Sexuality," p. 313.
44. See Susan Baker's article, "Biological Influences on Human Sex and Gender" (*Signs: Journal of Women in Culture and Society* 6, no. 1 [Autumn 1980], in press) for the one exception: Imperato-McGinley's work on the 5-reductase deficit of male pseudohermaphroditism.

gender roles seems to confirm Freud's "penile semantics."[45] Put less provocatively, one might say that the knowledge of two categories of beings permeates mental life even before knowledge of a sex difference, as such, exists. Since, in fact, gender roles and behaviors exist on a gradient, I would assume that their organization into two genders, which correspond to the two sexes, offers some cognitive advantage (the ready division into two opposites such as like and different, self and other).

Gender orders sexuality. Why else do those few genetic males misdiagnosed as females and raised as females grow up dreaming the dreams of women? Gender launches the individual into a particular psychosexual pathway; it is decisive for the shape of the oedipal configuration which is a crucial event in acculturation. In addition, socialization into passivity or activity, subordination or autonomy, is decisive for the way sexuality (sensuality) is experienced and for the fantasies that attach to it. Thus, gender training, not just the previous record of sensual experience, molds sexuality.

Sexuality, in turn, may be a mainstay for gender. Insofar as sexuality is a major component in the maintenance of gender, it is crucial to identity. There is a wealth of clinical evidence to suggest that, in this culture, genital sexual activity is a prominent feature in the maintenance of masculine gender while it is a variable feature in feminine gender. Thus an impotent man always feels that his masculinity, and not just his sexuality, is threatened. In men, gender appears to "lean" on sexuality. It is impossible to locate a physically intact man who has never achieved orgasm by any route whatsoever who does not have significant psychopathology. In males, the need for sexual performance is so great that performance anxiety is the leading cause of secondary impotence. The vast array of male "perversion" (in both types and numbers), in contrast to women, may be testimony to the male need to preserve sexuality against long odds. In contrast, whether or not a woman is orgasmic has few implications for personality organization. Put another way, there is a difference in the primacy of sexuality between men and women, at least in this culture. In women, gender identity and self-worth can be consolidated by other means.

This difference in the relationship between genital sexuality and gender is, I believe, the single most telling distinction between female and male sexuality. Whatever the causes of the difference it means that while women may suffer the consequences of sexual inhibition, sexual expression is not critical to personality development. Many women have the capacity to abstain from sex without negative psychological consequences. (The problem for women is that they are often denied the legal

45. Joel Fineman, "Psychoanalysis, Bisexuality, and the Difference before the Sexes," in *Psychosexual Imperatives: Their Roles in Identity Formation*, ed. Marie Coleman Nelson and Jean Ikenberry (New York: Human Science Press, 1979).

right of sexual refusal.) In men, there is such a rigid link between sexual expression and gender that their sexuality often appears driven rather than liberated.

Sex Print

The relationship between sexuality and identity is mediated not only through gender but also through what I have called the "sex print."[46] The sex print is an individual's erotic signature. It signifies that the individual's sexual potentiality is progressively narrowed between infancy and adulthood. This phenomenon has been alluded to by sexologists and analysts of markedly different persuasions. In Freud, the polymorphous perverse infant-child is metamorphosed into the heterosexual adult through psychosexual maturation and the aegis of the family. Eissler, while remarking on "perversions," noted that "biological knowledge has little value when it is observed that the pleasure premium is unconditionally tied to a rigid individual pattern. . . . Despite many other available channels for gratification the physical demand remains ungratified. . . . "[47] It is clear that this description is apt for nearly all individuals, obligatory heterosexuals, obligatory homosexuals, and so on. The sex print conveys more than just preference for a sexual object; it is an individualized script that elicits erotic desire. It also refers to the strong preference for specific erotic techniques, though this aspect of the sex print may prove to have a strong biological predisposition. Tripp notes that "people and lower animals both end up with sharply specific sex patterns, though in man these vary enormously from one individual to the next."[48]

From the subjective point of view the sex print is experienced as sexual "preference." Because it is revealed rather than chosen, sexual preference is felt as deep rooted and deriving from one's nature. To the degree that an individual utilizes sexuality (for pleasure, for adaptation, as the resolution of unconscious conflict) and to the degree that sexuality is valued, one's sexual "nature" will be experienced as more or less central to personality. To the extent that an individual's sex print "deviates" from the culture's prescription for sexuality, it may be experienced as even more central to identity (at least in this culture). So, for example, many transsexuals and transvestites report both relief and a sense of personality consolidation when "I found out what I am," when "I found out there were others like me."[49]

46. I use "sex print" in the sense of fingerprint, i.e., unchangeable and unique. I do not mean to apply anything about its origins, and it has no reference to imprinting.
47. Eissler, "Notes on Problems of Technique in the Psychoanalytic Treatment of Adolescents," pp. 236–37.
48. C. A. Tripp, *The Homosexual Matrix* (New York: New American Library), p. 17.
49. Person and Ovesey, "The Transsexual Syndrome in Males, Part I."

While sexual preference represents the narrowing of sexual potential, it is not experienced that way by most people. To some degree this is because sex printing is more pronounced (i.e., the script is more rigid) in the perversions, less pronounced in both heterosexuality and homosexuality. Furthermore, each individual usually has a cluster of effective erotic stimuli or fantasies so that it is possible to focus on one's own diversity rather than circumscription. It is also true that, within limits, one can add to one's effective sexual repertoire. Then, too, many people can perform effectively in many different situations, although without the subjective experience of excitement. Most important, heterosexuals have always had the advantage of viewing their sexuality as natural.

Even so, the sense of one's sexuality as bedrock derives not only from the shape of pleasure but also from the fact that the same erotic stimuli remain effective. So, for example, it is difficult for most heterosexuals to become bisexual even when they consciously make the effort out of intellectual or political conviction. In therapy, change in sexual orientation or even in sexual attitude (e.g., the insistence that a partner be "superior" in intellectual achievement) is achieved only with great difficulty and sometimes not at all. In some homosexual male patients who enter treatment in order to change their sexual orientation, it has been reported that the effective obstacle to change is not the inability to have intercourse with women, nor the preference for sex with men, but the unwillingness to give up a homosexual "identity."

The mechanism of sex printing is obscure, despite the obvious advantage in eliminating certain situations as sexual (some mechanism for the control of sexuality occurs in every species). Freud uses the explanatory concepts of repression, maturation, and fixation; however, his explanation depends on accepting the psychosexual stages of libido as inborn. Tripp suggests a neurological basis, nature unspecified, to account for the fact that each individual "loses his initial diversity of responses as his sexual interests become even more narrowed down to specific channels of expression."[50] Social sanction is often cited as the vector that socializes individuals toward obligatory heterosexuality. This explanation does not suffice. First, if sex printing were simply learned or conditioned, it could be readily unlearned or deconditioned. We have, in the relative irreversibility of sex print, the same problem as in the conceptualization of gender: the puzzle of why "learned" behavior is apparently irreversible. This form of "learning" is connected with the process of identity formation. The mechanism of this connection is a puzzle, which has led some theorists to arbitrary and unwarranted assumptions that imprinting occurs in humans. Second, the critical question is not why some patterns are strongly eroticized but, rather, why other erotic scripts are aversive. Third, social sanction cannot be used to explain sex

50. Tripp, p. 19.

printing in those individuals whose preferences depart from the conventional ones.

In sum, for the individual, both gender and sex print carry the subjective impression of being part of the private self, intact from external demands, autonomous. In this sense, they appear as part of the private realm, distinct from the public one. The importance attached to one's sexual "identity" may be even greater in a culture, such as ours, in which stabilizing features, such as rigid class distinction or geographical rootedness, are missing and cannot anchor personality. In other words, sexual identity draws its significance from individual development and as the repository of desire but becomes more important as other self-identifying features in the culture are attenuated.

Relevance of Sexual Paradigms to Issues of Female Sexuality

Sexual paradigms have relevance for at least three feminist concerns: (1) the importance of sexuality to individual development; (2) the relationship between sexuality, power, and dependency; and (3) the relationship of sexual liberation to the women's movement.

Sexuality and Individual Development

It is, in a sense, easier to prescribe for sexuality in some version of utopia than to grapple with intrinsic ambivalences attached to the expression of female sexuality in this culture. There are essentially two problematic areas in female sexuality: masochism and inhibition of sexuality. The issue of masochism has been dealt with extensively by a number of authors. They have demonstrated that masochism, insofar as it is an extensive part of female fantasy life, is secondary to the power relationships that exist in patriarchal society and is not intrinsic to female psychosexual development per se.[51]

Inhibition of sexuality has not received the same theoretical attention accorded masochism. Female sexual inhibition really refers to three separate orders of phenomena: first, inhibitions of assertiveness that take place in an interpersonal context; second, inhibition of sex per se as manifest by an inhibition of desire, arousal, or orgasm; and, third, low sexual "drive." The first set of inhibitions has little to do with sexuality; it is most often based on deference to the male and fear of him and includes such behaviors as "faking" orgasm, not insisting on adequate stimulation, assuming that male orgasm terminates a sexual encounter, and paying excessive attention to pleasing rather than to

51. See, e.g., Ethel Person, "Some New Observations on the Origins of Femininity," in *Women and Analysis,* ed. J. Strouse (New York: Grossman Publishers, 1974); Lionel Ovesey, "Masculine Aspirations in Women."

being pleasured. This set of inhibitions is usually easily resolved when a woman achieves greater assertiveness and a sense of autonomy. In fact, many so-called frigid women turn out to have no substantive problems with the achievement of arousal or orgasm; they either suffer from ignorance about what constitutes appropriate stimulation or from interpersonal intimidation. True female sexual inhibition refers to inhibition of desire, arousal, or orgasm, which arises out of psychological conflicts. Primarily, then, since most women are capable of orgasm, female sexual inhibition refers to low female "drive." So-called low drive is manifest in the low rates of female adolescent masturbation, the tendency to tie sexuality to intimacy, and the ability to tolerate anorgasmia. Here the tacit assumption is that male sexuality constitutes the norm and that women perform at a deficit.

The most striking difference in the behavioral manifestations of sexuality between the sexes occurs in adolescence. A comparison of induction into genital sexuality is of particular importance.[52] For some individuals sexual activity begins prior to adolescence; according to Kinsey, one-fifth of his male sample and one-tenth of his female sample experienced orgasm prior to age twelve.[53] For most individuals, though, sexuality emerges during adolescence under the impact of two factors: the hormonal shifts of puberty cause bodily changes that focus attention on emerging sexuality and may even result in spontaneous arousal and orgasm; next, social life is increasingly organized around disparate patterns of male and female interests and behaviors, which include imitations (rehearsals) of adult forms of social and sexual interactions.

In males, adolescence is characterized by the beginning of overt sexual activity and ejaculation. For most females, menstruation is the key event; for males, ejaculation. Menstruation may tend to inhibit sexual exploration, both for symbolic reasons and because it carries the threat of pregnancy. Whatever the reason, sex becomes organized differently for the two sexes. In males, over 80 percent have masturbated to orgasm by age fifteen, whereas only 20 percent of females have.[54] This discrepancy is still apparent in data collected twenty years later.[55] Thus masturbation in females is more erratic than it is in males; in females only about two-thirds ever masturbate to orgasm and, of those, half discover masturbation after having been introduced to orgasm in an interpersonal context. Explanations for the low level of female masturbation vary, but from the clinical point of view it is very significant. As has been noted previously, a male who has not achieved orgasm by either masturbation or coitus by the age of twenty almost certainly suffers from significant

52. This account is drawn from a superb section on adolescent sexuality by Gagnon and Simon (n. 18 above).
53. Kinsey's data reported by Gagnon and Simon, p. 55.
54. Kinsey's data reported by ibid.
55. Gagnon and Simon, p. 55, quoting work done previously with Berger.

sexual psychopathology, whereas no such conclusion can be drawn in the case of a female.

What consequences flow from these differences? It is generally assumed that the low rate of female masturbation reflects a problem. The advantages of the expression of sensuality and of genital sexuality in development are self-evident. The sense of autonomy is tied, at least subjectively, to the expression of sexuality in many individuals, and there is evidence in the clinical literature that masturbation in adolescent girls is related to high self-esteem and to the subsequent pursuit of career goals.[56] But it is unlikely that masturbation itself is so beneficial; more likely some general assertiveness plays a role in the exploration of both sexuality and role experimentation.

Low masturbation is not a problem per se; it is a problem only insofar as it reflects the female experience of sexuality as reactive rather than autonomous. Neither anorgasmia nor abstention necessarily bodes ill for women. There is no correlation between achievement of orgasm and mental health in women. Part of the confusion about the importance of sexuality is that the importance of sensual-erotic pleasure is not separated from the importance of orgasm. While orgasm does not seem crucial to achievement of high levels of personality integration in women, the absence of the capacity for sensual pleasure does not bode well for either sex.[57] Part of the confusion is because any discrepancy between female and male sexuality is viewed as problematic for females. The male model of sexuality, with its emphasis on orgasm and on sexuality as performance and achievement, is used as the sexual standard for both sexes. Consequently, hand in hand with the preoccupation with "sexual liberation," we see an almost fanatic preoccupation with the achievement of orgasm, multiple orgasms, and vaginal orgasms. The absence of focus on genitality, in some women, may reflect the psychobiographical fact that genitality (in contrast to sensuality) was never invoked.

In the individual woman, relative or absolute disinterest in genital sexuality does not constitute evidence for repression provided there is some capacity for sensual gratification. Genitality and orgasm do not seem to be crucial to psychological development in women. There are alternate routes for achieving autonomy and consolidating gender. This is not to deny that previously "frigid" women may experience ego expansion when they achieve orgasm for the first time or that many women

---

56. Abraham Maslow, "Self-Esteem (Dominance-Feeling) and Sexuality in Women," *Journal of Social Psychology* 16 (1942): 259–94, and "Dominance, Personality and Social Behavior in Women," *Journal of Social Psychology* 10 (1939): 3–39.

57. In this regard, see Ruth Moulton's interesting observation that aversion to having the breasts touched correlated with poor therapeutic results in her treatment sample of "frigid" women ("Multiple Factors in Frigidity," in *Science and Psychoanalysis*, vol. 10, ed. Jules Masserman [New York: Grune & Stratton, 1966]).

clinically have significant areas of repressed sexuality. Nor is it to deny that many people achieve their greatest sense of intimacy and union through sexuality. It is to argue that one must demonstrate repression rather than assume it, that periodic asexuality and anorgasmia seem consonant with mature ego development in women, and that one ought not dictate a tyranny of active sexuality as critical to female liberation.

The degree to which the difference in the primacy of genital sexuality between women and men represents a biological or cultural divergence is an open question. On one hand, as Gagnon and Simon point out, female capacity (for orgasm) does not predict rate, thus suggesting the primacy of the cultural input. On the other hand, the frequency of spontaneous ejaculation in adolescent males almost insures the integration of genital sexuality into psychosexual development and fantasy life, while the paucity of spontaneous orgasm in females may, in turn, be viewed as biological or cultural, pending evidence to establish one or the other position.[58]

Whatever the causes, there is a relative "muting of female erotic impulsivity"[59] in this culture. In libido theory, inhibition of female sexuality is understood as the result of either the circuitous path of libidinal development in females or diminished constitutional endowment. From the culturist perspective, it is viewed as the product of selective strictures. While it is undoubtedly true that direct cultural proscriptions influence attitudes, such strictures are not usually decisive in psychological life. Take, for example, the widespread occurrence of male adolescent masturbation in the Victorian era; while the strictures against masturbation were influential, they did not deter the entire male adolescent population.

It is probably more to the point that socialization for girls occurs in such a way that the record of internalized object relations will support the cultural bias. Fear of pregnancy (or fear of the pill) acts in the same direction. Female psychosexual development is only currently being reformulated.[60] One root of low "drive" originates in the particular configuration of the female oedipal constellation. The girl finds her erotic rival the source of dependent gratification, a situation which intensifies her oedipal rivalry. Furthermore, the fact that her first erotic object is

58. Ford and Beach (n. 15 above) claim that in all human societies which have been studied, "males are more likely than females to stimulate their own sexual organs" (p. 242). In both lower mammals and female primates, there is relatively low masturbation. Consequently, Ford and Beach support an "evolutionary" or biological component. With the same data available, Gagnon and Simon form a cultural interpretation.

59. The phrase is Dorothy Dinnerstein's in *The Mermaid and the Minotaur: Sexual Arrangements and Human Malaise* (New York: Harper & Row, 1976).

60. Dinnerstein's *The Mermaid and the Minotaur* is the most systematic exposition of this point of view to date. However, her account is hampered somewhat by its completely ahistorical perspective.

homosexual may lead some women to repress their earliest experiences of sensuality (this may be one reason some women regard certain sexual acts as shameful). It is only within the context of the specific female oedipal constellation that other psychological contributions to muted erotic sensibility can be understood. It is probable that females start life with as much sensual-erotic potential as males, but certain inhibitions implicit in female object relations countervail, inhibitions solidified by cultural biases and realistic consequences.

Emphasis on inhibition of female sexuality has almost precluded discussions about the quality of male sexuality, which often seems compulsive in the guise of liberated sexuality. While both sexes may display inhibited sexuality (e.g., orgasmic inhibition in women, impotence in men), among men one more often sees compulsive sexuality, and not just among men who have sexual "problems." What so stokes male sexuality that clinicians are impressed by the force of sexuality? Not libido, but rather the curious phenomenon by which sexuality consolidates and confirms gender. While it is unclear why this linkage occurs in men and not usually in women, the meaning of sexuality to men and the ways it is used are clear. First, sexuality represents domination; witness the widespread rape, control, and transgressive fantasies among men. Consequently, anxiety about any threat to masculine power can be assuaged by sexual encounter. Second, dependency needs can be disguised as sexual; this is especially important for men who are denied any legitimate outlets for dependency gratification. Third, reassurance against castration anxiety ought never to be underestimated as the motivation for a sexual encounter, particularly in such a competitive culture as ours. Fourth, the need to overcome a primary female identification (as is fostered by the custom of female monopoly of child care) may lead to an overvaluation of the penis and sexuality. In other words, relative gender fragility in men fosters excessive reliance on sexuality. Men appear to engage more in sex for sex's sake (sex shorn of interpersonal meaning) than women, yet sex carries many hidden symbolic valences for men. One can conclude that it is just as meaningful to talk about male hypersexuality as it is to talk about female hyposexuality.

Given a current liberal climate of thinking about sexuality there is a danger, not so much in an antierotic attitude, but in too much insistence on the expression of sexuality as the sine qua non of mental health and self-actualization. It is extremely difficult to separate ourselves from the current cultural standards and to judge how highly we should value the expression of sexuality per se. If one does not adhere to a belief in drive theory, one must question whether the overriding emphasis placed on sexuality is inevitable or even desirable. In any neutral discussion about sexuality, one would have to weigh not just the developmental advantages of active sexuality but also the adaptive advantages of the capacity for abstinence, repression, or suppression. This is particularly true because of the difference in the developmental and adult sexual patterns between women and men: it has been too easily assumed that the male pattern of sexuality is freer, beneficial, and more desirable. The way in which sexuality is integrated into personality has greater meaning than the rate of orgasm.

Sexuality, Power, and Dependency

Feminist analyses have verified the psychoanalytic insight that sexuality reflects multiple motives. Sexual fantasies are tied to both nonsexual motives, which arise from individual experience, and to personality styles that stem from gender role training. The nonsexual, nonaffectionate motives most often expressed are power and dependency motives. This is true of both actual behavior and dream images and fantasies. It is precisely because sexuality is so often the vehicle for the expression of power relations that sexuality is by its very nature a subject for political inquiry. Obviously, from the feminist and sexual liberationist points of view, the freeing of sexuality from other contaminating motivation is highly desirable. All three paradigms of sexual motivation described previously acknowledge the confluence of sexual and nonsexual motives in sexual and nonsexual behavior. What is extremely interesting, and somewhat paradoxical, is that in libido theory it is theoretically possible to experience sex as pure sex uncontaminated by other considerations provided one is able to dissolve cultural inhibitions and individual conflicts. This hope is at the heart of Wilhelm Reich's and Norman O. Brown's cultural prescriptions.

In contrast, in the third paradigm, the meaning of sexuality will always be linked to nonsexual meaning because of the infantile intertwining of sensuality and object relations and because sensual-sexual parts of the body (e.g., the mouth in sucking), have multiple meanings and functions in development. Sex qua sex, without these other meanings, is an impossibility. Sex will always be permeated with meanings that attach to individual and social parameters. In particular, because sensuality develops in the relatively dependent, helpless child, with the earliest gratification attached to powerful adults, it is unlikely that sexuality will ever be completely free of submission-dominance connotations. At the same time, it is possible that being female will not necessarily carry submissive connotations. In other words, the limitations to sexual "liberation," meaning liberation from power contaminants, do not reside in the biological nature of sexuality, or in cultural and political arrangements, and certainly not in the sex difference, but may lie in the universal condition of infantile dependence. It may be that the consequences of infantile dependence form the substance of tragedy; such a suspicion, of course, echoes Freud's pessimistic assessment of the human condition.

Sexual Liberation

While one might expect to be able to predict which groups would favor a historical analysis of sexuality and which a biological one, one is very frequently surprised. For example, one group of feminists postulates a feminine libido (as a version of biological substratum) as opposed to a masculine libido but may view the feminine as superior.[61] Some advocates of the rights of sexual minorities have utilized a "by nature" or congenital argument to justify their demands, yet many homosexuals favor a cultural analysis. With the development of the gay rights movement, the theoretical focus among gays has shifted from the causes of homosexuality to the causes of prejudice against it. Interest in this latter question parallels (and may be instrumental in) the heightened interest in historical and cultural variations of sexual practice and attitudes toward sexuality.

Despite the recent focus on the historical forces that shape sexuality and despite the extremely cogent criticisms of libido conceptualized as drive, Freud's paradigm remains paramount. While it is easy to understand that historical contingency limits our choices and opportunities, it is more difficult to accept the proposition that historical contingency forms a substantial part of the sexual self. We still tend to regard sexuality, as it exists, as representing human nature uncorrupted by social institutions. Take, for example, the enormous influence of the ideology of the sexual liberation movement.

It is a tenet of "sexual liberation" that society has caused the individual to repress her or his sexuality to the grave detriment of that individual. Such a belief is based on the assumption that sexuality is natural, an essence that seeks a particular expression out of its own nature and, furthermore, that repression of sexuality stunts the personality. In other words, sexual liberation draws on Freud's libido theory and on the theories of some Freudian revisionists (Brown, Marcuse) as its intellectual rationale. It is surprising how many people who consider themselves anti-Freudian or antipsychoanalytic agree fundamentally with the postulates of libido theory. Sexual liberation is strikingly espoused by several groups which have little else in common; one might even say that they border on hostility toward one another, as illustrated in the differences in assumptions among gay, S-M, and mainstream liberationists; feminists; pornography advocates; and practitioners in the sex therapy industry.

Sexual liberation is not the same as female liberation, an observation feminists have made for years.[62] It is clear from object-relations theory that sexuality is the vehicle for the expression of nonsexual motives. In this culture there may be a basic contradiction between sexual liberation

---

61. Hélène Cixous in a presentation to the Columbia University Seminar on Women and Society, October 8, 1979.

62. E.g., Kate Millett in *Sexual Politics* (New York: Doubleday & Co., 1970).

and personal liberation (or autonomy) for women insofar as sexuality as constructed expresses dependent or masochistic trends. Sexuality, even when abundantly expressed, in contrast to repressed sexuality, cannot be liberated as long as women have to define themselves vicariously through their relationship to men.[63] Sexuality then carries the inevitable distortions implicit in psychosexual development and the connotations of instrumental use as the major modality for securing a self-defining sexual liaison. Sexuality takes on too much meaning as interpersonal "glue," too little meaning as pleasure or self-expression.

If one is not an advocate of libido theory, one must take seriously the alternate proposition that sexuality as experienced is not as autonomous, independent, or natural as one subjectively feels it to be. The sexuality so often liberated is a product of sexist conditioning rather than the true individual core that sexuality is so often assumed to be. From the feminist point of view, sexual liberation can be a conservative force in society, insofar as it enshrines the status quo as bedrock. Any radical social critique must consider the possibility that 'id" itself, in part the repository of wishes, is not insulated from culture; although once consolidated, id may be largely immutable in any one individual. The feminist movement must deal not just with personal liberation but also with the institutions that shape desire.

Reserve about sexual liberation as a political movement can conflict with enthusiasm for individual sexuality. On one hand, it can be conceded that sexuality is plastic, not exclusively dictated by "nature"; on the other, the individual's sexuality is not endlessly plastic. Once subjectivity and sexuality are consolidated in the course of individual development, they are as nature to the individual, not to be changed lightly or with ease. Thus a healthy respect for eroticism as it is experienced is in order.

In sum, then, sexual liberation, while important and even crucial to some individuals, has significant limitations as social critique and political policy. At its worst, sexual liberation is part of the cult of individuality which only demands legitimization of the expression of the individual's needs, what appears to be her raw "impulse" life, against the demands of society without considering a political reordering of the social order itself. The achievement of the conditions necessary to female autonomy is a precondition for authentic sexual liberation.

Conclusion

Many psychoanalytic theorists currently view sexuality as a motivational system which is derivative, not from drive, but from the psychological record of sensual experience integrated through a series of object

63. Sexual liberation is often confused with sexual activity. Autobiographies such as Evelyn Keyes's *Scarlett O'Hara's Younger Sister: My Lively Life in and out of Hollywood* (Secaucus, N.J.: Lyle Stuart, Inc., 1977) inadvertently make this point abundantly clear.

relations. While the object-relations theory of sexuality does not preclude adherence to a drive theory of sexuality, it renders it superfluous. Even in this revised formulation, sexuality still appears to maintain a unique position in psychic development. In particular, sexuality is related to identity formation through the mediating structures of gender and sex print. One of the crucial differences between female and male sexuality is the invariable dependence of gender identity on sexuality in males, a dependence not invariably found in females. The mechanism of this association is unclear but may be related to the female monopoly of child care.

Theories of sexuality have relevance to issues of female sexuality and feminist theory in several ways. Female sexual inhibition or low female sexual "drive" reflects partly cultural intimidation, partly developmental issues. We must avoid using male sexuality as the norm; just as females may be hyposexual, male sexuality frequently appears driven rather than liberated. Male sexuality is often driven by the need to express dominance symbolically. While it may be difficult to "liberate" sexuality from power contaminants, it will represent an advance when dominance is not automatically linked with male sexuality, submission with female sexuality.

Although sexuality is experienced as autonomous, part of the self uncorrupted by social institutions, the fantasies attached to desire reflect interiorization from the culture. Therefore, some problematic aspects of sexuality are not immutable. Interiorization is not a singular reflection of cultural values. It occurs in the context of self and object relations. Sexual reform depends not just on attitudinal change regarding sexuality but on significant changes in child rearing and away from the stereotypic rendering of sex roles. Real sexual liberation will come out of female liberation, not the other way around.

Department of Psychiatry
Columbia University School of Medicine

Compulsory Heterosexuality and Lesbian Existence

Adrienne Rich

I

Biologically men have only one innate orientation—a sexual one
that draws them to women,—while women have two innate orientations, sexual toward men and reproductive toward their young.[1]

. . . I was a woman terribly vulnerable, critical, using femaleness as
a sort of standard or yardstick to measure and discard men. Yes—

In its first issue (Autumn 1975), *Signs: Journal of Women in Culture and Society* published
Carroll Smith-Rosenberg's now classic article, "The Female World of Love and Ritual:
Relations between Women in Nineteenth-Century America." The following summer ap-
peared Joan Kelly's "The Social Relation of the Sexes: Methodological Implications of
Women's History (*Signs: Journal of Women in Culture and Society,* vol. 1, no. 4 [Summer 1976]).
Among scholarly articles, these two provided, in different ways, a point of departure for
my thinking in this essay. I am deeply indebted also to the growing body of lesbian research
in other journals, including Blanche W. Cook's "Female Support Networks and Political
Activism," *Chrysalis* 3 (1977): 43–61; and Lorraine Bethel's " 'This Infinity of Conscious
Pain': Zora Neale Hurston and the Black Female Literary Tradition," lecture given at the
Harlem Studio Museum, May 1978, forthcoming in *Black Women's Studies,* ed. Gloria Hull,
Elaine Bell Scott, and Barbara Smith (Old Westbury, N.Y.: Feminist Press, 1980); by
several books published in the last few years: Kathleen Barry, *Female Sexual Slavery* (En-
glewood Cliffs, N.J.: Prentice-Hall, Inc., 1979): Mary Daly, *Gyn/Ecology: The Metaethics of
Radical Feminism* (Boston: Beacon Press, 1978); Susan Griffin, *Woman and Nature: The Roar-
ing Inside Her* (New York: Harper & Row, 1978); Diana Russell and Nicole van de Ven, eds.,
Proceedings of the International Tribunal on Crimes against Women (Millbrae, Calif.: Les Femmes, 1976); and by Susan Cavin's dissertation in sociology, "Lesbian Origins: An Hystorical
and Cross-cultural Analysis of Sex Ratios, Female Sexuality and Homo-sexual Segregation
versus Hetero-sexual Integration Patterns in Relation to the Liberation of Women" (Ph.D.
diss., Rutgers University, 1978).
   1. Alice Rossi, "Children and Work in the Lives of Women" (paper delivered at the
University of Arizona, Tucson, February 1976).

something like that. I was an Anna who invited defeat from men without ever being conscious of it. (But I am conscious of it. And being conscious of it means I shall leave it all behind me and become—but what?) I was stuck fast in an emotion common to women of our time, that can turn them bitter, or Lesbian, or solitary. Yes, that Anna during that time was . . .

[Another blank line across the page:][2]

The bias of compulsory heterosexuality, through which lesbian experience is perceived on a scale ranging from deviant to abhorrent, or simply rendered invisible, could be illustrated from many other texts than the two just preceding. The assumption made by Rossi, that women are "innately sexually oriented" toward men, or by Lessing, that the lesbian choice is simply an acting-out of bitterness toward men, are by no means theirs alone; they are widely current in literature and in the social sciences.

I am concerned here with two other matters as well: first, how and why women's choice of women as passionate comrades, life partners, co-workers, lovers, tribe, has been crushed, invalidated, forced into hiding and disguise; and second, the virtual or total neglect of lesbian existence in a wide range of writings, including feminist scholarship. Obviously there is a connection here. I believe that much feminist theory and criticism is stranded on this shoal.

My organizing impulse is the belief that it is not enough for feminist thought that specifically lesbian texts exist. Any theory or cultural/political creation that treats lesbian existence as a marginal or less "natural" phenomenon, as mere "sexual preference," or as the mirror image of either heterosexual or male homosexual relations, is profoundly weakened thereby, whatever its other contributions. Feminist theory can no longer afford merely to voice a toleration of "lesbianism" as an "alternative life-style," or make token allusion to lesbians. A feminist critique of compulsory heterosexual orientation for women is long overdue. In this exploratory paper, I shall try to show why.

I will begin by way of examples, briefly discussing four books that have appeared in the last few years, written from different viewpoints and political orientations, but all presenting themselves, and favorably reviewed, as feminist.[3] All take as a basic assumption that the social

2. Doris Lessing, *The Golden Notebook* (New York: Bantam Books [1962] 1977), p. 480.
3. Nancy Chodorow, *The Reproduction of Mothering* (Berkeley: University of California Press, 1978); Dorothy Dinnerstein, *The Mermaid and the Minotaur: Sexual Arrangements and the Human Malaise* (New York: Harper & Row, 1976); Barbara Ehrenreich and Deirdre English, *For Her Own Good: 150 Years of the Experts' Advice to Women* (Garden City, N.Y.: Doubleday & Co., Anchor Press, 1978); Jean Baker Miller, *Toward a New Psychology of Women* (Boston: Beacon Press, 1976).

relations of the sexes are disordered and extremely problematic, if not disabling, for women; all seek paths toward change. I have learned more from some of these books than from others; but on this I am clear: each one might have been more accurate, more powerful, more truly a force for change, had the author felt impelled to deal with lesbian existence as a reality, and as a source of knowledge and power available to women; or with the institution of heterosexuality itself as a beachhead of male dominance.[4] In none of them is the question ever raised, whether in a different context, or other things being equal, women would *choose* heterosexual coupling and marriage; heterosexuality is presumed as a "sexual preference" of "most women," either implicitly or explicitly. In none of these books, which concern themselves with mothering, sex roles, relationships, and societal prescriptions for women, is compulsory heterosexuality ever examined as an institution powerfully affecting all these; or the idea of "preference" or "innate orientation" even indirectly questioned.

In *For Her Own Good: 150 Years of the Experts' Advice to Women* by Barbara Ehrenreich and Deirdre English, the authors' superb pamphlets, *Witches, Midwives and Nurses: A History of Women Healers,* and *Complaints and Disorders: The Sexual Politics of Sickness,* are developed into a provocative and complex study. Their thesis in this book is that the advice given American women by male health professionals, particularly in the areas of marital sex, maternity, and child care, has echoed the dictates of the economic marketplace and the role capitalism has needed women to play in production and/or reproduction. Women have become the consumer victims of various cures, therapies, and normative judgments in different periods (including the prescription to middle-class

4. I could have chosen many other serious and influential recent books, including anthologies, which would illustrate the same point: e.g., *Our Bodies, Ourselves,* the Boston Women's Health Collective's best-seller (New York: Simon & Schuster, 1976), which devotes a separate (and inadequate) chapter to lesbians, but whose message is that heterosexuality is most women's life preference; Berenice Carroll, ed., *Liberating Women's History: Theoretical and Critical Essays* (Urbana: University of Illinois Press, 1976), which does not include even a token essay on the lesbian presence in history, though an essay by Linda Gordon, Persis Hunt, et al. notes the use by male historians of "sexual deviance" as a category to discredit and dismiss Anna Howard Shaw, Jane Addams, and other feminists ("Historical Phallacies: Sexism in American Historical Writing"); and Renate Bridenthal and Claudia Koonz, eds., *Becoming Visible: Women in European History* (Boston: Houghton Mifflin Co., 1977), which contains three mentions of male homosexuality but no materials that I have been able to locate on lesbians. Gerda Lerner, ed., *The Female Experience: An American Documentary* (Indianapolis: Bobbs-Merrill Co., 1977), contains an abridgment of two lesbian/feminist position papers from the contemporary movement but no other documentation of lesbian existence. Lerner does note in her preface, however, how the charge of deviance has been used to fragment women and discourage women's resistance. Linda Gordon, in *Woman's Body, Woman's Right: A Social History of Birth Control in America* (New York: Viking Press, Grossman, 1976), notes accurately that: "It is not that feminism has produced more lesbians. There have always been many lesbians, despite high levels of repression; and most lesbians experience their sexual preference as innate . . ." (p. 410).

women to embody and preserve the sacredness of the home—the "scientific" romanticization of the home itself). None of the "experts'" advice has been either particularly scientific or women-oriented; it has reflected male needs, male fantasies about women, and male interest in controlling women—particularly in the realms of sexuality and motherhood—fused with the requirements of industrial capitalism. So much of this book is so devastatingly informative and is written with such lucid feminist wit, that I kept waiting as I read for the basic prescription against lesbianism to be examined. It never was.

This can hardly be for lack of information. Jonathan Katz's *Gay American History*[5] tells us that as early as 1656 the New Haven Colony prescribed the death penalty for lesbians. Katz provides many suggestive and informative documents on the "treatment" (or torture) of lesbians by the medical profession in the nineteenth and twentieth centuries. Recent work by the historian Nancy Sahli documents the crackdown on intense female friendships among college women at the turn of the present century.[6] The ironic title, *For Her Own Good*, might have referred first and foremost to the economic imperative to heterosexuality and marriage and to the sanctions imposed against single women and widows—both of whom have been and still are viewed as deviant. Yet, in this often enlightening Marxist-feminist overview of male prescriptions for female sanity and health, the economics of prescriptive heterosexuality go unexamined.[7]

Of the three psychoanalytically based books, one, Jean Baker Miller's *Toward a New Psychology of Women*, is written as if lesbians simply do not exist, even as marginal beings. Given Miller's title I find this astonishing. However, the favorable reviews the book has received in feminist journals, including *Signs* and *Spokeswoman*, suggest that Miller's heterocentric assumptions are widely shared. In *The Mermaid and the Minotaur: Sexual Arrangements and the Human Malaise*, Dorothy Dinnerstein makes an impassioned argument for the sharing of parenting between women and men and for an end to what she perceives as the male/female symbiosis of "gender arrangements," which she feels are leading the species further and further into violence and self-extinction. Apart from other problems that I have with this book (including her silence on the institutional and random terrorism men have practiced on women—and children—throughout history, amply documented by

5. Jonathan Katz, *Gay American History* (New York: Thomas Y. Crowell Co., 1976).

6. Nancy Sahli, "Smashing: Women's Relationships before the Fall," *Chrysalis: A Magazine of Women's Culture* 8 (1979): 17–27. A version of the article was presented at the Third Berkshire Conference on the History of Women, June 11, 1976.

7. This is a book which I have publicly endorsed. I would still do so, though with the above caveat. It is only since beginning to write this article that I fully appreciated how enormous is the unasked question in Ehrenreich and English's book.

Barry, Daly, Griffin, Russell and van de Ven, and Brownmiller,[8] and her obsession with psychology to the neglect of economic and other material realities that help to create psychological reality), I find utterly ahistorical Dinnerstein's view of the relations between women and men as "a collaboration to keep history mad." She means by this, to perpetuate social relations which are hostile, exploitive, and destructive to life itself. She sees women and men as equal partners in the making of "sexual arrangements," seemingly unaware of the repeated struggles of women to resist oppression (our own and that of others) and to change our condition. She ignores, specifically, the history of women who—as witches, *femmes seules,* marriage resisters, spinsters, autonomous widows, and/or lesbians—have managed on varying levels *not* to collaborate. It is this history, precisely, from which feminists have so much to learn and on which there is overall such blanketing silence. Dinnerstein acknowledges at the end of her book that "female separatism," though "on a large scale and in the long run wildly impractical," has something to teach us: "Separate, women could in principle set out to learn from scratch— undeflected by the opportunities to evade this task that men's presence has so far offered—what intact self-creative humanness is."[9] Phrases like "intact self-creative humanness" obscure the question of what the many forms of female separatism have actually been addressing. The fact is that women in every culture and throughout history *have* undertaken the task of independent, nonheterosexual, woman-connected existence, to the extent made possible by their context, often in the belief that they were the "only ones" ever to have done so. They have undertaken it even though few women have been in an economic position to resist marriage altogether; and even though attacks against unmarried women have ranged from aspersion and mockery to deliberate gynocide, including the burning and torturing of millions of widows and spinsters during the witch persecutions of the fifteenth, sixteenth, and seventeenth centuries in Europe, and the practice of suttee on widows in India.[10]

Nancy Chodorow does come close to the edge of an acknowledgment of lesbian existence. Like Dinnerstein, Chodorow believes that the fact that women, and women only, are responsible for child care in the sexual division of labor has led to an entire social organization of gender inequality, and that men as well as women must become primary carers for children if that inequality is to change. In the process of examining, from a psychoanalytic perspective, how mothering-by-women affects the psychological development of girl and boy children, she offers documentation that men are "emotionally secondary" in women's lives; that

8. Susan Brownmiller, *Against Our Will: Men, Women and Rape* (New York: Simon & Schuster, 1975).
9. Dinnerstein, p. 272.
10. Daly, pp. 184–85; 114–33.

"women have a richer, ongoing inner world to fall back on. . . . men do not become as emotionally important to women as women do to men."[11] This would carry into the late twentieth century Smith-Rosenberg's findings about eighteenth- and nineteenth-century women's emotional focus on women. "Emotionally important" can of course refer to anger as well as to love, or to that intense mixture of the two often found in women's relationships with women: one aspect of what I have come to call the "double-life of women" (see below). Chodorow concludes that because women have women as mothers, "The mother remains a primary internal object [*sic*] to the girl, so that heterosexual relationships are on the model of a nonexclusive, second relationship for her, whereas for the boy they recreate an exclusive, primary relationship." According to Chodorow, women "have learned to deny the limitations of masculine lovers for both psychological and practical reasons."[12]

But the practical reasons (like witch burnings, male control of law, theology, and science, or economic nonviability within the sexual division of labor) are glossed over. Chodorow's account barely glances at the constraints and sanctions which, historically, have enforced or insured the coupling of women with men and obstructed or penalized our coupling or allying in independent groups with other women. She dismisses lesbian existence with the comment that "lesbian relationships do tend to re-create mother-daughter emotions and connections, but most women are heterosexual" (implied: more mature, having developed beyond the mother-daughter connection). She then adds: "This heterosexual preference and taboos on homosexuality, in addition to objective economic dependence on men, make the option of primary sexual bonds with other women unlikely—though more prevalent in recent years."[13] The significance of that qualification seems irresistible—but Chodorow does not explore it further. Is she saying that lesbian existence has become more visible in recent years (in certain groups?), that economic and other pressures have changed (under capitalism, socialism, or both?), and that consequently more women are rejecting the heterosexual "choice"? She argues that women want children because their heterosexual relationships lack richness and intensity, that in having a child a woman seeks to re-create her own intense relationship with her mother. It seems to be that on the basis of her own findings, Chodorow leads us implicitly to conclude that heterosexuality is *not* a "preference" for women; that, for one thing, it fragments the erotic from the emotional in a way that women find impoverishing and painful. Yet her book participates in mandating it. Neglecting the covert socializations and the overt forces which have channelled women into marriage and heterosexual romance,

11. Chodorow, pp. 197–98.
12. Ibid., pp. 198–99.
13. Ibid., p. 200.

pressures ranging from the selling of daughters to postindustrial economics to the silences of literature to the images of the television screen,
she, like Dinnerstein, is stuck with trying to reform a man-made
institution—compulsory heterosexuality—as if, despite profound emotional impulses and complementarities drawing women toward women,
there is a mystical/biological heterosexual inclination, a "preference" or
"choice" which draws women toward men.

Moreover, it is understood that this "preference" does not need to
be explained, unless through the tortuous theory of the female Oedipus
complex or the necessity for species reproduction. It is lesbian sexuality
which (usually, and, incorrectly, "included" under male homosexuality)
is seen as requiring explanation. This assumption of female heterosexuality seems to me in itself remarkable: it is an enormous assumption to
have glided so silently into the foundations of our thought.

The extension of this assumption is the frequently heard assertion
that in a world of genuine equality, where men were nonoppressive and
nurturing, everyone would be bisexual. Such a notion blurs and sen-
timentalizes the actualities within which women have experienced sexuality; it is the old liberal leap across the tasks and struggles of here and
now, the continuing process of sexual definition which will generate its
own possibilities and choices. (It also assumes that women who have
chosen women have done so simply because men are oppressive and
emotionally unavailable: which still fails to account for women who continue to pursue relationships with oppressive and/or emotionally unsatisfying men.) I am suggesting that heterosexuality, like motherhood,
needs to be recognized and studied as a *political institution*—even, or
especially, by those individuals who feel they are, in their personal experience, the precursors of a new social relation between the sexes.

II

If women are the earliest sources of emotional caring and physical
nurture for both female and male children, it would seem logical, from a
feminist perspective at least, to pose the following questions: whether the
search for love and tenderness in both sexes does not originally lead
toward women; *why in fact women would ever redirect that search;* why
species-survival, the means of impregnation, and emotional/erotic relationships should ever have become so rigidly identified with each
other; and why such violent strictures should be found necessary to
enforce women's total emotional, erotic loyalty and subservience to
men. I doubt that enough feminist scholars and theorists have taken the
pains to acknowledge the societal forces which wrench women's emotional and erotic energies away from themselves and other women and

from woman-identified values. These forces, as I shall try to show, range from literal physical enslavement to the disguising and distorting of possible options.

I do not, myself, assume that mothering-by-women is a "sufficient cause" of lesbian existence. But the issue of mothering-by-women has been much in the air of late, usually accompanied by the view that increased parenting by men would minimize antagonism between the sexes and equalize the sexual imbalance of power of males over females. These discussions are carried on without reference to compulsory heterosexuality as a phenomenon let alone as an ideology. I do not wish to psychologize here, but rather to identify sources of male power. I believe large numbers of men could, in fact, undertake child care on a large scale without radically altering the balance of male power in a male-identified society.

In her essay "The Origin of the Family," Kathleen Gough lists eight characteristics of male power in archaic and contemporary societies which I would like to use as a framework: "men's ability to deny women sexuality or to force it upon them; to command or exploit their labor to control their produce; to control or rob them of their children; to confine them physically and prevent their movement; to use them as objects in male transactions; to cramp their creativeness; or to withhold from them large areas of the society's knowledge and cultural attainments."[14] (Gough does not perceive these power-characteristics as specifically enforcing heterosexuality; only as producing sexual inequality.) Below, Gough's words appear in italics; the elaboration of each of her categories, in brackets, is my own.

Characteristics of male power include:

the power of men

    1. *to deny women* [our own] *sexuality*
        [by means of clitoridectomy and infibulation; chastity belts; punishment, including death, for female adultery; punishment, including death, for lesbian sexuality; psychoanalytic denial of the clitoris; strictures against masturbation; denial of maternal and postmenopausal sensuality; unnecessary hysterectomy; pseudolesbian images in media and literature; closing of archives and destruction of documents relating to lesbian existence];
    2. *or to force it* [male sexuality] *upon them*
        [by means of rape (including marital rape) and wife beating; father-daughter, brother-sister incest; the socialization of women to feel that male sexual "drive" amounts to a right;[15] idealization

14. Kathleen Gough, "The Origin of the Family," in *Toward an Anthropology of Women*, ed. Rayna [Rapp] Reiter (New York: Monthly Review Press, 1975), pp. 69–70.
15. Barry, pp. 216–19.

of heterosexual romance in art, literature, media, advertising, etc.; child marriage; arranged marriage; prostitution; the harem; psychoanalytic doctrines of frigidity and vaginal orgasm; pornographic depictions of women responding pleasurably to sexual violence and humiliation (a subliminal message being that sadistic heterosexuality is more "normal" than sensuality between women)];

3. *to command or exploit their labor to control their produce*
[by means of the institutions of marriage and motherhood as unpaid production; the horizontal segregation of women in paid employment; the decoy of the upwardly mobile token woman; male control of abortion, contraception, and childbirth; enforced sterilization; pimping; female infanticide, which robs mothers of daughters and contributes to generalized devaluation of women];

4. *to control or rob them of their children*
[by means of father-right and "legal kidnapping";[16] enforced sterilization; systematized infanticide; seizure of children from lesbian mothers by the courts; the malpractice of male obstetrics; use of the mother as "token torturer"[17] in genital mutilation or in binding the daughter's feet (or mind) to fit her for marriage];

5. *to confine them physically and prevent their movement*
[by means of rape as terrorism, keeping women off the streets; purdah; foot-binding; atrophying of women's athletic capabilities; haute couture, "feminine" dress codes; the veil; sexual harassment on the streets; horizontal segregation of women in employment; prescriptions for "full-time" mothering; enforced economic dependence of wives];

6. *to use them as objects in male transactions*
[use of women as "gifts"; bride-price; pimping; arranged marriage; use of women as entertainers to facilitate male deals, e.g., wife-hostess, cocktail waitress required to dress for male sexual titillation, call girls, "bunnies," geisha, *kisaeng* prostitutes, secretaries];

7. *to cramp their creativeness*
[witch persecutions as campaigns against midwives and female healers and as pogrom against independent, "unassimilated" women;[18] definition of male pursuits as more valuable than female within any culture, so that cultural values become embodiment of male subjectivity; restriction of female self-fulfillment to marriage and motherhood; sexual exploitation of women by male artists and teachers; the social and economic

16. Anna Demeter, *Legal Kidnapping* (Boston: Beacon Press, 1977), pp. xx, 126–28.
17. Daly, pp. 132, 139–41, 163–65.
18. Barbara Ehrenreich and Deirdre English, *Witches, Midwives and Nurses: A History of Women Healers* (Old Westbury, N.Y.: Feminist Press, 1973); Andrea Dworkin, *Woman Hating* (New York: E. P. Dutton, 1974), pp. 118–54; Daly, pp. 178–222.

disruption of women's creative aspirations;[19] erasure of female tradition];[20] and

8. *to withhold from them large areas of the society's knowledge and cultural attainments*

   [by means of noneducation of females (60% of the world's illiterates are women); the "Great Silence" regarding women and particularly lesbian existence in history and culture;[21] sex-role stereotyping which deflects women from science, technology, and other "masculine" pursuits; male social/professional bonding which excludes women; discrimination against women in the professions].

These are some of the methods by which male power is manifested and maintained. Looking at the schema, what surely impresses itself is the fact that we are confronting not a simple maintenance of inequality and property possession, but a pervasive cluster of forces, ranging from physical brutality to control of consciousness, which suggests that an enormous potential counterforce is having to be restrained.

Some of the forms by which male power manifests itself are more easily recognizable as enforcing heterosexuality on women than are others. Yet each one I have listed adds to the cluster of forces within which women have been convinced that marriage, and sexual orientation toward men, are inevitable, even if unsatisfying or oppressive components of their lives. The chastity belt; child marriage; erasure of lesbian existence (except as exotic and perverse) in art, literature, film; idealization of heterosexual romance and marriage—these are some fairly obvious forms of compulsion, the first two exemplifying physical force, the second two control of consciousness. While clitoridectomy has been assailed by feminists as a form of woman-torture,[22] Kathleen Barry first pointed out that it is not simply a way of turning the young girl into a "marriageable" woman through brutal surgery: it intends that women in the intimate proximity of polygynous marriage will not form sexual relationships with each other; that—from a male, genital-fetishist perspective—female erotic connections, even in a sex-segregated situation, will be literally excised.[23]

19. See Virginia Woolf, *A Room of One's Own* (London: Hogarth Press, 1929), and *Three Guineas* (New York: Harcourt Brace & Co., [1938] 1966); Tillie Olsen, *Silences* (Boston: Delacorte Press, 1978); Michelle Cliff, "The Resonance of Interruption," *Chrysalis: A Magazine of Women's Culture* 8 (1979): 29–37.

20. Mary Daly, *Beyond God the Father* (Boston: Beacon Press, 1973), pp. 347–51; Olsen, pp. 22–46.

21. Daly, *Beyond God the Father*, p. 93.

22. Fran P. Hosken, "The Violence of Power: Genital Mutilation of Females," *Heresies: A Feminist Journal of Art and Politics* 6 (1979): 28–35; Russell and van de Ven, pp. 194–95.

23. Barry, pp. 163–64.

The function of pornography as an influence on consciousness is a major public issue of our time, when a multibillion-dollar industry has the power to disseminate increasingly sadistic, women-degrading visual images. But even so-called soft-core pornography and advertising depict women as objects of sexual appetite devoid of emotional context, without individual meaning or personality: essentially as a sexual commodity to be consumed by males. (So-called lesbian pornography, created for the male voyeuristic eye, is equally devoid of emotional context or individual personality.) The most pernicious message relayed by pornography is that women are natural sexual prey to men and love it; that sexuality and violence are congruent; and that for women sex is essentially masochistic, humiliation pleasurable, physical abuse erotic. But along with this message comes another, not always recognized: that enforced submission and the use of cruelty, if played out in heterosexual pairing, is sexually "normal," while sensuality between women, including erotic mutuality and respect, is "queer," "sick," and either pornographic in itself or not very exciting compared with the sexuality of whips and bondage.[24] Pornography does not simply create a climate in which sex and violence are interchangeable; *it widens the range of behavior considered acceptable from men in heterosexual intercourse*—behavior which reiteratively strips women of their autonomy, dignity, and sexual potential, including the potential of loving and being loved by women in mutuality and integrity.

In her brilliant study, *Sexual Harassment of Working Women: A Case of Sex Discrimination,* Catharine A. MacKinnon delineates the intersection of compulsory heterosexuality and economics. Under capitalism, women are horizontally segregated by gender and occupy a structurally inferior position in the workplace; this is hardly news, but MacKinnon raises the question why, even if capitalism "requires some collection of individuals to occupy low-status, low-paying positions . . . such persons must be biologically female," and goes on to point out that "the fact that male employers often do not hire qualified women, *even when they could pay them less than men* suggests that more than the profit motive is implicated" [emphasis added].[25] She cites a wealth of material documenting the fact that women are not only segregated in low-paying, service jobs (as secretaries, domestics, nurses, typists, telephone operators, child-care workers, waitresses) but that "sexualization of the woman" is part of the job. Central and intrinsic to the economic realities of women's lives is the requirement that women will "market sexual attractiveness to men, who

24. The issue of "lesbian sadomasochism" needs to be examined in terms of the dominant cultures' teachings about the relation of sex and violence, and also of the acceptance by some lesbians of male homosexual mores. I believe this to be another example of the "double-life" of women.

25. Catharine A. MacKinnon, *Sexual Harassment of Working Women: A Case of Sex Discrimination* (New Haven, Conn.: Yale University Press, 1979), pp. 15–16.

tend to hold the economic power and position to enforce their pre-dilections." And MacKinnon exhaustively documents that "sexual harassment perpetuates the interlocked structure by which women have been kept sexually in thrall to men at the bottom of the labor market. Two forces of American society converge: men's control over women's sexuality and capital's control over employees' work lives."[26] Thus, women in the workplace are at the mercy of sex-as-power in a vicious circle. Economically disadvantaged, women—whether waitresses or professors—endure sexual harassment to keep their jobs and learn to behave in a complaisantly and ingratiatingly heterosexual manner be-cause they discover this is their true qualification for employment, what-ever the job description. And, MacKinnon notes, the woman who too decisively resists sexual overtures in the workplace is accused of being "dried-up" and sexless, or lesbian. This raises a specific difference be-tween the experiences of lesbians and homosexual men. A lesbian, clos-eted on her job because of heterosexist prejudice, is not simply forced into denying the truth of her outside relationships or private life; her job depends on her pretending to be not merely heterosexual but a hetero-sexual *woman,* in terms of dressing and playing the feminine, deferential role required of "real" women.

MacKinnon raises radical questions as to the qualitative differences between sexual harassment, rape, and ordinary heterosexual inter-course. ("As one accused rapist put it, he hadn't used 'any more force than is usual for males during the preliminaries.'") She criticizes Susan Brownmiller[27] for separating rape from the mainstream of daily life and for her unexamined premise that "rape is violence, intercourse is sexual-ity," removing rape from the sexual sphere altogether. Most crucially she argues that "taking rape from the realm of 'the sexual,' placing it in the realm of 'the violent,' allows one to be against it without raising any questions about the extent to which the institution of heterosexuality has defined force as a normal part of 'the preliminaries.'"[28] "Never is it asked whether, under conditions of male supremacy, the notion of 'con-sent' has any meaning."[29]

The fact is that the workplace, among other social institutions, is a place where women have learned to accept male violation of our psychic and physical boundaries as the price of survival; where women have been educated—no less than by romantic literature or by

26. Ibid., p. 174.

27. Brownmiller (n. 8 above).

28. MacKinnon, p. 219. Susan Schecter writes: "The push for heterosexual union at whatever cost is so intense that . . . it has become a cultural force of its own that creates battering. The ideology of romantic love and its jealous possession of the partner as property provide the masquerade for what can become severe abuse" (*Aegis: Magazine on Ending Violence against Women* [July–August 1979], pp. 50–51).

29. MacKinnon, p. 298.

pornography—to perceive ourselves as sexual prey. A woman seeking to escape such casual violations along with economic disadvantage may well turn to marriage as a form of hoped-for-protection, while bringing into marriage neither social or economic power, thus entering that institution also from a disadvantaged position. MacKinnon finally asks:

> What if inequality is built into the social conceptions of male and female sexuality, of masculinity and femininity, of sexiness and heterosexual attractiveness? Incidents of sexual harassment suggest that male sexual desire itself may be aroused by female vulnerability. . . . Men feel they can take advantage, so they want to, so they do. Examination of sexual harassment, precisely because the episodes appear commonplace, forces one to confront the fact that sexual intercourse normally occurs between economic (as well as physical) unequals . . . the apparent legal requirement that violations of women's sexuality appear out of the ordinary before they will be punished helps prevent women from defining the ordinary conditions of their own consent.[30]

Given the nature and extent of heterosexual pressures, the daily "eroticization of women's subordination" as MacKinnon phrases it,[31] I question the more or less psychoanalytic perspective (suggested by such writers as Karen Horney, H. R. Hayes, Wolfgang Lederer, and most recently, Dorothy Dinnerstein) that the male need to control women sexually results from some primal male "fear of women" and of women's sexual insatiability. It seems more probable that men really fear, not that they will have women's sexual appetites forced on them, or that women want to smother and devour them, but that women could be indifferent to them altogether, that men could be allowed sexual and emotional—therefore economic—access to women *only* on women's terms, otherwise being left on the periphery of the matrix.

The means of assuring male sexual access to women have recently received a searching investigation by Kathleen Barry.[32] She documents extensive and appalling evidence for the existence, on a very large scale, of international female slavery, the institution once known as "white slavery" but which in fact has involved, and at this very moment involves, women of every race and class. In the theoretical analysis derived from her research, Barry makes the connection between all enforced conditions under which women live subject to men: prostitution, marital rape, father-daughter and brother-sister incest, wife-beating, pornography, bride-price, the selling of daughters, purdah, and genital mutilation. She sees the rape paradigm—where the victim of sexual assault is held responsible for her own victimization—as leading to the rationaliza-

30. Ibid., p. 220.
31. Ibid., p. 221.
32. Kathleen Barry, *Female Sexual Slavery* (see unnumbered n. above).

tion and acceptance of other forms of enslavement, where the woman is presumed to have "chosen" her fate, to embrace it passively, or to have courted it perversely through rash or unchaste behavior. On the contrary, Barry maintains, "female sexual slavery is present in ALL situations where women or girls cannot change the conditions of their existence; where regardless of how they got into those conditions, e.g., social pressure, economic hardship, misplaced trust or the longing for affection, they cannot get out; and where they are subject to sexual violence and exploitation."[33] She provides a spectrum of concrete examples, not only as to the existence of a widespread international traffic in women, but also as to how this operates—whether in the form of a "Minnesota pipeline" funneling blonde, blue-eyed midwestern runaways to Times Square, or the purchasing of young women out of rural poverty in Latin America or Southeast Asia, or the providing of *maisons d'abattage* for migrant workers in the eighteenth arrondissement of Paris. Instead of "blaming the victim" or trying to diagnose her presumed pathology, Barry turns her floodlight on the pathology of sex colonization itself, the ideology of "cultural sadism" represented by the vast industry of pornography and by the overall identification of women primarily as "sexual beings whose responsibility is the sexual service of men."[34]

Barry delineates what she names a "sexual domination perspective" through whose lens, purporting objectivity, sexual abuse and terrorism of women by men has been rendered almost invisible by treating it as natural and inevitable. From its point of view, women are expendable as long as the sexual and emotional needs of the male can be satisfied. To replace this perspective of domination with a universal standard of basic freedom for women from gender-specific violence, from constraints on movement, and from male right of sexual and emotional access is the political purpose of her book. Like Mary Daly in *Gyn/Ecology,* Barry rejects structuralist and other cultural-relativist rationalizations for sexual torture and antiwoman violence. In her opening chapter, she asks of her readers that they refuse all handy escapes into ignorance and denial. "The only way we can come out of hiding, break through our paralyzing defenses, is to know it all—the full extent of sexual violence and domination of women. . . . In *knowing,* in facing directly, we can learn to chart our course out of this oppression, by envisioning and creating a world which will preclude female sexual slavery."[35]

"Until we name the practice, give conceptual definition and form to it, illustrate its life over time and in space, those who are its most obvious victims will also not be able to name it or define their experience."[36]

33. Ibid., p. 33.
34. Ibid., p. 103.
35. Ibid., p. 5.
36. Ibid., p. 100.

But women are all, in different ways and to different degrees, its victims; and part of the problem with naming and conceptualizing female sexual slavery is, as Barry clearly sees, compulsory heterosexuality. Compulsory heterosexuality simplifies the task of the procurer and pimp in worldwide prostitution rings and "eros centers," while, in the privacy of the home, it leads the daughter to "accept" incest/rape by her father, the mother to deny that it is happening, the battered wife to stay on with an abusive husand. "Befriending or love" is a major tactic of the procurer whose job it is to turn the runaway or the confused young girl over to the pimp for seasoning. The ideology of heterosexual romance, beamed at her from childhood out of fairy tales, television, films, advertising, popular songs, wedding pageantry, is a tool ready to the procurer's hand and one which he does not hesitate to use, as Barry amply documents. Early female indoctrination in "love" as an emotion may be largely a Western concept; but a more universal ideology concerns the primacy and uncontrollability of the male sexual drive. This is one of many insights offered by Barry's work:

> As sexual power is learned by adolescent boys through the social experience of their sex drive, so do girls learn that the locus of sexual power is male. Given the importance placed on the male sex drive in the socialization of girls as well as boys, early adolescence is probably the first significant phase of male identification in a girl's life and development. . . . As a young girl becomes aware of her own increasing sexual feelings . . . she turns away from her heretofore primary relationships with girlfriends. As they become secondary to her, recede in importance in her life, her own identity also assumes a secondary role and she grows into male identification.[37.]

We still need to ask why some women never, even temporarily, "turn away from heretofore primary relationships" with other females? And why does male-identification—the casting of one's social, political, and intellectual allegiances with men—exist among lifelong sexual lesbians? Barry's hypothesis throws us among new questions, but it clarifies the diversity of forms in which compulsory heterosexuality presents itself. In the mystique of the overpowering, all-conquering male sex drive, the penis-with-a-life-of-its-own, is rooted the law of male sex-right to women, which justifies prostitution as a universal cultural assumption on the one hand, while defending sexual slavery within the family on the basis of "family privacy and cultural uniqueness" on the other.[38] The adolescent male sex drive, which, as both young women and men are

37. Ibid., p. 218.
38. Ibid., p. 140.

taught, once triggered cannot take responsibility for itself or take no for an answer, becomes, according to Barry, the norm and rationale for adult male sexual behavior: a condition of *arrested sexual development.* Women learn to accept as natural the inevitability of this "drive" because we receive it as dogma. Hence marital rape, hence the Japanese wife resignedly packing her husband's suitcase for a weekend in the *kisaeng* brothels of Taiwan, hence the psychological as well as economic imbalance of power between husband and wife, male employer and female worker, father and daughter, male professor and female student.

The effect of male-identification means

> internalizing the values of the colonizer and actively participating in carrying out the colonization of one's self and one's sex. . . . Male identification is the act whereby women place men above women, including themselves, in credibility, status, and importance in most situations, regardless of the comparative quality the women may bring to the situation. . . . Interaction with women is seen as a lesser form of relating on every level.[39]

What deserves further exploration is the double-think many women engage in and from which no woman is permanently and utterly free: However woman-to-woman relationships, female support networks, a female and feminist value system, are relied on and cherished, indoctrination in male credibility and status can still create synapses in thought, denials of feeling, wishful thinking, a profound sexual and intellectual confusion.[40] I quote here from a letter I received the day I was writing this passage: "I have had very bad relationships with men—I am now in the midst of a very painful separation. I am trying to find my strength through women—without my friends, I could not survive." How many times a day do women speak words like these, or think them, or write them, and how often does the synapse reassert itself?

Barry summarizes her findings:

> . . . Considering the arrested sexual development that is understood to be normal in the male population, and considering the numbers of men who are pimps, procurers, members of slavery gangs, corrupt officials participating in this traffic, owners, operators, employees of brothels and lodging and entertainment facilities, por-

39. Ibid., p. 172.
40. Elsewhere I have suggested that male identification has been a powerful source of white women's racism, and that it has been women who were seen as "disloyal" to male codes and systems who have actively battled against it (Adrienne Rich, "Disloyal to Civilization: Feminism, Racism, Gynephobia," in *On Lies, Secrets, and Silence: Selected Prose, 1966–1978* [New York: W. W. Norton & Co., 1979]).

nography purveyors, associated with prostitution, wife beaters, child molesters, incest perpetrators, johns (tricks) and rapists, one cannot but be momentarily stunned by the enormous male population engaging in female sexual slavery. The huge number of men engaged in these practices should be cause for declaration of an international emergency, a crisis in sexual violence. But what should be cause for alarm is instead accepted as normal sexual intercourse.[41]

Susan Cavin, in her rich and provocative, if highly speculative, dissertation, suggests that patriarchy becomes possible when the original female band, which includes children but ejects adolescent males, becomes invaded and outnumbered by males; that not patriarchal marriage, but the rape of the mother by the son, becomes the first act of male domination. The entering wedge, or leverage, which allows this to happen is not just a simple change in sex ratios; it is also the mother-child bond, manipulated by adolescent males in order to remain within the matrix past the age of exclusion. Maternal affection is used to establish male right of sexual access, which, however, must ever after be held by force (or through control of consciousness) since the original deep adult bonding is that of woman for woman.[42] I find this hypothesis extremely suggestive, since one form of false consciousness which serves compulsory heterosexuality is the maintenance of a mother-son relationship between women and men, including the demand that women provide maternal solace, nonjudgmental nurturing, and compassion for their harassers, rapists, and batterers (as well as for men who passively vampirize them). How many strong and assertive women accept male posturing from no one but their sons?

But whatever its origins, when we look hard and clearly at the extent and elaboration of measures designed to keep women within a male sexual purlieu, it becomes an inescapable question whether the issue we have to address as feminists is, not simple "gender inequality," nor the domination of culture by males, nor mere "taboos against homosexuality," but the enforcement of heterosexuality for women as a means of assuring male right of physical, economical, and emotional access.[43] One of many means of enforcement is, of course, the rendering invisible of the lesbian possibility, an engulfed continent which rises fragmentedly to view from time to time only to become submerged again. Feminist research and theory that contributes to lesbian invisibility or marginality is

41. Barry, p. 220.
42. Cavin (see unnumbered n. above), chap. 6.
43. For my perception of heterosexuality as an economic institution I am indebted to Lisa Leghorn and Katherine Parker, who allowed me to read their unpublished manuscript, "Redefining Economics" (1980). See their article: "Towards a Feminist Economics: A Global View," *Second Wave* 5, no. 3 (1979): 23–30.

actually working against the liberation and empowerment of woman as a group.[44]

The assumption that "most women are innately heterosexual" stands as a theoretical and political stumbling block for many women. It remains a tenable assumption, partly because lesbian existence has been written out of history or catalogued under disease; partly because it has been treated as exceptional rather than intrinsic; partly because to acknowledge that for women heterosexuality may not be a "preference" at all but something that has had to be imposed, managed, organized, propagandized, and maintained by force, is an immense step to take if you consider yourself freely and "innately" heterosexual. Yet the failure to examine heterosexuality as an institution is like failing to admit that the economic system called capitalism or the caste system of racism is maintained by a variety of forces, including both physical violence and false consciousness. To take the step of questioning heterosexuality as a "preference" or "choice" for women—and to do the intellectual and emotional work that follows—will call for a special quality of courage in heterosexually identified feminists but I think the rewards will be great: a freeing-up of thinking, the exploring of new paths, the shattering of another great silence, new clarity in personal relationships.

III

I have chosen to use the terms *lesbian existence* and *lesbian continuum* because the word *lesbianism* has a clinical and limiting ring. *Lesbian existence* suggests both the fact of the historical presence of lesbians and our continuing creation of the meaning of that existence. I mean the term *lesbian continuum* to include a range—through each woman's life and throughout history—of woman-identified experience; not simply the fact that a woman has had or consciously desired genital sexual experience with another woman. If we expand it to embrace many more forms of primary intensity between and among women, including the sharing

44. I would suggest that lesbian existence has been most recognized and tolerated where it has resembled a "deviant" version of heterosexuality; e.g., where lesbians have, like Stein and Toklas, played heterosexual roles (or seemed to in public) and have been chiefly identified with male culture. See also Claude E. Schaeffer, "The Kuterai Female Berdache: Courier, Guide, Prophetess and Warrior," *Ethnohistory* 12, no. 3 (Summer 1965): 193–236. (Berdache: "an individual of a definite physiological sex [m. or f.] who assumes the role and status of the opposite sex and who is viewed by the community as being of one sex physiologically but as having assumed the role and status of the opposite sex" [Schaeffer, p. 231].) Lesbian existence has also been relegated to an upper-class phenomenon, an elite decadence (as in the fascination with Paris salon lesbians such as Renée Vivien and Natalie Clifford Barney), to the obscuring of such "common women" as Judy Grahn depicts in her *The Work of a Common Woman* (Oakland, Calif.: Diana Press, 1978) and *True to Life Adventure Stories* (Oakland, Calif.: Diana Press, 1978).

of a rich inner life, the bonding against male tyranny, the giving and receiving of practical and political support; if we can also hear in it such associations as *marriage resistance* and the "haggard" behavior identified by Mary Daly (obsolete meanings: "intractable," "willful," "wanton," and "unchaste" . . . "a woman reluctant to yield to wooing")[45]—we begin to grasp breadths of female history and psychology which have lain out of reach as a consequence of limited, mostly clinical, definitions of "lesbianism."

Lesbian existence comprises both the breaking of a taboo and the rejection of a compulsory way of life. It is also a direct or indirect attack on male right of access to women. But it is more than these, although we may first begin to perceive it as a form of nay-saying to patriarchy, an act of resistance. It has of course included role playing, self-hatred, breakdown, alcoholism, suicide, and intrawoman violence; we romanticize at our peril what it means to love and act against the grain, and under heavy penalties; and lesbian existence has been lived (unlike, say, Jewish or Catholic existence) without access to any knowledge of a tradition, a continuity, a social underpinning. The destruction of records and memorabilia and letters documenting the realities of lesbian existence must be taken very seriously as a means of keeping heterosexuality compulsory for women, since what has been kept from our knowledge is joy, sensuality, courage, and community, as well as guilt, self-betrayal, and pain.[46]

Lesbians have historically been deprived of a political existence through "inclusion" as female versions of male homosexuality. To equate lesbian existence with male homosexuality because each is stigmatized is to deny and erase female reality once again. To separate those women stigmatized as "homosexual" or "gay" from the complex continuum of female resistance to enslavement, and attach them to a male pattern, is to falsify our history. Part of the history of lesbian existence is, obviously, to be found where lesbians, lacking a coherent female community, have shared a kind of social life and common cause with homosexual men. But this has to be seen against the differences: women's lack of economic and cultural privilege relative to men; qualitative differences in female and male relationships, for example, the prevalence of anonymous sex and the justification of pederasty among male homosexuals, the pronounced ageism in male homosexual standards of

45. Daly, *Gyn/Ecology*, p. 15.

46. "In a hostile world in which women are not supposed to survive except in relation with and in service to men, entire communities of women were simply erased. History tends to bury what it seeks to reject" (Blanche W. Cook," '"Women Alone Stir My Imagination': Lesbianism and the Cultural Tradition," *Signs: Journal of Women in Culture and Society* 4, no. 4 [Summer 1979]: 719–20). The Lesbian Herstory Archives in New York City is one attempt to preserve contemporary documents on lesbian existence—a project of enormous value and meaning, still pitted against the continuing censorship and obliteration of relationships, networks, communities, in other archives and elsewhere in the culture.

sexual attractiveness, etc. In defining and describing lesbian existence I would hope to move toward a dissociation of lesbian from male homosexual values and allegiances. I perceive the lesbian experience as being, like motherhood, a profoundly *female* experience, with particular oppressions, meanings, and potentialities we cannot comprehend as long as we simply bracket it with other sexually stigmatized existences. Just as the term "parenting" serves to conceal the particular and significant reality of being a parent who is actually a mother, the term "gay" serves the purpose of blurring the very outlines we need to discern, which are of crucial value for feminism and for the freedom of women as a group.

As the term "lesbian" has been held to limiting, clinical associations in its patriarchal definition, female friendship and comradeship have been set apart from the erotic, thus limiting the erotic itself. But as we deepen and broaden the range of what we define as lesbian existence, as we delineate a lesbian continuum, we begin to discover the erotic in female terms: as that which is unconfined to any single part of the body or solely to the body itself, as an energy not only diffuse but, as Audre Lorde has described it, omnipresent in "the sharing of joy, whether physical, emotional, psychic," and in the sharing of work; as the empowering joy which "makes us less willing to accept powerlessness, or those other supplied states of being which are not native to me, such as resignation, despair, self-effacement, depression, self-denial."[47] In another context, writing of women and work, I quoted the autobiographical passage in which the poet H.D. described how her friend Bryher supported her in persisting with the visionary experience which was to shape her mature work:

> . . . I knew that this experience, this writing-on-the-wall before me, could not be shared with anyone except the girl who stood so bravely there beside me. This girl had said without hesitation, "Go on." It was she really who had the detachment and integrity of the Pythoness of Delphi. But it was I, battered and dissociated . . . who was seeing the pictures, and who was reading the writing or granted the inner vision. Or perhaps, in some sense, we were "seeing" it together, for without her, admittedly, I could not have gone on. . . .[48]

If we consider the possibility that all women—from the infant suckling her mother's breast, to the grown woman experiencing orgasmic sensations while suckling her own child, perhaps recalling her mother's

47. Audre Lorde, *Uses of the Erotic: The Erotic as Power*, Out & Out Books Pamphlet no. 3 (New York: Out & Out Books [476 2d Street, Brooklyn, New York 11215], 1979).

48. Adrienne Rich, "Conditions for Work: The Common World of Women," in *On Lies, Secrets and Silence* (p. 209); H. D., *Tribute to Freud* (Oxford: Carcanet Press, 1971), pp. 50–54.

milk-smell in her own; to two women, like Virginia Woolf's Chloe and Olivia, who share a laboratory;[49] to the woman dying at ninety, touched and handled by women—exist on a lesbian continuum, we can see ourselves as moving in and out of this continuum, whether we identify ourselves as lesbian or not. It allows us to connect aspects of woman-identification as diverse as the impudent, intimate girl-friendships of eight- or nine-year olds and the banding together of those women of the twelfth and fifteenth centuries known as Beguines who "shared houses, rented to one another, bequeathed houses to their room-mates . . . in cheap subdivided houses in the artisans' area of town," who "practiced Christian virtue on their own, dressing and living simply and not associating with men," who earned their livings as spinners, bakers, nurses, or ran schools for young girls, and who managed—until the Church forced them to disperse—to live independent both of marriage and of conventual restrictions.[50] It allows us to connect these women with the more celebrated "Lesbians" of the women's school around Sappho of the seventh century B.C.; with the secret sororities and economic networks reported among African women; and with the Chinese marriage resistance sisterhoods—communities of women who refused marriage, or who if married often refused to consummate their marriages and soon left their husbands—the only women in China who were not footbound and who, Agnes Smedley tells us, welcomed the births of daughters and organized successful women's strikes in the silk mills.[51] It allows us to connect and compare disparate individual instances of marriage resistance: for example, the type of autonomy claimed by Emily Dickinson, a nineteenth-century white woman genius, with the strategies available to Zora Neale Hurston, a twentieth-century black woman genius. Dickinson never married, had tenuous intellectual friendships with men, lived self-convented in her genteel father's house, and wrote a lifetime of passionate letters to her sister-in-law Sue Gilbert and a smaller group of such letters to her friend Kate Scott Anthon. Hurston married twice but soon left each husband, scrambled her way from Florida to Harlem to Columbia University to Haiti and finally back to Florida, moved in and

49. Woolf, *A Room of One's Own*, p. 126.

50. Gracia Clark, "The Beguines: A Mediaeval Women's Community," *Quest: A Feminist Quarterly* 1, no. 4 (1975): 73–80.

51. See Denise Paulmé, ed., *Women of Tropical Africa* (Berkeley: University of California Press, 1963), pp. 7, 266–67. Some of these sororities are described as "a kind of defensive syndicate against the male element"—their aims being "to offer concerted resistance to an oppressive patriarchate," "independence in relation to one's husband and with regard to motherhood, mutual aid, satisfaction of personal revenge." See also Audre Lorde, "Scratching the Surface: Some Notes on Barriers to Women and Loving," *Black Scholar* 9, no. 7 (1978): 31–35; Marjorie Topley, "Marriage Resistance in Rural Kwangtung," in *Women in Chinese Society*, ed. M. Wolf and R. Witke (Stanford, Calif.: Stanford University Press, 1978), pp. 67–89; Agnes Smedley, *Portraits of Chinese Women in Revolution*, ed. J. MacKinnon and S. MacKinnon (Old Westbury, N.Y.: Feminist Press, 1976), pp. 103–10.

out of white patronage and poverty, professional success, and failure; her survival relationships were all with women, beginning with her mother. Both of these women in their vastly different circumstances were marriage resisters, committed to their own work and selfhood, and were later characterized as "apolitical." Both were drawn to men of intellectual quality; for both of them women provided the on-going fascination and sustenance of life.

If we think of heterosexuality as the "natural" emotional and sensual inclination for women, lives such as these are seen as deviant, as pathological, or as emotionally and sensually deprived. Or, in more recent and permissive jargon, they are banalized as "life-styles." And the work of such women—whether merely the daily work of individual or collective survival and resistance, or the work of the writer, the activist, the reformer, the anthropologist, or the artist—the work of self-creation—is undervalued, or seen as the bitter fruit of "penis envy," or the sublimation of repressed eroticism, or the meaningless rant of a "manhater." But when we turn the lens of vision and consider the degree to which, and the methods whereby, heterosexual "preference" has actually been imposed on women, not only can we understand differently the meaning of individual lives and work, but we can begin to recognize a central fact of women's history: that women have always resisted male tyranny. A feminism of action, often, though not always, without a theory, has constantly reemerged in every culture and in every period. We can then begin to study women's struggle against powerlessness, women's radical rebellion, not just in male-defined "concrete revolutionary situations"[52] but in all the situations male ideologies have not perceived as revolutionary: for example, the refusal of some women to produce children, aided at great risk by other women; the refusal to produce a higher standard of living and leisure for men (Leghorn and Parker show how both are part of women's unacknowledged, unpaid, and ununionized economic contribution); that female antiphallic sexuality which, as Andrea Dworkin notes, has been "legendary," which, defined as "frigidity" and "puritanism," has actually been a form of subversion of male power—"an ineffectual rebellion, but . . . rebellion nonetheless."[53] We can no longer have patience with Dinnerstein's view that women have simply collaborated with men in the "sexual arrangements" of history; we begin to observe behavior, both in history and in individual biography, that has hitherto been invisible or misnamed; behavior which often constitutes, given the limits of the counterforce exerted in a given time and place, radical rebellion. And we can connect these rebellions and the necessity for them with the physical passion of woman

52. See Rosalind Petchesky, "Dissolving the Hyphen: A Report on Marxist-Feminist Groups 1–5," in *Capitalist Patriarchy and the Case for Socialist Feminism,* ed. Zillah Eisenstein (New York: Monthly Review Press, 1979), p. 387.

53. Andrea Dworkin, *Pornography: Men's Graphic Depiction of Whores* (New York: G. P. Putnam's Sons, 1981).

for woman which is central to lesbian existence: the erotic sensuality which has been, precisely, the most violently erased fact of female experience.

Heterosexuality has been both forcibly and subliminally imposed on women, yet everywhere women have resisted it, often at the cost of physical torture, imprisonment, psychosurgery, social ostracism, and extreme poverty. "Compulsory heterosexuality" was named as one of the "crimes against women" by the Brussels Tribunal on Crimes against Women in 1976. Two pieces of testimony, from women from two very different cultures, suggest the degree to which persecution of lesbians is a global practice here and now. A report from Norway relates:

> A lesbian in Oslo was in a heterosexual marriage that didn't work, so she started taking tranquillizers and ended up at the health sanatorium for treatment and rehabilitation. . . . The moment she said in family group therapy that she believed she was a lesbian, the doctor told her she was not. He knew from "looking into her eyes," he said. She had the eyes of a woman who wanted sexual intercourse with her husband. So she was subjected to so-called "couch therapy." She was put into a comfortably heated room, naked, on a bed, and for an hour her husband was to . . . try to excite her sexually. . . . The idea was that the touching was always to end with sexual intercourse. She felt stronger and stronger aversion. She threw up and sometimes ran out of the room to avoid this "treatment." The more strongly she asserted that she was a lesbian, the more violent the forced heterosexual intercourse became. This treatment went on for about six months. She escaped from the hospital, but she was brought back. Again she escaped. She has not been there since. In the end she realized that she had been subjected to forcible rape for six months.

(This, surely, is an example of female sexual slavery according to Barry's definition.) And from Mozambique:

> I am condemned to a life of exile because I will not deny that I am a lesbian, that my primary commitments are, and will always be to other women. In the new Mozambique, lesbianism is considered a left-over from colonialism and decadent Western civilization. Lesbians are sent to rehabilitation camps to learn through self-criticism the correct line about themselves. . . . If I am forced to denounce my own love for women, if I therefore denounce myself, I could go back to Mozambique and join forces in the exciting and hard struggles of rebuilding a nation, including the struggle for the emancipation of Mozambiquan women. As it is, I either risk the rehabilitation camps, or remain in exile.[54]

54. Russell and van de Ven, pp. 42–43, 56–57.

Nor can it be assumed that women like those in Carroll Smith-Rosenberg's study, who married, stayed married, yet dwelt in a profoundly female emotional and passional world, "preferred" or "chose" heterosexuality. Women have married because it was necessary, in order to survive economically, in order to have children who would not suffer economic deprivation or social ostracism, in order to remain respectable, in order to do what was expected of women because coming out of "abnormal" childhoods they wanted to feel "normal," and because heterosexual romance has been represented as the great female adventure, duty, and fulfillment. We may faithfully or ambivalently have obeyed the institution, but our feelings—and our sensuality—have not been tamed or contained within it. There is no statistical documentation of the numbers of lesbians who have remained in heterosexual marriages for most of their lives. But in a letter to the early lesbian publication, *Ladder*, the playwright Lorraine Hansberry had this to say:

> I suspect that the problem of the married woman who would prefer emotional-physical relationships with other women is proportionally much higher than a similar statistic for men. (A statistic surely no one will ever really have.) This because the estate of woman being what it is, how could we ever begin to guess the numbers of women who are not prepared to risk a life alien to what they have been taught all their lives to believe was their "natural" destiny—AND—their only expectation for ECONOMIC security. It seems to be that this is why the question has an immensity that it does not have for male homosexuals. . . . A woman of strength and honesty may, if she chooses, sever her marriage and marry a new male mate and society will be upset that the divorce rate is rising so—but there are few places in the United States, in any event, where she will be anything remotely akin to an "outcast." Obviously this is not true for a woman who would end her marriage to take up life with another woman.[55]

This *double-life*—this apparent acquiescence to an institution founded on male interest and prerogative—has been characteristic of female experience: in motherhood, and in many kinds of heterosexual behavior, including the rituals of courtship; the pretense of asexuality by the nineteenth-century wife; the simulation of orgasm by the prostitute, the courtesan, the twentieth-century "sexually liberated" woman.

Meridel LeSueur's documentary novel of the Depression, *The Girl,* is arresting as a study of female double-life. The protagonist, a waitress in a St. Paul working-class speakeasy, feels herself passionately attracted to

55. I am indebted to Jonathan Katz's *Gay American History* (n. 5 above) for bringing to my attention Hansberry's letters to *Ladder* and to Barbara Grier for supplying me with copies of relevant pages from *Ladder,* quoted here by permission of Barbara Grier. See also the reprinted series of *Ladder,* ed. Jonathan Katz et al. (New York: Arno Press); and Deirdre Carmody, "Letters by Eleanor Roosevelt Detail Friendship with Lorena Hickok," *New York Times* (October 21, 1979).

the young man Butch, but her survival relationships are with Clara, an older waitress and prostitute, with Belle, whose husband owns the bar, and with Amelia, a union activist. For Clara and Belle and the unnamed protagonist, sex with men is in one sense an escape from the bedrock misery of daily life; a flare of intensity in the grey, relentless, often brutal web of day-to-day existence:

> ... It was like he was a magnet pulling me. It was exciting and powerful and frightening. He was after me too and when he found me I would run, or be petrified, just standing in front of him like a zany. And he told me not to be wandering with Clara to the Marigold where we danced with strangers. He said he would knock the shit out of me. Which made me shake and tremble, but it was better than being a husk full of suffering and not knowing why.[56]

Throughout the novel the theme of double-life emerges; Belle reminisces of her marriage to the bootlegger Hoinck:

> You know, when I had that black eye and said I hit it on the cupboard, well he did it the bastard, and then he says don't tell anybody. ... He's nuts, that's what he is, nuts, and I don't see why I live with him, why I put up with him a minute on this earth. But listen kid, she said, I'm telling you something. She looked at me and her face was wonderful. She said, Jesus Christ, Goddam him I love him that's why I'm hooked like this all my life, Goddam him I love him.[57]

After the protagonist has her first sex with Butch, her women friends care for her bleeding, give her whiskey, and compare notes.

> My luck, the first time and I got into trouble. He gave me a little money and I come to St. Paul where for ten bucks they'd stick a huge vet's needle into you and you start it and then you were on your own. ... I never had no child. I've just had Hoinck to mother, and a hell of a child he is.[58]

> Later they made me go back to Clara's room to lie down. ... Clara lay down beside me and put her arms around me and wanted me to tell her about it but she wanted to tell about herself. She said she started it when she was twelve with a bunch of boys in an old shed. She said nobody had paid any attention to her before and she became very popular. ... They like it so much, she said, why shouldn't

56. Meridel LeSueur, *The Girl* (Cambridge, Mass.: West End Press, 1978), pp. 10–11. LeSueur describes, in an afterword, how this book was drawn from the writings and oral narrations of women in the Workers Alliance who met as a writers' group during the Depression.
57. Ibid., p. 20.
58. Ibid., pp. 53–54.

you give it to them and get presents and attention? I never cared anything for it and neither did my mama. But it's the only thing you got that's valuable. . . . [59]

Sex is thus equated with attention from the male, who is charismatic though brutal, infantile, or unreliable. Yet it is the women who make life endurable for each other, give physical affection without causing pain, share, advise, and stick by each other. (*I am trying to find my strength through women—without my friends, I could not survive.*) LeSueur's *The Girl* parallels Toni Morrison's remarkable *Sula,* another revelation of female double-life:

> Nel was the one person who had wanted nothing from her, who had accepted all aspects of her. . . . Nel was one of the reasons [Sula] had drifted back to Medallion. . . . The men . . . had merged into one large personality: the same language of love, the same entertainments of love, the same cooling of love. Whenever she introduced her private thoughts into their rubbings and goings, they hooded their eyes. They taught her nothing but love tricks, shared nothing but worry, gave nothing but money. She had been looking all along for a friend, and it took her a while to discover that a lover was not a comrade and could never be—for a woman.

But Sula's last thought at the second of her death is, "Wait'll I tell Nel." And after Sula's death, Nel looks back on her own life:

> "All that time, all that time, I thought I was missing Jude." And the loss pressed down on her chest and came up into her throat. "We was girls together," she said as though explaining something. "O Lord, Sula," she cried, "Girl, girl, girlgirlgirl!" It was a fine cry—loud and long—but it had no bottom and it had no top, just circles and circles of sorrow.[60]

The Girl and *Sula* are both novels which reveal the lesbian continuum in contrast to the shallow or sensational "lesbian scenes" in recent commercial fiction.[61] Each shows us woman-identification untarnished (till the end of LeSueur's novel) by romanticism; each depicts the competition of heterosexual compulsion for women's attention, the diffusion and frustration of female bonding that might, in a more conscious form, reintegrate love with power.

59. Ibid., p. 55.

60. Toni Morrison, *Sula* (New York: Bantam Books, 1973), pp. 103–4, 149. I am indebted to Lorraine Bethel's unpublished essay on *Sula* which first called it to my attention as a novel of woman-identification.

61. See Maureen Brady and Judith McDaniel, "Lesbians in the Mainstream: The Image of Lesbians in Recent Commercial Fiction," *Conditions,* vol. 6 (1979).

IV

Woman-identification is a source of energy, a potential springhead of female power, violently curtailed and wasted under the institution of heterosexuality. The denial of reality and visibility to women's passion for women, women's choice of women as allies, life companions, and community; the forcing of such relationships into dissimulation and their disintegration under intense pressure have meant an incalculable loss to the power of all women *to change the social relations of the sexes, to liberate ourselves and each other.* The lie of compulsory female heterosexuality today afflicts not just feminist scholarship, but every profession, every reference work, every curriculum, every organizing attempt, every relationship or conversation over which it hovers. It creates, specifically, a profound falseness, hypocrisy, and hysteria in the heterosexual dialogue, for every heterosexual relationship is lived in the queasy strobelight of that lie. However we chose to identify ourselves, however we find ourselves labeled, it flickers across and distorts our lives.[62]

The lie keeps numberless women psychologically trapped, trying to fit mind, spirit, and sexuality into a prescribed script because they cannot look beyond the parameters of the acceptable. It pulls on the energy of such women even as it drains the energy of "closeted" lesbians—the energy exhausted in the double-life. The lesbian trapped in the "closet," the woman imprisoned in prescriptive ideas of the "normal," share the pain of blocked options, broken connections, lost access to self-definition freely and powerfully assumed.

The lie is many-layered. In Western tradition, one layer—the romantic—asserts that women are inevitably, even if rashly and tragically, drawn to men; that even when that attraction is suicidal (e.g., *Tristan und Isolde,* Kate Chopin's *The Awakening*) it is still an organic imperative. In the tradition of the social sciences it asserts that primary love between the sexes is "normal," that women *need* men as social and economic protectors, for adult sexuality, and for psychological completion; that the heterosexually constituted family is the basic social unit; that women who do not attach their primary intensity to men must be, in functional terms, condemned to an even more devastating outsiderhood than their outsiderhood as women. Small wonder that lesbians are reported to be a more hidden population than male homosexuals. The black lesbian/feminist critic, Lorraine Bethel, writing on Zora Neale Hurston, remarks that for a black woman—already twice an outsider—to choose to assume still another "hated identity" is problematic indeed. Yet the lesbian continuum has been a lifeline for black women both in Africa and the United States.

62. See Russell and van de Ven, p. 40: " . . . few heterosexual women realize their lack of free choice about their sexuality, and few realize how and why compulsory heterosexuality is also a crime against them."

Black women have a long tradition of bonding together . . . in a Black/women's community that has been a source of vital survival information, psychic and emotional support for us. We have a distinct Black woman-identified folk culture based on our experiences as Black women in this society; symbols, language and modes of expression that are specific to the realities of our lives. . . . Because Black women were rarely among those Blacks and females who gained access to literary and other acknowledged forms of artistic expression, this Black female bonding and Black woman-identification has often been hidden and unrecorded except in the individual lives of Black women through our own memories of our particular Black female tradition.[63]

Another layer of the lie is the frequently encountered implication that women turn to women out of hatred for men. Profound skepticism, caution, and righteous paranoia about men may indeed be part of any healthy woman's response to the woman-hatred embedded in male-dominated culture, to the forms assumed by "normal" male sexuality, and to *the failure even of "sensitive" or "political" men to perceive or find these troubling.* Yet woman-hatred is so embedded in culture, so "normal" does it seem, so profoundly is it neglected as a social phenomenon, that many women, even feminists and lesbians, fail to identify it until it takes, in their own lives, some permanently unmistakable and shattering form. Lesbian existence is also represented as mere refuge from male abuses, rather than as an electric and empowering charge between women. I find it interesting that one of the most frequently quoted literary passages on lesbian relationship is that in which Colette's Renée, in *The Vagabond,* describes "the melancholy and touching image of two weak creatures who have perhaps found shelter in each other's arms, there to sleep and weep, safe from man who is often cruel, and there to taste *better than any pleasure, the bitter happiness of feeling themselves akin, frail and forgotten* [emphasis added]."[64] Colette is often considered a lesbian writer; her popular reputation has, I think, much to do with the fact that she writes about lesbian existence as if for a male audience; her earliest "lesbian" novels, the Claudine series, were written under compulsion for her husband and published under both their names. At all events, except for her writings on her mother, Colette is a far less reliable source on lesbian existence than, I would think, Charlotte Brontë, who understood that while women may, indeed must, be one another's allies, mentors,

63. Lorraine Bethel, "This Infinity of Conscious Pain" (see unnumbered n. above).
64. Dinnerstein, the most recent writer to quote this passage, adds ominously: "But what has to be added to her account is that these 'women enlaced' are sheltering each other not just from what men want to do to them, but also from what they want to do to each other" (Dinnerstein, p. 103). The fact is, however, that woman-to-woman violence is a minute grain in the universe of male-against-female violence perpetrated and rationalized in every social institution.

and comforters in the female struggle for survival, there is quite extraneous delight in each other's company and attraction to each others' minds and character, which proceeds from a recognition of each others' strengths.

By the same token, we can say that there is a *nascent* feminist political content in the act of choosing a woman lover or life partner in the face of institutionalized heterosexuality.[65] But for lesbian existence to realize this political content in an ultimately liberating form, the erotic choice must deepen and expand into conscious woman-identification—into lesbian/feminism.

The work that lies ahead, of unearthing and describing what I call here "lesbian existence" is potentially liberating for all women. It is work that must assuredly move beyond the limits of white and middle-class Western women's studies to examine women's lives, work, and groupings within every racial, ethnic, and political structure. There are differences, moreover, between "lesbian existence" and the "lesbian continuum"—differences we can discern even in the movement of our own lives. The lesbian continuum, I suggest, needs delineation in light of the "double-life" of women, not only women self-described as heterosexual but also of self-described lesbians. We need a far more exhaustive account of the forms the double-life has assumed. Historians need to ask at every point how heterosexuality as institution has been organized and maintained through the female wage scale, the enforcement of middle-class women's "leisure," the glamorization of so-called sexual liberation, the withholding of education from women, the imagery of "high art" and popular culture, the mystification of the "personal" sphere, and much else. We need an economics which comprehends the institution of heterosexuality, with its doubled workload for women and its sexual divisions of labor, as the most idealized of economic relations.

The question inevitably will arise: Are we then to condemn all heterosexual relationships, including those which are least oppressive? I believe this question, though often heartfelt, is the wrong question here. We have been stalled in a maze of false dichotomies which prevents our apprehending the institution as a whole: "good" versus "bad" marriages; "marriage for love" versus arranged marriage; "liberated" sex versus prostitution; heterosexual intercourse versus rape; Liebeschmerz versus humiliation and dependency. Within the institution exist, of course, qualitative differences of experience; but the absence of choice remains the great unacknowledged reality, and in the absence of choice, women will remain dependent upon the chance or luck of particular relationships and will have no collective power to determine the meaning and place of sexuality in their lives. As we address the institution itself, moreover, we begin to perceive a history of female resistance which has

65. Conversation with Blanche W. Cook, New York City, March 1979.

never fully understood itself because it has been so fragmented, miscalled, erased. It will require a courageous grasp of the politics and economics, as well as the cultural propaganda, of heterosexuality to carry us beyond individual cases or diversified group situations into the complex kind of overview needed to undo the power men everywhere wield over women, power which has become a model for every other form of exploitation and illegitimate control.

Montague, Massachusetts

Reproductive Freedom: Beyond "A Woman's Right to Choose"

Rosalind Pollack Petchesky

Introduction

" . . . that all the while the *Foetus* is forming . . . even to the Moment that the Soul is infused, so long it is absolutely not in her Power only, but in her right, to kill or keep alive, save or destroy, the Thing she goes with, she won't call it Child; and that therefore till then she resolves to use all manner of Art, to the help of Drugs and Physicians, whether Astringents, Diuretics, Emeticks, or of whatever kind, nay even to Purgations, Potions, Poisons, or any thing that Apothecaries or Druggists can supply. . . . "[1] The lengths to which women go to control their conditions of reproduction—whether, when, how, and with whom they would bear children—are amazing and persistent. As Angus McLaren shows us, behind Defoe's scathing condemnation of female malice in the act of abortion lies the presence of not only "right-to-life" antecedents in seventeenth-century England but the idea among women that abortion is a "woman's right." Linda Gordon, in *Woman's Body, Woman's Right,* lays

A shorter version of this paper was presented at "The Second Sex—Thirty Years Later: A Commemorative Conference on Feminist Theory" (September 27–29, 1979, New York University), sponsored by the New York Institute for the Humanities. My deepest thanks go to Hal Benenson and Zillah Eisenstein for their painstaking critical and supportive comments, which kept me on my path; and to Ellen Ross, Ros Baxandall, Meredith Tax, Nathan Pollack, Harriet Cohen, and Elsa Dixler for their encouragement and editorial help. In addition, I wish to acknowledge the organizational work and support of CARASA, the pioneering book of Linda Gordon, and time and resources provided by the Hastings Center, without which the paper could not have been. Most of all, the principal ideas in the paper and the need to take them seriously I learned from Sarah Eisenstein, who understood better than any of us the complexity of political thinking.

1. Quote from Daniel Defoe, *Conjugal Lewdness,* in Angus McLaren, *Birth Control in Nineteenth-Century England* (London: Croom Helm, 1978), pp. 34–35.

the groundwork of a feminist theory of reproductive freedom, observing that, throughout history, women have practiced forms of birth control and abortion; recurrent moral or legal prohibitions against such practices merely "forced women underground in their search for reproductive control."[2] Similarly, George Devereux, surveying 350 primitive, ancient, and preindustrial societies, asserts: "that there is every indication that abortion is an absolutely universal phenomenon, and that it is impossible even to construct an imaginary social system in which no woman would ever feel at least impelled to abort."[3]

The fact of universality in birth control practices, as Gordon emphasizes, helps us to understand that reproductive freedom for women is not simply a matter of developing more sophisticated techniques. While the ascent from "purgations, potions, and poisons" to vacuum aspiration doubtless represents a gain for women, abortion and reproductive freedom generally (of which safe, legal, funded abortion is but one small part) remain political, not technological, agendas—which feminists find necessary to mobilize over and over again, on different terrains and in different contexts. Because we are in the thick of that mobilization at present, it is important to examine the political ideas that have informed the movements for reproductive freedom historically and today.

Two essential ideas underlie a feminist view of reproductive freedom, ideas that have recurrently been implicit in all historical situations in which abortion, birth control, child care, maternity care, and the status of unmarried mothers and their children have become objects of political conflict. On the broadest level, these two ideas reflect the long-standing tension in feminist theory between an emphasis on *equality* and an emphasis on women's *autonomy*. The first is derived from the biological connection between women's bodies, sexuality, and reproduction. It is an extension of the general principle of "bodily integrity," or "bodily self-determination," to the notion that women must be able to control their own bodies and procreative capacities—that is, the reproductive and sexual uses to which their bodies are put. The second is a "historical and moral argument" based on the social position of women and the socially determined needs which that position generates. It states that, insofar as women, under the existing division of labor between the sexes, are the ones most affected by pregnancy, since they are still the ones responsible for the care and rearing of children, it is women who must decide about contraception, abortion, and childbearing.

It is apparent that these two ideas grow out of different philosophical traditions and have very different, sometimes contradictory, refer-

2. Linda Gordon, *Woman's Body, Woman's Right: A Social History of Birth Control in America* (Harmondsworth, Middlesex, and New York: Penguin Books, 1977), p. 47.
3. George Devereux, "A Typological Study of Abortion in 350 Primitive, Ancient, and Pre-industrial Societies," in *Abortion in America*, ed. Harold Rosen (Boston: Beacon Press, 1967), p. 98.

ence points and political priorities. The first emphasizes the *individual* dimensions of reproduction, the second the *social* dimensions. The first appeals to a "fixed" level of the biological person, while the other implies a set of social arrangements, a sexual division of labor that has developed historically and may therefore be changed under new conditions. Finally, one is rooted in the conceptual framework of "natural rights," while the other invokes the legitimating principle of "socially determined needs"; from this perspective, their links are to a liberal feminist and a Marxist tradition, respectively.

In what follows I shall attempt to analyze the origins and theoretical implications of these two ideas; to take account of the radical and conservative elements in each; and, by referring to particular historical experiences in which women's reproductive control has been at issue, to highlight certain tensions between them which may never be (nor should we wish them to be) totally resolved. My argument is that reproductive freedom—indeed, the very nature of reproduction itself—is irreducibly social and individual at the same time; that is, it operates "at the core of social life" as well as within and upon women's individual bodies. Thus, a coherent analysis of reproductive freedom requires a perspective that is both Marxist and feminist.[4] This dual perspective is also necessary on the level of political practice. For even if it were true, as some "right-to-lifers" have charged, that the women's movement is self-contradictory in demanding both control by women over reproductive matters and greater sharing of responsibility for such matters between women and men, it is also true that both these goals are indispensable to a feminist program for reproductive freedom. We have to struggle for a society in which responsibility for contraception, procreation, and child rearing is no longer relegated to women primarily; and, at the same time—as long as there is any connection between sex, reproduction, and women's bodies—we have to defend the principle of control over our bodies and our reproductive capacities. In the long run, we have to ask whether women's control over reproduction is what we want, whether it is consistent with equality; in the short run, we have never experienced the concrete historical conditions under which we could afford to give it up.

Controlling Our Bodies

The principle that grounds women's reproductive freedom in a "right to bodily self-determination," or "control over one's body," has, I will argue, three distinct but related bases: liberalism, neo-Marxism, and biological contingency. Its liberal roots may be traced to the Puritan revolution in seventeenth-century England. In that period, the Leveller

4. I am indebted to Zillah Eisenstein for this important clarification.

idea of a "property in one's own person" was linked explicitly to nature, and paralleled the idea of a "natural right" to property in goods: "To every individual in nature is given an individual property by nature, not to be invaded or usurped by any: for every one as he is himselfe, so he hath a selfe propriety, else could he not be himselfe, and on this no second may presume to deprive any of without manifest violation and affront to the very principles of nature, and of the Rules of equity and justice between man and man. . . ."[5] A person, to be a person, must have control over himself/herself, in body as well as in mind. This Leveller notion of individualism, individual selfhood, while phrased in masculine terms, had specific applications to the conditions of women in the seventeenth century: the enactment of the Puritan idea of marriage as a contract, restrictions against wife beating, and the liberalization of divorce.[6] It had other applications, however, that affected men and women both—for example, the introduction of habeas corpus in 1628 (bodies cannot be detained without cause); and, above all, a resistance to the idea of selling, or alienating, one's body to another through wage labor. Thus, the original notion of "property in one's person" was not only an assertion of individualism in an abstract sense but had a particular radical edge that rejected the commoditization of bodies through an emergent labor market. The Levellers (who, in fact, were mostly petty tradesmen and craftsmen, anxious to distinguish themselves from propertyless laborers) were saying: my body is not property, is not transferable; it belongs only to me.

While the liberal origins of the "bodily integrity" principle are quite clear, its radical implications, today as in the seventeenth century, should not be forgotten. In its more recent juridical expressions, for example, the so-called right to privacy, that principle has been usefully applied to defend prisoners from physical abuse, undocumented aliens from bodily searches, patients from involuntary treatment or medical experimentation, as well as in the more well-known "reproductive rights" cases *(Griswold* v. *Connecticut, Eisenstadt* v. *Baird,* and the original abortion decision, *Roe* v. *Wade).*[7] While privacy, like property, has a distinctly negative

5. Quoted in C. B. MacPherson, *The Political Theory of Possessive Individualism* (London: Oxford University Press, 1962), p. 140.

6. See Keith Thomas, "Women and the Civil War Sects," *Past and Present* 13 (1958): 332–52. For accounts of Leveller doctrine as well as the ideas of more radical sects about women and individualism in this period, see Christopher Hill, *The World Turned Upside Down* (New York: Viking Press, 1972), and *The Century of Revolution, 1603–1714* (New York: W. W. Norton & Co., 1961), chaps. 4, 7, and 8; MacPherson, chap. 3.

7. Griswold v. Connecticut, 381 U.S. 479 (1965); Eisenstadt v. Baird, 405 U.S. 438 (1972); Roe v. Wade, 410 U.S. 113 (1973); and Doe v. Bolton, 410 U.S. 179 (1973). See also the fine summary and analysis of these cases as well as the June 1977 Supreme Court decisions on abortion by Kristin Booth Glen ("Abortion in the Courts: A Laywoman's Historical Guide to the New Disaster Area," *Feminist Studies* 4 [February 1978]: 1–26).

connotation which is exclusionary and asocial, when applied to persons as persons—in their concrete, physical being—it also has a positive sense that roughly coincides with the notion of "individual self-determination." In other words, control over one's body is an essential part of being an individual with needs and rights, a concept which is, in turn, the most powerful legacy of the liberal political tradition.

This principle clearly applies to persons as persons and not only to women. Juliet Mitchell has argued forcefully, however, that it was the soil that nourished the growth of feminism in the eighteenth and nineteenth centuries, and that many of the positive gains sought by women under the rubrics of "liberty" and "equality" still have not been won.[8] I would go further and argue that a certain idea of individuality is also not antithetical to a Marxist tradition, which distinguishes between the idea of individual human beings as historically determined, concrete, and particular in their needs, and the ideology of "individualism" (i.e., "the individual" conceived as isolated, atomized, exclusive in *his* possessions, disconnected from larger social fabrics). This Marxist concept of a "concrete individuality" has been elucidated by Agnes Heller and Herbert Marcuse, who both recognize that the end of socialist transformation for Marx is ultimately the satisfaction of individual needs, which are always concrete and specific (unlike rights, which belong to "citizens" or "persons" in the abstract). Thus, according to Heller, "Marx recognizes no needs other than those of individual people"; and, while understanding needs as generally social or "socially produced," such needs nevertheless "are the needs of individual human beings": "When the domination of things over human beings ceases, when relations between human beings no longer appear as relations between things, then *every* need governs 'the need for the development of the individual,' the need for the self-realization of the human personality."[9]

Similarly, Marcuse, in his essay "On Hedonism," argues in favor of restoring a sense of individual "happiness" to a revolutionary ethic ("general happiness apart from the happiness of individuals is a meaningless phrase"). Through his analysis of contemporary forms of domination and repression that alienate individuals from a sense of connectedness with their own bodies and thus with the physical and social world, Marcuse arrives at a view of hedonism as containing a liberatory element. That element is a sense of "complete immediacy," of "sensuality," which, Marcuse suggests, is a necessary precondition for the "development of personality" and the participation of individuals in social life. The link between eroticism and politics is a "receptivity that is open and

8. Juliet Mitchell, "Women and Equality," in *The Rights and Wrongs of Women*, ed. Juliet Mitchell and Ann Oakley (Harmondsworth, Middlesex: Penguin Books, 1976).
9. Agnes Heller, *The Theory of Need in Marx* (New York: St. Martin's Press, 1976), pp. 67, 73.

that opens itself (to experience)."[10] Control over one's body is a fundamental aspect of this sense of immediacy, this "receptivity," a requirement of being a person and engaging in conscious activity. Understood
thus, it is a principle of a radical morality that should never be abandoned, under any social conditions.

The direct connection between the principle of "control over one's
body" and feminist claims regarding women's control over reproduction
seemed obvious to early birth control advocates. Long before Margaret
Sanger, Ezra Heywood, an anarchist birth controller in the 1870s, asserted "Woman's Natural Right to ownership of and control over her
own body-self—a right inseparable from Women's intelligent existence.
. . ."[11] This connection is as real today. Because pregnancies occur in
women's bodies (and are likely to for some time, Shulamith Firestone
notwithstanding), the continued possibility of an "unwanted" pregnancy
affects women in a very specific sense, not only as potential bearers of
fetuses, but also in their capacity to enjoy sexuality and to maintain their
health. As Judge Dooling held in *McCrae* v. *Califano,* a woman's right to
decide upon abortion when her health is at stake is "nearly allied to her
right to be."[12]

Reproduction affects women as women, in a way that transcends
class divisions and that penetrates everything—work, political and community involvements, sexuality, creativity, dreams. Gordon illustrates
this point with reference to the conditions that generated the
nineteenth-century birth control movement:

> The desire for and the problems in securing abortion and con-
> traception made up a *shared female experience.* Abortion technique
> was apparently not much safer among upper-class doctors than
> among working-class midwives. The most commonly used
> contraceptives—douches, withdrawal—were accessible to women of
> every class. And what evidence there is of the subjective experience
> of women in their birth-control attempts also suggests that the de-
> sire for spaced motherhood and smaller families existed in every
> class, and that the desire was so passionate that women would take
> severe risks to win a little space and control in their lives. *The individ-
> ual theory and practice of birth control stems from a biological female condi-
> tion that is more basic even than class.*[13]

It is surprising to find Gordon reverting to a "biological female
condition" in the midst of an analysis of the social construction of wom-

10. Herbert Marcuse, *Negations: Essays in Critical Theory* (Boston: Beacon Press, 1968),
pp. 166–71.

11. Gordon (n. 2 above), p. 66.

12. Joseph P. Fried, "Abortion Aid Limits for the Poor Ruled Unlawful by Judge,"
New York Times (January 16, 1980), pp. A1, B2.

13. Gordon (n. 2 above), p. 70 (my italics).

en's reproductive experience. Yet it reminds us that the "bodily integrity" principle has an undeniable biological component, inseparable from its social and moral aspects. As long as women's bodies remain the medium for pregnancies, the connection between women's reproductive freedom and control over their bodies represents not only a moral and political claim but also, on some level, a material necessity. This acknowledgment of biological reality should not be mistaken for biological determinist thinking about women; my point is simply that biology is a *capacity* as well as a limit.[14] The fact that it is women who get pregnant has been the source not only of our confinement (in all senses) but, in some measure, of our (limited) power. An abundance of feminist anthropological literature reminds us that pollution rituals, fertility cults, prohibitions against abortion, as well as chastity rules imposed upon wives and daughters are signs of men's envy and fear of women's reproductive capacity—of its imagined powers, yes, but also of its reality. Indeed, the current and vituperative attack on abortion in the United States and elsewhere in the West has been interpreted by some feminists as a massive recurrence of male "womb envy."

I would be the last to romanticize the control that comes from our biological connection to childbearing, or to underestimate its repressive social aspects for women. On the other hand, women's control over their bodies is not like preindustrial workers' control over their tools; it cannot be wrested away simply through changes in technology or legal prohibitions and repression—which is why no modern society has succeeded for long in outlawing abortion or birth control, only in driving it "underground." (Even women slaves retain the capacity to abort as an act of resistance—an act that derives from powerlessness, as I shall emphasize later, but also from a residual power.) The inability of societies, and men, to regulate totally women's reproductive control, or to mediate in an absolute way women's connection to their bodies, reflects the dialectical nature of the "biological female condition."

It is important, however, to keep in mind that woman's reproductive situation is never the result of biology alone, but of biology mediated by social and cultural organization. That is, it is not inevitable that women, and not men, should bear the main consequences of unintended pregnancy and thus that their sexual and reproductive expression be inhibited by it. Rather, it is the result of the socially ascribed primacy of motherhood in women's lives. Yet it is also true that biology as it is socially mediated by male-dominant institutions affects all women in a

14. Cf. Sara Ruddick: "Neither our own ambivalence toward our women's bodies nor the bigoted, repressive uses men, colonizers and racists have made of biology, should blind us to biology's possibilities. On the other hand, our belief in the biological body's psychosocial efficacy may be an illusion created by the fact that the people who engage in maternal practices almost always have female bodies" ("Maternal Thinking," *Feminist Studies* [1980], in press).

way that cuts across class divisions. In our own period there is prolific evidence of this "shared female experience." The cutbacks in abortion funding, whose initial and hardest impact has been on low-income women, have been the spearhead of a right-wing movement to curtail abortion services and reimbursements for most working-class and middle-class women living in various states and dependent on many different health insurance plans as well. While sterilization abuse has mainly been directed at poor, Third World, and mentally disabled women, the ultimatum to well-paid women chemical workers that they get sterilized or lose their jobs has widened our perspective on this issue.[15] Indeed, the fact that female sterilization, an irreversible procedure, has become the most widely used, medically encouraged, and economically reimbursable method of contraception among all but the very young in the United States,[16] as evidence grows of the pill's dangers to women's health and abortions are restricted, raises questions about reproductive "choices" for *most* women. This basic material condition of reproduction—that the two major birth control methods in current use are, on the one hand, irreversible, and on the other hand, dangerous to health—affects women of all classes. It is a condition set, not by reproductive technology, but by reproductive politics—a politics that seeks to curtail the efforts of women, as women, "to win a little space and control in their lives" and freely to express their sexuality.

The principle of "control over our bodies," then, has a material as well as a moral and a political basis. What I have called the "liberal," the "radical" or "neo-Marxist," and the "biological" elements of this principle should not be seen as alternatives to one another but rather as different levels of meaning that give the principle its force and complexity. Sorting out these different levels should make it easier for us to distinguish between situations when we are describing "control over our bodies" as a *material fact,* when we are asserting it as a *right,* and when (with, I believe, the most radical political implications) we are defining it as part of a larger set of socially determined *human needs.*

And yet, the idea of "a woman's right to choose" as the main princi-

15. "Four Women Assert Jobs Were Linked to Sterilization," *New York Times* (January 5, 1979); Rosalind Petchesky, "Workers, Reproductive Hazards and the Politics of Protection: An Introduction," *Feminist Studies* 5 (Summer 1979): 233–45; Michael J. Wright, "Reproductive Hazards and 'Protective' Discrimination," ibid., pp. 302–9; Wendy Chavkin, "Occupational Hazards to Reproduction—a Review of the Literature," ibid., pp. 310–25.

16. Committee for Abortion Rights and against Sterilization Abuse [CARASA], *Women Under Attack: Abortion, Sterilization Abuse, and Reproductive Freedom* (New York: CARASA, 1979); Rosalind Petchesky, "Reproduction, Ethics and Public Policy: The Federal Sterilization Regulations," *Hastings Center Report* 9 (October 1979): 29–42; Charles F. Westoff and James McCarthy, "Sterlization in the United States," *Family Planning Perspectives* 11 (May/June 1979): 147–52; Charlotte F. Muller, "Insurance Coverage of Abortion, Contraception and Sterilization," ibid., 10 (March–April 1978): 71–77.

ple of reproductive freedom is insufficient and problematic at the same time as it is politically compelling. For one thing, this principle does evade moral questions about when, under what conditions, and for what purposes reproductive decisions—for example, the abortion decision—should be made. Feminists writing on abortion usually have not claimed that a pregnant woman "owns" the fetus, or that it is part of her body (although right-to-lifers and others have interpreted the feminist position this way). On the contrary, feminists have generally characterized an unwanted pregnancy as a kind of bodily "invasion."[17] Recognizing a situation of real conflict between the survival of the fetus and the needs of the woman and those dependent on her, the feminist position says merely that women must decide, because it is their bodies that are involved, and because they still have primary responsibility for the care and development of the children born.

But determining who should decide—the political question—does not tell us anything about the moral and social values women ought to bring to this decision, *how* they should decide.[18] Should women get an abortion on the grounds that they prefer a different gender (which amniocentesis can now determine)? Such a decision, in my view, would be blatantly sexist, and nobody's claim to "control over her body" could make it right or compatible with feminist principles. That is, "a woman's right to control her body" is not abstract or absolute, but we have not developed a morality that is both socialist and feminist that would tell us what the exceptions should be. Admitting that we have not fully articulated a feminist morality of abortion, however, does not imply that all or most women who get abortions do so thoughtlessly or irresponsibly. On the contrary, women who seek abortions know and experience better than anyone else the difficulty of that decision. Much more serious is the potential danger in the assertion of women's right to control over reproduction as absolute or exclusive, insofar as it can be turned back on us to reinforce the view of all reproductive activity as the special, biologi-

17. "There is no way a pregnant woman can passively let the fetus live; she must create and nurture it with her own body, a symbiosis that is often difficult, sometimes dangerous, uniquely intimate. However gratifying pregnancy may be to a woman who desires it, for the unwilling it is literally an invasion—the closest analogy is to the difference between lovemaking and rape. ... Clearly, abortion is by normal standards an act of self-defense" (Ellen Willis, *The Village Voice* [March 5, 1979], p. 8). This is the most eloquent statement of the feminist position on abortion I have read. Cf. Judith Jarvis Thomson's classic essay, "A Defense of Abortion" (in *The Rights and Wrongs of Abortion*, ed. John Finnis et al. [Princeton, N.J.: Princeton University Press, 1974], pp. 10, 12), who uses philosophical sleight of hand to arrive at the same conclusion.

18. This point is made persuasively by Daniel Callahan, *Abortion: Law, Choice and Morality* (New York: Macmillan Publishing Co., 1970), p. 494; cf. Alison Jaggar, "Abortion and a Woman's Right to Decide," in *Women and Philosophy*, ed. Carol C. Gould and Marx W. Wartofsky (New York: Capricorn Books, 1976), p. 347.

cally destined province of women. Here it has to be acknowledged that this danger grows out of the concept of "rights" in general, a concept inherently static and abstracted from social conditions. Rights are by definition claims that are staked within a given order of things and relationships. They are demands for access for oneself, or for "no admittance" to others, but they do not challenge the social structure itself, the social relations of production and reproduction.[19] The claim for "abortion rights" seeks access to a necessary service, but by itself it fails to address the existing social relations and sexual divisions around which responsibility for pregnancy and children is assigned. And in real-life struggles, this limitation exacts a price, for it lets men and society neatly off the hook.

The notion of "rights" has tremendous polemical power, but "rights" tend to be seen as isolated, discrete goods rather than as part of a total revolutionary program. This is different from Marx and Engels's view of "bourgeois rights" as necessary preconditions and as means to building a class-conscious movement but not as ends in themselves (as feminists often think of them). It is also different from the more radical concept of control over one's body as a social and individual need, implicit in the requirements of personality and sensual "receptivity." Needs, unlike rights, exist only in connection with concrete individuals and within concrete historical circumstances. For a Native American woman on welfare, who every time she appears in the clinic for prenatal care is asked whether she would not like an abortion, "the right to choose an abortion" may appear dubious if not offensive.[20]

Finally, the idea of a "woman's right to choose" is vulnerable to political manipulation by the forces of conservatism and laissez-faire, as demonstrated in recent legislative and judicial debates. Thus "right-to-lifers" exploit the liberal concept of "informed consent" by promoting legislation that would require abortion patients to be "informed" in graphic detail of a fetus' physiological characteristics at each stage of development. Physicians opposing the federal, California, and New York City regulations to curb involuntary sterilization, particularly the requirement of a thirty-day waiting period, have claimed that such regulation is "paternalistic" and inhibits women's "right to choose" sterilization.[21] During hearings before the House Select Committee on Population in 1978, a spokesman for the Upjohn Company, manufacturer of Depo-Provera (an injectible contraceptive drug currently banned from U.S. distribution because of evidence it is carcinogenic), opposed FDA

19. Cf. Mitchell (n. 8 above), pp. 384–85.

20. Meredith Tax, citing a remark by Pat Bellanger, representative of WARN (Women of All Red Nations), St. Paul, Minnesota.

21. Patricia Donovan, "Sterilizing the Poor and Incompetent," *Hastings Center Report* 6 (October 1976): 5; and Petchesky, "Reproduction, Ethics and Public Policy," p. 35.

regulation of contraceptives on the ground that it "deprives the public of free choice": ". . . safety cannot be absolute—it can be defined *only in relative and personal terms*. The individual with advice from his or her physician—not a governmental regulatory agency—should decide which risks are 'reasonable' under these circumstances."[22]

The idea that judgments about contraceptive safety can only be made "in relative and personal terms" of course assails the commitment to establishing and enforcing generalizable, social standards of health and safety that transcend individual judgments. Moreover, when the risks include thromboembolisms, myocardial infarction, breast cancer, and cervical cancer, the need for social standards and their vigorous enforcement is a matter for women of life and death. Recent applications of laissez-faire ideology to reproductive policy are clearly part of a larger right-wing push that seeks "deregulation" in many spheres; seen within this general political context, they are to be expected. But the ease with which the principle of individuality and control over one's own body may be perverted into what is truly bourgeois individualism—and capitalist greed—should make us pause, clear our heads, and think through more rigorously the social conditions of individual control.

The Social Relations of Reproduction

The idea that biological reproduction itself is a social activity, distinct from the activity of child rearing and determined by its own changing material conditions and social relations, is essentially Marxist in inspiration. In *The German Ideology,* Marx defines "three aspects of social activity": along with "the production of material life" and "the production of new needs," human procreation—reproduction within the family—is also a "social relationship." That is, it involves not only "natural," or biological, relations but social, cooperative relations among men and women through sexual and procreative practices. That activity is social insofar as it is cooperative, purposive, and above all conscious.[23] While Marx clearly has in mind relations for the purpose of procreation, we can extend this view to human sexuality in general, which, whether heterosexual, homosexual, or bisexual, is fundamentally social, involving reciprocity, the conscious articulation and recreation of desire; not merely satisfying a need but doing so in an interactive context that people create together. Moreover, as recent writings by Rayna Rapp and

22. U.S. Congress, House, Select Committee on Population, *Fertility and Contraception in the United States,* 95th Cong., 2d sess., December 1978, p. 110.
23. Karl Marx, *The German Ideology,* in *Writings of the Young Marx on Philosophy and Society,* ed. Lloyd D. Easton and Kurt H. Guddat (Garden City, N.Y.: Anchor Books, 1967), pp. 419–22.

Ellen Ross, Jeffrey Weeks, Jean-Louis Flandrin, Michel Foucault, Gayle Rubin, and others attest,[24] sexual meanings and practices, like the meanings and practices of motherhood, vary enormously through history, across cultures, and within the same culture—indicating that these "natural" realms of human experience are incessantly mediated by social praxis and design.

If this variability characterizes sexual and maternal experience, how much more is it true of contraception, abortion, and child rearing practices—all domains which, throughout civilization, have been transformed by conscious human interventions.[25] A woman does not simply "get pregnant" and "give birth" like the flowing of tides and seasons. She does so under the constraint of definite *material conditions* that set limits on "natural" reproductive processes—for example, existing birth control methods and technology and access to them; class divisions and the distribution/financing of health care; nutrition; employment, particularly of women; and the state of the economy generally. And she does so within a specific network of *social relations* and social arrangements involving herself, her sexual partner(s), her children and kin, neighbors, doctors, family planners, birth control providers and manufacturers, employers, the church, and the state.

Georg Lukács is one Marxist theorist who takes up the idea of a "metabolism," or necessary interaction, between the natural and social aspects of human life. Lukács suggests that the progressive socialization of "natural being" through "social practice" is the very essence of history.[26] To dichotomize "nature" and "society" as the objects of two different sciences is, in this view, false; and, by inference, it is also false to assume a split between women's "biological" functions and her "social"

24. Rayna Rapp and Ellen Ross, "Sex and Society: A Research Note from Social History and Anthropology," *Comparative Studies in Society and History* (forthcoming); Jeffrey Weeks, *Coming Out: Homosexual Politics in Britain, from the Nineteenth Century to the Present* (London: Quartet Books, 1977); *Radical History Review*, vol. 20 (Spring/Summer 1979), special issue on "Sexuality in History," especially articles by Robert A. Padgug ("Sexual Matters: On Conceptualizing Sexuality in History," pp. 3–23) and Jeffrey Weeks ("Movements of Affirmation: Sexual Meanings and Homosexual Identities," pp. 164–79); Jean-Louis Flandrin, "Contraception, Marriage, and Sexual Relations in the Christian West," in *Biology of Man in History,* ed. Robert Forster and Orest Ranum (Baltimore: Johns Hopkins University Press, 1975); Michel Foucault, *The History of Sexuality,* vol. 1, *An Introduction* (New York: Pantheon Books, 1978); Gayle Rubin, "The Traffic in Women," in *Toward an Anthropology of Women,* ed. Rayna (Rapp) Reiter (New York: Monthly Review Press, 1975), pp. 157–210.

25. See, e.g., Gordon (n. 2 above), chaps. 1 and 2; Norman E. Himes, *Medical History of Contraception* (New York: Gamut Press, 1963); John T. Noonan, Jr., *Contraception* (Cambridge, Mass.: Harvard University Press, 1966); Devereux (n. 3 above); Steven Polgar, "Population History and Population Policies from an Anthropological Perspective," *Current Anthropology* 13 (April 1972): 203–11.

26. Georg Lukács, *The Ontology of Social Being—2. Marx* (London: Merlin Press, 1978), pp. 5–7, 38–39.

ones. Hilda Scott similarly reflects this view in paraphrasing the Czech demographer Helena Svarcova: "Marx's observation . . . suggests looking for the dialectical relationship between the natural and social sides of reproduction, instead of regarding them as two parallel but independent processes. In this view, human population is seen as the unity of biological and social aspects which condition each other, the social aspects being the chief but not the only factor."[27]

The attempt to develop a social conception of reproduction is, of course, not limited to Marxists. Demographers, for example, conventionally acknowledge the importance of social conditions in determining population, but within a set of completely mechanistic assumptions. A social phenomenon such as changing birth rates is thus viewed solely in terms of statistically measurable demographic events (numbers of women in a given childbearing cohort, numbers entering the labor force, availability and use of contraceptives, and so on) as though it were a natural, unintended occurrence.[28] Population-oriented anthropologists, on the other hand, emphasize not only the tremendous variability but the rational, deliberate character of methods for controlling population and fertility (infanticide, contraception, abstinence, marriage practices, withdrawal) among all societies, including the most primitive.[29] However, they view such activity from a functionalist perspective, as "adaptive mechanisms" adopted by the culture as a whole, undifferentiated by sexual divisions or divisions of power. Utterly lacking from this perspective is any sense that the methods and goals of reproduction, and control over them, may themselves be a contested area within the culture—particularly between women and men.

In contrast, an analysis of reproductive activity in terms of the "social relations of reproduction" would emphasize the historical dynamism of consciousness and social conflict and the historical agency of social groups. Social divisions, based on differing relationships to power and resources, mediate the institutional and cultural arrangements through which biology, sexuality, and reproduction among human beings are expressed, and such relations are essentially antagonistic and complex. At the most basic level they involve gender divisions, or the sexual division of labor (itself a predominantly cultural product, as feminist theorists such as Gayle Rubin and Nancy Chodorow have demonstrated); but in class-divided societies, they are also entangled with divisions based on class. Linda Gordon's book is laced with examples of the ways in which, in nineteenth- and twentieth-century America, women's birth control possibilities were directly affected by their class position,

27. Hilda Scott, *Does Socialism Liberate Women?* (Boston: Beacon Press, 1974), p. 159.
28. Thanks to Ellen Ross and Hal Benenson for reminding me of this point.
29. See Polgar, "Population History"; and Alexander Alland, *Adaptation in Human Evolution: An Approach to Medical Anthropology* (New York: Columbia University Press, 1970).

which determined their relationship to medical and family planning distribution systems. Thus, the diaphragm—"the most effective available contraceptive in the 1930s" (and, when we consider women's health and safety, among the best methods available today)—was virtually inaccessible to working class and poor women, due to material conditions such as the lack of privacy, running water, and access to the private clinics and medical instruction through which diaphragms were dispensed.[30] Today, class and race divisions in reproductive health care determine not only women's access to decent gynecological services, counseling, and the like, but their risk of exposure to involuntary sterilization, dangerous contraceptive drugs, or unnecessary hysterectomy.

The social relations of reproduction are also complicated by the different forms of consciousness and struggle through which they are expressed in different historical periods. Sometimes the antagonisms remain implicit or repressed; sometimes, under particular conditions which need to be understood more precisely, birth control and abortion become terrains of open sexual and class conflict. Anthropological and historical studies, while scant, record the particularity of reproductive relations to class and culture and the ways those relations are inherently ones of social division. Devereux, for example, describes a number of societies in which abortion, or retaliation against involuntary induced abortion, represented a clear act of female defiance.[31] Likewise, Flandrin, in his analysis of late medieval church views toward contraception and sexual relations (especially nonprocreative sex), points out that the evidence of widespread contraceptive practice among married as well as unmarried persons indicates that conscious, even unrepentant resistance to the dominant ecclesiastical morality must have been common in Europe from the fifteenth to the eighteenth centuries.[32]

In regard to a theory of reproductive freedom, these examples suggest that the critical issue for feminists is not so much the content of women's choices, or even the "right to choose," as it is the social and material conditions under which choices are made. The "right to choose" means very little when women are powerless. In cultures where "illegitimacy" is stigmatized or where female infants are devalued, women may resort to abortion or infanticide with impunity; but that option clearly grows out of female subordination. Similarly, women may have autonomy over reproduction and childbirth, as in New Guinea, while being totally excluded from everything else.[33] Or, like the women employees at

30. Gordon (n. 2 above), pp. 309–12.
31. Devereux (n. 3 above), pp. 113, 117.
32. Flandrin (n. 24 above), pp. 25–28.
33. Sherry B. Ortner, "The Virgin and the State," *Feminist Studies* 4 (October 1978): 25; and Gordon (p. 34), who cites similar examples from anthropological evidence and concludes: "These are women's choices, but hardly choices coming from positions of power."

the American Cyanimid plant in West Virginia, they may "choose" sterilization as the alternative to losing their jobs. To paraphrase Marx, women make their own reproductive choices, but they do not make them just as they please; they do not make them under conditions which they themselves create but under social conditions and constraints which they, as mere individuals, are powerless to change.[34] The fact that individuals themselves do not determine the social framework in which they act does not nullify their choices nor their moral capacity to make them. It only suggests that we have to focus less on the question of "choice" and more on the question of how to transform the social conditions of choosing, working, and reproducing.

At present, the organized forces that shape the class-specific socially constructed character of women's reproductive experience in the United States are powerful and diverse. The intervention of doctors, particularly obstetrician-gynecologists, in women's control over their reproductive lives has been pervasive, yet medical control over reproduction is far from monolithic. Private and governmental population control agencies have cooperated with the medical profession, as "medical indications" and "medical effectiveness" became euphemisms for technical efficiency in population control. But these agencies maintain a financial and institutional power base independent of doctors. Further, the large-scale commercialization of birth control products and services has meant that other interests, such as pharmaceutical and insurance companies, have become important influences on the kinds of methods available to women, their safety or risk, and whether or not they will be reimbursed.

The impact of this conjuncture of medical, corporate, and state interests on the "management" of reproduction has defined the choices of all women, but in a way that is crucially different depending on one's class and race. Still the major providers of birth control and abortion information and services to women, physicians are widely known to vary the kinds and amount of information they provide and the quality of services based on the class and race of their patients. For example, private doctors in Maryland were found to provide abortions with much greater regularity to their middle-class than to their lower-class patients.[35] Likewise, cases of sterilization abuse by physicians in the public health services have occurred almost entirely among Black, Native American, and Mexican American welfare recipients, as well as women who are prisoners or mentally retarded.[36] Low-income and non-

34. Karl Marx, *The Eighteenth Brumaire of Louis Bonaparte* (New York: International Publishers, 1963), p. 15.

35. Constance A. Nathanson and Marshall H. Becker, "The Influence of Physicians' Attitudes on Abortion Performance, Patient Management and Professional Fees," *Family Planning Perspectives* 9 (July/August 1977): 158–63.

36. Ad Hoc Women's Studies Committee against Sterilization Abuse, *Workbook on Sterilization and Sterilization Abuse* (Bronxville, N.Y.: Women's Studies, Sarah Lawrence College, 1978); and CARASA (n. 16 above), pp. 49–53.

English-speaking women are regularly denied information about safer, "nonmedical" methods of birth control because of racist and class-biased assumptions that they are not "competent" to "manage" such methods. Moreover, it is invariably poor, Third World women—in Latin America and Puerto Rico, or in the southern or southwestern United States—who are likely to be used as experimental subjects in international population control programs for testing or "dumping" contraceptive chemicals or implants (such as Depo-Provera) whose safety has been questioned by the FDA.[37] Finally, in a capitalist society, class is the mightiest determinant of the material resources that help to make having and raising children joyful rather than burdensome.

It would be wrong, however, to picture women of any class as the passive victims of medical, commercial, and state policies of reproductive control. In hearings before the House Select Committee on Population and in lawsuits, women have successfully challenged drug companies and doctors regarding the severe health hazards of the pill, Depo-Provera, and other synthetic hormones.[38] Groups of Mexican American, Native American, Black, and other women have joined with women's health and reproductive rights groups to fight against involuntary sterilization in the courts and through extensive new federal and state regulations. An active, vocal movement to defend women's reproductive freedom and "abortion rights" is growing in the United States and western Europe and is currently a major force in the women's movement. Reproductive politics is more than ever a terrain of active struggle.

What is "reproductive freedom," from the standpoint of historical materialism? On what principle is women's struggle to secure control over the terms and conditions of reproduction based? A materialist view of reproductive freedom would justify this struggle in terms of the principle of socially determined need—that is, from this view the moral imperative itself grows out of the historically and culturally defined position that women find themselves in through motherhood. Because it is primarily women—not fathers, not doctors, not "child care specialists," not the state—who are still the ones who bear the consequences of pregnancy and the responsibility for children, the conditions of reproduction and contraception affect them directly, and in every other aspect of their lives. Therefore, it is women primarily who should have control over whether, when, and under what conditions to have children. Moreover, an emphasis on the social rather than biological basis of reproductive activity implies that such activity is once and for all removed from any "privatized" or "personal sphere" and may legitimately be claimed for

37. See Barbara Ehrenreich, Mark Dowie, and Stephen Minkin. "The Charge, Gynocide; the Accused, the U.S. Government," reprinted in *CARASA News* 4 (January 1980): 13; Deborah Maine, "Depo: The Debate Continues," *Family Planning Perspectives* 10 (November/December 1978): 392.

38. U.S. Congress, House, Select Committee on Population (n. 22 above), pp. 109–10.

political and social intervention. That intervention may take the form of measures to protect or regulate reproductive health—for example, to assure the safety and voluntariness of contraceptive methods, or to transform the material conditions that presently divide women's reproductive options according to class and race.

On the other hand, a materialist view of reproductive freedom recognizes the historical contingency of the conditions in which women seek reproductive control for themselves. For most of history, women's "choices" over reproduction have been exercised in a framework in which reproduction and motherhood still determine their relationship to the rest of society. A materialist (and, I would argue, feminist) view looks forward to an eventual transcendence of the existing social relations of reproduction, so that gender is not ultimately determinant of responsibility. This implies that, should existing social arrangements change—should society be transformed so that men, or society itself, bear an equal responsibility for nurturance and child care—then the basis of the needs would have changed and control over reproduction might not belong primarily to women.[39]

It is here, however, that a contrary feminist sensibility begins to rankle and the limitations of a historical materialist, or traditional Marxist, framework for defining reproductive freedom become apparent. These limitations are disturbingly suggested in Alison Jaggar's "Marxist feminist" defense of abortion, which argues that the "right" of women to an abortion is "contingent" upon "women's situation in our society": " . . . if the whole community assumes the responsibility for the welfare of mothers and children, [then] the community as a whole should now have a share in judging whether or not a particular abortion should be performed. . . ."[40]

Can we really imagine the social conditions in which we would be ready to renounce control over our bodies and reproductive lives—to give over the decision as to whether, when, and with whom we will bear children to the "community as a whole"? The reality behind this nagging question is that control over reproductive decisions, particularly abortion, has to do not only with "the welfare of mothers and children" but very fundamentally with sexuality and with women's bodies as such. The analysis emphasizing the social relations of reproduction tends to ignore, or deny, the level of reality most immediate for individual women: that it

39. The position that is being presented here is obviously different from the technological determinism of Shulamith Firestone in *The Dialectic of Sex* (New York: Bantam Books, 1970). Firestone's simplistic view that women's position could be "revolutionized" by the introduction of in vitro fertilization, artificial uteruses, and other "advanced" features of reproductive technology ignores the social aspects of reproduction and the political question of who controls that technology, how control is organized socially and institutionally, and for what ends.

40. Jaggar (n. 18 above), pp. 351, 356, 358.

is their bodies in which pregnancies occur. Indeed, that analysis becomes false insofar as it disregards the immediate, sensual reality of individuals altogether. In order to make this connection, a theory of reproductive freedom has to have recourse to other conceptual frameworks, particularly that which has been more commonly associated with a feminist tradition and which asserts women's right to and need for bodily self-determination.

Reproductive Politics: Lessons of the Past and Visions of the Future

"Even if contraception were perfected to infallibility, so that no woman need ever again bear an unwanted child; even if laws and customs change—as long as women and women only are the nurturers of children, our sons will grow up looking only to women for compassion, resenting strength in women as 'control,' clinging to women when we try to move into a new mode of relationship."[41]

How do we break out of the apparent contradiction between "women's right to control" over reproduction, and their need not to be defined by reproduction? How do we begin to transform the social relations of reproduction, to bring men, as potential fathers, into those relations on an equal basis? How would such a transformation affect the principle of "control over our bodies"? It is the argument of this paper that, in practice, the two ideas of reproductive freedom discussed here must both be incorporated into a revolutionary feminist and socialist politics. Despite the real tensions between these ideas—that stressing changes in the social relations of reproduction, and that stressing women's control over their bodies—neither is dispensable for feminists, and both are essential. Yet no political movement for "reproductive rights" or women's emancipation, including our own, has yet sustained this double agenda in a full, systematic, and consistent way.

The failure to integrate these two ideas in practice in a political movement is illustrated quite dramatically by Attina Grossman's account of the abortion struggle that united feminists, socialists, and communists in Weimar Germany.[42] According to Grossman, "the Communist left and its women's movement" saw abortion as primarily "a class issue": the proposed law making abortion a criminal act would affect working-class women most severely, since middle-class women could both afford and get access to illegal abortion and contraception. Feminists, on the other hand, emphasized "women's right to sexual pleasure and control of their bodies," suggesting that maternity itself is a special female realm of experience that cuts across class divisions.

41. Adrienne Rich, *Of Woman Born* (New York: W. W. Norton & Co., 1976), p. 211.
42. Attina Grossman, "Abortion and the Economic Crisis: The 1931 Campaign against §218 in Germany," *New German Critique* 14 (Spring 1978): 119–37.

Grossman correctly stresses the positive aspects of this political campaign: that it brought together in a single coalition the women's movement and the working-class movement; that it appealed to women of all classes on the basis of their oppression as women in reproduction; that it moved even the German Community Party (KPD), for mainly tactical reasons, to put forward a feminist slogan: "Your body belongs to you." Yet the very different ideological bases on which different groups supported the abortion struggle implied differing senses of why that campaign was important and must have had an impact on the cohesiveness of the movement and its ability to make its ideas felt. As Grossman remarks, "the politics of reproduction were never . . . adequately integrated into Communist ideology";[43] that is, a theory that related the need of individual women for control over their bodies to the needs of the working class as a whole was not—nor has it yet been—articulated.

Reproductive politics in the context of actual socialist revolutions have been still less cohesive or consciously feminist. In general, where reforms such as liberalized abortion and divorce have been introduced as a fundamental aspect of socialist revolutions—for example, in the Soviet Union and eastern Europe—the purpose has been mainly to facilitate women's participation in industry and the breakup of feudal and patriarchal forms. Such measures have not been inspired by either of the ideas I have been examining, nor by a feminist movement self-consciously struggling to put those ideas into practice. Richard Stites's account of the Soviet Union in the 1920s and 1930s,[44] and Hilda Scott's of Czechoslovakia in the 1950s and 1960s,[45] both richly and poignantly

43. Ibid., p. 134.
44. Stites shows how the postrevolutionary Russian Family Code—which abolished illegitimacy, eased divorce, and recognized de facto marriages—worked to women's disadvantage in the absence of either adequate means of material support for women and children or a feminist politics emphasizing men's role in reproduction. Likewise, the liberalized abortion law of 1920 became a pretext not only for abandonment and non-recognition of paternity, but for the lax and exploitive sexual relations that characterized this period. In these conditions of insecurity, the return to a traditional sanctification of marriage and motherhood in the 1930s, with heavy restrictions on both abortion and divorce, was actually welcomed by many women themselves, insofar as the new (1936) provisions reinforced men's responsibility for providing protection to wife and children (Richard Stites, *The Women's Liberation Movement in Russia* [Princeton, N.J.: Princeton University Press, 1978], pp. 367–69, 374, 386–87).
45. Scott documents the introduction of liberal abortion laws during the 1950s in Czechoslovakia, Hungary, and Rumania and its repressive aftermath. Following a major birthrate decline, as well as an apparently significant increase in the abortion rate, in the 1960s policymakers and population "experts" in these countries not only blamed abortion for social and demographic problems but accused women of "selfishness" and irresponsibility for seeking abortion and getting pregnant in the first place. A series of "maternal incentive" policies was introduced, including extended paid maternity leave, housewives' allowances, bonuses for additional children, etc., and "abortions for other than medical reasons in the case of childless married women and those with one child" were restricted (Scott [n. 27 above], pp. 141, 132–33, 153).

illustrate the limits of "reproductive reforms" when they are neither accompanied by the necessary material changes that would augment women's real power in society, nor brought into effect through a mass independent women's movement. In these cases—foreshadowing recent experience in the United States since *Roe* v. *Wade*—such reforms were used in a later, reactionary period as a pretext for sexual and reproductive repression. The tendency these cases point to is a reactive chain of developments in which measures such as liberalized abortion and abolishing illegitimacy seem to unleash a rise in sexual activity, abortions, and divorce followed by a period of backlash, in which there is an outcry against the "breakup of the family," women are blamed and accused of "selfishness," and the society is chided by population experts about its declining birthrate. In the absence of either adequate material support (incomes, child care, health care, housing) or shared male responsibility for contraception and child rearing, women—particularly unskilled and low-income women—seem left, after these reforms, in some ways more vulnerable than before.[46] And so the reaction is reinforced by the very failure of the reforms to go far enough.

Scott's assessment of the situation in Czechoslovakia, while critical of the repressiveness for women of the later, backward shifts in abortion policy, tends nevertheless to focus the blame on abortion itself (and, by implication, on the women who got abortions). She intimates that abortion is intrinsically a method of birth control which puts women at a disadvantage and "encourages irresponsibility on the part of men": ". . . abortion as a birth control method puts all the responsibility for the future of the unborn child [*sic*] on the woman. She makes the application, she agrees to the operation, she pays the fee. If, as in Czechoslovakia, she must go before an interruption commission, she is the one who receives the lecture, is subjected to pressure to have the child, is reproached for getting herself 'into trouble.'"[47] Yet what is most striking in Scott's account of abortion in Czechoslovakia is the absence (as in Russia) of any women's organization, movement, or tradition that made reproductive freedom a value in its own right. Clearly, there is nothing inevitable, nothing written into "nature," about the presumed relationship between abortion and male "irresponsibility." One could perfectly well imagine a system of abortion decision making that involved potential fathers to the same degree as potential mothers, although whether women would or should give up their control over this decision

46. A very moving and amusing expression of this pattern, and of people's confusion and personal conflict over heterosexual relations, marriage, and abortion in the 1920s in Russia, is the fine Soviet film *Bed and Sofa*, or *Tretya Meschanskaya*, produced by V. Shklovsky and A. Room (1927).

47. Scott (n. 27 above), p. 144. Cf. Kristin Luker's similar argument that abortion reform in the United States in the early 1970s encouraged "male disengagement from responsibility," in *Taking Chances: Abortion and the Decision Not to Contracept* (Berkeley: University of California, 1975), pp. 134–35.

is another question. What reinforces male irresponsibility is the reliance on abortion *in a social context in which the sex-gender division itself (particularly around child care) remains unchanged,* and *in a political context in which that division remains unchallenged.*

That a socialist revolution is a necessary but far from sufficient basis for reproductive freedom is illustrated in a very different way by the current antinatalist drive in China. The effort of the Chinese government to limit births to two per couple, through a massive campaign of propaganda and education as well as economic incentives (both positive and negative),[48] raises numerous questions. While the political decision that the Chinese economy and educational system cannot support an increasingly young population may be rational on some level, one wonders, first, whether the economic sanctions on households are accompanied by as vigorous efforts to equalize the position of women in work, economic, and political life; or to develop birth control education and methods for men. Moreover, do the measures fall more heavily on some groups because of the existence of class and economic divisions, so that poorer families feel a greater pressure to comply? Finally, how and by whom were the decisions made? Were those most affected by them (parents) involved in the process? What is most disturbing about the Chinese policy is its emphasis on chemical contraceptives and IUDs for *women,* with all the known risks and side effects.[49] Once again it is women whose bodies are subjected to reproductive and contraceptive risk.

Strategies for establishing reproductive freedom must distinguish between different historical and political contexts. Under the conditions of advanced capitalism existing in the United States today—particularly as the right wing seeks to restore patriarchal control, through family, church, and state, over whether, how, and with whom women have children—women are compelled to defend their own control. Reproductive politics in this context necessarily become a struggle for control. Moreover, that struggle is greatly complicated by persistent class and race divisions. For most women in capitalist society, the very idea of reproductive "control" (or "choice") is unthinkable short of a vast array of social changes in health care, employment, housing, child care, etc.— changes that are themselves predicated upon a socialist revolution. In the meantime, "control" in a more limited sense may mean very different things to different groups of women (birth control information is one thing, possession of your reproductive organs and custody of your children is another). In a class- and race-divided society, "pronatalist"

48. James P. Sterba, "Chinese Will Try to Halt Growth of Population by End of Century," *New York Times* (August 13, 1979), p. A4; Walter Sullivan, "A Tough New Drive on Births in China," *New York Times* (October 10, 1979), pp. C1, C11.

49. Sullivan reports that "while various contraceptive preparations are taken by millions of Chinese women, only 10,000 men are taking the birth control substance gossypol experimentally." On the commune he visited, 95 percent of the sterilizations performed had been done on women (Sullivan, pp. C1, C11).

and "antinatalist" policies coincide (e.g., restrictions on abortion *and* involuntary sterilization), making it necessary for "reproductive rights" proponents to articulate continually that "reproductive freedom means the freedom to have as well as not to have children."[50] Because women are still subordinate economically, politically, and legally, a policy emphasizing male sharing of child rearing responsibility could well operate to divest women of control over their children in a situation where they have little else. (We are currently getting a foretaste of this danger, with increasing losses of custody fights by women, particularly lesbian mothers.) In such a defensive and reactionary context, the "collective" principle could play into the suggestions of "right-to-lifers" that the responsibility for childbearing is too important to be left to women.

On the other hand, because the sexual division of labor around child rearing still prevails and defines women's position, a policy emphasizing improved benefits and services in order to encourage childbearing—even among single heterosexual women and lesbians—may ease the material burdens of motherhood; but it may also operate in practice to perpetuate the existing sexual division of labor and women's social subordination. This has certainly been the case in Eastern Europe, according to Scott's testimony. Likewise, in the United States, it is easy to imagine an accretion of reforms—particularly with current fears among demographers and policymakers about the declining birthrate—such as pregnancy disability benefits, child care centers, maternity leave provisions, etc., which, if unaccompanied by demands for transforming the total position of women, particularly around child rearing, can be used to rationalize that position.[51] The point is not, of course, that present attempts to secure funded abortion, pregnancy and maternity benefits, child care services, and other reproduction-related reforms should be abandoned, but rather that those attempts must be moved beyond the framework of "a woman's right to choose" and connected to a much broader revolutionary movement that addresses all of the conditions for women's liberation.

A feminist and socialist transformation of the existing conditions of reproduction would seek to unleash the possibilities for material (economic and technological) improvements in reproduction from traditional family and sexual forms, to embed those positive material changes in a new set of social relations. Foremost among these new relations is

50. CARASA (n. 16 above), p. 9.
51. To offset the birthrate decline in the United States, Princeton demographer Charles Westoff suggests a variation on a pronatalist incentives policy which would divide all American women into one-third who would "never have any children" and another two-thirds who "would have to reproduce at an average rate of three births per woman to maintain a replacement." While the former group would presumably be channeled into full-time employment, the latter would be drawn into their role of "breeders" through "a serious investment in child-care institutions" and other government-sponsored reproductive subsidies ("Some Speculations on the Future of Marriage and Fertility," *Family Planning Perspectives* 10 [March/April 1978]: 79–82).

that concerned with the care of children. As Adrienne Rich declares, men must be "ready to share the responsibilities of full-time, universal child care as a social priority"—which is to say, the responsibility for children must be dissociated from gender, which necessarily means that it becomes dissociated from heterosexuality. The writings of feminist theorists like Rich, Nancy Chodorow, and Dorothy Dinnerstein,[52] unveiling the deeply rooted cultural and psychic bases of traditional child-rearing arrangements, help to explain why it is this aspect of presocialist patriarchy that seems most intractable in postrevolutionary societies. The changes we require are total; as Scott writes: ". . . no decisive changes can be brought about by measures aimed at women alone, but, rather, the division of functions between the sexes must be changed in such a way that men and women have the same opportunities to be active parents and to be gainfully employed. This makes of women's emancipation not a 'woman question' but a function of the general drive for greater equality which affects everyone. . . . The care of children becomes a fact which society has to take into consideration."[53]

Under different historical conditions from any that now exist, it may become possible to transcend some of the more individualist elements of feminist thinking about reproductive freedom—to move toward a conception of reproduction as an activity that concerns all of society. At the same time, the basis could be created for the genuine reproductive freedom of individuals, ending systems of domination that inhibit individuals' control over their bodies. We need to start envisioning what those conditions would be, even though they seem very far from present reality. At least three conditions would seem necessary in order for a socially based, "gender-free," and individually liberating norm of reproduction to be actualized. First, we would have to have the material prerequisites that would make having and raising children, or not doing so, a real alternative for *all* people: convenient, safe, and reliable methods of birth control; good-quality, publicly funded health care, maternal and prenatal, and child care; the elimination of reproductively hazardous environments where we work and live; and the provision of adequate jobs, incomes, housing, and education for all.[54]

But the kind of socialist and feminist transformation we want would require more than material and technological changes. It would require, second, fundamental changes in the social and sexual relations of reproduction, so that the feminist idea of collective, shared responsibility for sexuality, birth control, and child care becomes ingrained in socialist

52. Nancy Chodorow, *The Reproduction of Mothering* (Berkeley: University of California, 1975); Dorothy Dinnerstein, *The Mermaid and the Minotaur* (New York: Harper & Row, 1976).

53. Scott (n. 27 above), p. 190.

54. See "Principles of Unity," CARASA; and "Statement of Purpose," Coalition for the Reproductive Rights of Workers" (CRROW) (both available from CARASA, 386 Park Avenue South, Room 1502, New York, New York 10016).

ideology and in social practice. Under conditions of socialist transformation, unlike capitalism, there is a normative basis for maintaining the principle of collective (transgender) responsibility in the activity of reproduction and child rearing, as in everything else. The historical fact that, in most actual socialist societies, birth control and child care have remained women's primary domain, both ideologically and practically, should not be taken as evidence of an inherent incompatibility between socialism and women's liberation (the view that socialism is just one form of "patriarchy"). Rather, it should be seen as one dimension, among others, in which a full socialist transformation has not been achieved. The formal arrangements through which these transformed social relations would be expressed have not begun to be imagined. Between the patriarchal heterosexist nuclear family and the spartan barracks of War Communism, there is surely a copious range of sexual and caretaking possibilities.

Third, the historical conditions in which women might anticipate sharing reproductive responsibility with men, or with the "community as a whole," would need to be ones in which democratic principles and processes were built into reproductive (and all) decision making. That is, we would need a radical social democracy in which domination by bureaucrats and medical professionals would not be allowed to represss those whose lives are most immediately affected.

Given such a context, we might imagine a number of concrete situations in which collectively organized social intervention into reproductive, or even "population" matters in a narrower sense, would be not only legitimate but necessary. Society would have to deal with economic and social questions concerning the allocation of resources to communal child care facilities, the mobilization of men on a systematic basis into child care activity, and, most difficult of all, the relationship between the responsibilities of collective organizations and those of parents or other related adults for children. Indeed, unless we adopt a crude anti-Malthusian position that refuses to acknowledge any such thing as population problems, we would have to deal with certain real "quantitative" concerns—for example, the ways that the age structure of the population affects its capacity to provide collective child care and educational resources.[55] The view of reproduction and parenting as essentially social relationships implies not only a commitment to the legitimacy, in principle, of social regulation of those areas of human activity, but also a rejection of the idea that there is a "natural right" to procreate indefinitely or to procreate at all. That idea must be distinguished sharply from the idea of a socially determined need (of both men and women) to participate in the care and rearing of children, as a very distinct and

---

55. See Steven Polgar, "Birth Planning: Between Neglect and Coercion," in *Population and Social Organization,* ed. Moni Nag (The Hague: Mouton Publishers, 1975), p. 197.

special part of human existence. The latter, it seems to me, is absolutely essential to a feminist and socialist vision of the future. The former is a remnant of biological determinist thinking (akin to "mother-right") that should have no place in feminist thought.

And yet, even in a society where the collective responsibility for reproduction and child rearing is taken seriously at all levels of public and interpersonal life, would there not still be aspects of reproductive and sexual relations that remain a "personal affair"? In particular, would women not still retain a preemptive claim to reproductive autonomy, especially around questions of abortion and childbearing, based on the principle of "control over one's body"? Even in the context of new, revolutionary social relations of reproduction, it would never be legitimate to compel a person to have sex or to bear a child, to have an abortion or be sterilized, to express or to repress sexuality in some prescribed way, or to undergo surgical or chemical or other bodily intervention for reproductive or contraceptive purposes. A sense of being a person, with personal and bodily integrity, would remain essential to the definition of social participation and responsibility, under any historical conditions I can imagine.

To deny that there will always be a residual conflict or tension between this principle—which is the idea of concrete individuality, or subjective reality—and that of a social and socially imposed morality of reproduction seems to me not only naive but dismissive of an important value. In any society, there will remain a *level of individual desire that can never be totally reconciled with social need,*[56] without destroying the individual personalities whose "self-realization," as Heller and Marcuse stress, is the ultimate object of social life. How would an individual woman's desire to have a child, or not to have a child, be harmonized in every case with a social policy that determines, on the basis of social need, the circumstances in which people should or should not have and raise children? Even if reproduction and pregnancy were technologically relegated to the laboratory, in the vision of Firestone, there would no doubt remain women who resisted the "technological revolution" as usurping a process that belonged to them individually, personally, to their bodies. The provision of adequate, universal child care services or male sharing in child rearing will eliminate neither the tension between the principles of individual control and collective responsibility over reproduction, nor the need to make reproductive choices that are hard. On the other hand, this very tension can be for feminism—and through feminism, socialism—a source of political vitality.

School of Metropolitan and Community Studies
Ramapo College

56. Heller (n. 9 above), p. 45.

Menstruation and Reproduction: An Oglala Case

Marla N. Powers

The purpose of this paper is to show the relationship between female puberty ceremonies and so-called menstrual taboos. Anthropologists have usually treated these rites independently and have regarded taboos associated with menstruation as symbols of a woman's defilement. However, in my view, the notion of defilement has more often been based on a priori notions regarding menstruation as interpreted by Western standards than on empirical evidence. Although menstruation may be regarded as symbolic of defilement in some societies, such a negative attitude toward menstruation does not necessarily exist in all of them. Treating one Native American society, the Oglala,[1] I will demonstrate that myths and rituals related to female puberty in general and to menstruation in particular are aspects of the same phenomenon, which

An earlier version of this essay was presented at the Thirty-fifth Annual Plains Conference, Lincoln, Nebraska, in November 1977 as part of a symposium entitled "Women's Role and Status in Plains Culture." I am indebted to Ximena Bunster B. and Andrew P. Lyons for their comments and for their initial support and encouragement, to Robin Fox and Lionel Tiger for providing an academic milieu conducive to exploring new ideas, and especially to William K. Powers whose insightful work with the Oglala has provided the foundation for my work and with whom discussions have proved invaluable in helping me to clarify my own ideas.
1. The Oglala live in the Pine Ridge reservation in southwestern South Dakota. My information is based on my own fieldwork on the Pine Ridge reservation in July–August 1976 and on Joseph Epes Brown, *The Sacred Pipe* (1953; reprint ed., Baltimore: Penguin Books, 1971); Alice Fletcher, "The White Buffalo Festival of the Uncpapas," *16th and 17th Annual Report of the Peabody Museum, Harvard* 3, nos. 3 and 4 (1884): 260–75; William K. Powers, *Oglala Religion* (Lincoln: University of Nebraska Press, 1977); J. R. Walker, "The Sun Dance and Other Ceremonies of the Oglala Division of the Teton-Dakota," *Anthropological Papers of the Museum of Natural History*, vol. 16, pt. 2 (1917); and Clark Wissler, "Societies and Ceremonial Associations in the Oglala Division of the Teton-Dakota," *Anthropological Papers of the Museum of Natural History*, vol. 11, pt. 1 (1912).

emphasizes the importance of the female reproductive role. Often in the anthropological literature ideologies and rituals associated with menstruation are extracted and analyzed separately from their cultural context, a technique which has led anthropologists to focus on negative or polluting aspects of menstruation. Although references to the menstrual cycle are abundant in Oglala cosmology and cosmogony,[2] I will restrict my analysis to, first, myths and rituals related to the puberty ceremony known variously as the Buffalo Ceremony[3] (or, in Lakota, *Išnati Awicalowanpi* [they sing over her (first) menses])[4] and, next, to myths related to menstruation and/or rules for sexual conduct focusing on two important mythological characters: *Anukite* (Double-faced Woman) and *Sinte Sapela Win* (Deer Woman). The relationship between buffalo and women, prevalent in Oglala myths and rituals, substantiates my thesis that it is the female's reproductive role in society that is being emphasized rather than her catamenial period, which has been analyzed variously as taboo, pollution, and defilement.

Theoretical Orientation

In his famous work, *The Rites of Passage* (1909), Arnold Van Gennep provided a means of analyzing life crises according to certain recurring patterns. Each life crisis in Van Gennep's scheme proceeds in a threefold manner, which he termed (1) preliminal, or rite of separation; (2) liminal, or rite of transition; and (3) postliminal, or rite of incorporation. This tripartite division was collectively called the schema of the rites of passage. Van Gennep considered puberty ceremonies "to be primarily rites of separation from an asexual world, followed by rites of incorporation into a sexual world."[5] He also distinguished between "first rites" and "recurring rituals." As it relates to my thesis, menarche would be regarded as a first rite, subsequent rituals associated with it as recurring rituals. In both cases a female is symbolically or physically isolated from the rest of society (preliminal), the ceremony takes place in a special lodge (liminal), and after appropriate rituals have been performed she is reincorporated into society (postliminal). Although Van Gennep's model fits well for the analysis of both rituals, I break with anthropological tradition and, in addition to analyzing both puberty ceremonies (first rites) and menstrual cycle rituals (recurring rituals) at the microlevel, I also apply Van Gennep's three-stage model to the total life cycle of a woman. Only at this macro level of analysis can the relationship between

2. J. Owen Dorsey, "A Study of Siouan Cults," *Eleventh Annual Report of the Bureau of Ethnology* (Washington, D.C., 1889), pp. 351–544; Powers; Walker.

3. Walker.

4. Brown.

5. Arnold Van Gennep, *The Rites of Passage* (Chicago: University of Chicago Press, 1960), p. ix.

the initial puberty ceremonies and subsequent menstrual cycle rituals be explained adequately.

Menstruation

Menstrual taboos restrict the behavior of women (and men) during menstruation. It generally has been reported in the anthropological literature that menstrual blood and the menstruating woman are considered polluted and dangerous, and therefore both must be avoided lest they contaminate men and their belongings. These notions have been attributed to tribal societies in relatively modern times; however, anti-menstrual attitudes have a long history in Western thought.[6] I suggest, therefore, that some anthropologists, educated in the Western tradition, have explained tribal menstrual rites in light of their own pre-suppositions, not those of the tribal cultures.

The most misinterpreted aspect of the menstrual taboo is seclusion of the woman. This isolation has been interpreted by Western investigators as a sign of defilement and degradation. Young and Bac-dayan equate the "degrading aspect of the [menstrual] customs" (mainly seclusion) to the social separation and abasement imposed on ethnic groups and low-caste persons. "While it is possible that women do not object to being so restricted and very likely become accustomed to the rules, it is probable that they submit to such customs only because the male-dominated system of social control leaves them no alternative."[7] This misinterpretation is due to a common misconception that *values* placed on certain behaviors in Western society can be equated with values placed on those same behaviors in non-Western society. For example, Ortner considers the limitations put on participation in ceremonial events by menstruating women among the Crow a symbol of defilement,[8] although there is no empirical evidence that the Crow themselves share her interpretation.

A non-Western perspective provides a different picture, at least with respect to American Indians. For example, among the Indians of California a girl at her first menstruation was thought to possess supernatural power.[9] The onset of menstruation is regarded by the Navajo as a time for rejoicing, and the young woman becomes a tribal symbol of

6. See, for example, Janice Delaney, *The Curse* (New York: E. P. Dutton, 1976).

7. Frank W. Young and A. A. Bacdayan, "Menstrual Taboos and Social Rigidity," in *Cross-cultural Approaches, Readings in Comparative Research,* ed. Clelland Ford (New Haven, Conn.: HRAF Press, 1967), p. 100.

8. Sherry B. Ortner, "Is Female to Male as Nature Is to Culture?" in *Woman, Culture and Society,* ed. M. Z. Rosaldo and Louise Lamphere (Stanford, Calif.: Stanford University Press, 1974).

9. Sir James G. Frazer, *The Golden Bough* (1922; abridged ed., New York: Macmillan Co., 1963), vol. 1.

fecundity.[10] Underhill reports that among the Papago a menstruating woman is the vessel of supernatural power—the power that allows her to give birth. "This power is so different from a man's power that the two must be kept apart."[11] One of Underhill's informants stated that she looked forward to her days of separation. Philip Deere, a Muskogee from Oklahoma, stated that "woman is the same as man—but at a certain age she changes into another stage of life. During this stage she *naturally* purifies herself each month. During their monthly time women *separate themselves* [my emphasis] from men. Men must sweat [take a sweat bath] once a month while women are naturally purifying themselves to keep their medicine effective."[12]

Frazer reported that in primitive societies ritual observances concerning ceremonial purity were the same for divine kings and chiefs as for mourners and girls at puberty. He rationalized this by stating that while Western (civilized) man would consider one group holy and the other unclean, in the savage mind concepts of holiness and pollution were not yet differentiated. Douglas speaks to this point: "Perhaps our ideas of sanctity have become very specialized and . . . in some primitive cultures the sacred is a very general idea meaning little more than prohibition. In that sense the universe is divided between things and actions which are subject to restrictions and others which are not; among the restrictions some are intended to protect divinity from profanation and others to protect the profane from the dangerous intrusion of divinity."[13]

While it is useful to reconsider our definition of the sacred as Fraser and Douglas suggest, the problem is not only semantic. Misinterpretation arises from considering individual rites in isolation rather than as a part of a dynamic whole. Puberty ceremonies and menstrual taboos of a culture are never isolated conceptually, and any piecemeal interpretation of them is bound to fail.

Išnati Awicalowanpi

The following is a summary of a girl's puberty rite called *Išnati Awicalowanpi* ("they sing over her [first] menses"). *Išnati* literally means "to dwell alone" and refers both to the act of menstruation and the isolation in which women live during their menstruation.[14] The cere-

10. Charlotte J. Frisbee, *Kinaalda, A Study of the Navaho Girl's Puberty Ceremony* (Middletown, Conn.: Wesleyan University Press, 1967); Flora L. Bailey, *Some Sex Beliefs and Practices in a Navaho Community* (Cambridge, Mass.: Peabody Museum of American Archaeology and Ethnology, Harvard, 1950), vol. 40, no. 2.

11. Ruth M. Underhill, *Red Man's Religion* (Chicago: University of Chicago Press, 1965), p. 51.

12. Personal interview with Philip Deere.

13. Mary Douglas, *Purity and Danger* (Harmondsworth, Middlesex: Routledge & Kegan Paul, 1966), p. 18.

14. Powers, p. 101.

mony has been treated fully by Brown, Fletcher, Powers, and Walker. At menarche a young Oglala woman was secluded alone in a new tipi outside the camp circle. An older kinswoman or another female, chosen by the family for her impeccable reputation, usually attended to her needs and instructed her in her new duties as a potential wife and mother. The Oglala believed that the influences that surrounded a young woman during her first menses had a profound effect on her throughout her lifetime.

The Buffalo ceremony was performed to invoke the spirit of the buffalo and thereby secure for the initiate the virtues most desired in an Oglala woman—chastity, fecundity, industry, and hospitality—and also to announce to the people that the girl was now a woman. The ceremony was conducted by a shaman about ten days after the young woman's first menstrual period at the request of the girl's father.

The day before the ceremony the young woman's mother and her female relatives erected another tipi to serve as a ceremonial lodge for *Išnati Awicalowanpi*. The lodge was erected with its doorway toward the east. The women built a fire north of the lodge out of cottonwood to protect the initiate from the evil influences of Anukite (described later) and Waziya, the wizard. Meanwhile, the young woman took her menstrual bundle and placed it in a plum tree (a symbol of fruitfulness) to safeguard it from the evil influences of Inktomi.[15] The young woman's father made an altar between the *catku* (place of honor—the west) and the fireplace in the center of the tipi, and placed the ritual paraphernalia in the lodge: a buffalo skull with horns attached, a pipe, tobacco, a wooden bowl, sweet grass, sage, an eagle plume, a fire carrier, dried chokecherries, dried meat, a drum, two rattles, a clout, and a new dress for the young woman.

The shaman wore only a breech clout, leggings, moccasins, and a buffalo headdress with horns. From the rear of the headdress hung buffalo skin with a buffalo tail attached which hung below the shaman's knees when he stood. His hands, body, and face were painted red, and three perpendicular black stripes were painted on his right cheek. He carried a pipe and a staff made of chokecherry wood.

During the ceremony, the shaman prayed as he smoked the pipe which he then passed around to the people gathered in and around the lodge. While they smoked he painted the right side of the buffalo skull red and then painted a red stripe from the occipital region to the middle of the forehead. He filled the nasal cavities with sage and blew smoke into them, thus symbolically imparting life to the skull, and prayed to the buffalo god and the four winds. The young woman was brought into the lodge and instructed by the shaman to sit cross-legged—as men and children sit—between the altar and the fireplace.

15. Inktomi, the spider, is the trickster/culture hero who is capable of transforming himself into human or other nonhuman forms.

The shaman then prayed to the sun, the moon, the earth, and the four winds. "We are about to purify and to make sacred a virgin ["virgin" refers to prepubescent females] from whom will come the generations of our people."[16] He then said, "Bull buffalo—I have painted your woman's [the buffalo skull] forehead red and have given her a red robe. . . . Command her to give her influence to this young woman so that she may be a true buffalo woman and bear many children." He then turned to the young woman: "You have abided alone for the first time. You are now a woman and should be ashamed to sit as a child. Sit as a woman sits."[17] She then moved her legs to one side and sat as women do.

Then the shaman prayed that the young woman would be industrious like the spider, wise like the turtle, and cheerful like the meadowlark. With these attributes she would be chosen by a brave man who would provide well for her. Then he began to act like a buffalo bull toward the initiate, saying, "I am the buffalo bull and you are a young buffalo cow."[18] He bellowed and red smoke (like the dust emitted by a buffalo giving birth to a calf) came out of his mouth. He blew smoke on the girl until the tipi was filled with it. He danced toward the young woman lowing like a buffalo bull during the rutting season. He repeatedly sidled up to her like a buffalo performing a mating ritual. Each time that he did this her mother placed sage under her arms and in her lap. The shaman placed the wooden bowl filled with chokecherries and water on the ground to simulate a water hole on the Plains and bade the young woman to get on her hands and knees and drink like a buffalo with him.

The young woman was then told to remove her dress, and her mother was instructed to arrange her hair so that it fell in front like a woman's. The shaman painted the part of her hair and the right side of her forehead red like the buffalo skull and said, "Red is a sacred color. Your first menstrual flow was red. Then you were sacred. This is to show that you are akin to the buffalo god and are his woman. You are now a buffalo woman—you are entitled to paint your face in this manner."[19] He tied an eagle plume in her hair and gave her a staff of cherrywood. Her mother removed the belt that had held the menstrual bundle and the ceremony ended with giveaways and a feast in the girl's honor.

Exegesis

To the Oglala the buffalo was the most important of all animals. It provided them with food, clothing, shelter, and even fuel for their fires.

16. Brown, p. 119.
17. Walker, p. 146.
18. Ibid., p. 147.
19. Ibid., p. 149.

It was a natural symbol of the universe for symbolically contained within it was the totality of all manifest forms of life, including people. Bushotter[20] furnishes two stories about the buffalo. According to one story the buffalo originated under the earth. In the cosmogony we find that the buffalo and the Oglala are one. Another story tells us that the Oglala believe that a man who dreams of buffalo and so acts like a buffalo has a buffalo inside him and a chrysalis lies near his shoulder blade so that no matter how often he is wounded he does not die.[21] The chrysalis symbolizes that the buffalo (man/woman) has the power to renew himself (procreate). Metamorphosis, therefore, is perpetual. There are many correspondences between woman and buffalo in myth and ritual. For instance, the buffalo ceremony establishes the initiate's relationship with the White Buffalo Calf Woman,[22] a woman who in her sexual prime brought the sacred ceremonies to the Oglala so that they might live.

Thus we see what Turner calls "multivocality" in the symbol of the buffalo; the symbol has no singular meaning, but rather a number of latent meanings from which one emerges in response to particular emotional needs of people. There is a symbolic relationship between males and females (buffalo bull and buffalo cow), and the importance of sexual reproduction is emphasized. Both women and buffalo are associated with creating and sustaining life. The sexual nature of initiation ceremonies cannot be denied since symbolically these rites transform an individual into a man or woman. These, like all other "rites of passage are always founded on the same idea, the reality of change in the participants' social condition."[23] *Išnati Awicalowanpi* is clearly a rite of separation from the asexual world and incorporation into the world of sexuality. Prior to the ceremony, during her menstrual period the young woman is separated from the profane world. While she is in her menstrual hut, she is isolated and maintained both physically and symbolically in an intermediate state until the actual ceremony takes place.

During the ceremony itself, the initiate goes through all of Van Gennep's stages in this rite of passage, the preliminal (asexual) stage. She

20. George Bushotter was a Teton Sioux employed by the Bureau of American Ethnology for the purpose of writing his memoirs in his native language. He completed 259 texts which were translated by the ethnologist James Owen Dorsey between 1887 and 1888.

21. Ibid.

22. In the cosmology *Woȟpe* (Falling Star), the daughter of the Sun and the Moon, drops out of the cosmos and turns into the White Buffalo Calf Woman. (*Woȟpe* resides in the lodge of [marries] the South Wind.) The White Buffalo Calf Woman brings the original sacred ceremonies to the Oglala. After giving the people the ceremonies and the sacred pipe she leaves the camp. As she leaves she turns into three different kinds of buffalo: red and yellow (red, north where woman comes from; yellow, east-surprise), white (south, at the center), and black (west); then she disappears over the hill (sunset). This represents the path of the Sun, which at midday is directly over the fireplace (in the center) representing creation.

23. Van Gennep, p. 141.

sits cross-legged like men and children, she is wearing her hair like a child's, and a dress that she wore prior to her menses. During the liminal stage she is both girl and woman (asexual and sexual). She sits at the *catka* which in a tipi is the place of the west wind whose breezes and rains cleanse. She now is sitting like a woman but the arrangement of her hair and her dress are still a girl's. She subsequently removes her dress which is associated with her old status and thus is separated from the world of the child (asexual). Her mother removes the belt that held her menstrual bundle (which symbolizes the liminal stage) and hands it to the shaman who in turn gives it to the girl's father indicating that the marginal (dangerous) period has passed (the girl has been separated from the liminal stage) and men need not fear contamination. She enters the postliminal (sexual) stage. Her hair is arranged like a woman's and her face and hair are painted like a buffalo woman's. The songs and feasts in her honor reincorporate her into the profane world with a new status, that of a woman—a buffalo woman (to the Oglala, one who creates life). During the ceremony the shaman is both buffalo bull (during the simu-lated mating ritual) and buffalo woman (since the shaman's face is painted like that of the buffalo skull and the buffalo skull is symbolic of a buffalo woman). This is substantiated linguistically since in a ritual con-text the term for buffalo is *pte,* "buffalo cow" (female buffalo).

In the ceremony the red water (chokecherries and water) is sacred, meant for buffalo women and a sign of life. Again we see the connection being made symbolically between buffalo women (sexual or pubescent women, those who have the power to create life) and life. Moreover, if red is sacred and sacred water and menstrual blood are red, then sym-bolically sacred water *is* menstrual blood. If sacred water is life, menstrual blood also symbolizes life. When the shaman as the buffalo bull and the initiate as a buffalo woman drink the sacred water, the two become one as buffalo people (incorporation) and at the same time the initiate ingests symbolically the sacred menstrual blood which had left the body, thus replicating the cycle of life. I believe that taboos associated with pregnancy and childbirth serve the same function. We find many similarities in the taboos. Both menstruating women and women giving birth are secluded in special lodges, for instance; both are attended by postmenopausal females; and the placenta, like the menstrual bundle, is placed in a tree.

"Anukite Ihanblapi," the Double Woman Cult

Another example of female symbolism is found in a mythological character called *Anukite,* who plays an important role in the supernatural affairs of the Oglala. In the cosmology *Ite* (Face) is very beautiful and is married to *Tate* (the Wind). *Ite* has an affair with the Sun, who at the time is married to the Moon. Because of her infidelity *Ite* is punished and given an ugly face. On one side she is still beautiful, on the other ugly. She thus becomes *Anukite* (Double Face), who, according to Powers, "appears to men in visions and in the real world in the form of a deer or two deer women, one white and the other black. The two faces of Double Face and the two Deer Women represent proper and improper sexual conduct. . . . Men become disorderly or crazy when they have [improper] sexual relations with deer women."[24]

Women who dream of *Anukite* have unusual powers to seduce men. These women were considered wakan (sacred). The Oglala say that if a man meets a lone woman in the woods or on the prairie he must avoid her, for she may be a deer woman. The myth attributes to the deer a peculiar scent in the hoof that becomes a fine perfume when the deer becomes a woman. The perfume then acts as a medicine and works an evil spell on men. Sometimes even wishing to make love to a deer woman can be fatal.[25] Deer women often appear as beautiful creatures who, after enticing men to have improper sexual relations with them, turn into deer and run away. After this the man goes insane or dies.

Lunar and Solar Symbols

According to the medicine man, Black Elk, "The power of woman grows with the moon and comes and goes with it."[26] As they do in other societies, many correspondences exist between the moon and menstruation. In the cosmology we find that as a result of the Sun's adulterous affairs with *Ite*, the Sun and Moon separate. Linguistically *wi* (moon, female) was preeminent. When the Moon is given her own domain, the undifferentiated *wi* becomes month. Thus *wi* (female) is isolated from the Sun during the month just as women are isolated from men during their menstrual period. According to Powers, "*Ite* is sent away from the Sun as punishment because she *sat in the place of the moon*. Metaphorically . . . Man does not have sexual relations with a woman who sits in the place of the moon, that is, during her menstrual period."[27] Among many American Indian tribes, semen is perceived as being finite; thus proscriptions about male sexual relations with menstruating women ensure that semen will not be "wasted" on a woman at times when she cannot conceive. Since these tribes are comparatively small groups concerned with maintaining a stable population, to "waste" semen would be fatal to the society's ability to reproduce itself.

24. Powers, p. 197.
25. Wissler, p. 94.
26. John G. Neihardt, *Black Elk Speaks* (Lincoln: University of Nebraska Press, 1961), p. 212.
27. Powers, p. 194.

In Native North America the two most common proscriptions regarding menstruating women are: (1) that they be secluded, metaphorically, kept out of the sun; and (2) that they not cook for their husbands, that is, that they not go near the fireplace. In Oglala cosmology the Sun passes over the fireplace at midday; thus a woman using the fireplace symbolically risks having improper sexual relations with the Sun (just as *Ite* did). That both the Sun and fireplace symbolize creation is underscored by the fact that when the White Buffalo Calf Woman left the Oglala she followed the path of the Sun. Symbolically her place was in the center, as a symbol of fecundity, and the birth of the Oglala (who emerged from the center) for the White Buffalo is found at the center of the herd (universe). Names for months of the year also reflect the relationship between the Moon (menstruation) and creation. For example, November is known as moon when deer copulate, or Winter Moon. In *waniyetu* (winter), the radical element *ni* means life or breath. Winter is also associated with North, and the North Wind has predominantly female characteristics. Nine months later, August is known as moon when seeds ripen (give birth, bring forth fruit), or the Harvest Moon.

The Oglala regard the moon as having influence over berdaches (men who dressed like women and who assume female behaviors), who were considered to have auspicious powers related to childbirth and childrearing. Often they were called upon to name children. Berdaches were men who dreamed of a *wakan* (sacred [menstruating] woman) or who repeatedly dreamed of *pte winkte*. Although *pte winkte* has been glossed as hermaphrodite buffalo, according to Beuchel the literal translation is fat, dry buffalo cow[28] (or a cow who cannot nourish/sustain life). Again we see a relationship between menstruating women and life. An ambiguity exists, however, since menstruation symbolizes the potentiality for life (the ability to conceive) and the absence of life (not having conceived).

Macro-Level Analysis

So far I have focused on the female puberty ceremony and myths and rituals associated with menstruation at the micro level of analysis. However, at the macro level the entire female life cycle may also be analyzed in terms of Van Gennep's rites of passage. At this level the relationship between the puberty ceremony and menstrual taboos becomes clear. According to the literature and my own informants, Oglala women can take an active role in a number of rituals only during prepubescent and postmenopausal stages of their lives. During their re-

28. Eugene Beuchel, S.J., *Lakota-English Dictionary* (Pine Ridge, S.D.: Holy Rosary Mission, 1970).

productive stage restrictions are placed on their participation. For example: only "virgins" (prepubescent girls) are permitted to touch or carry the sacred sun dance pole. They also may handle the sacred pipe and other sacred paraphernalia normally proscribed for pubescent women. Postmenopausal women may assist in ritual curing, pick sacred herbs, and instruct young women at puberty and childbirth. The Oglala divide the female life cycle into four stages: *wicincala* "young girl" (prepubescent); *wikoškalaka*—"young woman (pubescent); *winyan*—"woman" (married woman); and *winnunłcala*—"old woman" (postmenopausal).[29] Two of the stages are decidedly unambiguous, the first and the last, in which the female is not sexually reproductive. The second and third stages are ambiguous in the sense that a distinction is made between two types of sexually reproductive females, both physiologically mature and hence capable of bearing children, of whom only one is considered "socially" mature (i.e., "the woman," or married woman). These ambiguous stages may be seen together as a dialectic between pre- and postreproductive stages. In Van Gennep's terms the second and third stages may be viewed as liminal.

By substituting a new set of terms for Van Gennep's three stages, we may analyze the female life cycle as shown in table 1. If the liminal stage

Table 1

Van Gennep's Schema	Stage in Life Cycle	Oglala Names
Preliminal	Prereproductive (prepubescent)	*wicincala*
Liminal	Reproductive (pubescent female, unmarried)	*wikoškalaka*
	(pubescent female, married)	*winyan*
Postliminal	Postreproductive (postmenopausal)	*winunłcala*

29. Similarly, there are corresponding male stages: *hokšila*—"young boy," *koškalaka*—"young man," *wicaša*—"married man," *wicałcala*—"old man." Furthermore, among the Oglala the sexual distinction between males and females is underscored in prescriptions and proscriptions for participation in sacred rituals. Thus we see that prepubescent girls and postmenopausal women perform sacred duties while they are in profane states while males perform sacred duties during that period of their life that parallels the reproductive stage of the women. We also see that neither young boys nor old men take an active part in ritual.

	Prereproductive	Reproductive	Postreproductive
Female	*wicincala**	*wikoškalaka*†/*winyan*†	*winunłcala**
Male	*hokšila*†	*koškalaka**/*wicaša**	*wicałcala*†

*Indicates prescription for active participation in ritual.
†Indicates proscription against active participation in ritual.

is sacred, we may conclude that the female's entire reproductive stage is also sacred, because during this time the woman is in a continuous state of ambiguity, that is, if she does not reproduce, she menstruates, if she does not menstruate, she reproduces.

Compared to the pre- and postreproductive stages which are continuous (uninterrupted by the potential of reproduction), the entire reproductive stage, beginning with the puberty ceremony and including each menstrual period, can be viewed in terms of Victor Turner's notion of *communitas,* or antistructure. This is a time when people are released from cultural constraints "only to return to structure revitalized by their experience of *communitas*."[30] But Turner tells us that *communitas* cannot be sustained, that our perceptions of reality must be structured in order for there to be reality.[31] The function of the menstrual taboo then is not to enunciate the pollutive nature of the female but to give structure to what otherwise is a period of antistructure.

Conclusion

I have shown that viewed as part of a dynamic whole rather than isolated events, female puberty ceremonies and menstruation among the Oglala are both aspects of the same phenomenon and serve to emphasize the female's reproductive role. Nowhere in the data is there evidence that practices associated with menstruation are in any way considered a sign of defilement or degradation toward the menstruating female.

It would be useful to reexamine the data from other societies in the same way that I have treated the Oglala to ascertain whether or not conclusions regarding rituals related to puberty ceremonies and menstruation are based on empirical evidence or, as in the case among American Indian groups, represent the imposition of Western values on behaviors in non-Western societies. Perhaps a reevaluation will point us toward a better understanding of what may only be Western concepts of misogyny. By viewing menstruation in a larger context and seeing it merely as one of many components in a female symbolic system, we may learn to desensitize ourselves from Western negative notions of female physiology and address ourselves to the need to make a *unified* analysis of women's symbolic and material lives.

Department of Anthropology
Rutgers University

30. Victor Turner, *The Ritual Process* (Chicago: Aldine Publishing Co., 1969), p. 129.
31. Ibid.

Pornography and Repression: A Reconsideration

Irene Diamond

"Porn Is Here to Stay," sociologist Amitai Etzioni could assert with complete confidence in 1977,[1] by assuming that any attempt to abolish pornography would be tantamount to trying to eliminate sexual impulses. Pornography may in fact have the staying power suggested by Etzioni, not because of the "naturalness" of sexuality but rather because of the resiliency of the political and economic institutions which structure and shape sexual expression. If we regard pornography primarily as a medium for expressing norms about male power and domination which functions as a social control mechanism for keeping women in a subordinate status, then we have to question the prevailing liberal attitudes toward the issue of pornography and repression, which Etzioni and other social scientists hold. My purpose here is to examine the assumptions and data upon which the liberal model rests.

Historically, efforts to control the distribution of pornography have emanated from societal forces bent on suppressing all sexual matters—from birth control to sex education to scientific studies—while opposing efforts have come from those promoting openness in sexual matters. Moreover, since John Wilkes's *An Essay on Woman* in the eighteenth century, pornography has been used as a vehicle for criticizing the prevailing social order. As a consequence of this history, contemporary wisdom in the social science and "progressive" intellectual communities chastizes all plans to control pornography as attempts to repress sexuality and maintain the established order by those who have unenlightened and unhealthy sexual attitudes. Predictably, Etzioni dismisses a 1976 poll indicating that a substantial majority of Americans approves of crackdowns on pornography by declaring that most of these persons

1. Amitai Etzioni, "Porn Is Here to Stay," *New York Times* (May 17, 1977), p. 35.

"have difficulty accepting their own sexuality and feel that unless the
authorities keep the lid on, their urges may erupt. A democratic society
requires holding at bay these sexual anxieties and their repressive political expressions."[2] Leaving aside the genuine motivations of such persons, which we cannot presume to know, Etzioni's statement contains the
conventional assumption that the content of pornography is sex and that
the genre is essentially a medium for sexual expression. For example, in
his history of pornography, H. Montgomery Hyde writes: "It is generally
agreed that the essential characteristic of pornography is its sexuality. In
order to come within the category of pornography, material must have
the power to excite sexual passions."[3] Since free and unfettered sexual
expression is valorized as a force leading to human liberation, liberals
have associated pornography with the progressive and the good. For
instance, Al Goldstein, editor of *Screw,* one of the many tabloids of the
1960s designed to expose the hypocrisies of society by shocking its sensi-
bilities, has described pornography as "one of the most sane manifestations of the human condition."[4] And Paul Goodman, though obviously
not a "porn pusher," shared Goldstein's presumptions regarding the
"progressive" model and could call on the Supreme Court in 1961 to "set
aside the definition of pornography as obscenity—just as it set aside the
doctrine of separate but equal facilities—and to clarify and further the
best tendency of the sexual revolution."[5] Interestingly, many commentators consider pornography a uniquely modern phenomenon which
emerged during the seventeenth century in response to the strains of
modernization.[6] Steven Marcus has argued that the social process accompanying industrialization and urbanization led to the splitting off of
sexuality from the rest of life. It was in response to this increasingly
repressive situation that pornography, which Marcus describes as "nothing more than a representation of the fantasies of infantile sexual life,"[7]
emerged and flourished. Although the "newness" of pornography is by
no means accepted by pornography historians or sexual historians, it is
nonetheless an article of faith in the conventional wisdom that the so-
called excesses of pornography—its tendency toward what has been
euphemistically termed the "unaesthetic"—are solely attributable to the
repression of sexuality in the society at large.

    2. Ibid.
    3. H. Montgomery Hyde, *A History of Pornography* (New York: Farrar, Straus & Gir-
oux, 1965), p. 1.
    4. Cited by Robert Yoakum in "An Obscene, Lewd, Lascivious, Indecent, Filthy, and
Vile Tabloid Entitled *Screw*," *Columbia Journalism Review* (March/April 1977), p. 46.
    5. Paul Goodman, *Utopian Essays and Practical Proposals* (New York: Random House,
1962), p. 57.
    6. David Foxon, "Libertine Literature in England, 1660–1745," *Book Collector* 1–3
(Spring, Summer, Winter, 1963): 306.
    7. Steven Marcus, *The Other Victorians* (New York: Basic Books, 1964), p. 286.

The Emerging Critique

In recent years, the conventional liberal interpretation of pornography has come under attack. The generally held presumption that pornography is about sexuality has been called into question. Reflecting on his brief career in a "porno-fac," Burton Wohl concluded: "The letting of blood, violence, is porno's bottom line and not even the insatiable marquis could get beyond it. Power depends on violence, bloodshed. And power is what pornography celebrates, illuminates—above all sublimates. The other stuff, the tumid-humid-licking-sticking-writhing-and fall is peripheral, a catalogue of ornaments like the botanical and architectural doodling in Renaissance painting."[8] This primacy of power and violence in pornography was first underscored in *Sexual Politics* (1970), where Kate Millett dramatically demonstrated the centrality of male domination and female subjugation in literary descriptions of sexual activity. Others before her may have noted the sadistic aspects of pornography, but no one had linked sexuality and cruelty to the maintenance of patriarchy. Moreover Millett argued that the growing permissiveness in sexual expression during the twentieth century had given greater latitude to the expression of male hostility.[9] Whereas Millett dealt with avant-garde pornographic literary artists of the twentieth century, Robin Morgan in "Goodbye to All That" (1970) exposed the woman hatred of Left-hippie underground papers such as *Rat:* "It's the liberal co-optative masks on the face of sexist hate and fear worn by real nice guys we all know and like, right? We have met the enemy, and he's our friend. And dangerous. . . . A genuine left doesn't consider anyone's suffering irrelevant or titillating."[10] Morgan was also one of those arrested in 1970 for invading Grove Press, a so-called pioneer publisher of erotic literature, on the grounds that "Grove's sadomasochistic literature and pornographic films dehumanize and degrade women."[11] Expanding on these critiques of pornographic avant-garde literature and underground newspapers, Andrea Dworkin wrote in 1974: "*Suck* is a typical counter-culture sex paper. Any analysis of it reveals that the sexism is all-pervasive, expressed primarily as sadomasochism, absolutely the same as, and not counter to, the parent cultural values."[12] Dworkin also stressed the effects of pornography on the self-images of women and men, but she never explicitly connected the violence of fiction to what

8. Burton Wohl, "The Reluctant Pornographer," *Harper's Magazine* (December 1976), p. 91.
9. Kate Millett, *Sexual Politics* (New York: Doubleday & Co., 1969), pp. 42–45.
10. Robin Morgan, "Goodbye to All That," in *The American Sisterhood,* ed. Wendy Martin (New York: Harper & Row, 1972), p. 361.
11. Nancy Moran, "Nine Women Arrested in Five-Hour Sit-In at Grove Press," *New York Times* (April 14, 1970), p. 55.
12. Andrea Dworkin, *Woman Hating* (New York: E. P. Dutton, 1974), p. 78.

she termed "herstory, the underbelly of history." It was Susan Brownmiller, in her examination of the history of rape (1975) who made the connection when she defined pornography as "the undiluted essence of anti-female propaganda" and equated its philosophy to that of rape. She charged that the open display of pornography promoted a climate in which acts of sexual hostility were not only tolerated but ideologically encouraged. Calling attention to the systematized, commercially successful propaganda machines dominating the Forty-Second Streets of the nation's cities,[13] Brownmiller became the first feminist since the social purity advocates of the 1870s to call for government censorship of pornography.

With the appearance of *Snuff* in 1975, a porn film which purported to show an actual sexual assault, murder, and dismemberment of a woman, feminist activities began to focus on the portrayal of sexual violence. The relationship between increased violence in pornography and the media and the increasing rate of rape was emphasized; in Robin Morgan's words: "Pornography is the theory, and rape the practice."[14] Moreover, feminists began to argue that the increasing degree of violence was a male response to feminism itself. Diana Russell, who helped to organize the first International Tribunal on Crimes against Women in 1976 and subsequently helped to form a San Francisco group called "Women against Violence in Pornography and Media," claimed that "the great proliferation of pornography since 1970—particularly violent pornography and child pornography—is part of the male backlash against the women's liberation movement. Enough women have been rejecting the traditional role of being under men's thumbs to cause a crisis in the collective male ego. Pornography is a fantasy solution that inspires non-fantasy acts of punishment for uppity females."[15] And in a similar vein Ellen Willis wrote: "The aggressive proliferation of pornography is . . . a particularly obnoxious form of sexual backlash. The ubiquitous public display of dehumanized images of the female body is a sexist, misogynist society's answer to women's demand to be respected as people rather than exploited as objects. All such images express hatred and contempt, and it is no accident that they have become more and more overtly sadomasochistic. . . . Their function is to harass and intimidate, and their ultimate implications are fascistic."[16]

This newly emerging analysis of pornography differs in several respects from conventional interpretations. For feminists, the "what" of pornography is not sex but power and violence, and the "who" of concern are no longer male consumers and artists but women. In the conventional model, women are invisible. No concern is expressed for

13. Susan Brownmiller, *Against Our Will* (New York: Simon & Schuster, 1975), p. 394.
14. Robin Morgan, *Going Too Far* (New York: Random House, 1977), p. 169.
15. Diana Russell, "On Pornography," *Chrysalis* 4 (1977): 12.
16. Ellen Willis, "Sexual Counterrevolution I," *Rolling Stone* (March 24, 1977), p. 29.

women being degraded or abused in pornographic films, photographs, or shows; nor the women who might become the real-life victims of nonfantasy acts; nor women in general whose oppression is reinforced by distorted views of their nature. The invisibility of women in this conventional model is attributable to several factors: (1) the tendency of patriarchal society to define reality in terms of men's activities, (2) the tendency in liberal society to discuss pornography in relationship to abstract rights and principles disconnected from pornography's grim reality in actual communities; and (3) the belief shared by traditional moralists and liberationists alike that human sexuality has a fixed "naturally" given shape. Feminists maintain that women as a class are victimized in an ideological sense by pornography and that this leads to the actual physical victimization of individual women. Although feminists reject the "traditional moralist" notion that pornography is primarily about sex, and therefore evil, they tend to agree with the moralist argument that the effects of pornography are harmful. And yet, the two positions differ fundamentally in their definition of the wrongness of pornography: for the moralist pornography is a pleasure which substitutes for "higher" pleasures, thus destroying the "virtue" of the viewer; it is wrong because of what it does *not* lead to. According to Charles B. Keating, Jr., head of one of the most active national antipornography organizations: "The traditional Judeo-Christian ethic does not condemn pleasure as an evil in itself; it does condemn the pursuit of pleasure for its own sake, *as an end* rather *than a means,* deliberately excluding the higher purposes and values to which pleasure is attached. [The sex drive] serves the individual and the common good of the human race, only when it is creative, productive, when it ministers to love and life. When, however, it serves only itself, it becomes a perversion. . . . Every word by which the organs of sex are designated bears out this statement: genital, generative, reproductive, procreative."[17] The possibility that pornography may have consequences for victims other than the viewer is not the moralist's primary concern since patriarchal religions view the abused wife, rape victim, or brutalized actress as fallen women who are in large part responsible for their fate. The feminist, on the other hand, who is predominantly concerned with female victims, insists that pornography contributes to actual violence against women. Feminist analysis interprets pornography not merely as the reflection of men's sexual fantasies but primarily as one of the mechanisms that has sustained the systemic domination of women by men throughout history. Pornography, then, is not unique to a particular historical period; nevertheless, because it serves political purposes, its quantity and violent nature will proliferate in response to efforts to disturb power relationships between

17. Statement of Charles H. Keating, Jr., in the *Report of Commission on Obscenity and Pornography* (Washington, D.C.: Government Printing Office, September, 1970), p. 516; emphasis added.

men and women. Moreover, feminists consider the so-called excesses of pornography a manifestation of a backlash rather than the conventional argument concerning the "repression of sexuality." These are the propositions suggested by a feminist interpretation of pornography. Does the available evidence support these propositions? If not, why not?

Pornography and Violent Behavior

In 1969 the President's Commission on the Causes and Prevention of Violence concluded that media violence can induce persons to act aggressively. However, a year later the Commission on Obscenity and Pornography concluded that exposure to pornography does not seriously promote antisocial behavior. Since 1970, this latter report has been continuously acclaimed within the liberal social science community for having definitely documented the benignity of pornography.[18] At worst pornography is harmless; at best it provides for "more agreeable and 'increased openness' in marital communications."[19] Thus, whereas the report on violence confirmed the accepted liberal credo that environment is an important determinant of human behavior, the report on obscenity and pornography rejected this notion. A social learning model was deemed appropriate in explaining the impact of violence in the media but was not deemed applicable to the impact of pornography. The disparate models and conclusions of two major government research reports produced by leading social scientists can only be understood in light of the prevailing liberal ideology of the late 1960s: violence by ordinary citizens in the midst of civil disorders and a purported crime wave was viewed unfavorably, while sex in the midst of the so-called sexual revolution was viewed most favorably. The respective commissions framed their research questions and designs accordingly.

As we might expect, the Pornography Commission assumed that its subject of concern was "explicit sexual materials." In fact the commission chose not to use "pornography" in its report because it felt that the term connoted disapproval of the materials in question.[20] By employing a neutral term the commission could also use its investigations to document the need for sex education. However, this seemingly genuine concern became confused with its primary goal of proving that anything associated with the expression of sexuality was good. These "biases" influenced the final report in several ways: the choice of research designs employed by the various investigators, the interpretation of the individual data sets, and the integration of the individual studies into the actual

18. For instance, Etzioni's claims which appeared in several leading newspapers around the country in 1977 were based on the findings of the commission report.

19. *Report of the Commission*, p. 194.

20. Ibid., p. 3.

report. Because of the commission's agenda only a small percentage of the materials in both the report and its accompanying ten technical volumes actually deals with the impact of pornography on human behavior.

Attitude Surveys

The commission's investigators undertook a wide variety of surveys designed to discover different populations' *attitudes* toward pornography and its effects. Opinion data, however interesting in terms of descriptive information, do not address the question of the empirical consequences of visual materials. By comparison, the violence commission did not conduct polls to determine which persons believed that the effects of violence in the media were harmful. The thrust of the pornography commission's attitude studies did suggest that educated persons, young persons, and men tended to believe that pornography was harmless and that it provided information about sex. That this information became the first data section of the effects-panel report suggests the conventional premise: "If enough of the right people believe it to be so, then it is so." Data indicating that sex offenders more often than nonoffenders also expressed agreement with pornography's socially desirable or neutral effects were not included.[21] The final report did not explore some of the fascinating material which surveys did uncover with regard to the politics of porn usage.[22]

Retrospective Studies

Due to the ethical problems involved in human experimentation, retrospective studies are often used in social research, although it is very difficult if not impossible to establish causal relationships through the use of such designs. Here again it is worth noting that the Violence Commission did not undertake a single study that attempted to identify violent offenders and then to trace their use of violent materials. The Pornography Commission, however, conducted several retrospective studies of sex offenders, some with appropriate control groups and

21. R. F. Cook and R. H. Fosen, "Pornography and the Sex Offender: Patterns of Exposure and Immediate Arousal Effects of Pornographic Stimuli," in *Technical Reports of the Commission on Obscenity and Pornography* (Washington, D.C.: Government Printing Office, 1970), 7:168.

22. For instance, Alan Berger and his colleagues in their survey of high school students concluded that "it is the boys who introduce the girls to these movies, and this suggests that dating may be one of the major mechanisms by which boys manage the introduction" (A. S. Berger, J. H. Gagnon, and W. Simon, "Pornography: High School and College Years," in *Technical Reports of the Commission*, 9:168).

some without, and arrived at the conclusion that "empirical research . . . has found no reliable evidence to date that exposure to explicit sexual materials plays a significant role in the causation of delinquent or criminal sexual behavior among youth or adults."[23] This conclusion relied on the findings that sex offenders and "sex deviants" reported less exposure to erotica during adolescence than other adults, and that during adulthood sex offenders did not have significantly different exposure to erotica or report greater likelihood of engaging in "sociosexual" behavior following exposure.[24]

However, the technical reports reveal different usages of the term "sex offender" which are sometimes liberal and sometimes restrictive. In two of the four studies where controlled comparisons were made between offenders and other groups, rapists constituted a minority of the offenders, and exhibitionists, pedophiles, persons convicted of "taking indecent liberties," and homosexuals formed the majority.[25] Only in these studies do the data indicate fairly conclusively that "sex offenders" had less exposure to pornography during adolescence. In the Walker study, where "sex offenders" referred only to rapists, we find that with a total group of sixty incarcerated rapists use of pornographic materials during adolescence was not examined other than to determine at what age subjects first saw various kinds of pornography. The investigators indicate no statistically significant differences in age of first exposure but then note that "visual inspection of the means [of exposure] revealed a tendency . . . for the comparison groups to be exposed to pornography at an earlier age." Rapists indicated less frequent usage during adulthood, but of course these incarcerated subjects also reported that "pornography was not easy to obtain."[26] Rapists did report *collecting* pornography for a significantly longer time than other men's groups, but no data are presented as to whether collecting is more common among the one group or the other. And yet, on the basis of such data the investigators conclude that "sex offenders, if anything, tend to have less experience with pornography than other groups."[27]

Goldstein et al., the other study which isolated sex offender rapists, attempted a more sophisticated analysis of pornography usage. Twenty rapists plus a variety of different control groups were questioned about their use of pornographic materials during the past year, the rapists being asked to report on the year prior to their incarceration. On the basis of

23. *Report of the Commission*, p. 139.
24. Ibid., p. 242.
25. In Cook and Fosen, the group of sixty-three sex offenders included sixteen rapists and ten attempted rapists, while in W. T. Johnson, L. Kupperstein, and J. Peters, "Sex Offenders' Experience with Erotica," in *Technical Reports of the Commission*, 7:164, the forty-seven sex offenders included eighteen rapists.
26. C. E. Walker, "Erotic Stimuli and the Aggressive Sexual Offender," in *Technical Reports of the Commission*, 7:111.
27. Ibid., p. 130.

data derived in this manner the investigators concluded that rapists had less exposure to all stimuli and media.[28] During adolescence there were few significant differences. However, in the investigators' own published book, and not the official report, they discovered what they term "dramatic" differences during preadolescence (six to ten years): 30 percent of the rapists, as opposed to 2 percent of the control groups, reported exposure to hard-core pornographic photos. Also cited here is the finding that "only rapists stand out in reporting a significantly earlier age of peak experience," and "the rapists only report more frequent exposure than controls for the most vivid experience."[29]

In both the Goldstein and Walker studies, data on the question of behavioral impact tend to be questioned and interpreted away. The Walker study indicates that rapists "reported more frequently than the control group that pornography had led them to commit a sexual crime," but this response, it is argued, represents a "convenient, ready-made explanation" for their current situation (although the control group comprised incarcerated non-sex offenders). Moreover, although Walker notes that the ratings on the projective inkblot test "were only minimally reliable and demonstrated essentially no validity," he nevertheless concludes: "Expert clinical judges did not rate the fantasy productions of the sex offenders in response to projective stimuli as indicating significantly more pathological sexual thought, sexual arousal, or aggressive sexual inclinations."[30] Somewhat similarly, the Goldstein study notes that "only the rapists stand out from all other groups in containing a higher percentage who wished to imitate the portrayed activity." Yet, because only 57 percent of the rapists as opposed to 85 percent of the controls actually attempted to imitate some feature of their peak erotic stimulus, the rapists are then characterized as having "low-beam performance" in contrast to their high interest statements.[31] The crucial question of the circumstances under which "performance" occurs is not explored. Thus when only rapists are categorized as sex offenders the actual data do not suggest that rapists have typically been deprived of pornography, nor is there firm evidence that rapists do not imitate portrayed behavior.

That some of the deficiencies in the report are attributable to the restrictive categorization of rapists is also apparent in Propper's survey of young male (aged sixteen to twenty-one) reformatory inmates. The

28. M. J. Goldstein et al., "Exposure to Pornography and Sexual Beavior in Deviant and Normal Groups," in *Technical Reports of the Commission*, vol. 7. The authors indicated that the data in the report were not completely analyzed, which presumably explains why the preadolescence material only appears in their 1973 book.

29. Michael J. Goldstein and Harold Stanford Kant with John J. Hartman, *Pornography and Sexual Deviance* (Berkeley: University of California Press, 1973), p. 73.

30. Walker, p. 128.

31. Goldstein and Kant, p. 75.

data that show these inmates reporting considerable experience with sexual materials are footnoted in the report with the comment: "*Only* 3% of the sample had been incarcerated for assault, and *only* 2% for sex offenses"[32] (emphasis added). Not included in the report itself are data indicating that 62 percent of these "juveniles" scored high on a "peer sex behavior index," which included such items as "gang-bangs" and "intentionally getting a girl drunk." Since scores on this index positively related to exposure to "erotic materials," Propper himself concluded that "contrary to the opinion that high exposure may inhibit sexual practices, the data suggest a greater amount of activity among those who are more highly exposed."[33]

Experimental Laboratory Studies

Unlike the various commissions which have studied the impact of violence, the Pornography Commission did not undertake a single controlled laboratory study involving children. The commission noted this gap in its call for "Needed Additional Research" but explained that fears about the consequences of such studies had precluded them. Garry Wills has commented on the irony of this attitude: "The group first deferred to a social instinct that childhood exposure to 'pornography' would have a powerful effect, before going on to argue that exposure has no such effect—all on the basis of tests invalidated by that first deference to the view that it has such an effect!"[34] The fourteen laboratory studies which were conducted used either male college students or married couples as subjects, and only three of these studies were designed in a way that permitted exploration of the possible relationship between pornography and aggressive behaviors. Most examined the impact of viewing pornography on attitudes, reported feelings of sexual arousal, or reports of sexual behavior outside the laboratory,[35] and were not designed to consider the matter of aggressive sexual behavior. Moreover, in many of the experiments the materials which subjects were shown might be classified more properly as sex-education materials rather than the amalgam of sex, violence, and woman hatred which typifies pornography.

Of the three experiments that did deal with aggression, two were conducted by Donald L. Mosher and lacked the most elemental features

32. *Report of the Commisson*, p. 221.

33. M. M. Propper, "Exposure to Sexually Oriented Materials among Young Male Prison Offenders," *Technical Reports of the Commission*, 9:363.

34. Garry Wills, "Measuring the Impact of Erotica," *Psychology Today* (August 1977), p. 33.

35. It is worth noting that in one study of married couples 11 percent of the women reported that they sought therapy after viewing hard-core porn films with their husbands. Cited in J. Mann, J. Sidman, and S. Starr, "Effects of Erotic Films on Sexual Behaviors of Married Couples," *Technical Reports of the Commission*, 8:217.

of standard laboratory research—a control group. His designs were clearly derived from the popularly held theory that if persons are provided with a "safety outlet" for expressing their "normal" feeling of hostility and aggression toward women they will be less inclined to act on those feelings. On the basis of his finding that males who exhibited highly "sex-calloused" attitudes showed a decline in such attitudes after viewing pornography, the commission concluded that "fears" about learning such attitudes from the medium were "unwarranted." The fact that these subjects might have shown the same decline after watching "Mr. Rogers' Neighborhood" was simply ignored.[36]

Only one study was modeled on the extensively used experiments which enabled violence researchers to conclude that aggressive behaviors are learned from media presentations of aggression. Tannenbaum found that subjects delivered stronger shocks to a confederate after viewing an "erotic" film sequence than did subjects who viewed neutral or aggressive films. And even more significantly, when aggressiveness and eroticism were joined in the same presentation, subjects delivered the most intense shocks.[37] The commission's brief reference to this study was counterbalanced with the findings from Mosher's other study,[38] which lacked the most basic ingredient of experimental design and yet purported to show that subjects were less inclined to aggress verbally against a female after viewing pornography. No less questionable was the commission's extensive reliance on the now famous satiation study conducted by Howard, which has often been offered in the popular media as proof of the catharsis theory of aggression. Howard found that college students exhibited a decreased interest in pornographic materials after being fed large amounts in a short period of time.[39] Presumably, after getting a proper "dosage" interest is satisfied. The commission never questioned the validity of this experiment even though its own surveys indicated that pornography consumers are habitual consumers in the real world.

Social Indicator Statistics

The final type of evidence upon which the commission relied was longitudinal data on the availability of pornography and reported sex offenses in both the United States and Denmark. The commission argued that the number of rapes known to the police in the United States was a "crude" measure, in comparison with the more "refined" measure

36. *Report of the Commission*, p. 201.
37. P. H. Tannenbaum, "Emotional Arousal as a Mediator of Communication Effects," *Technical Reports of the Commission*, 8:340.
38. *Report of the Commission*, p. 208.
39. J. L. Howard, C. B. Reifler, and M. B. Liptzin, "Effects of Exposure to Pornography," *Technical Reports of the Commission*, 8:97–133.

of arrests for rape.[40] Although rape and pornography had both increased during the decade, the commission concluded that if availability were related to the incidence of rape "one would have expected an increase of much greater magnitude than the available figures indicate." It must be said that the commission also noted that the data did not disprove a causal connection. Since the publication of the commission's report, however, it is the Danish data which have been proclaimed positive proof for the catharsis of "safety-outlet" theories. The Danes had gradually removed all legal restrictions on pornography during the 1960s, and the data appeared to indicate that sex crimes had taken a dramatic turn downward. Further research has shown, however, that certain crimes such as homosexual prostitution were no longer being included in the statistics, thus artificially deflating the overall sex-crime figure. More importantly, it is now evident that the incidence of rape did not decline but in all likelihood increased.[41] The effects report of the commission demonstrated a decline in rape in Denmark by combining the statistics for "rape" and "attempted rape." These data were "adapted" from statistics in the technical report by Ben-Veniste;[42] his raw data indicated a decline in "attempted rape," but he himself did not discuss the issue of a decline in rape.[43] Kutschinsky, in his study, reported slightly different figures for "rape" and concluded that the overall decline in sex-crimes *had not* occurred in the area of rape.[44] In 1976 both J. H. Court of Australia and Victory Bachy of Belgium published papers which reported new rape statistics released by the Copenhagen police that were considerably higher than those cited by Kutschinsky. According to Court, "the trend since 1969 indicates that there has been a rise to a new level higher than anything experienced in the previous decade."[45] The Danish experiment, then, has *not* proven that the proliferation of pornography leads to a decline in sexual assaults against women.

*   *   *

In retrospect, the conclusions of the Commission on Pornography and Obscenity that pornography is harmless are not warranted on the basis of the actual data that were available to it. One might well wonder

40. *Report of the Commission*, p. 229.

41. J. H. Court notes these changes in "Pornography and Sex Crimes: A Re-Evaluation in the Light of Recent Trends around the World," *International Journal of Criminology and Penology* 5 (1976): 129–57.

42. *Report of the Commission*, p. 231.

43. R. Ben-Veniste, "Pornography and Sex Crime—the Danish Experience," *Technical Reports of the Commission*, 7:253.

44. B. Kutschinsky, "Sex Crimes and Pornography in Copenhagen: A Survey of Attitudes," *Technical Reports of the Commission*, 7:3.

45. Court, p. 143; Victor Bachy, "Danish 'Permissiveness' Revisited," *Journal of Communication* 26, no. 1 (1976): 40–43.

why the Goldstein report to the commission contained partially analyzed data or why rape statistics were gathered so hastily, but the fact remains that the commission's dubious conclusions cannot be attributed to its lacking the advantages of more recent data. Instead of pointing out the defects of the report, social scientists such as Etzioni who adhere to the conventional model of pornography and repression argued that the commission's data provided incontrovertible support for their belief in the harmless impact of pornography. The power of the prevailing liberal model has effectively limited the quality of research in the area, but more valuable studies are now emerging. Edward Donnerstein and John Hallan, for example, in a variation of a typical laboratory study where subjects are angered by a confederate, report that subsequent exposure to erotica increases aggression against females more so than against males.[46] And work by Seymour Feshback and his students indicates that males exposed to sadomasochistic stories are more likely to be sexually aroused by rape stories, more likely to believe that victims enjoy rape, and more likely to say that they would behave like fictional rapists when assured of nonpunishment.[47] Other data which may also support the proposition that pornography contributes to actual violence against women include reports from some cities that areas with large numbers of pornography outlets tend to have disproportionately high rape rates, statements from police officers that rapists are often found with pornographic materials, and reports that wife batterers are often devotees of pornographic literature.[48]

At this point there are no systematic quantitative data to support the proposition that pornography will proliferate in response to efforts to increase women's power. However, I would argue that the relationship between pornography and violence against women is inexplicable without the assumptions of this second proposition. Recognition of an in-

46. Edward Donnerstein and John Hallan, "The Facilitating Effects of Erotica on Aggression against Women," *Journal of Personality and Social Psychology* (in press).
47. Seymour Feshbach, "Sex, Aggression, and Violence toward Women" (paper delivered at the American Psychological Association Annual Meeting, Toronto, September 1978). See also Neal Malamuth, Scott Haber, and Seymour Feshback, "Testing Hypotheses Regarding Rape: Exposure to Sexual Violence, Sex Differences, and the Normality of Rapists," *Journal of Research in Personality* (in press).
48. Data on areas from Cleveland (Police Department memo, Captain Carl I. Delau, August 1977), and Los Angeles (City Planning Department, "Study of the Effects of the Concentration of Adult Entertainment Establishments in the City of Los Angeles," June 1977 [mimeographed]); Mildred Daley Pagelow reported on wife batterers as devotees in *Women against Violence in Pornography and Media Newspage* 1, no. 7 (December 1977): 2; and in response to my question during a public talk on wife abuse (Detroit, November 1976), Commander James Bannon of the Detroit Police Department (also a holder of a Ph.D. in sociology with a specialization in sex roles) responded that "often we find that the man is trying to enact a scene in some pornographic pictures." Liberals have tended not to believe the opinions of police officers; this may explain why the commission ignored their reports about rape and pornography which were available to the commission.

stitutionalized sexual hierarchy where men are in the dominant position provides the only adequate explanation for the repeated selection of women as victims in both pornography and the real world. Liberal social science has tended not to document these patterns because its models do not acknowledge the existence of patriarchy. This crucial theoretical gap also leaves liberals unable to explain why the legitimization of the pornography trade in the 1970s has not resulted in the predicted loss of interest and sales. (Estimates for this trade in Los Angeles were $15 million in 1969 and $85 million in 1976. Shops increased from eighteen to 143.)[49] If, however, we do accept the idea that pornography is a political and economic mechanism for sustaining patriarchal power relationships between men and women, we must also consider the possibility that when women take on new economic roles and destabilize existing relationships there will be an increase in the use of violence and repression against women. To recognize these dynamics is to understand why pornography appears to grow both in its quantity and its violence in certain historical periods. F. E. Kenyon, a British psychiatrist, has argued: "The considerable output of pornography in Victorian times may have resulted not only from the repressive, puritanical and hypocritical society, but also as a reaction to emerging female emancipation. Similarly today the further threat of 'Women's Liberation' could be partly responsible for another outpouring of pornography."[50] Of course, not all classes of women were drawn out of the home in the nineteenth century, and the challenges to the sexual status quo were neither as widespread or fundamental as those occurring today. Thus sexual backlash may not have been a predominant feature of the Victorian period. Moreover, technological advances in the capacity to produce pornographic materials are a contributing factor to growth and can determine differences between various historical periods. And yet, since technology is not an autonomous force, printing advances have taken particular forms because of prevailing power relationships.

One final factor is relevant in considering the proliferation of pornography in the contemporary period. Capitalism has advanced to a consumer stage where its economic goals are readily served by the commoditization and exploitation of sexuality, although the structural dynamics specific to capitalism did not necessitate this particular mechanism for achieving the goals of increased consumption. Sexuality has been appropriated as the particular mechanism because of preexisting patriarchal relationships. But pornography may serve the interests of capitalism in yet another way, a notion which is dramatized in Pamela

49. J. H. Court, "Rape and Pornography in Los Angeles" (paper presented at the annual conference of Australian Psychological Society, Flinders University, South Australia, August 1977), p. 7.

50. F. E. Kenyon, "Pornography, Law, and Mental Health," *British Journal of Psychiatry* 126 (March 1975): 226.

Hansford Johnson's comments on German fascism: "When the Nazis took on the government of Poland, they flooded the Polish bookstalls with pornography. This is a fact. Why did they do so? They did so on the theory that to make the individual conscious only of the need for personal sensation would make the social combination of forces more difficult. . . . The Nazi scheme was the deliberate use of pornography to the ends of social castration. The theory was, and it is worth considering that—permit all things for self-gratification, and you are likely to encourage withdrawal from any sort of corporate responsibility."[51] Although Johnson is calling attention to the consequences of self-indulgence, her analysis does suggest that the reaffirmation of male power and control promoted by pornography and the behaviors thereby encouraged serve to deflect attention from the complete absence of control which most men have over their economic roles within capitalist society.

Ultimately, however, any understanding of the nature of pornography will have to include new conceptualizations of human sexuality. For there are those who acknowledge that violence is endemic to pornography, and that men often act on these fantasies, but who still view these connections as a "natural" expression of human sexuality. Robert Stoller, a psychoanalyst, writes: "An essential dynamic in pornography is hostility. Perhaps the most important difference between more perverse and less perverse ('normal') pornography, as between perversion and 'normality,' is the degree of hostility (hatred and revenge fantasies) bound or released in the sexual activity. One can raise the possibly controversial question whether in humans (especially males) powerful sexual excitement can ever exist without brutality also being present."[52] Although Stoller recognizes the complexity of the prevailing pattern of male "sexual" behavior in patriarchal society, he does not acknowledge the possibility that this "natural" dynamic may in fact be structured by patriarchy. Admittedly, this is an extremely difficult proposition to test because patriarchy has been so universally dominant. In fact, in the laboratory it is difficult to distinguish sexual and violent arousal, a seeming confirmation of the "nature" argument. However, as far as I am aware, no experimental studies have considered how these arousal mechanisms are themselves conditioned by sexist attitudes. I would propose a laboratory study akin to the Tannenbaum experiment mentioned earlier,[53] with the crucial addition of a measure for subjects' adherence to patriarchal values to test whether there is any variability in the apparent physiological interconnection between violent and sexual arousal,

51. Pamela Hansford Johnson, *On Iniquity* (New York: Charles Scribner's Sons, 1967), p. 26.

52. Robert Stoller, *Perversion: The Erotic Form of Hatred* (New York: Pantheon Books, 1975), p. 88.

53. See above (n. 37).

and if so, whether attitudinal predispositions can account for the way the two covary. Admittedly such a study, no matter how imaginative and sensitive its design, would still be a very crude approximation of complex biohistorical processes, thus careful historical study in combination with field studies of noncapitalist-patriarchal systems might provide a more appropriate test. These suggestions are predicated on the belief that sexuality, as well as relations between the sexes, is a product of social existence and as such is subject to human will. From this perspective, arguments contending that pornography is only about violence and oppression, and has nothing in common with erotica, are no less limited than arguments which recognize only pornography's sexual nature. In fact, the simplified equation of pornography and violence may well gain a degree of political legitimacy, for it reinforces the traditional view that pornography is evil without necessarily challenging anyone's fundamental beliefs about sexuality. By comparison, the argument that pornography is intimately related to sexual life as presently constructed and cannot be understood apart from that reality promotes the notion that even the raw material of sex is shaped by society and its relations of domination. This more inclusive perspective points to the futility of efforts to discover the "true" or "natural" form of sexuality, highlights the partial truths contained within traditional moralist and liberationist beliefs, and further elucidates the feminist claim that the sexual revolution is not our revolution.

Department of Political Science
Purdue University

The Politics of Prostitution

Judith R. Walkowitz

In this essay, I shall outline some historical precedents for the current feminist attack on commercial sex, as represented by the Women against Pornography campaign.[1] The radical feminist attack on commercial sex has its roots in earlier feminist campaigns against male vice and the double standard. Past generations of feminists attacked prostitution, pornography, white slavery, and homosexuality as manifestations of undifferentiated male lust. Their campaigns were brilliant organizing drives that successfully aroused female anger, stimulated grass-roots organizations, and mobilized women not previously brought into the political arena. The vitality of the women's suffrage movement of the late nineteenth and early twentieth centuries cannot be understood without reference to the revivalistic quality of these antivice crusades, which often ran in tandem with the struggle for the vote.

Nonetheless, these earlier moral campaigns were in many ways self-defeating. Frequently, they failed to achieve their goals; feminists started a discourse on sex and mobilized an offensive against male vice, but they lost control of the movement as it diversified. In part, this loss resulted from contradictions in their attitudes; in part, it reflected feminists' impotence to reshape the world according to their own image.

Preparation of this essay was facilitated by a grant from the National Library of Medicine, PHS-LM 2574-03. I would also like to thank Phyllis Mack, Christine Stansell, Rayna Rapp, Gayle Rubin, and Daniel Walkowitz for their critical suggestions and advice.

1. Of course, the Women against Pornography campaign protests against sexual violence as well as commercial sex. However, earlier feminist crusaders also protested against sexual violence, although their efforts often victimized the women they were seeking to protect.

Four recent works illuminate this process in Great Britain and the United States. Deborah Gorham's "The Maiden Tribute of Modern Babylon Re-examined"[2] and Edward Bristow's *Vice and Vigilance*[3] explore the unhappy alliance between British feminists and repressive moralists in the agitation against white slavery during the social purity crusade of 1870–1918. The public discourse on prostitution is also the subject of Mark Connelly's *The Response to Prostitution in the Progressive Era,*[4] while *The Maimie Papers,*[5] an edited collection of letters by a former prostitute, sheds light on the lives and self-perceptions of prostitutes themselves. These studies tell us how feminists and others mobilized over prostitution and how their campaigns helped to define and construct sexuality in the late nineteenth century; they also delineate the relationship between public intervention and definitions of deviance.

In both Britain and America, feminist moral crusades against male vice began with a struggle against the state regulation of prostitution.[6] In 1864, the British Parliament passed the first of three statutes providing for the sanitary inspection of prostitutes in specified military depots in southern England and Ireland. Initially, this first Contagious Diseases Act, as it was obliquely entitled, aroused little attention. However, public opposition to regulation surfaced in the 1870s, when a coalition of middle-class nonconformists, feminists, and radical workingmen challenged the acts as immoral and unconstitutional, and called for their repeal. The participation of middle-class women in repeal efforts fascinated and shocked many contemporary observers, who regarded this female rebellion as a disturbing sign of the times.

Under the leadership of Josephine Butler, the Ladies National Association was founded in late 1869 as a separatist feminist organization. A "Ladies Manifesto" was issued, which argued that the acts not only deprived poor women of their constitutional rights and forced them to submit to a degrading internal examination, but they officially sanctioned a double standard of sexual morality. Like earlier female-reform efforts, the feminist attack on state regulation reinforced women's self-

2. Deborah Gorham, "The 'Maiden Tribute of Modern Babylon' Re-examined: Child Prostitution and the Idea of Childhood in Late-Victorian England," *Victorian Studies* 21 (Spring 1978): 353–69.

3. Edward Bristow, *Vice and Vigilance: Purity Movement in Britain since 1700* (Dublin: Gill & Macmillan, 1977).

4. Mark Connelly, *The Response to Prostitution in the Progressive Era* (Chapel Hill: University of North Carolina Press, 1980).

5. *The Maimie Papers,* ed. Ruth Rosen and Sue Davidson (Old Westbury, N.Y.: Feminist Press, 1977).

6. My perspective on the history of feminist moral crusades is informed not only by the material available in the works under review, but by my ongoing research on the politics of prostitution in late-Victorian and Edwardian Britain. See Judith R. Walkowitz, *Prostitution and Victorian Society: Women, Class and the State* (New York: Cambridge University Press, 1980).

conscious participation in a distinct female subculture. The feminist campaign also drew hundreds of women into the political arena for the first time by encouraging them to challenge male centers of power, such as the police, Parliament, and the medical and military establishments that were implicated in the administration of the acts. Feminists thus rallied to the defense of members of their own sex, while opposing the sexual and political prerogatives of men. They rejected the prevailing social view of "fallen women" as pollutants of men and depicted them instead as victims of male pollution, as women who had been invaded by men's bodies, men's laws, and by that "steel penis," the speculum.

This entailed a powerful identification with the fate of prostitutes. Mid-Victorian feminists treated prostitution as the end result of the artificial constraints placed on women's social and economic activity; inadequate wages and restrictions of their industrial employment forced women on to the streets, where they took up the "best paid industry,"[7] prostitution. Prostitution also served as a paradigm for the female condition; it established the archetypal relationship between men and women, repeated in a more subtle manner within genteel society. Feminists realized that the popular sentimentalization of "female influence" and motherhood only thinly masked an older contempt and distrust for women as "The Sex," as sexual objects to be bought and sold by men. The treatment of prostitutes under the acts epitomized this underlying misogyny.

As "mothers" and "sisters," feminists insisted on their right to defend prostitutes, thereby invoking two different kinds of authority relationships. The assertion of a mother's right to defend "daughters" was both an extension of women's traditional role within the family and a political device aimed at subverting patriarchal authority: it gave mothers, not fathers, the right to control sexual access to the daughters.[8] But it also sanctioned an authority relationship between older, middle-class women and young working-class women that, although caring and protective, was hierarchical and custodial. In other contexts, feminist repealers approached prostitutes on a more egalitarian basis, as sisters, albeit fallen ones, whose individual rights deserved to be respected and who had the right to sell their bodies on the streets unmolested by the police. This was the radical message of the repeal campaign, one that was linked to an enlightened view of prostitution as a voluntary and temporary occupation for adult working-class women.

Although capable of enunciating a radical critique of prostitution, middle-class feminists still felt ambivalent about prostitutes and the right of working-class women to control their own sexuality. By and large, these anxieties remained submerged during the libertarian struggle

7. Josephine Butler to Mary Priestman, May 4, 1874, no. 3327, Butler Collection, Fawcett Library, London.
8. I would like to thank Carroll Smith-Rosenberg for this observation.

against state regulation, but they soon surfaced in the more repressive campaign against white slavery. After the suspension of the Contagious Diseases Acts in 1883, Butler and her circle turned to the agitation against the foreign "traffic in women" and the entrapment of children into prostitution in London. When Parliament refused to pass a bill that would raise the age of consent and punish traffickers in vice, Butler and Catherine Booth of the Salvation Army approached W. T. Stead of the *Pall Mall Gazette* for assistance. The result was the "Maiden Tribute of Modern Babylon," published in the summer of 1885.

The "Maiden Tribute" was one of the most successful pieces of scandal journalism published in Britain during the nineteenth century. In prurient detail, it documented the sale of "five pound" virgins to aristocratic old rakes, graphically describing the way, according to Gorham, the "daughters of the people" had been "snared, trapped and outraged either when under the influence of drugs or after prolonged struggle in a locked room" (p. 353). The series had an electrifying effect on public opinion. A public demonstration (estimated at 250,000) was held in Hyde Park to demand the passage of legislation raising the age of consent for girls from thirteen to sixteen. For one brief moment, feminists and personal rights advocates joined with Anglican bishops and socialists to protest the aristocratic corruption of young innocents.

In their examination of the "Maiden Tribute" episode, both Gorham and Bristow part company with most historians, who, as Gorham notes, have traditionally "accepted the definition of the problem that the reformers themselves offered" (p. 362). Other commentators have accepted as a fact the existence of widespread involuntary prostitution among British girls at home or abroad; they have also assumed that in pressing for age-of-consent legislation, moral reformers were motivated by a simple desire to protect innocent victims from sexual violence.

Gorham and Bristow delineate the vast discrepancy between the reformers' view and the reality of prostitution. Both observe that the evidence of widespread involuntary prostitution of British girls in London and abroad is slim. During the 1870s and 1880s, officials and reformers were able to uncover a small traffic in women between Britain and the continent, although the women enticed into licensed brothels in Antwerp and Brussels were by no means the young innocents depicted in the sensational stories. Similarly, there undoubtedly were some child prostitutes on the streets of London, Liverpool, and elsewhere; most of these young girls were not victims of false entrapment, as the vignettes in the "Maiden Tribute" would suggest.

Why, then, did feminist reformers endorse this crusade and ally with repressive moralists and antisuffragists who were as anxious to clear the streets of prostitutes as to protect young girls from vicious aristocrats? Gorham brilliantly untangles the complex motives of feminists and others in taking up the question of involuntary and child prostitution. Her study is a model of cultural analysis, which examines middle-class views of childhood, gender, and sexuality in the context of ongoing political struggles and social divisions within Victorian society. Although sensitive to the distinct political agenda of feminists in the campaign, Gorham shows how their professed solidarity with working-class women was undermined by their allegiance to hierarchical notions of authority that divided women along class and generational lines.

Like the instrumental violation of registered women under the Contagious Diseases Acts, the story of aristocratic corruption of virgins "generated a sense of outrage with which a wide spectrum of public opinion found itself in sympathy" (p. 354). Feminist repealers undoubtedly believed they could manipulate this popular anger first to secure the full repeal of the Contagious Diseases Acts (they were finally removed from the statute books in 1886) and then to launch an assault on the double standard. They were also attracted to the radical message in Stead's exposé of aristocratic vice. The disreputable performance of members of Parliament during the debates over the age of consent simply confirmed their worst suspicions about "the vicious upper classes." At the same time, this focus on licentious aristocrats and child victims inhibited a more searching and critical analysis of prostitution. By portraying young prostitutes as sexually innocent and passive victims of individual evil men, the reformers were able to assuage middle-class guilt without implicating members of their own class in the sexual oppression of working-class women and girls. "Had they allowed themselves," suggests Gorham, "to see that many young girls engaged in prostitution not as passive, sexually innocent victims, but because their choices were so limited, the reformers would have been forced to recognize that the causes of juvenile prostitution were to be found in an exploitative economic structure" (p. 355).

According to Gorham, feminists tended to share the same feelings of anxiety over youthful female sexuality as other members of the middle class. Although they felt obliged to redress the sexual wrongs done to working-class girls by men of a superior class, they registered the same repugnance toward incorrigible girls as they had earlier toward unrepentant prostitutes. For them, as well as for more repressive moralists, the desire to protect young girls thinly masked coercive impulses to control their voluntary sexual responses and to impose a social code on them in keeping with the middle-class view of female adolescent dependency.

Bristow considers the legal and institutional legacy of the "Maiden Tribute" in *Vice and Vigilance*. Although he traces the history of antivice crusades back to the Society for the Reformation of Manners of the 1690s, he concedes that the "heart" of his study lies in the period 1880–1918, when the social purity movement erupted on the national scene and altered the climate of opinion about sex. *Vice and Vigilance* is witty, informative, and well researched, but it does not offer a rigorous interpretation of modern sexuality, nor does it fully explore the meaning and timing of these antivice crusades. Caught between a popular narrative and a scholarly project, Bristow is at his best when describing the infrastructure of purity organizations and their political maneuverings at the national and municipal level.

The public furor over the "Maiden Tribute" forced the passage of the Criminal Law Amendment Act of 1885, a pernicious piece of omnibus legislation which raised the age of consent for girls from thirteen to sixteen but also gave police far greater summary jurisdiction over poor working-class women and children, a trend that Butler and her circle had always opposed. Finally, it contained a clause making indecent acts between consenting male adults a crime, thus forming the basis of legal prosecutions of male homosexuals in Britain until 1967.

Despite the public outcry against corrupt aristocrats and international traffickers, the new bill was mainly enforced against the working-class women, not their social betters or foreigners. Under pressure from local vigilance associations, police officials cracked down on streetwalkers and brothel keepers. The prosecution of brothels increased fourteenfold, and similar drives against solicitation were instituted in the capital and major provincial cities.

Bristow simply reports these developments, but does not suggest how legal repression affected the structure and organization of prostitution. Although we still await a detailed study of late-Victorian prostitution, some preliminary generalizations are possible. By providing for easy, summary proceedings against brothel keepers, the 1885 act helped to drive a wedge between prostitutes and the poor working-class community. Prostitutes were uprooted from their neighborhoods and had to find lodgings in other areas of the city and in the periphery. Their activity had become more covert. Cut off from other sustaining relationships, increasingly they were forced to rely on pimps for emotional security and for protection against legal authorities. Indeed, the wide prevalence of pimps in the early twentieth century meant that prostitution had shifted from a female- to a male-dominated trade, and there existed a greater number of third parties with an interest in prolonging women's stay on the streets.[9]

In the wake of Stead's "shocking revelations," the National Vigilance Association (NVA) was formed. First organized to ensure the local enforcement of the Criminal Law Amendment Act, the NVA soon turned its attention to burning obscene books and to attacking music halls, theaters, and nude painting. It condemned the works of Balzac, Zola, and Rabelais and successfully prosecuted their British distributors; it

9. See Abraham Flexner, *Prostitution in Europe* (New York: Century Co., 1914).

attacked birth-control literature and advertisements for "female pills" (abortifacient drugs) on the same grounds. To these moral crusaders, "pornographic literature," broadly defined, was a vile expression of the same "undifferentiated male lust"[10] that ultimately led to homosexuality and prostitution. As Bristow observes, the fact that pornography was now available in cheap editions heightened middle-class concern. They visualized the masses, whose political loyalty they doubted, perusing works that might further weaken their allegiance to the dominant moral order.

While the social purity movement served middle-class interests, it is a common error among historians to assume, as Gorham does, that working-class support for social purity was "ephemeral" or that both "before and after the summer of 1885 [social purity] remained almost exclusively a middle-class movement" (p. 378). Middle-class evangelicals may have predominated in the National Vigilance Association, but Bristow presents suggestive evidence that the values of social purity were internalized among some portions of the working class in the late nineteenth century.

By the mid-eighties, Ellice Hopkins, the female pioneer in social purity, had already organized 200 ladies' rescue committees and male chastity leagues. She spoke on male chastity before meetings of workingmen, and she and others recruited thousands of respectable workingmen into White Cross armies, dedicated to promoting the single standard of chastity and attacking vice. The prescriptive literature distributed by social purity groups seems also to have influenced child-rearing practices of the time. Edwardian working-class parents were notable for their strict schedules, puritanical treatment of masturbation, and for the severe restrictions they placed on their teenage daughters' social and sexual behavior. Although the late-Victorian and Edwardian years represented a "germination" period for the "new sexuality," the available "facts" about adult sexuality in this period, the general decline in both venereal disease and prostitution, the high age of marriage and low illegitimacy rates, and the apparently limited use of contraceptives among the working classes would seem to support Bristow's hypothesis that "sexual restraint" was indeed "spreading down through society" (p. 125). As we shall see in the American case, certain countervailing tendencies were perceptible as well.

Why was social purity so attractive to respectable workingmen? As Bristow notes, it provided an avenue of social mobility for some men, like William Coote, a former compositor who became the national secretary of the National Vigilance Association. Sexual respectability became a hallmark of the labor aristocrat, anxious to distance himself from the

10. Jeffrey Weeks, *Coming Out: Homosexual Politics in Britain, from the Nineteenth Century to the Present* (London: Quartet Books, 1977), p. 18.

"bestiality" of the casual laboring poor, as increased pressure was placed on the respectable working class to break their ties with "outcast" groups. Other structural factors were at work as well, although Bristow does not elaborate on them. Changing employment patterns seem to have reinforced patriarchal tendencies among skilled sectors of the working class by the end of the century, as the proportion of married women working outside the home declined and the family wage for male workers became a demand of trade unions. Seen in this context, social purity, which called upon men to protect and control their women, served as the ideological corollary of the family wage, morally legitimating the prerogatives of patriarchy inside and outside the family. Thus, social purity served to undermine working-class solidarity, while tightening definitions of gender among respectable workingmen and working women.

What was the subsequent relationship between feminism and social purity? Initially, feminists filled many committee positions of the National Vigilance Association, but this connection was short-lived for Butler and her circle, who resigned when the repressive direction of the NVA became apparent. Throughout the late eighties and nineties, Butlerites warned their workers to "beware" of the repressive methods of the social purity societies, but their warnings were too late. The new social purity movement had passed them by, while absorbing a goodly number of the Ladies National Association rank and file.

Conservative suffragists like Millicent Fawcett and Elizabeth Blackwell still remained within the ranks of social purity, but they never controlled the direction of the movement. On the other hand, social purity permanently left its imprint on the women's movement; its theme of the sexual wrongs perpetrated against women by men permeated later feminist consciousness. After the 1880s, the "women's revolt" became "Puritan and not Bohemian. It is uprising against the tyranny of organized intemperance, impurity, mammonism, and selfish motives."[11]

These, then, are the historical links between feminism and repressive crusades against prostitution, pornography, and homosexuality. Begun as a libertarian struggle against the state sanction of male vice, the repeal campaign helped to spawn a hydra-headed assault against sexual deviation of all kinds. The struggle against state regulation evolved into a movement that used the instruments of the state for repressive purposes. It may be misleading to interpret these later crusades as "blind" repressive attacks on sexuality, as Bristow suggests; rather, they extended the meaning of sexuality. According to Michel Foucault, this discourse on sex was a strategy for exercising power in society.[12] By ferreting out new areas of illicit sexual activity and defining them into

11. "The New Woman," *Woman's Signal* (November 29, 1894).
12. Michel Foucault, *The History of Sexuality*, vol. 1, *An Introduction*, trans. Robert Hurley (New York: Pantheon Books, 1978).

existence, a new "technology of power" was created that facilitated control over an ever-widening circle of human activity. However, power is not immanent in society; it is deployed by specific human agencies. During the repeal campaign, feminist leaders were able to control and shape the public discourse on sex; but, according to Bristow, they "rapidly lost control of a spreading and diversifying movement and social purity had begun to lose sight of [Butler's] ideal of the 'supremacy of conscience' with its non-repressionist implications. Purity reform came to mean the harassing of prostitutes and systematic blind repression in the arts and entertainment" (p. 77).

The story is much the same in America.[13] In the 1860s and 1870s, American feminists and other moral reformers were able to forestall the introduction of regulation for prostitutes in U.S. cities. The one exception was St. Louis, where systematic medical inspection of prostitutes was established in 1870; within a few years, however, purity forces overturned the city ordinance. Out of the antiregulationist struggle grew the social purity movement (which Josephine Butler always regarded as a characteristically American phenomenon transplanted to British soil). Like its British counterpart, purity reform in America was particularly concerned with youthful sexuality, hostile to working-class culture, and ready to use the state to enforce a repressive sexual code. American feminists helped propagate the message of social purity, and were drawn to what seemed to be an attack on aggressive male sexuality and the double standard. But it is unclear how much they dictated public policy. More than in Britain, corporate interests, as represented by the corporation executives who bankrolled Anthony Comstock and by John D. Rockefeller's Bureau of Social Hygiene, came to dominate antivice efforts at the national level and in some locales. In 1913, for example, the Bureau of Social Hygiene sponsored George Kneeland's investigation into *Commercialized Vice in New York*,[14] which gave added momentum to the repression of street solicitation and brothel keeping in New York. The heavy involvement of corporate philanthropy in purity efforts undoubtedly reflects the more advanced stage of capitalist development in progressive-era America than in Britain and the power of monopoly capitalism at this time.

Mark Connelly's *The Response to Prostitution in the Progressive Era* is less concerned with feminist participation in purity work than with the widespread phenomenon of "anti-prostitution." The book has the virtues, and some of the vices, of traditional cultural history. Connelly astutely dissects literary genres associated with discourse on prostitution during the progressive era: white-slave narratives, vice commission reports, medical literature on venereal disease, even the clauses of the

13. For an interpretation of the American social purity movement, see David Pivar, *Purity Crusade: Sexual Morality and Social Control* (Westport, Conn.: Greenwood Press, 1976).
14. George Kneeland, *Commercialized Vice in New York* (New York: Century Co., 1913).

Mann Act. His discussion of that "rare exotic literary genre," the white-slave tract, is superb. These narratives served as "spicy cultural counter-part to the stuffy vice commission reports"; they were "vicarious 'tour guides' to the red-light districts for individuals who would not go there in person." Like the exposés of child prostitution in the "Maiden Trib-ute," the child-woman figure of the white-slave tract "reflected an in-ability to confront prostitution as a manifestation of *adult* sexuality totally outside the prescription of civilized morality. Childish victims were perhaps easier to deal with psychologically than libidinous men and women" (p. 127). Connelly also provides a judicious guide to the more "scientific" vice commission reports. As social documents, these reports can not be read "straight"; but if properly decoded, they can yield a wealth of information about the social profile of prostitutes, their material cul-ture, and community life. By focusing exclusively on the documents as texts, however, Connelly fails to use them to construct a rounded descrip-tion of prostitutes and their response to the crisis precipitated by the police crackdowns.

Whereas Bristow presents a breezy narrative of the personages and events of British social purity, Connelly is committed to the task of un-covering the larger cultural meaning of the public discourse on Ameri-can prostitution. In trying to do so, Connelly homogenizes the progres-sives, whose specific identities are rarely discussed, who all seem to be last-ditch defenders of Victorian morality, riddled by the same psycho-logical blind spots. They may have employed different literary tableaux, but fundamentally they spoke with one voice. When he considers why the theory that women resorted to the streets because of inadequate wages enjoyed such currency among progressives, Connelly concludes that "anxiety seems as strongly provoked by the fact that women were working in industrial jobs at all as by the low wages they received." "This is not to dismiss," he hastens to add, "the very genuine concern over the economic plight of working women expressed by many who addressed the wages-and-sin issues" (p. 35). Yet he never tells us who in fact held these varying positions, under what conditions these differences were ex-pressed, and why one opinion prevailed over another. The discourse on prostitution represented a power struggle among distinct social con-stituencies, inside and outside the bourgeoisie. As the British case dem-onstrates, that conflict reflected both class and gender divisions. Con-nelly's generalized discussion of cultural anxiety posits a bourgeois hegemony, but ignores Raymond Williams' critical reminder that the "reality of any hegemony . . . is that while by definition it is always domi-nant, it is never either total or exclusive."[15] The struggle between cul-

15. Raymond Williams, *Marxism and Literature* (Oxford: Oxford University Press, 1977), p. 113.

tures is a dynamic historical process; unfortunately, Connelly's well-crafted book tends to obscure that process.

This problem aside, Connelly's book illuminates many aspects of prostitution that interest feminist scholars. His discussion of clandestine prostitution is particularly insightful. The obsession with "clandestines" or "amateurs," Connelly argues, was a reaction to changing sexual and social mores. Even before the First World War, traditional moralists were shocked by the perceptible increase in "flappers," female adolescents in open rebellion against rigid Victorian sexual standards. The free and easy sexual habits of this small vanguard were symptomatic of the more widespread departure of women from traditional social and economic roles. Although the majority of young, single women working and living alone in the city were not conscious feminists, and though they had as their goal marriage and child rearing, "they nevertheless had achieved a degree of autonomy outside the context of a male-oriented or domestic setting and, at least for several years in the late teens and early twenties, led lives markedly different from their mothers" (p. 39).

The desire of young working women to lead lives different from those of their mothers may have constituted an unprecedented change in popular female consciousness. This partial break with traditional gender roles took many forms. In the early twentieth century, a new leadership cadre of trade-union organizers, suffragists, and radical agitators was recruited from the ranks of working-class women. But can one equate the sexual rebellion of flappers with these more self-conscious, focused, and politicized acts of emancipation?

Let us consider the case of Maimie Pinzer, a former prostitute and author of the letters collected in the *Maimie Papers*. Maimie's letters to Fanny Howe, a Boston patrician and philanthropist, constitute a brilliant autobiography of a survivor struggling to maintain her independence and self-respect against terrible odds. Written between 1910 and 1922, they reveal little of Maimie's experience in prostitution (she was never a streetwalker but seems to have carried on a discreet trade with gentlemen in the afternoon). The letters do, however, tell us a great deal about her subsequent working life outside prostitution, and about the circumstances that might have impelled "self-respecting errant girls" like herself to move into prostitution.

As Ruth Rosen notes in her sensitive introduction, Maimie's social background closely paralleled that of other working-class girls in the progressive era. A crisis in the family economy, caused by the death of her father; an estranged relationship with her mother; early sexual experiences with men of her own class—all forced Maimie and thousands of her contemporaries to leave their families and strike out on their own in their late teens. Many of these young working women eventually drifted into prostitution as a temporary solution to uneasy circumstances. Their move into prostitution, Rosen reminds us, was still a choice, because prostitutes were not simply "passive victims of impersonal economic and social forces" (p. xxv), but active historical agents, women who made their own history, albeit under restrictive conditions.

Judging from Maimie's experience, however, one should not underestimate the practical impediments to female self-sufficiency. Maimie tried all the options available to women at the time: marriage, prostitution, female employment within the tertiary sector, from office work to rescue work. In New York, Montreal, and Philadelphia, Maimie confronted sexual harassment on the job, dead-end positions, seasonal employment, and grossly inadequate wages. Having lived comfortably off the "wages of sin," she subsequently found the exploitative conditions of respectable employment unbearable. As she explained, "My trouble is that I am a working girl who has lived like a 'lady' and it's hard to curb my desires and live as the working girl should" (p. xxix).

Ironically, her most satisfying venture turned out to be rescue work. In 1913, with financial backing from middle-class benefactors, she opened a mission in Montreal for "self-respecting errant girls" like Stella Phillips, the "most beautiful girl in Montreal" and Maimie's alter ego. Maimie interpreted Stella's move into prostitution as an act of self-assertion: "That her parents and environment are sordid is an accepted fact; and that [she and her type] have refused to drop into the same rut and have an idea to outgrow the conditions they were born into, makes them 'different'" (p. 272). For Maimie, sexual expression represented a form of female rebellion. Although she evinced little interest in politics and feminism, she had this much in common with the female political activists of her generation: Maimie, like Rose Schneiderman of the Women's Trade Union League (WTUL) or Annie Kenney of the Women's Social and Political Union (WSPU), struggled personally against the fatalism and acquiescence of her class and gender.

By 1922, when the correspondence ends, Maimie had closed the mission and settled into a monogamous, privatized relationship with her second husband, Ira Benjamin. Her life continued to parallel larger historical developments, for the postwar years witnessed the disappearance of segregated red-light districts and the demise of a self-conscious women's culture that had earlier energized the women's rights movement and antivice crusades. In the 1920s, women were told that they had achieved emancipation and that happiness lay in working out a close, intimate relationship with a man. Concern over prostitution, Connelly tells us, "dissipated almost as rapidly as it had emerged two decades earlier." It remains to be seen, however, whether the 1920s truly marked the end of an era. Although the market for prostitution may have altered since the prewar period, the same modes of class and gender domination organize social relations today. As the Women against Pornography campaign demonstrates, commercial sex can still arouse female anger and mobilize women into symbolic crusades against male vice.

Yet, if there is any moral lesson to be learned from these moral crusaders, it is that commercial sex is a hot and dangerous issue for feminists. In their defense of prostitutes and concern to protect women from male sexual aggression, earlier generations of feminists were still limited by their own class bias and by their continued adherence to a "separate sphere" ideology that stressed women's purity, moral supremacy, and domestic virtues. Moreover, feminists lacked the cultural and political power to reshape the world according to their own image. Although they tried to set the standards of sexual conduct, they did not control the instruments of state that would ultimately enforce these norms. There were times, particularly during the antiregulationist campaign, when feminists were able to dominate and structure the public discourse on sex and arouse popular female anger at male sexual license. Yet this anger was easily diverted into repressive campaigns against male vice and sexual variation, controlled by men and corporate interests whose goals were antithetical to the values and ideals of feminism.

Department of History
Rutgers University

The Front Line: Notes on Sex in Novels by Women, 1969–1979

Ann Barr Snitow

Women Have Only Just Begun to Write about Sex

In the history of fiction in English, it was only the day before yesterday that male novelists had the license or the desire to write about sex explicitly, seriously, as an experience in itself. It was only yesterday that the women novelists who are my subject could begin to think that they, too, had such license and such desire. The publication of Lawrence's *Lady*

Thanks to the following who, with patience and generosity, discussed some of the ideas in this piece with me: Dorothy Dinnerstein, Kate Ellis, Elizabeth Fisher, Daniel Goode, Gail Kuenstler, Dena Leiter, Bob Schaffer, Alix Kates Shulman, Meredith Tax, and Sharon Thompson. The generalizations and examples in this piece are drawn from the following novels: Renata Adler, *Speedboat* (New York: Random House, 1971); Margaret Atwood, *Surfacing* (New York: Popular Library, 1972); Rita Mae Brown, *Rubyfruit Jungle* (Plainfield, Vt.: Daughters Inc., 1973); Dorothy Bryant, *The Garden of Eros* (Berkeley, Calif.: Ata Books, 1979); Marilyn Coffey, *Marcella* (New York: Charterhouse Books, 1973); Constance De Jong, *Modern Love* (New York: Standard Editions, 1977); Jane De Lynn, *Some Do* (New York: Collier Books, 1978); Diane Di Prima, *Memoirs of a Beatnik* (New York: Olympia Press, 1969); Rosalyn Drexler, *To Smithereens* (New York: Signet Books, 1972); Marilyn French, *The Women's Room* (New York: Harcourt Brace Jovanovich, Inc., 1977); Gail Godwin, *The Odd Woman* (New York: Alfred A. Knopf, Inc., 1974); Mary Gordon, *Final Payments* (New York: Ballantine Books, 1978); Lois Gould, *A Sea Change* (New York: Avon Books, 1976); Sharon Isabell, *Yesterday's Lessons* (Oakland, Calif.: Women's Press Collective, 1974); Diane Johnson, *The Shadow Knows* (New York: Pocket Books, 1974); Erica Jong, *Fear of Flying* (New York: Signet Books, 1973); Ella Leffland, *Mrs. Munck* (New York: Pocket Books, 1970), and *Love Out of Season* (New York: Atheneum Publishers, 1974); Kate Millett, *Sita* (New York: Ballantine Books, 1976); Toni Morrison, *The Bluest Eye* (New York: Pocket Books, 1970), and *Sula* (New York: Bantam Books, 1973); Joyce Carol Oates, *Them* (New York: Fawcett Book Group, 1969); Iris Owens, *After Claude* (New York: Warner Paperback Library, 1973); Marge Piercy, *Woman on the Edge of Time* (New York: Alfred A. Knopf, Inc., 1976), and *High Cost of Living* (New York: Fawcett Crest Books, 1978); Sylvia Plath, *The Bell Jar* (New York: Bantam Books, 1971); Anne Roiphe, *Torch Song* (New York: Signet Books, 1977); Judith

Chatterley's Lover (1928) can stand as a first date for male novelists;[1] to name such a first date for women novelists is more difficult. One cannot go much further back than Doris Lessing's *The Golden Notebook* (1962) for a public, detailed, and influential exploration of how sex fits into a modern woman's life.[2] But that great study of social fragmentation is above

---

Rossner, *Looking for Mr. Goodbar* (New York: Pocket Books, 1975); Lynda Schor, *Appetites* (New York: Warner Books, 1975); Ann Shockley, *Loving Her* (New York: Avon Books, 1974); Ellen Schwamm, *Adjacent Lives* (New York: Avon Books, 1978); Alix Kates Shulman, *Memoirs of an Ex-Prom Queen* (New York: Bantam Books, 1972), and *Burning Questions* (New York: Bantam Books, 1978); Ellease Southerland, *Let the Lion Eat Straw* (New York: Charles Scribner's Sons, 1979); Kate Stimpson, *Class Notes* (New York: Times Books, 1979); Anne Tyler, *A Slipping Down Life* (New York: Popular Library, Inc., 1969); Alice Walker, *Meridian* (New York: Pocket Books, 1977). Obviously other books by these authors and others have influenced the research at a greater remove. Among the regrettable omissions are: Kathy Acker, Lisa Alther, June Arnold, Ingrid Bengis, E. M. Broner, Suzy McKee Charnes, Barbara Chase-Riboud, Francine Du Plessix Gray, Gael Greene, Bertha Harris, Elaine Kraf, Ursula LeGuin, Lucy Lippard, Alison Lurie, Janet Rule, and Joanna Russ. Another missing element is the short story. Look, e.g., at the diffused sexual longing in Sally George's "Joy through Strength in the Bardo" (*Heresies* [Fall 1977]); at the stories in *A Woman's Touch: An Anthology of Lesbian Eroticism and Sensuality for Women Only*, ed. Cedar and Nelly (Eugene, Oreg.: Woman-Share Books, 1979); and in Charleen Swansea and Barbara Campbell, eds., *Love Stories by New Women* (Charlotte, N.C.: Red Clay Books, 1978). See also Grace Paley, Toni Cade Bambara, and the work coming out in feminist journals. Women's poems, too, are pouring out in response to social changes and to the growth in conscious female community. Both stories and poems, explicit and exploratory about sex in ways quite different from the novel, deserve a separate study. All the writers are American, except for one Canadian, Margaret Atwood. Discussions of Lessing (English) and Atwood belong here because both have been important and suggestive to American women writing and publishing between 1969 and 1979. The method here is literary analysis: the best strategy for understanding what a woman writer means by discussing the constellation of things, "sex," is to look at *where* she situates sexuality in her books—thematically, structurally, and symbolically. Tone, too, is a subtle indicator of how particular novelists situate sex in the scheme of things. Is sex the climax, hence a climactic experience? Or is sex embedded in other experiences, perhaps sometimes overwhelmed by other elements in life?

1. Of course there are earlier explicit mentions of sex in the English novel. *Tom Jones* is ribaldry. But Fielding was naughty about sex while taking it for granted. Sex in the twentieth century is a consciously, anxiously reinterpreted mystery. The publication of *Ulysses* (1922) predates *Lady Chatterley's Lover* by several years, but Lawrence seems the better choice of date here, because he polemically insisted on sex as a major, serious theme for the traditional novel, as a subject in itself.

2. Other candidates for early, influential examples are: Mary McCarthy, *The Group* (New York: Harcourt, Brace & World, 1963) (a chapter published in 1954 taught a whole college generation about the diaphragm); Sylvia Plath, *The Bell Jar* (written in the fifties, published in England in 1963 [London: William Heinemann, Ltd.], in the United States in 1971 [New York: Bantam Books]); Diane DePrima, *Memoirs of a Beatnik* (a joyous parody of male pornography that treats free female sex play as similar to men's, an Olympia Press book, hence a dirty book, of 1969); and Erica Jong, *Fear of Flying*, which, as late as 1973, was hailed as a first in the female writing tradition. However, though Lessing is English, *The Golden Notebook* was probably the most inclusive of these. For all of its wonderful detail and daring, *The Group* is not a good germinal example because it flirts with what Lawrence in protest against censorship called "the dirty secret." This problem with tone persists: being funny or witty or ironic about sex without being self-deprecating is still, in 1979, causing

all the story of the many ways in which women are disappointed. It documents why women like its heroine, Anna, cannot integrate sex with love, or family, or work, or political consciousness.

Lessing also made several observations about women's sexual situation in *The Golden Notebook* that continue to be made in more recent women's novels: deeply arousing sex is scarce; sex that calls forth those deep feelings is the kind worth having; sexual arousal is an impulse that comes from the whole configuration of a person's experience. This last point is a feminist reinterpretation of the old cliché that women want love more than sex and its corollary: women are not as interested in graphic descriptions of sexual parts as they are in descriptions of social context.

The way in which *The Golden Notebook* develops these themes embodies the two major stylistic strains to be found in subsequent female writing about sex. On the one hand, Lessing is encyclopedic in her description of social texture; on the other, Lessing uses sex symbolically. In the realm of metaphor Anna's sexual experience is more positive than in its more literal embodiment. At this level, sex has the power to reassure and rejuvenate. Anna's final love affair is the occasion of a mental reorganization and passes as a happy ending.

When it became legally and socially possible for serious women novelists like Lessing to write about their sexual feelings, when they no longer paid a high social or economic price for having dared both to sleep with more than one man and to discuss this fact in public, the effect was not as if a lid had been taken off a pot so that rich, active sexual experiences could bubble out. Instead, alongside hope and occasional ecstacy, their books are about the pain of women, their social oppression and sexual repression. Women, for so long equated with sex, did not immediately leap at the chance to tell their side of the sex story. There were not, after all, many real inducements for them to throw away privacy, anonymity, and shame.[3] The decision of writers in the generations of Katherine Ann Porter, Caroline Gordon, Eudora Welty, Carson McCullers, or Elizabeth Hardwick not to be graphic also made sense at a

---

difficulty in the tonal balance of women's novels. Of course, women have written pornography and erotica, but women novelists like Gertrude Stein, Djuna Barnes, and Anais Nin were all expatriots, living in Colette's country. Many of their books were underground or obscure. See Djuna Barnes, *The Ladies Almanack* (New York: Harper & Row, 1972); Anais Nin, *The Delta of Venus* (New York: Harcourt Brace Jovanovich, Inc., 1977), and *The Little Birds* (New York: Harcourt Brace Jovanovich, Inc., 1979); and Elizabeth Fifer, "Is Flesh Advisable? The Interior Theatre of Gertrude Stein," *Signs: Journal of Women in Culture and Society* 4, no. 3 (Spring 1979): 472–83, for a discussion of Gertrude Stein's erotica.

3. Men tried to invent a new, friendly, eager female sexuality in what has been called the sexual revolution of the sixties. But after that experimental decade, the feminist movement emerged to challenge men's motives, insisting that the command to be sexually warm was as oppressive as the earlier command to be cold and pure. The pressures that gave rise to those inventions remain.

time when all women were seen as primarily sexual beings, routinely banished from other areas of knowledge, insight, or power. They tried to break the equation that linked them to private domestic and sexual experience. They wanted to be visionary artists, not limited women.

So recent is it that sex has stopped meaning pregnancy for most women that the post-Lessing writers now in their twenties, thirties, and forties—childbearing years—are a significant first generation. The idea that women can have sex and the world too is still exotic, but writers can now explore this possibility in their work, all of which has been touched in some way by the resurgence of feminist consciousness.

The realist novel has always been the novel of such first phases. Since the inception of the form, novels have been "how-to" manuals for groups gathering their identity through self-description. The discursive novels of family life, the *bildungsroman*, the stories of first success and first sexual exploits (though unlike their nineteenth-century counterparts they tend to end, not with weddings, but with divorces) are typical productions in 1969–79.[4] They set out to record changes in sexual manners. The novel of manners requires an audience with a shared body of experiences and values. Female community, a major social development of the decade, provides women writers with that audience, eager to recognize itself.

4. This description leaves out some female modernists and experimentalists, e.g., Kathy Acker, Constance De Jong, Barbara Guest, Bertha Harris, Fanny Howe, Elaine Kraf, Lucy Lippard, and Susan Sontag. Feminism and postmodernism have largely ignored each other, perhaps to the detriment of both. There are efforts to make connections in a feminist journal like *Heresies;* and Lucy Lippard's novel *I See/You Mean* (Los Angeles: Chrysalis Books, 1979) bridges these intellectual worlds. However, some novels that work inside the symbolic and structural vocabulary of modernism, like Joan Didion's *Play It as It Lays* (New York: Simon & Schuster, 1970), or Renata Adler's *Speedboat* (New York: Random House, 1971), have been closemouthed about gender in general. This reticence may well have to do with problems and contradictions in the way modernism descended in the female line, an aspect of literary history that needs further analysis. Elaine Showalter has established a useful starting point for this work in her criticism of Virginia Woolf's "secession" from the realist tradition of women like Charlotte Brontë and George Eliot (see *A Literature of Their Own: British Women Novelists from Brontë to Lessing* [Princeton, N.J.: Princeton University Press, 1977], p. 240 et passim). A longer version of this study will include some more experimental writers, particularly those who, by making innovation in form, suggest new ways to imagine or situate sexual experience in life. (Michel Foucault and Robert J. Stoller suggest further areas for exploration in describing how sexuality is presented in works of the imagination.) Postmodern experimentation in form is only one of the directions these innovations may take. In the construction of their own new forms, women may well react against some elements in modernism and will almost certainly challenge some current definitions of what an artist does and what her relationship to her audience can be. One direction that already seems to be attractive to innovative novelists is science fiction. See, for example, Doris Lessing, *Memoirs of a Survivor* (New York: Alfred A. Knopf, Inc., 1975), and *Shikasta* (New York: Alfred A. Knopf, Inc., 1979); Marge Piercy, *Woman on the Edge of Time* (New York: Alfred A. Knopf, Inc., 1976); Suzy McKee Charnes, *Motherlines* (New York: Berkley Publishing Corp., 1979); Joanna Russ, *The Female Man* (New York: Bantam Books, 1975); Ursula Le Guin, *The Left Hand of Darkness* (New York: Ace Books, 1976).

Do Women Write about Sex Differently from Men?

Sex is not one *thing*. Women have always intimated this, since their particular dependency on male protection and affection diffused the sexual moment into all aspects of social experience. The still common male insistence that sex is an animal function, a distinct drive, an organ with a private life, is related to our society's fetishism of objects in general. Just as labor in industrial society seems to disappear, leaving only the product of labor, so do the social interactions that form human sexual experience evaporate, leaving only organs and instincts. A large group of male novelists write and rewrite the *ur* story that comes from seeing sex this way.

Male novelists who have rejected this simplification have tended to go to the other extreme, making the sexual experience a symbol of failed transcendence. In a straight line of descent from F. Scott Fitzgerald to Philip Roth and Saul Bellow, male novelists have been using sexual disappointments to symbolize deceleration in the forward thrust of life in general. This group continues to show men seducing, betraying, possessing, and being bored by their possession, moving on to the next woman while obsessing continuously about that one in a million who cannot be bought or possessed, who has betrayed them and driven them out of the garden of Eden.[5] Doris Lessing, for all her doubts about her heroine's prospects for happiness, allows her Anna to draw more positive energy from a sexual encounter than most novelists in this second group allow their heroes. Lessing has more friendliness toward men, more hope for detente in the sex war.

Interestingly enough, women novelists seldom, if ever, write at either of these extremes: they neither reduce sex to an animal function nor elevate it to a symbol of ultimate triumph or defeat. Perhaps this is because the *act* of sex has not been women's primary testing ground as it has been for the male ego. Getting the man has been far more important to them than proving they can have orgasms with him. In fact, until recently, getting the man often included pretending lack of interest or actually repressing interest in orgasm. Women are perhaps lucky that their real sexuality was so secondary an issue that no such monolithic importance has been ascribed to it.

A common insight about sex excitement to be found in many women's novels is that each person's history is an encoded set of reasons for arousal. Particular textures, gestures, words are charged with the intensity of infancy, of puberty, of past sexual experience. Sex is an impulse that comes from the whole configuration of a person's life, part of a densely populated context. This is true for men, too, of course, but

5. For versions of this plot, see Jerzy Kozinski, Walker Percy, Kurt Vonnegut, Philip Roth, Saul Bellow, John Hawkes, and others.

they seem more reluctant to acknowledge the psychological and social roots of their sexual impulses. This would be to admit to outside controls, a weakness in men's eyes.

Sex Is Both Private and Social

In Ellease Southerland's *Let the Lion Eat Straw,* a young black woman with happy childhood memories of the South meets a man in New York City who comes from down home: "His voice, smooth purple, seemed to come from inside her heart. She breathed cautiously. He spoke. Her head afloat, somewhere in a Florida place" (p. 83). In those few moments, Abeba Williams falls in love with Daniel Torch. Her mother warns her that Torch is a country boy, but this is precisely why Abeba loves him. Sex is a chain reaction that begins in childhood when Abeba's grandmother "stroked the little girl, shoulders, back, hips" and Abeba clutched her grandmother's "soft, wrinkly body" (pp. 8–9). Sex that feels good in the novel is all sex in the family, that makes babies (Abeba eventually has fifteen), and that is sanctioned by church and home and community, by the warm world that recalls the shared life in the South.

There is another kind of sex in the novel, too. In what is a recurring primal scene described by many black women writers, Abeba is raped by her uncle when she is fifteen. He comes every week for a year and rapes her, because there is no father, no protection. Sex unprotected by family values is terrifying, evil, symbolized by the insinuating blues music so different from the hymns Abeba loves in church:

> I asked you for a kiss
> You gave me a smack
> Honey babe you got to learn
> To kiss back.
>
> [P. 49]

Arousal is only possible for Abeba if the chain of associations works, if the cues of family, church, and childhood are in place. The rest is not sex but exploitation, forming the associative chain: New York City, men drinking in bars or on street corners, the blues, which to Abeba are sleazy, the evil music of black men at loose ends.

Kate Stimpson's *Class Notes* offers a quite different illustration of the same point—that sexual feelings are elaborate creations, both social and private, rather than physical givens. The novel is one woman's early sexual history, step by faltering step. The heroine, Harriet, has to *learn* that there are lesbians, and that the current of her sexual feelings means she is one. Harriet cannot easily invent this idea of love for herself, though she is repeatedly disappointed by devastatingly described antierotic encounters with male lovers. Sex is social; in the male-worshiping world of Harriet's youth there are no sexual mores structured with a woman in mind.

Another example of an isolated yet socially mediated sexual development, *Yesterday's Lessons* by Sharon Isabell, is narrated by a young working-class woman who is poor and has little education. Gradually the narrator, Sharon, learns that the feeling she has for other women is called lesbianism, but the taboos surrounding her sexual longings for her girlfriend are numbing. Her social efforts to connect get converted into drinking bouts that make her sick or into double dates that are frustrating because it is the other girls who move and interest Sharon. But discrimination against women loving women is a very small part of what goes wrong for her as she tries again and again to get a sexual identity and a sexual life. Every time she tries to climb out of her social and sexual deprivation, she is thrown back again. She has good times; she is capable of deep feeling; but these things are like flowers stuck in a jar with hardly any water. By the end, it is clear that no matter what someone's particular erotic history may be, in this world each person's share in the pleasure of life is going to be small. "Where is the happiness? Who's got it? It doesn't have anything to do with being straight or gay" (p. 205).

There is a growing understanding among feminists that the recognition of gender as a significant political category in no way bypasses the crucial differences among women; of class, race, and sexual preference. Hence we would expect to find black women's descriptions of sexual experiences qualitatively different from white women's, working class from middle class, and, above all, straight women from gay women. However, recognition of these differences, though necessary, is not sufficient to predict what a person's sexual experience is like. In fact, these essential and politically important categories can be misleading, encouraging the already popular idea that each of these groups has unique sexual mores that isolate them from everyone else. They all share a gender training that is overwhelmingly pervasive. One can only insist that the novels exemplify the paradox which feminist theoreticians still struggle to understand: the personal is political, but this is not a simple equation. Sex is both more private and more public than is popularly acknowledged. On the one hand, the novelists describe how many sexual cues are asocial and arbitrary, the products of an individual's private sexual history, as unique as a fingerprint, as compelling as the imprinting of a duckling. On the other, they insist that sexual experiences are shared, social phenomena; they describe the unnecessarily desperate and lonely character of a sexual life that is isolated from the rest of experience, that is hidden behind social denial.

The black mother in *Let the Lion Eat Straw*, the repressed lesbian college girl in *Class Notes*, and the hard-bitten working-class girl of *Yesterday's Lessons* have little in common. However, in describing them, Southerland, Stimpson, and Isabell share a vision: None can locate her characters in a world where female sexuality has much chance of being explored or expanded. All three write of heroines who live with scarcity or assault and gradually find a way to survive in spite of it. They would agree that, in different ways, the conditions for *everyone's* sexuality are execrable.

Women, Too, Objectify Their Lovers: Sexism and Self-Hatred

Although women refuse to strip sex of its social and personal layers of meaning, a caveat: inevitably women novelists are mired in the very social contradictions they are concerned to name. Various permutations of sexist clichés about both men and women appear in the novels routinely, where they are often only half recognized, half examined. For example, will women really be destroyed if they explore anonymous sex, as the heroine of Judith Rossner's *Looking for Mr. Goodbar* is destroyed? Is male lustfulness murderous, as that book implies? Or are male lust and male murderousness falsely equated, in this novel and elsewhere, as part of our society's treasured illusion that male sexuality is like a bludgeon or a speeding train? A number of novels do begin to criticize received ideas about male sexuality. Anne Tyler, Ella Leffland, and Marge Piercy treat men and their sexual problems with a surprising degree of complexity and sympathy, considering the amount of enmity and distance between the sexes their books also assume. But it is as difficult for women as for men to imagine the sexual other. Women, traditionally adept at empathy, cannot finally claim a superiority in this field. Beyond male and female, objectification of others is a human dilemma, an urgent political issue confronting the entire species.

However, sexism toward men, including the objectification of male characters, is an insignificant category next to women's sexism toward women. If empathy has always been the female job, some of the novels have subtle ways of showing more sympathy to male characters than to female. For example, in *Adjacent Lives,* Ellen Schwamm has the versatility to enter a male consciousness. While there, she accepts everything. She loves her male hero almost as much as his mistress, her heroine. This is a novelistic triumph only until one sees the hero's wife through his eyes and then through Schwamm's. Schwamm hates the busty, dependent, insecure, yet lustful and lively wife as much as her hero does. Under the mask of empathy for a male hero, disgust for femaleness comes flowing out in a way that is old and sadly familiar, a crossing of the fine line between describing female self-consciousness, female self-dislike, and entering it, embracing it, accepting it without recourse to other ideas.

If *Adjacent Lives* is a novel that trembles on the verge of female self-loathing, Kate Millett's *Sita*[6] is a book that sinks right under. A daily, sometimes hourly, account of the painful end of a lesbian love affair, *Sita* is numbing to read but instructive to study. The more Millett admits she is wallowing in sexist clichés the more one expects this admission to turn into some kind of acknowledgment that there is danger in this self-hatred. But, amazingly, the book concludes by romanticizing the pain inherent in all love affairs based on sexist plays for power. Objectification of the loved one, gross belief in several forms of the double standard, covert phallic worship, solipsistic and paranoid sexual obsessions—all these are finally accepted because they are the truth and can be turned into art. Art is offered as the only kind of transcendence besides romanticized, pained sexuality.

Finally, though, attacking *Sita* is a cheap shot. If the book did not exist one would have to invent it as the extreme point of female sexism. No other writer has been so unapologetic about her female lust for power, her female boredom as soon as the loved one capitulates, her female romantic expectations—the notes, roses, phone calls meant to keep the relationship ritualized and mystified—to sharpen emotions and orgasms that would otherwise lose their edge. Let *Sita* stand as a sort of exorcism for the whole group of novels being discussed here. They necessarily reflect the sexism that is. It is a political task—not that of novels—to make the old sexual contract different. Women have had to enjoy sex in ways that were destructive to them. Instead of calling this masochism, one might say that it has been life affirming for women to embrace sex even on painful terms, to find ways to enjoy sex in spite of sexism, including their own.

Sex to Get Something Else

In *Memoirs of an Ex-Prom Queen,* Alix Kates Shulman writes about instrumental sex exchanged for a man's protection and support for childbearing and rearing. This traditional female compromise founds a family, which, in turn, becomes an alternative erotic center for the wife. For Shulman's heroine, Sasha, sex is displaced by children by an essential law of the female life cycle. The many women of Marilyn French's *The Women's Room* also sleep with their husbands to get the job of wife, and have children to keep the job. Unlike Shulman's, French's children are

6. Though *Sita* is autobiography, it also shows one direction the realist novel is taking. It represents an extreme point in the general interest in psychological realism, in reporting exactly how something feels.

those who come too soon, are difficult, and tie their mothers to the house like slaves.

If Shulman's novel is a novel of the cold war between wives and husbands, in French that war has become hot. Shulman's Sasha fakes orgasms, but French's women are so depressed and alienated that they are beyond this friendly/hostile subterfuge. In French, sex in the service of something else has become a frightful thing. Even the most serious efforts at love between men and women are hopelessly undermined as erotic encounters by the characters' despair and the author's cynicism.

These two novels have had an immense readership, but they are expressions of a kind of instrumental bond between the sexes that is in the process of decay. Few women now in their twenties can make the male-female bargain Sasha made in the 1950s and hope to have it kept. Outside prostitution, instrumental sex is a dwindling female option (though it can still be a female fate in the form of sexual harrassment at work). A few contemporary novels are self-conscious celebrations of the end to this ancient female dependence on erratic male chivalry. Almost all reflect this change at some level by the amount of space they lavish on exploring sex outside the boundaries of the old heterosexual contract.

Sex as Symbol

If women are wily and pragmatic about sex and its uses, some are also interested in writing about it symbolically. Sex has always been the sphere in which women were enjoined to find their meaning, the arena for their symbolic self-creation. However, the male tradition puts certain stumbling blocks in the way of this effort. Men's idea of sex as transcendence, sex as transformation, has often been linked to the kind of mystification that conceals fear of women and the desire to repress their sexuality. The move toward using sex as a metaphor for something beyond the flesh has usually culminated in the glorious moment when the male writer leaves his catalyst, the woman, behind. Some women writers, rebelling against this tradition of sex as transcendence, are writing about it as an irreducible experience, as a drama between people that resists the symbolic elaborations traditionally heaped upon it. Others are examining it for what it can imply. They find spiritual renewal, and other promises, hidden in sexual experience.

Like Lessing, a number of novelists make sex a central episode in a more general rejuvenation. Erica Jong's *Fear of Flying* is a fulsome and hectic version of this sex-as-rejuvenation idea. Leaving her husband behind, Jong's heroine follows one Adrian Goodlove who tells her, "I offer you an experience that could really change you" (p. 138). Jong satirizes this cult of experience, while cheerfully believing in it, too. Sex has been her reward for daring and is the yardstick on which her liberation is measured.[7]

In *Mrs. Munck,* Ella Leffland uses the same symbolic configurations with far greater subtlety than Jong. Her Mrs. Munck is driven by a desire for revenge against her first ravisher, an older man who quite literally ruined her life. After years of planning, when she gets her chance, she discovers that revenge is not particularly satisfying. Instead, she starts to discover the ways in which she once was and has continued to be complicitous with her destroyer. Being sexually dried up has hurt no one but herself. Instead of killing the old man, Mrs. Munck begins to explore the world again. She sleeps with a neighbor; she reassesses her body and its amazing capacities. The book's structure is based on the gradual thawing of a furious, frozen woman's body.

In contrast, Diane Johnson's *The Shadow Knows* represents a whole group of novels in which sex symbolizes male threat and female sexuality has no chance. The recently divorced heroine, N., lives in a cement-block housing project with her four small children. The reader has no way of knowing for certain if N.'s growing suspicions that someone is trying to kill her are the paranoid delusions of an abandoned, exhausted, anxious woman trapped at home with four children, or the rational constructions of a mind putting the evidence of slashed tires, besmirched front doors, and anonymous attacks together to form a logical whole. Near the end of the novel, N. is raped rather than murdered. The result is relief; a tension has been removed. By this meaningful placement, Johnson has described sex as an unwanted assault, one that is nevertheless sometimes a welcome relief. Laughably, this profound paradox has been called female masochism, the love of the attacker. Here, sex is the thing that keeps women indoors.

A number of these symbolic representations of sex confront each other in dialectical conversation in Mary Gordon's *Final Payments.* Because Isabel, the heroine, is Catholic, sex has always had an elaborate set of symbolic meanings for her. It is sin, woman's shame, selfishness. When Isabel falls in love, guilt overwhelms her sexual passion. Spiritual renewal depends on her finding some way to experience this passion without compromising her other fierce desire—for virtue. The novel's moral resolution is that of a lapsed Catholic who is, nonetheless, Jesuitical. Sex is recognized as a good in itself, a proper human cross to bear,

7. Kate Ellis makes the following important point: "[In the middle-class women's novels of the seventies,] the idea of female virtue rewarded by marriage is still present, in modified form, with sexual pleasure the new sign of membership in the feminist elect." In contrast, in Toni Morrison's novels "magnificent, poetic sex is experienced by . . . multifaceted misfits," in other words, sex is a part of life quite separate from any idea of reward or punishment. Black women characters are not punished by scarcity as often as white women; for them sex is usually an inevitable fate, varying from good to bad by laws that are beyond individual control (*In These Times* 4, no 6 [December 19, 1979–January 8, 1980], p. 23).

containing both ecstasy and sorrow. The novel insists on several levels of sexual feeling: the need to avoid assaultive, desperate sex and the sex which is mere relief; the need for spiritual rightness, for transcendent meaning in sexual contact; and the need to follow the body's lead, the body's own sense of propriety.

Given the variety of meanings symbolically assigned to sex in the novels, it is interesting that one traditional symbolic elaboration of sexuality is almost universally avoided: romance. There is a sharp split between high culture and low on this point.[8] While millions of women are reading popular romances that evoke magical feelings about male power and male protection, self-conscious women artists have long since firmly dismissed romantic excitement, routinely undercutting it by irony or parody or self-conscious criticism whenever it appears as an aspiration in their characters.[9]

Expansion: Sex Is Not the Only Profound Bodily Experience

"Sex" has usually meant genital sex. This, to some of the novelists, seems much too narrow an expression of the erotic potential in life. Certainly, sex is only a part of that general erotic rapture which stokes life's energies.[10] Sometimes in the novels, true eroticism is located elsewhere, perhaps in pregnancy, in birth, or in a variety of experiences with other women. The most sexually charged scene in Toni Morrison's *Sula* is between two pubescent girls who dig a hole together in the muddy earth, then cover it over again. Later in life these two recognize that their friendship was the depth experience, the sensually joyous, fruitful experience of their lives. In many of the other novels genital sex is similarly beside the point, not so much rejected as found limited or unavailable.

8. Few of the novels discussed here are likely to find their way into the hands of working-class women, white or black. Instead, many women read romantic fiction in which sex is carefully dished out, either as pleasurable rape or as a reward for the heroine when she has brought an essentially animalic man to heel. See Ann Barr Snitow, "Mass Market Romance: Pornography for Women Is Different," *Radical History Review* 20 (Spring/Summer 1979): 141–62; and Tania Modleski, "The Disappearing Act: A Study of Harlequin Romances," *Signs: Journal of Women in Culture and Society* 5, no. 3 (Spring 1980): 435–48. The plots of these novels depict the set of social moves necessary before a woman can relax her guard and enjoy sex. In this sense, these books, too, insist on the problem of proper emotional and social context in order for female sexual feelings to unfold.

9. The female skepticism about romance has a long history: the chastening of romantic illusion is a major theme of Jane Austen's *Northanger Abbey* and *Emma*, of Charlotte Brontë's *Villette*, and of George Eliot's *Middlemarch*. Black women writers have their own history of skepticism in relation to romance, since white women, not black, were the mystified objects of romance. See, e.g., Toni Morrison.

10. I am indebted to Dorothy Dinnerstein for discussing with me the differences between sex and eroticism: sex is only one of the possible expressions of the erotic, of the pleasures of infancy recalled.

Some of the fault lies in the very structure of heterosexual relations, in all those antierotic rituals and power plays the novels describe so devastatingly. But for a large number of the novelists, genital sex is not enough; they see women's expectations for ecstacy as having been pared down.

Dorothy Bryant's *Garden of Eros* enters the stream of consciousness of a blind woman having her baby alone on the floor of a rough cabin in the woods. Her husband, mysteriously and all too casually absent, is very present in her mind during the first few hours of contractions. She tenderly remembers their courtship, their first lovemaking. As the night progresses and the pains come faster and harder, she begins to get angry at her husband, only to forget him altogether as necessity calls forth a strength and simplicity of purpose in her. She gathers together all the things she will need—a piece of string to tie the cord, some water, a blanket. The baby comes well before the husband returns. He is a shadow beside the baby, beside the strength of the mother. Her rhythmic movement toward giving birth pushes the novel forward, a stirring physical event before which all other so-called procreative acts pale.

This passion emerges in a similar way in Margaret Atwood's *Surfacing.* In the early parts of the book, sexism and sex are so close as to be indistinguishable: "Prove your love, they say. You really want to marry me, let me fuck you instead. You really want to fuck, let me marry you instead. As long as there's a victory, some flag I can wave . . ." (p. 104). But the spiritually deadened heroine, the long-time victim of this kind of power-ridden sex, comes alive in the course of the book. She finds what she wants sex to be:

> I lie down, keeping the moon on my left hand and the absent sun on my right. He kneels, he is shivering. . . . He turns to curve over me; his eyes glint, he is shaking, fear or tensed flesh or the cold. I pull him down, . . . Heavy on me, warm stone, almost alive.
> "I love you," he says into the side of my neck, catechism. Teeth grinding, he's holding back, he wants it to be like the city, baroque scrollwork, intricate as a computer, but I'm impatient, pleasure is redundant, the animals don't have pleasure. I guide him into me, it's the right season, I hurry. [Pp. 190–91]

The use of a matriarchal goddess cult here, "the moon on my left hand . . . the sun on my right," is of a piece with a more general move among some feminists toward reasserting the very old idea that there is magical power in the female body, in female procreativity and nurturance. Whether or not the goddess can offer women an image of what profound bodily experiences are for, *Surfacing* has been a germinal book. If atavistic, it is also about a promise of human evolution. The Baroque sex of the city is civilized only in the worst sense of that word; it is dreary, decadent. Atwood's heroine returns to nature and myth looking for another outward path for human development.

The writers of this group have used their new freedom to be explicit about genital sex with skepticism and are not clear what a specifically female sexual openness will look like. Some are more sure than others that they want such a category to exist and to be lovingly elaborated, but all want to know, if men are unstable, a vanishing species, what other kinds of erotic richness life offers women besides closeness to these elusive or destructive others.

The novels that try to extend the boundaries of sexuality are expressing what until now has been primarily a female article of wisdom: the body is an animal that needs to be fed, to be held, also to be loved; one can never forget about it, pretend it is not there. Women, whose vocation it has been to be attuned to the slightest physical change in themselves (pregnancy), in their families (illness), in their infants (the need for constant nurturance), are quite naturally the sex to suggest that the varied joys of living in the body could and should be explored and extended.

Scarcity: The Enforced Sacrifice of Sex

Whatever the particular meaning allotted to sex, treating it symbolically and extending its range are acts of self-esteem. Nevertheless, the general point made earlier still prevails: most women novelists writing now are less interested in defining sex's elemental nature or value than in looking at how sex *happens* in a woman's life, at how it emerges as one element in a larger drama, the daily experiences of women.

For a number of these novelists, looking at how sex happens leads almost immediately to looking at how sex disappears from women's lives.[11] Where does it go? For the fortunate and the middle class, it goes into children, as in Shulman's *Memoirs of an Ex-Prom Queen* and Anne Tyler's *A Slipping Down Life;* it may also go into dedication to work and friends, as in Gail Godwin's *The Odd Woman.* For the poor, sex is overwhelmed by anxieties and struggles, as in Joyce Carol Oates's *Them,* Alice Walker's *Meridian,* and Marge Piercy's *The High Cost of Living.* Walker's heroine, Meridian, is one of the large number of women in these novels forced by circumstances to give up on sex. She begins as a young black girl who is curious about men and wants to love them; she ends up as a symbolic political catalyst for other black people, abandoning her interest in a private life. Walker does not romanticize this transformation. The man Meridian loves and who can arouse her deeply is the charming, sophisticated, politically active Truman. But a shared, sexual life with

11. Male writers also describe scarcity, the sexual elusiveness of women; the fact that both sexes share an obsession with the other's unavailability is a subject for further study.

Truman proves impossible. He cannot recognize what she is; cannot imagine her comradeship in the cause of black people; cannot, therefore, love her. His failure dooms them both to isolation and great sorrow. She is his destiny, but only in some future time neither of them will live to see. " 'I hate to think of you always alone' [Truman says to Meridian]. 'But that is my value,' said Meridian. 'Besides, all the people who are as alone as I am will one day gather at the river' " (p. 220).

Perhaps Marge Piercy, whose characters cannot even be romantic about a time when they will "gather at the river," is the clearest example of these writers who actively refuse to be metaphysical about sex. In *The High Cost of Living,* she insists instead that sex is a luxury some people in our society cannot afford. Good sex requires time, money, even education. Piercy's heroine, Leslie, is a graduate student in history first, a karate expert second, a lesbian third, and a feminist activist fourth. This order of things is not what she would wish, but it is necessary for her survival. Because she is female, gay, and working class, getting a chance to do interesting work means starving whole regions of her being. Eagerly upwardly mobile, Leslie is gradually disillusioned by what she sees of success, romance, and family. But she cannot figure out what else to want. Piercy shows both love and sex to be clearly inadequate when asked to fill a cultural gap this wide; she has measured Leslie's deprivations of spirit, of community, of money and found them too many. Love has starved.

Sex Is a Part of Life: Making the Best of the Unavoidable

While some of the novelists write about the scarcity of unalienated sexual experiences as a great sorrow, others take sex more for granted. Far from unattainable, it is unavoidable. In this group the problem is not how to find sex, the rare jewel, but how to convert as much of the steady stream of sex in which many women live into as good an experience as possible. Marilyn French, Diane Johnson, Toni Morrison, Joyce Carol Oates, Judith Rossner, Anne Tyler, and Ellease Southerland could be placed in this group. Another example is Lynda Schor, who, in her series of loosely connected stories, *Appetites,* assumes sex as a given in life and then searches for pleasurable possibilities hidden in this human condition. What interests Schor is that heterosexual sex is a shared ecstatic activity between two known enemies, man and woman, a situation either tragic or ridiculous. Schor emphasizes the ridiculous, but she is a serious satirist of the transaction between the sexes. In the story "Louise's Brownies," Lynda, a divorced woman with three children, and Alan, a divorced man, also with children but at a distance, are trying to have a love affair. When they sleep at his house, they have peace and brownies made by his maid Louise. But it is hard for Lynda to get a babysitter. When they sleep at her house, Lynda does not need a sitter, but then there are her three kids and the memory of Louise, that other exhausted housekeeper, cooking and cleaning for Alan on the other, richer side of town.

> We kiss, and then I shut the door to Alex's [a child's] room, as it's very close to mine and mine doesn't have a door that shuts, as it's also the living room and is connected with the kitchen and a small dining room. . . . By the time I'm finished, which is about two seconds, Alan is gone. Then I see his face peering down at me from the edge of my sleeping loft, which was built by my husband before we separated. . . . Alan is helping me remove my shirt when I notice a cockroach walking slowly along the molding ten feet above the ground, but directly above my head. I pick up my white diaphragm case and smash it. [Pp. 97–98]

Can there be sex within this architecture? In spite of the circumstances, Lynda wants Alan and Alan wants Lynda. They try very hard to ignore the fact that they disagree about everything and are living in utterly different social conditions. Things are too easy for Alan, too hard for Lynda. Her sexual feelings cannot survive in this unfriendly medium: "In a panic, I run through all my girl friends, trying to imagine which ones I might have a sexual relationship with in case I can't be civil to men anymore" (p. 108). The story ends when sex between Lynda and Alan has finally become impossible.

Nevertheless, in Lynda Schor's work, sex keeps coming back. There is reliability in the sudden flare-ups of sexual feelings right in the middle of the hostile territory of the sex war. It often takes the exhausted heroine by surprise that the irritated or irritating man she happens to be with—husband or lover—suddenly propels himself in her direction. But for all the inconvenience, sex is a momentary pleasure, a truce that she enjoys, a necessary part of life, like taking care of the children and eating.

Conclusions and Projections

What generalizations emerge about the women novelists now conceptualizing female sexual experiences? All are breaking new ground by openly describing female desires and female deprivations, but none universalizes sex. The women's movement has removed the universal "I" from their vocabulary. Most are acutely sensitive to women's shifting social reality. They write about sexuality, not as an isolated entity, but as a complex occasion in which certain words, thoughts, rooms, memories, and predictable tensions between men and women play as large a part as the body or any ideal of love.

Most of the novels treat the relationship between the sexes as a situation in crisis. While both romance and the sex that is only to get something else have been analyzed, criticized, and largely rejected, new sexual contracts between men and women have not been written. Instead, almost all the novelists describe sex with men as so encrusted with difficulties that only the sacrifice of self can make it work. This price now seems too high. A sexual episode is pleasant, but after the first burst of excitement, too many things have to go right before sexual feelings can deepen. The new female mobility and feminist ideology have only exacerbated the contradictions in standing gender arrangements. The atmosphere is increasingly experimental. Women are more and more openly writing about how they love each other and make love to each other. They are also looking for erotic pleasure in other experiences besides genital sex. If some of their experiments are forced on them by oppression, others are exploratory and freely chosen.

In the realm of the symbolic and the visionary, many wish to put together in their novels experiences which cannot yet cohabit in any actual woman's life. This making of visionary recombinations is one species of political work. In 1979 feminist theorists do not agree on whether their long-term goal is to maximize female identity or to·reject gender as a primary category. Novelists can explore the possible consequences of these very different directions. In *Surfacing,* for example, Margaret Atwood sacrifices sexual pleasure to motherhood as the more profound experience and source of female identity. In *Woman on the Edge of Time,* Marge Piercy examines the opposite choice, showing a society of the future in which mothering has been diffused into the life of the community freeing sexuality to become an area of both play and profound feeling.

A whole crop of still younger writers, their roots firmly in the women's movement, are refusing to accept the splits and compromises so carefully catalogued by the present transitional generation. This newest work is not properly the subject of this piece. Most of it is to be found in stories, those telegrams from the front line of change. But, though novels gestate slowly, increasingly women novelists are imagining ways of joining the physical, social, and spiritual dimensions of existence. They are also insisting on the fusion of the realistic and the visionary in the form of their art. Doris Lessing, Toni Morrison, Margaret Atwood, Marge Piercy, and a number of others begin with the traditional female concern with personal relationships and the details of daily life and then expand these concerns to include a wider and wider swath of human experience. A prediction: social realism, every group's first phase of artistic self-consciousness in the novel form, will not be abandoned by women novelists but enlarged by them to include visionary projections, recreations of the very idea of gender.

Department of English
Livingston College, Rutgers University

Review Essay

Biological Influences on Human Sex and Gender

Susan W. Baker

The central question of this review essay is the degree to which sex dimorphic behaviors are environmentally or biologically determined. Asking such a question need not, nor should it, compromise the search for equality between men and women. The term "sex dimorphic behaviors" needs clarification, for they comprise not one, but three groupings of behavioral or psychic phenomena: (1) gender identity, generally defined as the unified and persistent experience of one's self as male, female, or ambivalent; (2) gender-role behavior, the actions and activities that indicate to the self or others the degree to which one is male, female, or ambivalent; and (3) sexual object choice, usually heterosexual, homosexual, or bisexual. (For reasons of space, this review will take up neither transsexualism nor sex differences in cognition.)[1] Researchers in the field of psychoendocrinology investigate to what extent, and in what ways, biology or rearing influences each of these different phenomena.

Despite the fact that this field of inquiry is relatively new, a certain amount of knowledge is commonly held to be true. First, dimorphic biological development, which differentiates females from males, follows certain patterns in animals and humans. Except for the brain, which has yet to be studied in humans, a striking concordance seems to exist be-

1. Obviously, this review essay cannot cover every aspect of a complex field. Instead, it attempts to outline some central issues and present some important data concerning them.

tween animal and human development in this area. Next, these unfolding sequences consist of particular stages. They are: (*a*) The genetic, a female pattern of XX sex chromosomes or a male pattern of XY chromosomes. Later, we will deal with another genetic variant, XO, in Turner's syndrome. (*b*) Gonadal differentiation, from the primordial gonad in the fetus to ovaries in the female and testes in the male. (*c*) The prenatal hormonal environment. The male in utero is exposed to a high level of virilizing hormones, androgens, and testosterones, while the female is not. (*d*) The anatomical. The fetus, which has had the potential for both female (Müllerian) and male (Wolffian) internal reproductive systems, develops one of them. An absence of high levels of androgens leads to the Müllerian system; the presence of them in quantity to the Wolffian. Normally, external genitalia next appear from a structure, with a dimorphic capacity, called the genital tubercle. Again, the absence of androgens results in a development along female lines; a presence of androgens in development along male lines (see fig. 1). However, as we shall see below, in some clinical syndromes the anatomy of the external genitalia is ambiguous. Accordingly, sex anatomy itself becomes one of parameters along which we are usually forced to make the distinction between female and male. (*e*) The postnatal hormonal environment. The biological importance of this becomes especially clear during adolescence, where elevated levels of specific female and male hormones are responsible for secondary sex characteristics. This is also the time during which the gonads assume their mature reproductive capacity.

As the individual, both before and after birth, goes through these five stages, he or she normally has "concordance." That is, the chromosomes, the gonads, the prenatal hormonal environment, the reproductive systems, and the postnatal secondary sex characteristics all line up consistently in female, or male, patterns. However, some individuals are

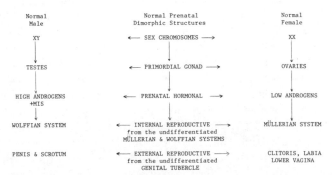

FIG. 1.—Prenatal sex dimorphic development in normal males and females. The androgen produced by the testes which cause the undifferentiated reproductive systems to differentiate along male lines is testosterone. The testes also make a Müllerian Inhibiting Substance (MIS), which causes regression of the Müllerian system in males.

"discordant." That is, at some stages they receive female, at other male, biological influences. The data base for the literature that we will survey has been these discordant individuals. Contemporary psychoendocrinology has focused on those who break, rather than represent, the statistical average. In other words, nature has contrived errors in the usual human development that in some ways mimic the experiments animal researchers have devised in their laboratories.

Six categories of discordancy, or six special human populations, emerge from a study of the literature. Four represent diagnosed, clinical syndromes of some genetic or endogenous, that is, internal, disorder of prenatal development: congenital, adrenal hyperplasia (CAH); complete androgen insensitivity, or testicular feminization (TF); partial androgen insensitivity, or Reifenstein's syndrome; and Turner's syndrome, or gonadal dygenesis (see fig. 2). The other two have disorders of the prenatal environment, which may never have been diagnosed and which the exogenous (i.e., external) administration of feminizing or virilizing hormones during the mother's pregnancy has induced. Each population reflects a different interaction between the three sex dimorphic behaviors and the influence of biological or environmental factors upon them. Moreover, each population has contributed data that have allowed various hypotheses to be generated about human sex and gender and about the importance of biological and environmental variables.

Before our presentation of the data and discussion, we wish to note that sex dimorphic behaviors are only those generally found to be more descriptive than not, more often than not for *groups* of normal males and females. The range of individual variation, and the overlap between the behavioral modes, is enormous among those persons with no known "abnormality" of prenatal environment. The "dimorphic" behaviors are those tendencies that differentiate large groups of females and males adequately enough to be labeled.

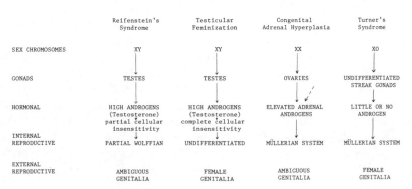

	Reifenstein's Syndrome	Testicular Feminization	Congenital Adrenal Hyperplasia	Turner's Syndrome
SEX CHROMOSOMES	XY	XY	XX	XO
GONADS	TESTES	TESTES	OVARIES	UNDIFFERENTIATED STREAK GONADS
HORMONAL	HIGH ANDROGENS (Testosterone) partial cellular insensitivity	HIGH ANDROGENS (Testosterone) complete cellular insensitivity	ELEVATED ADRENAL ANDROGENS	LITTLE OR NO ANDROGEN
INTERNAL REPRODUCTIVE	PARTIAL WOLFFIAN	UNDIFFERENTIATED	MÜLLERIAN SYSTEM	MÜLLERIAN SYSTEM
EXTERNAL REPRODUCTIVE	AMBIGUOUS GENITALIA	FEMALE GENITALIA	AMBIGUOUS GENITALIA	FEMALE GENITALIA

FIG. 2.—Prenatal sex dimorphic development in four clinical syndromes

Hypotheses

Psychoendocrinologists have been working with three major hypotheses:

1. Gender identity is *not* determined by chromosomes or by gonadal or prenatal hormonal influence but by rearing. Further, there is a critical period, between eighteen months and two years of life, after which successful sex reassignment will be difficult, if not impossible. However, it is not known if this irreversibility after two years is determined by the child's experience or by the parents' needs. Gender identity is essentially consolidated by three to four years of age.

2. In contrast, gender-role behavior is influenced by prenatal hormonal environment. This difference in biological influence may be related to the fact that gender identity, unlike gender-role behaviors, requires a psychic state of self-awareness, for which there is no known analogue in the nonhuman animal world and for which there may be no biological etiology.

3. Sexual orientation is generally subsumed under gender role. For our purposes now, it is better considered separately as a dimorphic behavior of sexual object choice that usually appears in adolescence, with obscure relationships to antecedents or influences in earlier behavior.[2] Most researchers in this field think that rearing (i.e., social and environmental factors) determines sexual orientation more than chromosomal, gonadal, or hormonal factors.

Evidence from Clinical Studies

Evidence from the six discordant populations has led to these hypotheses. Let us summarize the evidence from each population in turn.

1. *Children and adolescents with a history of elevated prenatal androgens.* The only clinical population that has been systematically studied with a history of endogenous prenatal virilization in genetic females is CAH, which is a genetically transmitted condition. The adrenal cortex, unable to produce normal amounts of cortisol from early in fetal life, is therefore overstimulated by the brain to produce elevated amounts of adrenal androgens. The condition occurs in both males and females, but males look normal at birth. In contrast, the elevated levels of adrenal androgens have prenatally acted on the genital tubercle in females, who are then born with ambiguous genitalia. Thus females are usually identified at birth and require early surgical correction of the external genitalia for

2. F. Whitam, "Child Indicators of Male Homosexuality," *Archives of Sexual Behavior* 6 (1977): 89–96.

a normal female appearance. All affected individuals require lifelong management with cortisone replacement to avoid continued postnatal virilization. The internal reproductive system that differentiates (in females) is female, implying that affected girls do not have sufficient androgens during the earlier prenatal critical period for Wolffian reproductive systems to develop.

The relevant evidence from this population for the hypotheses we have outlined follows. Two clinical follow-up studies used semistructured interviews with mothers and affected female children to assess long-term (current and retrospective) behavior patterns in affected children versus experimental controls.[3] Both studies found that gender identity was female in all cases, and that affected children differed significantly from the controls in various areas of gender-role behaviors, with highly increased incidence of tomboyism, elevated activity level, preference for boys as playmates, little interest in doll play, and generally low interest in infants, etc. Sexual orientation was not examined, because the children were too young; only a very few were adolescents in either sample. However, Ehrhardt and Baker reported an adolescent follow-up of the same sample of affected children, now with a mean age of sixteen years.[4] The general pattern of findings was that both interest in and experience with such heterosexual activities as dating, necking, petting and intercourse was delayed. Of the five girls who were not interested, four were the four youngest included in the study. The fifth was a twenty-year-old socially withdrawn girl who avoided close relationships with both men and women. Only one woman reported homosexual fantasies or experiences. She had had both heterosexual and homosexual relationships. It was interesting that while in childhood most of the affected children had reported little interest in their appearance and devoted minimal effort in self-grooming and dressing attractively, this had changed in about half the girls at the time of the follow-up.

Money and Schwartz also reported findings in an adolescent follow-up study of CAH girls.[5] Their findings were quite similar overall, but with a slightly higher incidence of homosexual relationships. How-

3. A. Ehrhardt, R. Epstein, and J. Money, "Fetal Androgens and Female Gender Identity in the Early Treated Andrenogenital Syndrome," *Johns Hopkins Medical Journal* 123, no. 3 (1968): 160–67; A. A. Ehrhardt and S. W. Baker, "Fetal Androgens, Human Central Nervous Differentiation, and Behavioral Sex Differences," in *Sex Differences in Behavior,* ed. R. C. Friedman, R. M. Richart, and R. L. Vande Wiele (New York: John Wiley & Sons, 1974).

4. A. A. Ehrhardt and S. W. Baker, "Prenatal Androgen Exposure and Future Adolescent Behavior" (paper presented at the International Congress of Sexology, Montreal, 1976).

5. J. Money and M. Schwartz, "Dating, Romantic and Nonromantic Friendships, and Sexuality in 17 Early-treated Adrenogenital Females, Aged 16–25," in *Congenital Adrenal Hyperplasia,* ed. P. A. Lee et al. (Baltimore: University Park Press, 1977), pp. 419–31.

ever, the incidence remained quite low, and it cannot be concluded that the incidence is significantly greater than would be found in a nonrandom appropriate control sample of equal size. Neither study used a control group, but both demonstrated nonetheless that the affected children's histories of generally tomboyish behavior in no way *determined* a homosexual object choice in adolescence. Most girls were heterosexual in orientation.

The CAH girls in the above studies were all reared as females. What happens to such girls if the syndrome is not accurately diagnosed in early life and they are mistakenly reared as males? The virilization of the external genitalia can be sufficient at times for this to occur. Money and Daley reported findings on a sample of CAH females unambiguously reared as males.[6] They all had a male gender identity, appropriate male gender-role behaviors, and a heterosexual (for gender identity and rearing) sexual object choice.

Thus, from clinical studies on fetally virilized genetic females gender identity was concordant with sex of rearing, gender-role behaviors appeared to be influenced by prenatal environment but were within the range of normal tomboyish girls' behaviors and in no way bizarre, and sexual orientation in most cases was heterosexual to rearing and gender identity.

2. *Children and adolescents with a history of androgen insensitivity.* Two clinical populations that have been studied fall into this category: the syndrome of complete androgen insensitivity or testicular feminization (TF) and partial androgen insensitivity (Reifenstein's syndrome). Testicular feminization is a quite rare genetically transmitted condition. Individuals with it have (see fig. 2) normal male chromosomes, gonads, and prenatal hormonal levels. However, the cells of their bodies are unable to respond to the elevated gonadal androgens prenatally, and as a result they do not virilize. The testes in normal males make an additional substance called the Müllerian Inhibiting Substance (MIS), produced normally in TF individuals, which is responsible for the lack of differentiation of the Müllerian system. Thus, these individuals in later life do not have reproductive capacity but can have a normal sexual relationship (as the external genitalia are female) and adopt their babies. Masica, Money, and Ehrhardt studied a clinical sample of ten TF girls reared as females.[7] On follow up, gender identity was female in all cases; gender-role behaviors were female, that is, not characterized by the "virilized"[8]

6. J. Money and J. Daley, "Hyperadrenocortical 46 XX Hermaphroditism with Penile Urethra: Psychological Studies in Seven Cases, Three Reared as Boys, Four as Girls," in Lee et al., pp. 433–46.

7. D. Masica, J. Money, and A. A. Ehrhardt, "Fetal Feminization and Female Gender Identity in the Testicular Feminizing Syndrome of Androgen Insensitivity," *Archives of Sexual Behavior* 1, no. 2 (1971): 131–42.

8. The term "virilization" is generally used in the animal and human literature for

behavior patterns reported in the CAH-affected individuals. Sexual orientation was heterosexual (by sex of rearing and gender identity) in all cases. Many went on to marry and adopt babies.

3. *Reifenstein's syndrome.* These individuals have a genetically trans-mitted syndrome of partial androgen insensitivity. These individuals, like the CAH females, are identified at birth because of abnormal (am-biguous) genitalia. Genetic and gonadal males who were incompletely virilized prenatally, they have been raised as either males or females. Ideally the decision as to rearing would depend upon the viability of the development of the external genitalia for future sexual functioning. However they have been raised, they generally require some surgical correction of the genitalia. Money and Ogunro interviewed ten subjects with partial androgen insensitivity, eight reared as males and two as females.[9] Nine of the ten subjects' gender identity was concordant with sex of rearing, in spite of severe functional genital difficulties, with four of those raised as males having a "clitoral-sized phallus." One female reported herself as ambivalent about her gender identity. She had three affected siblings who had publically reannounced their gender identity from female to male in adulthood. The authors speculated that this may have contributed to her ambivalence. Gender-role behaviors were gen-der appropriate to sex of rearing in all cases. Sexual orientation was exclusively heterosexual in eight of the nine subjects with any sexual experience. Several subjects were married and were parents by adop-tion. One subject, who had one lesbian experience of brief duration early in her teen years, expressed no interest in having another lesbian ex-perience, but she also had severe doubts about being accepted coitally as a woman.

4. *Turner's syndrome, or gonadal dysgenesis.* This is the last of the clini-cal populations with a genetic or endogenous disorder that we will dis-cuss. Turner's-syndrome individuals represent something of a special case compared with the other clinical groups; these individuals are miss-ing the second sex chromosome completely, or are genetically mosaic (i.e., some cells are missing the second sex chromosome, some cells may have a normal chromosomal complement, and some have other combi-nations of normal or abnormal sex chromosomal complements). Indi-

---

those hormonally responsive behaviors that are generally assumed to be most characteristic of males (such as a high degree of rough-and-tumble play in childhood in nonhuman primate males). Defeminization is used to describe a situation where behaviors generally assumed to be more characteristic of females are decreased in frequency by a hormonal manipulation. Most of the human dimorphic behavioral changes we refer to seem to fall most appropriately into the nomenclature of virilization rather than defeminization. An example in humans of defeminization rather than virilization would be if fetally virilized females had loss or severe impairment of menstrual cyclicity.

9. J. Money and B. Ogunro, "Behavioral Sexology: Ten Cases of Genetic Male Inter-sexuality with Impaired Prenatal and Pubertal Androgenization," *Archives of Sexual Behav-ior* 3, no. 3 (1974): 181–205.

viduals with this clinical condition are also not necessarily identified at birth. There is no abnormality of the external genitalia, but there are other associated features which may lead to an early diagnosis and always lead to a diagnosis by early adolescence. The associated features can include kidney and heart abnormalities and other dysmorphic features such as a webbed neck and moderate short stature. The degree to which an affected child displays any or all of these features varies widely. The chromosomal abnormality leads to undifferentiated or poorly differentiated gonads prenatally. Thus these children do not have reproductive capacity and do not develop secondary sex characteristics or menstruate without hormone replacement. It is for this reason the condition is recognized in early adolescence.

Ehrhardt, Greenberg, and Money evaluated developmental behavior patterns in fifteen Turner's-syndrome girls, using matched controls.[10] All subjects were unambiguously reared as females, and all had a female gender identity. If prenatal hormonal environment plays a predispositional influencing role in later preferred gender-role behaviors (hypothesis 2), one would assume that Turner's girls would be the least "defeminized," as they are the most likely to have the lowest amounts of prenatal gonadal hormones that could have any defeminizing effect on the brain. In this study, gender-role behaviors of affected subjects differed significantly from controls in the areas of an elevated interest in appearance, a lower frequency of active outdoor play, and decreased fighting. The nonsignificant trends in gender-role behaviors were all in the expected direction of a lower frequency of being labeled a tomboy, preferring or content to be a girl, a higher interest in "frilly dresses," extensive preference for girls rather than boys as playmates, play with only dolls versus boys' toys, and a strong, actively expressed interest in infant care. Although the sample was young, among those who were adolescents there were no reports of homosexual fantasies or experiences in either affected children or controls.

5. *Children exposed to exogenous feminizing hormones prenatally.* In certain animal species, in both males and females, progesterone can antagonize androgen action under certain circumstances.[11] Therefore, it was hypothesized that progesterone might have a similar effect in humans. Yalom, Green, and Fisk, in a double-blind study of the offspring of diabetic mothers treated with diethylbestrol plus progesterone during pregnancy, reported findings that seem to support the hypotheses of an antiandrogenizing effect of progesterone upon some aspects of human

10. A. Ehrhardt, N. Greenberg, and J. Money, "Female Gender Identity and Absence of Fetal Gonadal Hormones: Turner's Syndrome," *Johns Hopkins Medical Journal* 126, no. 5 (1970): 237–48.
11. J. A. Resko, "Fetal Hormones and Their Effect on the Differentiation of the Central Nervous System in Primates, *Federation Proceedings* 34 (1975): 1650–55.

gender-role behavior.[12] The twenty hormone-exposed males (aged sixteen to seventeen) were compared with a matched control group. The treated males were reported to be somewhat less assertive and aggressive and had decreased athletic coordination, decreased overall "masculine" interests, and less heterosexual experience compared with controls.

There were similar findings in a second study.[13] Here the subjects had been exposed to progesterone prenatally in mothers with preeclamptic toxemia. The authors reported findings on both males and females with a matched control group: male subjects had a significantly decreased interest in dating and marriage, females a decreased interest in tomboyish behavior and an increased interest in appearance. The most recent study in this area was reported by Meyer-Bahlburg, Grisanti, and Ehrhardt and Ehrhardt, Grisanti, and Meyer-Bahlburg.[14] The authors looked at males ($N=13$) and females ($N=15$) exposed prenatally to medroxy-progesterone acetate (MPA) in a double-blind study with matched controls. Because the subjects were eight to fourteen years of age, data on sexual orientation were not available. As in previous studies, gender identity was not affected, but there were some apparent treatment effects associated with gender-role behaviors in girls. Treated girls showed a lower incidence than the controls of being labeled a tomboy and a greater preference for feminine clothing styles. Hormone-exposed boys did not differ from controls.

6. *Children exposed to erogenous virilizing hormones prenatally.* Ehrhardt and Money reported findings on ten genetic females exposed prenatally to exogenously administered synthetic progestins.[15] The hormones were given to the mothers during pregnancy because of threatened miscarriages. Some of the children evidenced signs of the prenatal virilization at birth, having an enlarged clitoris. Those who required surgery had it within the first year of life. There was no question of postnatal virilization, and these girls did not require medical follow-up or management. Subjects were matched with controls; the age range at follow-up was four to fourteen years. All girls had a female gender identity.

12. I. Yalom, R. Green, and N. Fisk, "Prenatal Exposures to Female Hormones: Effect on Psychosexual Development in Boys," *Archives of General Psychiatry* 28 (1973): 554–61.

13. J. U. Zussman, P. P. Zussman, and K. Dalton. "Post-pubertal Effects of Prenatal Administration of Progesterone" (paper presented at the meeting of the Society for Research in Child Development, Denver, 1975).

14. H. F. L. Meyer-Bahlburg, G. C. Grisanti, and A. A. Ehrhardt, "Prenatal Effects of Sex Hormones on Human Male Behavior: Medroxyprogesterone Acetate (MPA)," *Psychoneuroendocrinology* 2 (1977): 381–90; A. A. Ehrhardt, G. C. Grisanti, and H. F. L. Meyer-Bahlburg, "Prenatal Exposure to Medroxyprogesterone Acetate (MPA) in Girls," ibid., pp. 391–98.

15. A. A. Ehrhardt and J. Money, "Progestin-induced Hermaphroditism: IQ and Psychosexual Identity in a Study of Ten Girls," *Journal of Sexual Research* 3 (1967): 83–100.

The gender-role findings were similar to those in the populations of CAH girls, with a significant tendency in the subject population, as opposed to controls, toward a higher activity level, long-term tomboyish behavior, etc.

This study is important in that it decreases the possibility that post-natal virilization or long-term medical management, with the consequent parental anxiety, is responsible in any way for the gender-role findings in the CAH children. The genital ambiguity at birth was also less severe and more easily correctable with one procedure in those cases requiring surgery. Thus, the parents were less likely to have long-term lurking fears regarding their daughters as being in any way "at risk" for later problems.

Reinisch and Karow, using the Cattell Personality Inventory, studied twenty-six boys and forty-five girls aged five to seventeen who had been exposed prenatally to various combinations of synthetic progestogens and estrogens.[16] They used untreated siblings as controls. No treated children evidenced any sign of a genital anomaly. Many of the mothers did not recall having taken any drugs during pregnancy. The authors found significant treatment effects: male and female subjects *mainly* exposed to progestogens were more "independent," "sensitive," "self-assured," "individualistic," and "self-sufficient," while male and female subjects exposed primarily to estrogens were more "group oriented" and "group dependent." The authors did not report findings on gender identity or gender-role behaviors. However, the reported findings are of interest in that they indicate a behavioral consequence to prenatal hormone exposure in areas not generally considered sex dimorphic. This study raises the possibility that general temperamental predispositions in human behavior may be influenced by aspects of the prenatal hormonal environment.

The 5 α-reductase deficit of male pseudohermaphroditism. The "state of the art" was at the point we have described when the Imperato-McGinley et al. study of a new population of male pseudohermaphrodites was published.[17] The controversial study has been widely publicized, with accompanying distortions and misrepresentations in the popular press. This is not that surprising, for the authors offered findings and proposed conclusions that challenged the basic tenets of the field and leaned very far toward "biological determinism," a view with important sociopolitical implications that prior psychoendocrine findings had never supported. For these reasons, the study merits a separate and detailed treatment here.

16. J. M. Reinisch and W. G. Karow, "Prenatal Exposure to Synthetic Progestins and Estrogens: Effects on Human Development," *Archives of Sexual Behavior* 6 (1977): 89–96.
17. J. Imperato-McGinley et al., "Androgens and the Evolution of Male-Gender Identity among Male Pseudohermaphrodites with 5 α-Reductase Deficiency," *New England Journal of Medicine* 300, no. 22 (1979): 1233–70.

Imperato-McGinley and their co-workers identified a group of thirty-eight male pseudohermaphrodites from twenty-three interrelated families in the Dominican Republic whose condition is genetically transmitted as an autosomal recessive trait. Affected males are born with a clitoris-like phallus and a bifid (incompletely developed) scrotum, with the testes either descended or not. Their enzymatic defect (the 5 α-reductase deficit) affects the conversion of the normal amounts of testosterone that the gonads make prenatally into another androgen, dihydrotestosterone, which is meant to act directly on the prenatal genital tubercle and to cause differentiation along male lines. The authors were able to interview thirty-three affected subjects and obtained retrospective data in two villages by interviewing subjects and other men and boys from those villages as controls. Other family members, wives, and girl friends were interviewed whenever possible.

The major findings from their interview data were: (1) Nineteen out of thirty-three subjects from the two villages had been "unambiguously reared" as females. (2) Adequate interview data were available on eighteen of the nineteen subjects. Of these eighteen, seventeen had successfully changed to a male gender identity and sixteen to a male gender role. (3) The seventeen subjects who changed gender identity recalled awareness of being different from other girls from age seven to twelve. (4) This awareness was usually associated in their minds with some incontrovertible evidence of body differences, for example, testes descending, lack of breast development, virilization of the body with the onset of adolescence. (5) The change in gender role to a male pattern generally took place either during puberty or in the postpubertal period. (6) The change in gender identity had an earlier onset, was more gradual, and spanned a longer period of time as the affected individual's body underwent the progressive development of male rather than female secondary sex characteristics of adolescence. (7) The age of onset of sexual behaviors, masturbation, morning erections, intercourse, etc., was not different between those subjects raised as girls and those raised as boys and not appreciably different from normal male controls. (8) Only one subject maintained a female gender identity. (9) All but two subjects displayed "heterosexual" sexual behavior, that is, attraction to and sexual relationships with women, following the change in gender identity to male.

The authors concluded from these findings: (1) In man, the relative influences of hormonal factors and environmental factors in the determination of gender identity remains unanswered. (2) In a laissez-faire environment, when sex of rearing is contrary to the testosterone-indicated biologic sex, the biologic sex prevails if the normal testosterone-induced activation of puberty is permitted to occur. (3) The extent of androgen exposure of the brain in utero, during the early postnatal period, and at puberty has more effect in determining male

gender identity than does sex of rearing. (4) Gender identity is not
unilaterally fixed in early childhood but evolves until stabilized with the
events of puberty.

The first question this provocative study raises is, "Are these affected children truly unambiguously reared?" It is necessary to establish
firmly that they are if the data are conclusively to challenge the "critical
period" hypothesis which delineates an age, the outside limits of which
are widely believed not to extend beyond three to four years of life,
within which gender identity is firmly and irrevocably fixed if rearing
has been unambivalent. Other discussions of these data have pointed out
that the 5 α-reductase affected subjects are not genitally normal as
females at birth.[18] All have clitoromegaly (an enlarged clitoris) and a
bifid scrotum with a urogenital sinus. In a retrospective study, it is impossible to assess clearly how the parents and extended family encompass or explain the observable facts of abnormal genital morphology at
birth. Further, in a highly sex-stereotyped culture where girls marry
early (often by the age of thirteen) and have a relatively rigid role definition of bearing children and taking care of the home, what fantasies of
the future for these children do the parents have where the affected
children lack a vagina, obviously making them incapable of normal
intercourse and childbearing?

The authors note that after enough affected children had undergone puberty, the dramatic transitions of virilization rather than feminization, the culture labeled the affected children both retrospectively and
at birth as "guevedoce" (eggs at twelve), "guevote" (penis at twelve), or
"machihembra" (first woman, then man). Where no treatment or medical intervention is available, cultures must encompass and explain deviant individuals. Over some period of time, this apparently happened in
the Dominican Republic. The question, however, as to whether the affected children were actually experienced from infancy on as completely
normal females by family and peers, and reared as such prior to this
labeling, appears unanswerable using the methods available in this study
of human subjects. Even if it were possible to do the requisite prospective
study, we have very little idea of how the self-sense of gender identity is
conveyed to children. For example, babies, by seven months of life, are
able to distinguish male faces from female faces.[19] We do not know,
however, whether this perceptual feat is learned in some way or represents a behavioral expression of some biologically given internal
schemata.

In summary, it appears unlikely that the genital malformation was
completely unnoticed by the surrounding culture. The affected children

18. J. Wilson, "Sex Hormones and Sexual Behavior," *New England Journal of Medicine*
300, no. 22 (1979): 1269–70.
19. J. F. Fagan, "Infants' Recognition of Invariant Features of Faces," *Child Development* 47 (1976): 627–38.

were not normal girls until they were affected by the male hormonal activation of puberty. Next, we can assume that the affected children in early childhood most likely did not behave like most girls in that culture. The authors report that girls and boys play together until the age of about seven, at which point girls are expected to begin doing some prescribed female domestic tasks. If the affected children behave according to the gender-role patterns in childhood of other fetally virilized children, we would expect these children to be somewhat resistant to the change other girls experienced and also to be engaged in active early play more typical of male playmates than female playmates. In fact, the two 5 α-reductase children followed at The New York Hospital by New and Levine had exactly this pattern of early and long-term tomboyish, active, rough-and-tumble play, in spite of the fact that both had their testes removed early in life. These data would seem to indicate that whatever the parents' experience of their affected child's genital appearance, their reactions and questions, even if largely repressed or unconscious, could be exacerbated by the child's behavioral proclivities throughout childhood.

As is true in the study of any clinical population, there are issues regarding the interpretations and generalizations of these data for the accurate understanding of the affected individuals and their families. Since these data come from another culture, there may be relevant factors and issues that will not come to light without the inclusion of anthropological studies. Moreover, it has been of less importance to have all the data to be able to make appropriate medical decisions, as long as medical management is unavailable to these affected individuals in other cultures. However, as more of these individuals have access to medical facilities and are diagnosed early, having full information is critical since the medical decisions that might be made will have enormous implications for the individuals' lives. For example, if the authors are correct in regarding the "prescriptive" role of biology in these affected individuals, one would have to recommend to parents that the children be reared as males, in spite of the fact that they would grow up with an obvious irreparable severe genital anomaly and would not be able to have normal intercourse or reproductive capacity in adulthood.

The other major issue pertaining to the 5 α-reductase individuals is that of the interpretations and generalizations made from these data and applied within the field of psychoendocrine studies and more broadly by other researchers interested in the nature/nurture controversy. This research represents the first time that a biological "prescription" for later dimorphic behavior in humans has been proposed as a scientific fact based on a study of humans. This study has been related to discussions of nature and nurture for unaffected individuals by many individuals both in and outside of the scientific community, and many proponents of this view draw heavily on evidence from the animal studies, which the human studies in some ways parallel. However, it is far from clear that what we learn from human studies can be translated easily to animal studies or vice versa. For example, (1) we do not know yet if there are morphologic sex differences in human brains (or the implications of such differences if they exist) as have been found in nonhuman animals; (2) as previously mentioned, many of the "dimorphic" behaviors studied in humans have no known analogies in other species, such as gender identity and some gender-role behaviors.

In the process of making theories one always hopes to be able to compare animal findings with findings from human studies in order to utilize the carefully controlled, methodologically sophisticated animal work. For example, the data from animal studies indicating differences in female and male brains raise the question as to whether this is true for humans, etc. It is critically important to keep in mind that although we study individuals who have clinical conditions that in some ways re-semble some features of the carefully controlled studies in other mam-mals, we do *not* know (1) how or if data from nonhuman mammals relate to human beings; (2) to what extent the human data accurately parallel features of the animal studies (as we are unable to use biologic controls to limit compounding effects of biological and environmental factors in humans); or (3) the degree to which our observations, mostly retrospec-tive of "deviant" behavior patterns in humans, represent "pure biologic" influences, or possibly relatively mild biological predispositional factors that then are inextricably confounded by the subsequent inter-relationship of child's disposition and parental and other environmental reactions.

While it *is* appropriate to make hypotheses and attempt to generate principles from these data, psychoendocrinology is a relatively young science. It would be a mistake to overgeneralize these hypotheses to rules or laws that apply to unaffected individuals, or to overgeneralize from an affected group with one hormonal history to another group with a different hormonal history. One of the immediate incalculable benefits of this research, instigated by John Money at Johns Hopkins over two decades ago, has been for these affected individuals themselves. Money's pioneering research provided the data base for appropriate clinical de-cisions to be made early in life in various groups of hormonally and genitally deviant infants.

For example, physicians were no longer required to advise parents of a chromosomally male child, born with genitals that would never be sexually functional for a normal sexual relationship, that the genetic makeup required that the child be raised as a male. One repercussion of the study on 5 α-reductase individuals has been the uncertainty not only as to what the findings may mean about biological influences on normal development, but also whether this study in some way mitigates the findings from other clinical samples. For example, are these data adequate to revise our prior understanding regarding the central importance of rearing on the formation of gender identity? (That is, the assumption that in cases of ambiguous sexual morphology, clinical decisions as to sex assignment or reassignment can be made successfully based purely on the decision that will allow the affected child the most normal life. As long as the child is "unambiguously" reared, gender identity will be concordant with rearing regardless of the chromosomal, gonadal, or prenatal hormonal situation.) This principle is so well established from clinical experience that it should not be in jeopardy as applied to these populations.

The data from the Imperato-McGinley study do not apply to the biological constraints on gender identity formation in normal males and females in any sense unless one is absolutely certain these children were viewed as completely normal girls. As previously discussed, this is unlikely. There is ample evidence from clinical cases that ambivalently reared individuals often consolidate their gender identity around the time of adolescence. In the study of the 5 α-reductase individuals the authors concluded that the gender identity decision in adolescence was not only a reversal but also the result of the biological "activation" of the brain responding to androgens, the male hormones. An animal model for the "activation" principle in lower mammals exists; that is, adult female animals given testosterone exhibit a greater frequency of mounting behaviors than control females, and male castrate animals given estrogens exhibit more frequent lordosis (female receptive) behaviors than control males. It is clearly acceptable to hypothesize that humans may have the potential for a similar activation and on that basis attempt to formulate studies that would support or disconfirm the hypothesis.

However, much of the real value of the Imperato-McGinley study is lost if other hypotheses are not also considered and evaluated. It is quite possible, for example, that the high androgens of prenatal hormonal environment did, in some way, decrease biologic vulnerability to the impact of environmental factors that contribute to gender identity, either through extending the critical period or, more likely, creating a greater "predisposition" toward "maleness" in gender role and gender identity. The predispositional hypothesis has support in terms of biological influences on preferred gender-role behaviors but has never been demonstrated as a factor in gender identity formation. Examination of this hypothesis could lead to data that might illuminate other conditions of gender identity confusion that presently lack a known biological association.

We would agree with Imperato-McGinley that their study raises provocative questions regarding a possible role of prenatal (and/or postnatal) hormonal environment in reducing, under some circumstances, a later plasticity of the brain, which could manifest itself as decreased vulnerability of the affected individuals to environmental prescriptions in the area of gender identity. This is related to the authors' conclusion that gender identity is continually evolving. We would agree that one's experience of oneself as male or female evolves over time, throughout childhood, and certainly to adolescence with its integration of a new awareness of one's self as a sexual being. We do not feel, however, that the Imperato-McGinley study proves that those changes in self-awareness are biologically programmed rather than consequences of the bringing together of environmental influences with maturation, including increased cognitive awareness.

Discussion

In general, the studies of clinical populations indicate a rather consistent picture. In females, prenatal exposure to abnormally high levels of androgens or other virilizing hormones results in some behavioral-temperamental consequences, particularly those dimorphic behaviors generally subsumed under the category of gender-role behaviors. In males, androgen insensitivity or prenatal exposure to sufficient levels of hormones that antagonize androgen action results also in behavioral temperamental consequences.

The bulk of the evidence from human studies does *not* support the thesis that prenatal environment is responsible for choice of sex object in adolescence. In fact, with the better controlled, more elaborate studies in nonhuman mammals, where much higher amounts of hormones are given throughout the various critical periods, no one has yet succeeded in producing "homosexual" animals. In those human studies where any subjects in the sample had bisexual or homosexual experiences, no control groups were used, and it is not known, but is unlikely, that the frequency was higher than it would be in other nonrandom appropriate control groups.

In the area of gender identity formation, in all systematic studies of human populations except one, gender identity was concordant for sex of rearing regardless of the chromosomal, gonadal, or prenatal hormonal situation. The exception, reporting findings of a gender identity "reversal" in male pseudohermaphrodites and postulating a purely biological explanation, did *not* demonstrate unambivalent rearing in their subjects. In fact, no study to date has been able to exclude confounding environmental factors where there was any visible abnormality at birth. Furthermore, such "proof" would require anthropological and sophisticated prospective studies (which have not been done), and knowledge of the operational environmental variables responsible for formation or imposition upon the infant of a sense of self that is gender-specific. To date we do not know how this information is either communicated by the parents (presumably) or processed by the infant.

There are many difficulties with the human studies, among them the confounding effects of medical condition, frequent use of retrospective interview data, the difficulty of providing adequate controls, and small sample sizes. However, acting within the constraints of ethical human investigation requires many of these limitations. Low subject availability in rare genetic syndromes or other hormonally exposed individuals is also an expectable limitation. In future studies, we hope, a greater range of more sophisticated methodologies may mitigate some of the other limitations in human research.

In spite of the problems, psychoendocrine research has provided a foundation of data that indicates that biological factors, such as hormonal environment before birth, can be a real influence on at least some behavioral and/or temperamental proclivities throughout life. Future research ought to define more clearly the range and limitations of these biological influences. It will probably also investigate the human brain. A wealth of *animal* data indicates differences between male and female brains—in cell nuclear size in specific areas of the brain, and axonal and dendritic growth, both of which are hormonally sensitive during early critical periods and later in life.[20] We also know that the brain has specific receptors for dissimilar hormones, with concentrations of the various receptors in functionally different parts of the brain.[21] It is relatively parsimonious to assume that many of these biologic facts in nonhuman species are probably also true for humans,[22] although to date there are no human data in any of these areas of research. When we have elucidated some of these issues of dimorphic brain structure in humans, we may then be able to approach the issues of the association between structure and function in humans and the roles of biology and environment in shaping both.

Department of Pediatrics
The New York Hospital—Cornell Medical College
and
Department of Human Development and Family Studies
Cornell University

20. R. A. Gorski, "Long-Term Hormonal Modulation of Neuronal Structure and Function," in *The Neurosciences: 4th Study Program*, ed. F. O. Schmidt and F. Worden (Cambridge, Mass.: M.I.T. Press, 1979), pp. 969–82.

21. B. McEwen, "Gonadal Steroids and Brain Development," *Biology of Reproduction* 22 (1980): 43–48.

22. R. W. Goy and P. A. Goldfoot, "Neuroendocrinology: Animal Models and Problems of Human Sexuality," *Archives of Sexual Behavior* 4 (1975): 405–20.

Review Essay

Behavior and the Menstrual Cycle

Richard C. Friedman, Stephen W. Hurt, Michael S. Aronoff, and John Clarkin

Because of the existence of multiple individual and environmental factors influencing a person's behavior, no one study can provide a complete analysis of the complex relationships that exist between behavior and the menstrual cycle. In studying that we must focus on influences on the individual arising from biological, psychological, and sociocultural factors. All three have the capacity to modify an individual woman's responses, and some factors may be more important than others in accounting for any one woman's behavioral changes. Thus dramatic biological changes, perhaps in nerve-cell receptor response to changing hormone levels, may be of such importance in the case of one individual that personality and sociocultural features may be relatively inconsequential. Alternatively, constellations of psychopathological syndromes may be primarily responsible for magnifying the effects of normal variations in hormone levels or receptor sensitivities.

In this review, we will focus on selected research studies that have attempted to explore the relationship between behavior and the menstrual cycle. Our purpose is to give an overview of the spectrum of information available. Further resource material will be noted throughout the text for those readers with a particular interest in any of the topics discussed. In considering each study, we shall devote some attention to the kind of individuals studied, the techniques employed in

We would like to acknowledge the most helpful assistance of Pat Cobb in the preparation of this manuscript.

gathering the data, and the context in which the study took place. Our review focuses first on studies of women without demonstrable physical or mental illness; that is, "normal" women. Here we examine three types of behavior: (1) mood, (2) task performance, and (3) sexual performance. Later we turn our attention to studies of women suffering from what are considered mental health problems, that is, "abnormal" women.

Findings in "Normal" Women

Fluctuations in Mood

Fluctuations in women's emotional state at different points in the menstrual cycle received the earliest systematic research attention. Clinical reports of mood disturbances related to the menstrual cycle suggested that irritability, depression, anxiety, and hostility were most prominent during the premenstrual (two to seven days prior to menstruation) and menstrual (from onset to cessation of the menstrual flow) phases of the cycle. Research in this area has demonstrated that most women experience at least some increase in "negative" feeling states during these two phases of the menstrual cycle. A complete bibliography of studies on this topic would include data on several thousand women from many different cultural groups. These studies have employed a number of research techniques, including retrospective self-reports and periodic, objective assessments of speech samples in both structured and unstructured settings. As a point of reference, the eight-day interval, from four days prior to onset of menstruation to four days following its onset, has been termed the "paramenstruum." Substantial evidence exists that mood tends to be more "positive" in some sense during the intermenstrual interval than during this paramenstrual interval.

Contemporary interest in menstrual-cycle symptomatology has resulted in the development of several self-report questionnaires, the most widely used of which is the Menstrual Distress Questionnaire (MDQ) developed by Moos and his collaborators.[1] The questionnaire includes forty-seven descriptive items thought to fluctuate with the menstrual cycle. These items include physical symptoms such as headache and cramps, emotional symptoms such as irritability and depression, and changes in behavior such as napping, decreased efficiency, and difficulty concentrating. Women were asked to "rate their experience of each of the 47 symptoms on the MDQ on a six-point scale ranging from no experience of the symptoms to an acute or partially disabling experience

1. R. H. Moos, "The Development of a Menstrual Distress Questionnaire," *Psychosomatic Medicine* 30 (1968): 853–66.

of the symptoms." Ratings are made separately for "the menstrual (during menstrual flow), premenstrual (the week before the beginning of menstrual flow), and intermenstrual (remainder of cycle) phases of her most recent menstrual cycle and for her worst menstrual cycle."

Moos's original report on 839 wives of graduate students at a large university in the western United States showed that scores for negative affect (a combination of the scores for crying, loneliness, anxiety, restlessness, irritability, mood swings, depression, and tension) differed significantly from their intermenstrual level during both the premenstrual and menstrual phases. Because the women filled out the questionnaire at different points in their menstrual cycle, the possibility that there existed a systematic effect of this variable on report of symptom severity was tested and rejected. Moos also reported that these retrospective accounts of symptom severity were not affected by the amount of time that elapsed between their occurrence and their report. These two findings, taken together, lend credence to the use of retrospective accounts to gather data on menstruation and behavior.

Other investigators have focused on the development of non–self-report measures of negative affects. In the early 1960s, Gottschalk devised a method for measuring anxiety based on the analysis of tape-recorded transcripts of verbal narratives.[2] Subjects spoke freely on a topic of their own choosing for five minutes, and the material was scored according to a scale of established reliability and validity. In a small investigation involving six women (two women studied over three cycles, two women studied over two cycles, and two women studied over one cycle), a tendency was noted for anxiety to decrease during ovulation. Ivey and Bardwick subsequently investigated a larger sample using the Gottschalk technique as well as additional questionnaires.[3] Twenty-six college students were studied at ovulation and premenstrually for two cycles. The average anxiety scores for all subjects were higher premenstrually than at ovulation. Moreover, in three of five cases in which anxiety was unexpectedly higher at ovulation, it was felt that this was attributable to coincidental psychosocial stress. An analysis of thematic content revealed that these women's self-perceptions of their adequacy fluctuated with the cycle. All subjects felt less able to cope with the problems of daily living during the premenstrual period compared with the ovulatory period.

In suggesting that affective changes during the menstrual cycle may be related to coincident events, the Ivey and Bardwick study represents recent trends in menstrual-cycle research. Perhaps because much of this

2. L. Gottschalk et al., "Variations in Magnitude of Emotion: A Method Applied to Anxiety and Hostility during Phases of the Menstrual Cycle," *Psychosomatic Medicine* 24 (1962): 300–311.

3. M. Ivey and J. Bardwick, "Patterns of Affective Fluctuation in the Menstrual Cycle," *Psychosomatic Medicine* 30 (1968): 336–45.

research had been conducted by biologically oriented investigaors, one hypothesis has been that periodic, negative emotional fluctuations might be determined primarily by fluctuations in the activity of female sex hormones. While biological factors clearly play a role in affective changes during the menstrual cycle, recent studies have attempted to determine the degree to which nonhormonal events modify affective changes during the menstrual cycle. These investigations have focused on such factors as the quantity and quality of environmental events, attitudes about menstruation, and personality traits.

A convincing demonstration of the influence of external events on one's interpretation of physiological change is the elegant study reported by Schachter and Singer.[4] Although not specifically directed at menstrual-related emotional changes, this study is relevant to the larger issue of understanding individual perception of physiological events. These researchers were able to demonstrate that, after inducing a state of physiological arousal with an injection of adrenalin, subjects' subsequent evaluations of their emotional state depended on the explanation of the state that the subject adopted rather than the degree of physiological arousal per se.

Demonstrations of the influence of external events on the self-report of negative affects during different phases of the menstrual cycle have recently appeared. Wilcoxon and her co-workers studied thirty-three undergraduates who filled out daily self-reports on pleasant activities, stressful events, moods, and somatic changes for thirty-five days.[5] Subjects included eleven males, eleven females taking oral contraceptives, and eleven females not taking oral contraceptives. Males were randomly assigned a "premenstrual" day from among the thirty-five study days. This day and the next three days were designated as each male's "premenstrual" period. The five days following this interval were assigned to the "menstrual" phase. Data from the males showed no fluctuations related to menstrual cycle "phase." Among the women, negative affects were found to be more intense during the paramenstruum, with the peak for no-pill women occurring during menstruation and that for pill women occurring during the premenstrual phase. However, Wilcoxon et al. found that for both groups of women, the experience of negative affects was more responsive to the presence of stressful external events than to the specific timing of the menstrual-cycle phase. They also noted that differences among women in the amount of negative affect experienced were still large despite their attempts to explain them on the basis of cycle phase, contraceptive status, or amount of stress experi-

4. S. Schachter and J. E. Singer, "Cognitive Social and Physiological Determinants of Emotional State," *Psychological Review* 69 (1962): 379–99.
5. L. A. Wilcoxon, S. L. Schrader, and C. W. Sherif, "Daily Self-Reports on Activities, Life Events, Moods and Somatic Changes during the Menstrual Cycle," *Psychosomatic Medicine* 38 (1976): 399–417.

enced. Further research regarding the influence of situational factors on reports of mood fluctuations during the menstrual cycle should enhance our understanding.

This also appears to be the case with studies of the experience of menstruation and attitudes and beliefs related to menstruation itself. Paige studied 102 women, some taking oral contraceptives, using the content-analysis technique of Gottschalk et al.[6] Her data indicate that, regardless of contraceptive status, premenstrual increases in anxiety were characteristic of women with normally heavy menstrual flow but were less pronounced in women with reduced flow. This relationship could not be explained by differences in physical symptoms of distress which were of equal magnitude in the reduced-flow and normal-flow groups. In another study, Brooks, Ruble, and Clark collected self-report questionnaire data from 232 undergraduate women at a private university in the eastern United States.[7] Subjects were asked to complete the MDQ twice, once "as if" they were in the premenstrual phase and once "as if" they were in the intermenstrual phase. They also completed an attitude survey in which they were asked to agree or disagree with forty-six statements constructed to represent "beliefs about physiological and psychological concomitants of menstruation, style of dealing with menstruation, menstrual-related effects on performance, and general evaluations of menstruation." As expected, differences in negative affect were recorded, with subjects responding with higher scores for the "as if" premenstrual period. Analysis of the attitudinal variables in relation to the differences between premenstrual- and intermenstrual-symptom scores revealed that reports of increased negative affect during the menstrual phase were associated with the view of menstruation as a debilitating and predictable event.

A statistical association between two sets of data, in this case attitudes and expectations related to menstruation and reports of an increase in negative affect during the premenstrual phase, does not imply causation. This association can be explained in one of three ways: (1) because women expect to have more difficulty premenstrually, they are more aware of and more likely to report such difficulties; (2) prior experience of difficulty during the premenstrual phase has produced a negative change in attitudes regarding this phase of the menstrual cycle; or (3) attitudes about the premenstrual phase and the increase in negative affect reported during this phase are both related to a third factor which is responsible for their association with one another (e.g., personality or biological factors). Data from the Brooks et al. study do not permit us to

6. K. Paige, "Effects of Oral Contraceptives on Affective Fluctuations Associated with the Menstrual Cycle," *Psychosomatic Medicine* 33 (1971): 515–37.

7. J. Brooks, D. Ruble, and A. Clark, "College Women's Attitudes and Expectations concerning Menstrual-related Changes," *Psychosomatic Medicine* 39 (1977): 288–98.

determine which of these three possibilities is responsible for the observed association. Because the possibilities are not mutually exclusive, one or all of them may contribute to the association.

Fluctuations in mood during the menstrual cycle have also been studied in relation to personality factors. A large-scale study was conducted in 1963 by two British researchers, Coppen and Kessel, who found that mood changes during the premenstruum were associated to a moderate degree with the Maudsley Personality Inventory factor of "neuroticism."[8] This factor is described as tapping the personality traits of emotional overreactivity and a tendency to develop various neurotic symptoms generally. Subsequent studies of menstruation using the Maudsley Personality Inventory have tended to confirm the findings of Coppen and Kessel. Similar personality traits measured by other instruments and using American samples have also shown a moderate association with negative mood changes during the premenstrual or menstrual phase.[9] These studies, in general, characterize those women who report the largest mood changes as high strung, sensitive, concerned about bodily functioning, emotionally labile, and having difficulty understanding human motivations. These personality traits have been found to be more closely associated with mood changes during the paramenstruum than with physical changes during this phase such as water retention, swelling of the breasts, or pain.

These have been studies of moderate to large-sized samples of women. Consequently, the personality variations within each sample are large. Generally, care is taken to see that the range of scores spans the entire range of normal personality variation. Across the entire range, it is the women with the extreme, but not abnormal, scores on the personality traits described above that report the largest negative mood changes during the paramenstruum. An alternative strategy was employed by Golub.[10] She studied fifty parous women between thirty and forty-five years of age who were not using oral contraceptives. A battery of psychological tests was administered to each woman four days prior to the next expected period and again two weeks after the onset of menstruation. Half the women were tested first premenstrually, half were tested first intermenstrually. The women chosen for the study were selected on the basis of demonstrated capacity to function at above-average levels of psychosocial competence. In addition, the instruments in the test battery

8. A. Coppen and N. Kessel, "Menstruation and Personality," *British Journal of Psychiatry* 109 (1963): 711–21.

9. G. H. Gruba and M. Rohrbaugh, "MMPI Correlates of Menstrual Distress," *Psychosomatic Medicine* 37 (1975): 265–72; E. E. Levitt and B. Lubin, "Some Personality Factors Associated with Menstrual Complaints and Menstrual Attitudes," *Journal of Psychosomatic Research* 11 (1967): 267–70.

10. S. Golub, "The Effects of Premenstrual Anxiety and Depression on Cognitive Function," *Journal of Personality and Social Psychology* 34 (1976): 99–105.

were chosen carefully and included two instruments for measuring anxiety. One of these has been shown to reflect anxiety proneness, a stable, dispositional feature of an individual's personality makeup. The second anxiety measure reflects the degree of anxiety currently experienced. An individual's scores on the first test show a good degree of similarity across time, while scores on the second test fluctuate in response to life events. Both instruments have been used to test men and women under a wide variety of circumstances and across a wide range of personality styles. This means that normative data for both tests are available and the scores of the women in Golub's study could be compared with the scores of women with different psychopathological diagnoses and with women tested under differing environmental conditions. Golub found that the amount of anxiety experienced by the women premenstrually was greater than that experienced intermenstrually. The level of premenstrual anxiety reported was found to be on a par with that reported by female college students experiencing mild situational stress. The degree of "anxiety proneness" in these women was found to be lower than that reported for the general population and was not significantly associated with the degree of "transient premenstrual anxiety" reported.

These selected findings illustrate the influence of psychological and sociocultural factors on affective changes during the menstrual cycle. While these factors play a significant role for some women, the results of these studies cannot be generalized to exclude the potential influence of hormonal factors. Beumont et al. gathered data on twenty-five women (nineteen to forty-six years old; mean age twenty-eight) with regular periods and compared them with data from seven women (twenty-six to forty-seven years old; mean age thirty-five) who had undergone hysterectomy with conservation of the ovaries one to five years previously.[11] These latter women continued to exhibit characteristic hormone fluctuations but did not menstruate. Data collected from all women included daily ratings of depression and associated symptoms, other psychological and emotional states, and physical symptoms. For the menstruating women, Beumont et al. reported significant symptomatic changes in all three areas during the menstrual cycle with a paramenstrual increase in symptoms reported. In the hysterectomized women, Beumont et al. report the same trend for the data on depression and other psychological and emotional states but not for physical symptoms. A comparison of the paramenstrual and intermenstrual scores of the hysterectomized women shows roughly the same proportion of change for depression and other psychological symptoms but, interestingly enough, not for physical symptoms. In addition, the mean symptom scores for the hysterec-

11. P. J. V. Beumont, D. H. Richards, and M. G. Gelder, "A Study of Psychiatric and Physical Symptoms during the Menstrual Cycle," *British Journal of Psychiatry* 126 (1975): 431–34.

tomized sample tend to be higher than those of menstruating women during both the paramenstruum and the intermenstruum. These data are suggestive of hormonal influences on mood and other psychological characteristics in women *regardless of menstruation* but clearly require additional study and replication before being widely accepted.

With respect, then, to the relationship between fluctuations in mood and the menstrual cycle, the following conclusions seem warranted. Almost all women experience some increase in negative affects during the premenstrual or menstrual phase of the cycles. Furthermore, the amount of change in negative affects during the premenstrual or menstrual phase in comparison with the intermenstrual phase appears to be related to some degree to a woman's current psychosocial experience and more enduring features of her psychological makeup such as attitudes about menstruation and personality factors as well as menstrual-cycle-related hormonal changes.[12]

Task Performance

As a general rule, people's performance is influenced by the way they feel. It seems hardly surprising, then, that investigators have explored the relationship between menstruation and task performance. Sommer's recent review of the area summarizes the findings to date.[13] The research shows a consistent trend. Studies utilizing objective performance measures generally fail to demonstrate menstrual-cycle-related changes. Studies based on performance measures, including academic examinations, simple reaction-time measures, and quantity and quality of factory production all fail to demonstrate menstrual effects.

In reviewing this area, however, Sommer noted that there appeared to be a difference between women's subjective reports of their ability to perform either premenstrually or menstrually and objective measures of their performance. Some women feel that their performance paramenstrually is worse than their performance intermenstrually. Unfortunately, none of the studies cited included both subjective reports and objective data on performance. We know of no demonstration of a relationship between paramenstrual changes in self-perceived performance capacity and changes in objective task performance during the same phase. Sommer's conclusion is, however, consistent with both retrospective and daily self-report data from several other studies which report impaired concentration and decreased cognitive arousal, two fac-

12. See Wilcoxon et al., Paige, Brooks et al., Coppen and Kessel, Gruba and Rohrbaugh, Levitt and Lubin, and Golub.

13. B. Sommer, "The Effect of Menstruation on Cognitive and Perceptual Motor Behavior: A Review," *Psychosomatic Medicine* 35 (1973): 515–34.

tors which presumably affect a person's subjective estimate of her ability to perform.

The relationship between self-perception of performance ability during the paramenstruum and objective evaluation of performance deserves more careful research attention. The discrepancy between subjective evaluation and objective performance may be related to sociocultural attitudes and expectations. If so, such attitudes appear to have limited impact on actual performance, but this possibility requires experimental investigation before it can be claimed as a fact.

Sexual Performance

Sexual behavior appears to be influenced by menstrual-cycle changes. Although there is some inconsistency in the findings of various investigators, the major changes in sexual behavior are located in the midcycle, ovulatory phase and the paramenstrual phase. In general, there is an increase in both sexual feelings and frequency of intercourse at both points in the cycle. During the ovulatory phase, these changes are an obvious reproductive advantage and in nonhuman, mammalian species, are associated with externally observable, physical signs of the presence of estrus that are hormonally based. Investigators who have noted a peak in human sexual activity during the paramenstruum have speculated that this peak may be related to cognitive rather than hormonal factors. Coital frequency may increase because of the absence of impregnation fears and because of sexual abstinence during menstruation.

Early studies of human sexual activity, which focused on changes in coital frequency, were not methodologically sophisticated. Their reliance on retrospective accounts and their focus on coital frequency as an adequate measure of sexual activity made it difficult to detect nontrivial, but nonetheless small, changes in sexual activity. Later studies, particularly those that have used daily self-reports and have included autoerotic and fantasy activity in addition to reports of coitus, have more consistently demonstrated menstrual-cycle-related changes. The postmenstrual peak in coital frequency seems to be the most firmly established alteration noted in both early and more contemporary studies. Changes in sexual behavior during the ovulatory phase have been shown, although less frequently; more often confirmed are increases in sexual feelings during this phase of the menstrual cycle. However, more recent studies which have cataloged sexual activity in detail have been able to demonstrate small but statistically significant increases during the ovulatory phase.

Adams, Gold, and Burt felt that the inability of previous investigators to demonstrate a midcycle elevation in sexual activity was a result of their focus on predominantly male-partner initiation as the measure of female sexual activity.[14] Adams et al. studied thirty-five white, college-educated women between twenty-one and thirty-seven years of age. All women filled out daily questionnaires on their sexual experiences, including information on the initiator of each sexual episode and whether the advance was rejected. Type of sexual behaviors recorded were intercourse, caressing, masturbation, fantasy, and sexual arousal from books, films, magazines, or dreams. The thirty-five subjects provided data on 171 cycles with a median of 4.2 cycles studied per subject. The data from this study show a midcycle ovulatory peak in female- plus mutually initiated heterosexual behavior but not in male-initiated sexual behavior. Autosexual activity was increased during the midcycle phase as well. These elevations were characteristic of those women in the study whose method of contraception was not hormonal regulation but were absent in women who used oral contraceptives.

Data from the Adams et al. study suggest that female-initiated sexual activity is most pronounced during the ovulatory phase of the menstrual cycle and appears to be under some degree of biological control. They speculated that the important biological factors were changes in female sex hormones, particularly estrogen, as it is this hormonal system that is modulated by the use of oral contraceptives. Other hormonal systems, however, also appear to play a role in human sexual activity as well.

Eleven couples aged twenty-one to thirty-one years and married for at least one year were studied over three menstrual cycles by Persky.[15] Subjects were interviewed individually twice weekly and blood samples were taken and assayed for plasma levels of testosterone and cortisol in both husbands and wives and for progesterone and estradiol in wives only. The interviews were rated independently by two psychiatrists for degree of sexual initiation, avoidance, couple interaction, and mood. Wives also rated themselves for degree of sexual gratification. They found that both the husbands' and wives' initiation sources were related to their spouses' responsivity scores, as might be expected. When these relationships were studied in association with the hormonal data, however, it appeared that testosterone levels played a greater role in explaining the strength of the association between initiation and clinically rated responsivity than did either estradiol or progesterone levels. In addition, intercourse frequency was related to wives' testosterone levels at their ovulatory peak, and wives' testosterone levels correlated significantly with their self-ratings of sexual gratification.

14. D. B. Adams, A. R. Gold, and A. D. Burt, "Rise in Female-initiated Sexual Activity at Ovulation and Its Suppression by Oral Contraceptives," *New England Journal of Medicine* 229 (November 23, 1978): 1145–50.

15. H. Persky et al., "Plasma Testosterone Level and Sexual Behavior of Couples," *Archives of Sexual Behavior* 7 (1978): 157–73.

Conclusions: Findings in Normal Women

Studies of menstruation and behavior in normal women have revealed a complex set of relationships. That the menstrual cycle is capable of altering behavior pattens in regular ways appears to be an incontrovertible fact. Women may experience increases in feelings of sexual desire as ovulation approaches. Female-initiated heterosexual activity and autosexual activity appear to increase at this point. There are some data suggesting that this might be related to midcycle androgen effects, but further studies are needed in this area.

As women approach the paramenstruum, they generally report increases in negative feeling states such as anxiety, irritability, depression, and tension as well as changes in their self-perception of performance capacity and ability. Interestingly, the intensity of negative affect experienced by women who are psychologically normal tends, as a rule, to be mild. Despite the fact that self-perception of performance might fluctuate, no objective fluctuation in menstrual task performance has been established. Despite these general tendencies, there remains a good deal of individual variability in response, across women within a menstrual cycle and across menstrual cycles for a single woman.

Findings in "Abnormal" Women

The term "premenstrual tension" was introduced in the 1930s by Frank and emphasizes one component of a painful-feeling picture.[16] Subsequent literature in the field refers either to "premenstrual tension syndrome" or "premenstrual affective syndrome." We favor the latter term, which is more inclusive and refers to a quantitative, significant difference in the severity of observable mood changes during the paramenstruum from that observed in "normal" women. For reasons that are unclear, the premenstrual affective syndrome appears to be most common and most severe roughly between ages twenty-five and forty.[17] Some investigators have suggested that this syndrome may be present in at least 25 percent of the menstruating population, and others have speculated that it is even more common.[18] Although data characterizing the population of women who are prone to suffer from extreme emotional distress during the cycle are limited, they suggest that such

16. R. T. Frank, "The Hormonal Causes of Premenstrual Tension," *Archives of Neurology and Psychiatry* 26 (1931): 1053–57.

17. J. L. Kramp, "Studies on the Premenstrual Syndrome in Relation to Psychiatry," *Acta Psychiatrica Scandinavica* 203 (suppl.; 1968): 261–67.

18. L. Rees, "Premenstrual Tension Syndrome in Relation to Personality, Neurosis, Certain Psychosomatic Disorders and Psychotic States," in *Psychoendocrinology,* ed. M. Reiss (London: Grune & Stratton, 1958).

women are likely to suffer from other psychopathology *not* in itself specifically linked to the menstrual cycle.[19] This must be qualified, however, because other studies suggest that some women, not well characterized to date, may manifest cyclical, recurrent, extremely painful moods at certain points in the cycle and not suffer from additional global forms of pathology.[20]

In moving on to a more detailed discussion of psychopathology and the menstrual cycle, we stress that there may well be qualitative differences between subgroups of pathological individuals and normals. We emphasize, however, the necessity for caution in generalizing from data on normal women to pathological subgroups and vice versa. Psychopathology is a rapidly changing field. Strict criteria for diagnosing psychiatric illnesses have been specified relatively recently. The types of behavioral conditions considered diagnosable illnesses have also changed as knowledge has accumulated. The clinical literature in any area of psychiatry contains articles about conditions similar in name but different in form and reports from investigators using different methods to study a variety of populations. Given these limitations of a rapidly growing area of knowledge, it is perhaps surprising that a trend has emerged.

Many studies suggest that depression-anxiety-irritability-tension often covary together and become more severe premenstrually. When fluctuations in intensity are repetitive and severe, these feelings constitute the "premenstrual affective syndrome" and may be associated with significant distress and impairment of functioning. Interestingly, the mood changes reported in the clinical literature seem to account for some but not all of the variance in behavioral symptomatology. Other types of behavioral symptoms (such as decreased impulse control, multiple somatic complaints, or psychotic symptoms) also appear to be linked to the menstrual cycle in some subgroups of subjects.

A number of investigators have noted a relationship between psychopathology linked to the menstrual cycle and neurotic character structure. Perhaps the most dramatic observations dealing with this relationship were made by Benedek and Rubenstein.[21] They were able to

19. Coppen and Kessel.

20. J. Cullberg, "Mood Changes and Menstrual Symptoms with Different Gestagen/Estrogen Combinations: A Double-Blind Comparison with a Placebo," *Acta Psychiatrica Scandinavica* 236 (suppl.; 1972): 1–86; R. F. Haskett et al., "Severe Premenstrual Tension: Delineation of the Syndrome (paper presented at the Thirty-Fourth Annual Scientific Program, Society of Biological Psychiatry, Chicago, May 12, 1979).

21. T. Benedek and B. B. Rubenstein, "Correlations between Ovarian Activity and Psychodynamic Processes. I. The Ovulative Phase," *Psychosomatic Medicine* 1 (1939): 245–70; see also pt. 2, "The Menstrual Phase," ibid., pp. 461–85. This work is also summarized in T. Benedek, *Studies in Psychosomatic Medicine: Psychosexual Functions in Women* (New York: Ronald Press, 1952).

predict cycle phase by analyzing the content of therapy sessions of fifteen patients in psychoanalysis. The investigators described a pattern in which the first part of the cycle, prior to ovulation, was a period of increased self-esteem and desire for erotic activity during which the individual's self-image was active. Following a period when active and passive-receptive tendencies were optimally fused at ovulation, the luteal phase of the cycle was characterized by passivity and more procreational interest in sex. During the few days immediately preceding menstruation, the investigators observed that regression occurred, and ego defensive strength decreased. The overall orientation of the patients tended to be more primitive. Painful feelings such as irritability, anxiety, and depression increased and tended to remit with the onset of menstruation.

Benedek and Rubenstein went beyond merely concluding that women's psychological state changes with the cycle to propose that the specific characteristics of a woman's sexual fantasy life are regulated by the same biological forces that control fertility and thereby maximize the synchrony between mind and body. Unfortunately, this 1939 study has never been replicated. The findings raise the question whether there might not be a relationship between the dramatic and often marked behavioral fluctuations noted by Benedek and Rubenstein and neurosis itself. Until this investigation is replicated, the question of whether the specific fantasies that motivate sexual behavior are in fact correlated with the hormonal events of the menstrual cycle, even in neurosis, must be considered open.

Other investigators have also noted that a correlation between psychopathological *traits,* particularly neurotic character structure, and psychopathological *states* that fluctuate with the cycle might exist. An important task for future research is to clarify this relationship from both descriptive and etiological perspectives.

In addition to the study by Coppen and Kessel mentioned above, in which the relationship between psychological symptoms, character structure, and the phases of the menstrual cycle were studied, Kramp conducted psychiatric interviews with 131 women who had applied for abortion. Sixty-six had a well-characterized "premenstrual tension syndrome" (PMT), 52 percent of whom had specific neurotic symptoms in childhood. Only 26 percent of the sixty-five patients without PMT had such symptoms.[22] Rees observed that in 145 neurotic patients with the premenstrual syndrome, there was a positive correlation between severity of neurosis and severity of cyclic affect distress. Rees suggested, however, that severe premenstrual tension could exist in normal women "of stable personality," and he noted that many severely neurotic women did

22. Kramp.

not suffer from it.[23] This finding has been emphasized by others as well.

This conclusion is compatible with an observation of Cullberg's.[24] In a study he conducted, 320 women received varying doses of one type of sex steroid, "gestagen," in combination with a fixed dose of estrogen, or placebo, in a controlled study of the effect of sex steroids on behavior. The prevalence of cyclic premenstrual complaints prior to ingestion of medication was high. Forty percent of the subjects were felt to have the premenstrual syndrome. Of these, approximately 26 percent had high scores for neuroticism on personality tests. Cullberg suggested that these individuals were "high reactors" who easily experience symptoms and who might constitute a majority of cases of premenstrual syndrome that are seen clinically. It is noteworthy that the remaining 74 percent had a clinically detectable premenstrual syndrome despite low scores for neuroticism on psychological tests.

Moos et al.'s investigation of fluctuations of symptoms and moods during the menstrual cycle illustrates the importance of describing the intermenstrual behavioral state of women with premenstrual difficulties.[25] Of fifteen married nulliparous women, seven complained of high premenstrual tension and eight stated they had low premenstrual tension on a questionnaire. The subjects completed self-rating scales during nine days in each of two consecutive cycles. The results were generally consistent with the observations of Benedek and Rubenstein for all women. Feelings of pleasantness, activation, and sexual arousal increased during the first half of the cycle. Fear, tension, and general discomfort were greatest premenstrually. Relative consistency existed from cycle to cycle. Importantly, it was observed that intermenstrual differences between the two groups of women existed. Anxiety, depression, and negative affect generally were higher intermenstrually for women with high premenstrual tension than for women with low premenstrual tension. These data support the argument that psychological-state differences between women must be interpreted in the context of more stable psychological-trait characterization.

The preceding studies suggest that neurotic women may be particularly *prone* to develop behavioral symptoms correlated with the menstrual cycle. However, many neurotic women do not experience such cyclical symptom occurrence. The features that might discriminate these two neurotic populations are not clear at present. The percentage of neurotic women who could be expected to fall into each subgroup is also not certain. O'Conner, Shelly, and Stern have observed that charac-

23. L. Rees, "Psychosomatic Aspects of the Premenstrual Syndrome," *Journal of Mental Science* 99 (1953): 62–73, and "The Premenstrual Syndrome and Its Treatment," *British Medical Journal* 1 (1953): 1014–16.

24. Cullberg.

25. R. B. Moos et al., "Fluctuations in Symptoms and Moods during the Menstrual Cycle," *Journal of Psychosomatic Research* 13 (1963): 37–44.

ter typology has never really been studied by interview methods to determine whether women with certain types of character defenses (such as hysterical) might differ in their emotional responsivities during the cycle from women with different types of character defenses (such as obsessions).[26] This is an intriguing area for future research, as is the systematic description of psychopathology among individuals who behave in clearly deviant ways during the paramenstruum.

Many investigators interested in the relationship between illness and the menstrual cycle have counted the frequency of certain types of behavior in relation to each woman's phase of the cycle. It can then be determined whether such behaviors cluster at particular phases of the cycle or are distributed randomly across all phases. This technique can be applied to any behavior of interest to an investigator.

When a wide variety of behaviors are looked at systematically, there seems to be a relationship between the occurrence of deviant acts and cycle phase. That is, of a population of women who commit a clearly pathological act, more are likely to be in the paramenstrual phase of the cycle than can be expected by chance. This has been shown to be true for calls to a suicide prevention center, suicide attempts, successful suicide acts, commission of nonviolent and violent crimes, disorderly conduct in schools and prisons, requests for psychiatric assistance, admission to a hospital with a psychiatric illness, and accidents.[27] As Parlee has noted, these correlations say nothing about the probability of normal women committing pathological acts as a consequence of cyclicity of psychohormonal functioning.[28] This clinical literature, taken in total, says nothing about what "women in general" are likely to be like paramenstrually. The samples studied aberrant and probably psychopathological subgroups. This is an important distinction to emphasize, in view of the evidence that the performance of normal women, at a variety of tasks, has not been shown to fluctuate with the cycle. Data garnered from deviant subgroups can be used in a biased and even a prejudicial fashion, if they are inappropriately applied. Given this reservation, however, there seems little doubt that, within the universe of potential pathological-act committers, the paramenstrual period is a time of relatively high expectancy for the occurrence of the act in question.

Parlee has also appropriately emphasized that there are no comparable studies correlating cycle phase with unusually positive behaviors,

26. J. F. O'Conner, E. M. Shelly, and L. O. Stern, "Behavioral Rhythms Related to the Menstrual Cycle," in *Biorhythms and Human Reproduction,* ed. M. Fern et al. (New York: John Wiley & Sons, 1974).

27. S. L. Smith, "Mood and the Menstrual Cycle," in *Topics in Psychoendocrinology,* ed. E. J. Sachar (New York: Grune & Stratton, 1975); and O'Connor et al. Also of interest is K. Dalton, *The Premenstrual Syndrome* (London: William Heinemann, 1964). The O'Conner study summarizes studies on a total of 1,339 women.

28. M. B. Parlee, "The Premenstrual Syndrome," *Psychological Bulletin* 80 (1973): 454–65.

such as acts of heroism or great creativity. It is possible that data about behavioral events and cycle phase reflect a bias since investigators in this area have tended to be clinicians interested in psychopathology per se. This possible bias should not obscure the fact that data on behavioral abnormality and cycle phase has, in our view, added a helpful perspective toward understanding psychopathology. However, in the studies referred to above, the individuals who have committed the deviant acts often have not been well diagnosed or examined with standard psychological tests. This dimension will no doubt be added in future studies.

Intriguing questions are open in the area of psychopathology and the menstrual cycle. Given the present state of the field, we think it will be helpful to present our own, often speculative, point of view. We refer the reader who wishes additional discussion to recent reviews in the scientific literature.[29]

From the psychodynamic point of view, if Benedek and Rubenstein's observations that the luteal phase is associated with increased interest in maternalism are accurate, it follows that women with neurotic conflicts about maternalism and pathological identifications with their mothers would have periodic exacerbations of intrapsychic conflicts during the luteal phase. Such women would be likely to suffer from severe neurotic symptoms as a result of cyclical fluctuations in the intensity of intrapsychic conflict. One hallmark of neurosis is the presence of unresolved oedipal conflicts. If intensity of sexual desire fluctuated with the cycle, so, presumably, would symptoms resulting from unconscious anxiety mobilized by desire. The same type of cyclical fluctuation could be expected to result from aggressive urges, stemming from unresolved oedipal conflicts and resulting in cyclical anxiety and symptom formation. If the hypotheses above are valid, one would expect that waxing and waning of symptoms would be triggered by physiological changes during the cycle, but the choice of particular symptoms would be determined by the form of the patient's neurosis.

Recovery time is a confounding issue when one assumes that behavioral symptoms wax and wan on a monthly basis. Chaotic and painful social interactions could begin paramenstrually, but their consequences could extend into the intermenstrual period. From the clinician's point of view, it would take an unusual woman, in an unusual social network, to manifest severe premenstrual behavioral symptoms regularly and yet function intermenstrually in a way that was comparable to normal control subjects.

Another area that warrants attention in our view is the relationship between a psychopathological diagnostic category known as the "border-

29. Smith; Parlee; O'Connor et al.; M. Steiner and B. J. Carroll, "The Psychobiology of Premenstrual Dysphoria: Review of Theories and Treatments," *Psychoneuroendocrinology* 2 (1977): 321–35; R. H. Moos, *The Menstrual Distress Questionnaire Manual* (Stanford, Calif.: Stanford University, 1977), and Sommer (n. 13 above).

line syndrome" and the menstrual cycle. By way of explanation, the preceding discussion has referred to patients with character pathology and/or neurosis. One type of character disorder is that in which certain personality traits are hypertrophied and rigid to the point where they become maladaptive; another is that in which certain healthy traits (such as the capacity to be empathic, to feel guilt, to restrain antisocial impulses) are deficient or even absent. In either case, although the person's optimal functioning may be severely impaired, mental mechanisms responsible for reality testing continue to function adequately. Neurosis, a term of much recent controversy, traditionally has referred to conditions in which distress and impaired functioning result from unconscious irrational anxiety in such a way, however, that the individual's ability to test and evaluate reality adequately is maintained.

Only recently have patients been described who seem to fluctuate widely with regard to the effectiveness and maturity of their characterological defenses. These patients appear to have well-integrated personality structures at some times and at other times appear to function at an extremely primitive level. They often suffer from transient affective dysphoria, identity diffusion, and perceptual difficulties and might manifest loss of reality testing for brief periods.[30] Criteria for defining this borderline syndrome have been agreed upon so recently that its relationship to the menstrual cycle remains to be systematically investigated. We speculate that many borderline individuals might be unusually sensitive to the normal physiological changes of the menstrual cycle and might manifest a wide variety of symptoms, even transient psychotic symptoms, during the cycle as a consequence. Thus the character defenses of borderline individuals do not appear to function smoothly over time. Hormones and neurotransmitters that fluctuate with the menstrual cycle theoretically have the capacity to impose a strain on behavioral homeostatic mechanisms. It is possible that some borderline individuals are unable adaptively to buffer against this strain. Such individuals might manifest unusual behavioral sensitivity to alterations in physiological state. Furthermore, clinical experience suggests that borderline individuals are often quite sensitive to the effects of psychoactive drugs. Whether they are equally sensitive to endogenous fluctuations of substances possessing behavioral activity remains to be seen. It should be noted that women with character neuroses and those with the borderline syndrome constitute a potentially large number of patients, particularly in outpatient treatment.

We have thus far presented two models for conceptualizing the relationship between psychopathology and the menstrual cycle. Both

30. R. L. Spitzer, J. Endicott, and M. Gibbon, "Crossing the Border into Borderline Personality and Borderline Schizophrenia," *Archives of General Psychiatry* 36 (1979): 17–25; J. G. Gunderson and J. E. Kolb, "Discriminating Features of Borderline Patients," *American Journal of Psychiatry* 135 (1978): 792–97.

our "cyclical neurosis" model and our "nonspecific overreaction" model are compatible with a modified version of Schachter and Singer's well known model for the determinants of emotional state. Schachter and Singer noted that similar physiological changes often occur in different emotional states. They suggested that the relationship between a state of physiological arousal and a cognition, appropriate to that state of arousal, resulted in a specific emotional state.[31] According to this model, individuals provide meaning to physiological change by interpreting it within its psychosocial context.

We suggest that for most women, *the fact* that fluctuation in the intensity of affect states occur is a direct result of primary (although unknown) biological determinants. We hypothesize that fluctuations in irritability, tension, depression, possibly in sexual desire, and other affects as well occur because of cyclical fluctuation in the biological activities of substances that impact on those parts of the central nervous system that regulate affect states. However, the psychosocial and intrapsychic consequences of such fluctuations all depend on cognitive state, itself a product of social context and psychobiographical determinants. We emphasize that with regard to the etiology of *intensity* of affect (i.e., how much change, how depressed in relation to controls), we see no reason to think in terms of single causes. In many cases, intrapsychic-psychosocial-cognitive interactions could certainly determine or greatly influence intensity, while in others biological factors could predominate.

We hypothesize that the subgroups may be even further subdivided with regard to the intensity of fluctuations in depression in comparison with fluctuations in other dysphoric affect states. Fluctuations in neurotic or borderline symptoms might theoretically occur as a result of fluctuations in a number of affect states other than depression (such as irritability or sexual desire). Some investigators have suggested, however, that a relatively specific relationship might exist between women who suffer from premenstrual affective symptoms and women who suffer from depression generally. In one study of headache patients at a neurology clinic, Kashiwagi, McClure, and Wetzel found a significant association between history of depression and premenstrual affective syndrome.[32] Other studies have found that not only are individuals with premenstrual affective syndrome more likely to have a history of depression in general, but their family members were also more likely to have histories of depression.[33] The number of studies in this area is still rather limited. Nonetheless, these data, as well as data on the relationship be-

31. Schachter and Singer (n. 4 above).

32. T. Kashiwagi, J. M. McClure, and R. B. Wetzel, "Premenstrual Affective Syndrome in Psychiatric Disorders," *Diseases of the Nervous System* 37 (1976): 116–19.

33. M. A. Schuckit et al., "Premenstrual Symptoms in Depression in a University Population," *Diseases of the Nervous System* 36 (1975): 516–17; R. D. Wetzel et al., "Premenstrual Affective Syndrome and Affective Disorder," *British Journal of Psychiatry* 127 (1975): 219–21.

tween suicide and the cycle, support the hypothesis that such a relationship might exist. This hypothesis is intriguing since it may lead to
research on the basis for depression itself and on the reasons for sex
differences in depression.

There is suggestive evidence that some schizophrenic patients may
be prone potentially to relapse paramenstrually.[34] However, schizo-
phrenics have not been shown to suffer from a high increase of
paramenstrual affective syndrome. It is possible, of course, that
paramenstrual affective symptomatic manifestations are distorted in
their expression because of schizophrenia. Despite some suggestive case
reports, manic-depressive illness has not been shown to fluctuate in severity during the menstrual cycle.[35] However, there has been relatively
little systematic study of this area. We suspect that the absence of positive
correlations reflects lack of detailed attention rather than a negative
finding.

Researchers have suggested that various pathophysiological mechanisms have etiological significance in producing fluctuations in psychological symptoms associated with the menstrual cycle. These have recently been reviewed by Smith, who emphasized, as we have, that the
behavioral changes associated with the cycle do not represent a unitary
phenomenon.[36] Since women may develop cyclic psychic distress for a
variety of reasons, no single "cause" is likely to be of unique importance.
Etiological factors frequently cited in the literature are: relative excess of
estrogen in relation to progesterone, endogenous sensitivity to estrogen
occurring premenstrually, increased body water, increased capillary
permeability, activation of the renin-angiotensin-aldosterone system,
hypoglycemia, sex-steroid withdrawal effects, and cyclical fluctuations in
brain neurotransmitters, particularly catecholamines.

In an extensive review, Steiner and Carroll have also emphasized
that the etiology of premenstrual dysphoria is not known, and no single
method of treatment has proved effective. Investigators summarize
work on the possible role of prolactin, a pituitary hormone, in producing
the premenstrual syndrome and the role of a dopamine agonist and
prolactin-suppressing agent, bromoergocryptine, in its treatment. As
Steiner and Carroll note, clinical trials of the treatment of premenstrual
syndrome with bromoergocryptine have been promising. Nonetheless,
data collection is still in preliminary stages. The role of prolactin in
producing the syndrome and of bromoergocryptine in treating it remain
important areas for future research.[37]

34. A. Coppen, "The Prevalence of Menstrual Disorders in Psychiatric Patients,"
British Journal of Psychiatry 111 (1965): 115–67; I. D. Glick, personal communication.
35. S. B. Diamond et al., "Menstrual Problems in Women with Primary Affective
Illness," *Comprehensive Psychiatry* 17 (1976): 541–48.
36. Smith (n. 27 above).
37. Steiner and Caroll (n. 29 above).

In reviewing the literature on psychopathology and the menstrual cycle, we see an analogy between this field and the more general area of depression. Like fleeting feelings of depression which are virtually universal, paramenstrual dysphoric affects may be minimal and unassociated with other symptoms. Feelings of depression may be severe enough to be quite painful and may lead to impaired social effectiveness. Similarly, the dysphoric feelings of the paramenstrual affective syndrome may be repetitively so severe that they warrant designation as symptoms. Depression may be associated with somatic symptoms, as may paramenstrual affective syndrome.

Depression is not a unitary concept. Different subgroups of depression have different etiologies and often have different treatments. The relationship between known biological determinants of depression and psychosocial determinants is a complex one. Thus some groups of depression result from primary biochemical lesions in the central nervous system, others result primarily from psychosocial determinants. In many, perhaps most, cases, interactions between physiological predisposition and psychosocial stress determines the form of the resultant psychopathology. We suspect that a similar matrix of complete etiologies of premenstrual affective syndrome will one day be identified. Future study of this interesting and important area should enhance our understanding of affect disorders, and perhaps even more important, of the mechanisms regulating affects in general.

Department of Psychiatry
New York Hospital–Cornell University Medical College

Review Essay

Pregnancy

Myra Leifer

Pregnancy is a unique period, since psychological changes and dramatic changes in physiology, appearance and body, and social status are all occurring simultaneously. However, we still know relatively little about the way in which normal women respond to this life stage because, until recently, feminine development has been regarded by most personality theorists as unimportant, deviant, or a minor variation of the male-determined stages of life. Female psychoanalytic theorists such as Helene Deutsch, Grete Bibring, and Therese Benedek were the first authors to deal extensively with the psychology of pregnancy and motherhood.[1]

No other stage in a woman's life is as replete with cultural stereotypes as pregnancy. Indeed, attitudes toward pregnancy have been one of the most prevalent sources of discrimination against women. The birth of a first child still creates the greatest discontinuity in the work lives of women. Although the situation improved with the amendment of the U.S. Civil Rights Act of 1964 to prohibit discrimination against the pregnant worker in hiring and fringe benefits, the fact that large numbers of employees who take maternity leaves each year do not return suggests that discrimination toward the pregnant woman continues.[2]

1. Helene Deutsch, *Psychology of Women* (New York: Grune & Stratton, 1945); Grete Bibring, "A Study of the Psychological Processes in Pregnancy and the Earliest Mother-Child Relationship," *Psychoanalytic Study of the Child* 16 (1961): 9–44; Therese Benedek, *Psycho-Sexual Functions in Women* (New York: Ronald Press, 1952).

2. Sue Mittenthal, "After Baby, Whither the Career?" *New York Times* (February 14, 1979).

Although the maternal role is changing rapidly, thus changing also the social context of pregnancy, much psychological research continues to report on women having reproductive difficulties or psychiatric problems.[3] In this essay, I will review those studies assessing the response of normal women to salient aspects of pregnancy.

The Motivation for Motherhood

Literature on the motivation for motherhood has been dominated by psychoanalytic theory, which regards such motivation as inevitable and biologically based.[4] Although previously discredited, the concept of maternal instinct has been revived again with the resurgence of sociobiological theories of human behavior. The seriousness with which it is now being considered is indicated by a recent paper by Alice Rossi.[5] Rossi, a feminist scholar who earlier had developed a social-role analysis of motherhood,[6] has attempted to restore biology to a central place in our understanding of maternal behavior. She argues that the universality of women's mothering may be due to an innate physiological disposition supported by a long evolutionary heritage.

However, social historians, sociologists, and cross-cultural researchers have related maternal attitudes to a broad range of socioeconomic phenomena and have underscored the importance of cultural pressures for parenthood.[7] Nancy Chodorow proposes that women are psychologically prepared for mothering through the developmental situation in which they grow up and in which women mother them.[8] She concludes that maternal behavior stems primarily from the structure of gender personality.

In studying the motivations for parenthood, many fertility researchers have adopted a cost-benefit approach derived from economic

3. See Roxanne Van Dusen and Eleanor B. Sheldon, "The Changing Status of American Women: A Life Cycle Perspective," *American Psychologist* 31 (1976): 106–15, for a review of current demographic trends affecting the role of motherhood.

4. See Deutsch for a discussion of the psychoanalytic view of motivation for pregnancy.

5. Alice Rossi, "A Biosocial Perspective on Parenting," *Daedalus* 106 (Spring 1977): 1–31.

6. Alice Rossi, "Transition to Parenthood," *Journal of Marriage and the Family* 30 (February 1968): 26–39.

7. Edward Shorter, *The Making of the Modern Family* (New York: Basic Books, 1975); Robert A. LeVine, *Culture Behavior and Personality* (Chicago: Aldine Publishing Co., 1973); Lois W. Hoffman and Martin L. Hoffman, "The Value of Children to Parents," in *Psychological Perspectives on Population,* ed. James T. Fawcett (New York: Basic Books, 1973); Edward W. Pohlman, *The Psychology of Birth Planning* (Cambridge, Mass.: Schenkman Publishing Co., 1969), pp. 19–76.

8. Nancy Chodorow, *The Reproduction of Mothering: Psychoanalysis and the Sociology of Gender* (Berkeley and Los Angeles: University of California Press, 1978).

theory. In this approach, birth-planning behavior is seen as the product of a decision-making process in which the benefits and values of children are weighed against their costs. Fawcett reviews some current studies in this vein;[9] the evidence suggests that situational, sociocultural, and psychological factors all differentially influence childbearing decisions. Sex-role attitudes and women's involvement in the workforce also have impact not only upon the number of children desired but also on the meaning attributed to parenthood.[10]

Although psychoanalytic theory maintains that motivation for motherhood is related to the way in which pregnancy is experienced, it appears that there may be only a limited relationship between these variables. The findings of several studies suggest that although a pregnancy may be undesired at the time of its inception, an attitude of acceptance develops as pregnancy progresses.[11]

Physical Aspects of Pregnancy

Somatic Symptomatology during Pregnancy

Although physicians have claimed that nausea and vomiting during pregnancy are caused or aggravated by psychological factors, research evidence regarding this assumption is inconclusive and contradictory.[12] It is not yet known what proportion of women actually experience these symptoms, nor do researchers agree on the biological, psychological, or sociological factors associated with them.[13] Elaine Grimm points out that the biochemical changes occurring in pregnancy create a lowered threshold for vomiting and concludes that nausea and vomiting in early pregnancy are not signs of maladjustment or rejection of the preg-

9. James T. Fawcett, "The Value and Cost of the First Child," in *The First Child and Family Formation,* ed. Warren B. Miller and Lucille Newman (Chapel Hill, N.C.: Carolina Population Center, 1978).

10. Lois W. Hoffman, Arland Thornton, and Jean Manis, "The Value of Children to Parents in the United States," *Journal of Population* 1 (Spring 1978): 91–131; John H. Scanzoni, *Sex Roles, Life Styles and Childbearing* (New York: Free Press, 1975).

11. Henriette Klein, Howard Potter, and Ruth Dyk, *Anxiety in Pregnancy and Childbirth* (New York: Paul B. Hoeber, 1950); Naomi Wenner and E. Ohaneson, "Motivation for Pregnancy" (paper read at the American Orthopsychiatric Association, New York, April 1967); George Winokur and Jack Werboff, "The Relationship of Conscious Maternal Attitudes to Certain Aspects of Pregnancy," *Psychiatric Quarterly* 30 (Fall 1959): 61–73.

12. See Julia A. Sherman, *On the Psychology of Women: A Survey of Empirical Studies* (Springfield, Ill.: Charles C. Thomas, 1971), for a review of studies of somatic symptomatology during pregnancy.

13. W. H. Trethowan and S. Dickens, "Cravings, Aversions and Pica of Pregnancy," in *Modern Perspectives in Psycho-Obstetrics,* ed. John Howells (New York: Brunner/Mazel, Inc., 1972).

nancy.[14] However, the persistence of the belief that pregnancy-related symptoms are of psychogenic origin has resulted in their being treated inadequately or with derision by medical personnel.[15]

In varying ways, recent studies have shown that sociocultural definitions of pregnancy and female sexuality influence the extent and severity of physical symptoms during pregnancy. Rosengren's findings suggest that the tendency of pregnant women to adopt a sick role is most marked among women who are socially mobile, perhaps because they lack a social network to provide clear-cut norms for behavior during pregnancy.[16] A number of other researchers also point to cultural expectations of the pregnant woman, the image of pregnancy presented by the peer group, the quality of the marriage, and the status of women in the particular culture as factors influencing the extent to which somatic symptomatology will be present.[17] The fact that husbands of pregnant women also report stress and somatic symptoms suggests that the social meaning of the physical changes in pregnancy is as important as the biological changes themselves.[18] The symptoms that men show during pregnancy are usually viewed as representing negative responses to their wives' pregnancies. However, one study found that the expectant fathers showing somatic symptomatology during pregnancy were more positive about their wives' pregnancies and later participated more in child care.[19]

The tenor of research on pregnancy as a sickness implies that women themselves cause their own somatic difficulties. The fact that pregnant women routinely visit a hospital clinic or physician's office

14. Elaine Grimm, "Psychologic and Social Factors in Pregnancy, Delivery and Outcome," in *Childbearing—Its Social and Psychological Aspects,* ed. Stephen Richardson and Alan Guttmacher (Baltimore: Williams & Wilkins, 1967).

15. K. Jean Lennane and R. John Lennane, "Alleged Psychogenic Disorders in Women," *New England Journal of Medicine* 288, no. 8 (1973): 288–92.

16. William Rosengren, "Social Sources of Pregnancy as Illness or Normality," *Social Forces* 39 (1961): 260–67, "Social Instability and Attitude toward Pregnancy as a Social Role," *Social Problems* 9 (1962): 371–78.

17. Margaret Mead, *Male and Female* (New York: William Morrow & Co., 1949); Esther Goshen-Gottstein, *Marriage and First Pregnancy: Cultural Influences and Attitudes of Israeli Women* (London: Tavistock Publications, 1966); Jean Thrasher, *The Subculture of Pregnancy in a College Community* (Durham: University of North Carolina Press, 1963); J. B. McKinlay, "The Sick Role: Illness and Pregnancy," *Social Science and Medicine* 6 (July 1972): 561–72.

18. Beatrice Liebenberg, "Expectant Fathers," *American Journal of Orthopsychiatry* 49 (1967): 358–59; Robert L. Munroe and Ruth H. Munroe, "Male Pregnancy Symptoms and Cross-Sex Identity in Three Societies," *Journal of Social Psychology* 84 (1971): 11–25; W. H. Trethowan, "The Couvade Syndrome: Some Further Observations," *Journal of Psychosomatic Research* 12 (1968): 107–15; Pauline Shereshefsky and Leon Yarrow, *Psychological Aspects of a First Pregnancy and Early Postpartum Adaptation* (New York: Raven Press, 1973).

19. Ruth H. Munroe, "Pregnancy Symptoms among Expectant American Fathers: An Inquiry into the Psychological Meaning" (Ph.D. diss., Harvard University, 1964).

which they have previously associated with disease can in itself enhance their perception of pregnancy as illness. As Lorber convincingly argues, the medical monopolization of pregnancy means that the normal pregnant woman is by definition sick.[20] She concludes that the view of female patients as deviants is an integral part of the medical ideology in which women are defined as ill by virtue of their reproductive functions, held responsible for what is disabling, and finally blamed for reacting emotionally to their physical condition.

Bodily Changes

Although pregnancy is the only period in adult life in which major bodily changes occur with startling rapidity and under normal circumstances, there has been little research on this aspect of pregnancy, and the data that exist are conflicting. Some studies indicate that the pregnant woman is more positive about her body, others that she is more conflicted or that no discernible trend regarding appearance exists.[21]

Emotional Response to Pregnancy

Surprisingly, few psychological studies have dealt with women's subjective reactions to pregnancy. Indeed, the most vivid accounts of what pregnancy and motherhood mean to women themselves have come not from the psychological literature but from feminist scholars, most notably Adrienne Rich, from the women's health movement, and from descriptive accounts written by new mothers.[22]

Current research does not yet provide an adequate picture of normal psychological change during pregnancy. Often limited by methodological problems, the empirical findings are contradictory and inconsistent. Some studies suggest that pregnancy is experienced as a

20. Judith Lorber, "Women and Medical Sociology: Invisible Professionals and Ubiquitous Patients," in *Another Voice*, ed. Marcia Millman and Rosabeth Moss Kanter (New York: Anchor Books, 1975).

21. Daniel Venezia, "Correlates of Body Attitude Change in Pregnancy," *Dissertation Abstracts International*, vol. 33, no. 3 (1972) (University Microfilms no. 72-24245); Alexander Tolor and Paul Di Grazia, "The Body Image of Pregnant Women as Reflected in Their Human Figure Drawings," *Journal of Clinical Psychology* 33 (1977): 556–71; O. McConnell and P. G. Daston, "Body Images Changes in Pregnancy," *Journal of Projective Techniques* 25 (July 1961): 451–56.

22. Adrienne Rich, *Of Woman Born* (New York: W. W. Norton & Co., 1976); Boston Women's Health Book Collective, *Our Bodies, Ourselves* (New York: Simon & Schuster, 1976); Virginia Barber and Merrill Skaggs, *The Mother Person* (New York: Bobbs-Merrill Co., 1975); Jane Lazarre, *The Mother Knot* (New York: McGraw-Hill Book Co., 1976). Two empirical studies that provide extensive material from women themselves are Ann Oakley, *Becoming a Mother* (London: Martin Robertson & Co., 1980); and Myra Leifer, *Psychological Effects of Motherhood: A Study of First Pregnancy* (New York: Praeger Publishers, 1980).

period of unusual well-being.[23] Severe psychopathology decreases throughout this period, pregnant women commit suicide much less frequently than women in comparable age groups, psychotic reactions are rare during pregnancy, and admissions to psychiatric hospitals fall at this time even though they rise rapidly for postpartum women.[24] Other studies report increased anxiety during pregnancy and present evidence that pregnancy is characterized by emotional upheaval and may be experienced as a psychological crisis.[25]

The divergence in these findings may stem from the fact that many studies have viewed the emotional changes of pregnancy as a negative phenomenon and ignore their adaptive meanings. Earlier studies, as Dana Breen notes, focus on changes such as increased "neuroticism" and view the normal outcome of pregnancy to be a return to the prepregnant psychological status.[26] In contrast, developmental theorists characterize pregnancy as a period of psychological activity and maintain that the emotional disequilibrium of pregnancy often mirrors psychological growth in preparation for motherhood.[27] Supporting this view, Reva Rubin describes a number of psychological operations pregnant women commonly engage in as they gradually assume a new sense of identity as a mother.[28] Breen found that women who report more depression and anxiety during pregnancy are more likely to adapt well to motherhood than are women who experience little psychological change during pregnancy.[29] In my own work, I have found increased self-preoccupation, anxiety, and emotional lability to be experienced by normal women throughout their pregnancies.[30] Anxiety directed toward the unborn child was found to be a significant reflection of the developing maternal bond, not an indication of pathology or neuroticism.

Many studies have focused exclusively on the psychological re-

23. Bernard Lubin, Sprague Gardener, and Aleda Roth, "Mood and Somatic Symptoms during Pregnancy," *Psychosomatic Medicine* 37 (1975): 136–46.

24. R. S. Paffenbarger, "Epidemiological Aspects of Parapartum Mental Illness," *British Journal of Preventive and Social Medicine* 18 (1964): 189–95; T. F. Pugh et al. "Rates of Mental Disease Related to Childbearing," *New England Journal of Medicine* 286 (1963): 1124–28.

25. Niles Newton, *Maternal Emotions* (New York: Paul B. Hoeber, 1955); Grete Bibring et al., "Considerations of the Psychological Processes in Pregnancy," *Psychoanalytic Study of the Child* 15 (1959): 113–21; Gerald Caplan, "Emotional Implications of Pregnancy and Influences on Family Relationships," in *The Healthy Child,* ed. H. Stuart and D. Preigh (Cambridge, Mass.: Harvard University Press, 1960); J. Loesch and N. Greenburg, "Some Specific Areas of Conflict Observed during Pregnancy," *American Journal of Orthopsychiatry* 32 (1962): 624–43.

26. Dana Breen, *The Birth of a First Child* (London: Tavistock Publications, 1975).

27. Deutsch; Bibring; Benedek (all cited in n. 1 above); Caplan.

28. Reva Rubin, "Attainment of the Maternal Role," *Nursing Research* 16 (1967): 237–53.

29. Breen.

30. Leifer.

sponse to pregnancy and ignored the social context in which these responses occur. The degree to which pregnancy is experienced as a time of well-being or stress may be critically related to the quality and extent of social and interpersonal support received. Margaret Mead and Niles Newton observe that markedly less help is given to childbearing women and infants in modern American society than in other societies.[31] A number of other studies underscore the effect of emotional support from the social network or the husband on the way in which the pregnancy is experienced.[32]

A range of social factors can influence a woman's response to pregnancy. Women pregnant for the first time tend to derive more satisfaction from their pregnancies than do women who have children. The less socioeconomic stress upon a woman, the more likely she is to enjoy her pregnancy.[33] Cross-cultural research has also begun to document the impact of social definitions of pregnancy.[34]

Hilary Graham describes the social image of pregnancy as characterized by ambiguity.[35] The pregnant woman is seen as strong and powerful because of her demonstrated fertility and fulfilled identity. However, she is simultaneously viewed as vulnerable and frail, allowed to indulge in normally prohibited activities and to abstain from her normal responsibilities; since her behavior is seen as not being fully under her own control she is regarded as somewhat dangerous and irrational. A recent series of studies found that women are socially stigmatized for being visibly pregnant and that reactions to pregnant women very closely parallel those to the physically disabled.[36]

The emotional changes of pregnancy have been most commonly

31. Margaret Mead and Niles Newton, "Cultural Patterning of Perinatal Behavior," in Richardson and Guttmacher, eds. (n. 13 above).

32. Mabel Blake Cohen, "Personal Identity and Sexual Identity," *Psychiatry* 29 (1966): 1–14; K. B. Nuckolls, J. Cassel, and B. H. Caplan, "Psychosocial Aspects, Life Crises and the Prognosis of Pregnancy," *American Journal of Epidemiology* 95 (1972): 431–41; Johanna D. Gladieux, "Pregnancy and the Transition to Parenthood: Satisfaction with the Pregnancy Experience as a Function of Sex Role Conceptions, Marital Relationships and Social Network," in Miller and Newman, eds. (n. 9 above); Shereshefsky and Yarrow (n. 18 above).

33. Richard Gordon and Katherine Gordon, "Some Social-Psychological Aspects of Pregnancy and Childbearing," *Journal of the Medical Society of New Jersey* 54 (May 1957): 569–72.

34. Eugene B. Brody, "The Meaning of the First Pregnancy for Working Class Jamaican Women," in Miller and Newman, eds.; Goshen-Gottstein (n. 17 above); Jane Hubert, "Belief and Reality: Social Factors in Pregnancy and Childbirth," in *The Integration of a Child into a Social World,* ed. Martin P. Richards (London: Cambridge University Press, 1974).

35. Hilary Graham, "The Social Image of Pregnancy: Pregnancy as Spirit Possession," *Sociological Review* 24 (1976): 291–308.

36. Shelley Taylor and Ellen Langer, "Pregnancy: A Social Stigma?" *Sex Roles* 3 (1977): 27–35; Ellen Langer et al., "Stigma, Staring and Discomfort: A Novel Stimulus Hypothesis," *Journal of Experimental Social Psychology* 12 (1976): 451–63.

attributed to hormonal changes, which are the most dramatic in a woman's lifetime. Both estrogen and progesterone levels are high. Following childbirth there is a sharp reduction in both of these hormones, and it may take several months for them to normalize. Parlee, in a review of research on the relationship between hormonal levels and mood throughout the menstrual cycle, reports that most studies have focused on negative affect, have failed to explore a broader range of mood, and have ignored the impact of social beliefs regarding hormonal effects.[37] She concludes that the relationship between hormonal levels and mood tone has not yet been convincingly demonstrated. Evidence that husbands of pregnant women also experience considerable psychological disequilibrium also points to the significance of social factors in influencing moods throughout pregnancy.[38]

Interpersonal Changes

Psychoanalytic theorists suggest that major shifts occur in the pregnant woman's interpersonal relationships, especially with her own mother and with her husband. The findings of the few studies that have investigated the pregnant woman's relationship with her own mother suggest that its quality may affect a woman's response to the role of mother.[39] Breen, for example, found that women who showed better adaptation to motherhood saw themselves as more similar to their own mothers after childbirth than before. However, as Adrienne Rich observes, few women growing up in patriarchal societies feel "mothered" enough themselves or have viable models for the complex role of motherhood.[40]

Few researchers have assessed the response of prospective fathers to pregnancy, and fewer still have attempted to describe its impact on the couple's interaction.[41] There is some evidence that marital satisfaction declines during pregnancy and that this is more marked for the husband than for the wife; that the pregnant woman shows a decline in sexual

37. Mary Brown Parlee, "Psychological Aspects of Menstruation, Childbirth and Menopause," in *Psychology of Women: Future Directions of Research,* ed. Julia A. Sherman and Florence I. Denmark (New York: Psychological Dimensions, Inc., 1979).

38. Arthur Colman and Libby Colman, *Pregnancy: The Psychological Experience* (New York: Herdes & Herdes, 1971); Liebenberg (n. 18 above); Shereshefsky and Yarrow (n. 18 above).

39. Celia J. Falicov, "Interpersonal Changes Accompanying First Pregnancy" (Ph.D. diss., University of Chicago, 1971); Judith W. Ballou, *The Psychology of Pregnancy* (Lexington, Mass.: Lexington Books, 1978); Breen (n. 26 above).

40. Rich (n. 22 above).

41. See Robert Fein, "Men's Experiences before and after the Birth of a First Child" (Ph.D. diss., Harvard University, 1974), for a review of research regarding the reactions of husbands to pregnancy.

interest, activity, and orgasmic functioning; and that husbands of pregnant women experience a parallel decline in sexual interest.[42] The
findings of a small, exploratory study of couple interaction during pregnancy suggest that pregnancy generates significant disequilibrium. Important changes were found to occur in the couple's sense of identity,
communication patterns, and role behavior; a striking shift to a more
traditional division of roles occurred with the birth of the baby.[43]

   Although some evidence indicates that relationships with female
friends may change during pregnancy or significantly influence the experience, this important area of research, too, has been neglected.[44]

The Relationship between Response to Pregnancy, Postpartum Reaction, and Status of the Infant

   To what extent is the way a woman experiences pregnancy related
to her response to motherhood and to her infant? Is the health or temperament of the infant related to maternal characteristics evident during
pregnancy? A growing body of research addresses questions such as
these.

   A number of investigators conclude that personality variables measured early in pregnancy are predictive of later emotional reactions, that
women who react positively to their female sexuality are more likely to
experience pregnancy positively. Niles Newton has made the important
distinction between cultural and biological femininity and argues that
pregnancy, childbirth, and breast feeding all require women to be active.[45] Breen found that those women in her study who had the most
problems coping with motherhood had attitudes that were traditionally
feminine.[46] Yet the bias of equating femininity with good adaptation to
motherhood has been so strong that researchers often ignore or distort
contradictory evidence.[47]

   42. Alexander Tolor and Paul Di Grazia, "Sexual Attitudes and Behavior Problems
during and following Pregnancy," *Archives of Sexual Behavior* 5, no. 6 (1976): 539–51; Don
Solberg, Julius Butler, and Nathaniel Wagner, "Sexual Behavior in Pregnancy," *New England Journal of Medicine* 288 (March 1973): 1098–1103; Shereshefsky and Yarrow (n. 18
above).
   43. Carolyn Cowan et al., "Becoming a Family: The Impact of a First Child's Birth on
the Couple's Relationship," in Miller and Newman, eds. (n. 9 above).
   44. Thrasher (n. 17 above); Falicov (n. 39 above).
   45. Niles Newton, "Interrelationships between Sexual Responsiveness, Birth and
Breast Feeding," in *Contemporary Sexual Behavior: Critical Issues in the 70s,* ed. J. Zubin and J.
Money (Baltimore: Johns Hopkins University Press, 1973).
   46. Breen (n. 26 above).
   47. As an example of this, see Ake Nilsson, "Paranatal Emotional Adjustment," in
Psychosomatic Medicine in Obstetrics and Gynaecology, ed. N. Morriss (Basel: Karger Press,
1972).

The research evidence is less clear about the relationship of personality characteristics, attitudes toward pregnancy, and eventual response to motherhood at postpartum. Work done by Gordon and Gordon during the 1950s indicated that experiencing stressful life circumstances (e.g., poverty or divorce) during pregnancy is highly predictive of later difficulty in adapting to motherhood. Other studies have confirmed an association between reaction to pregnancy and maternal attitudes.[48] Nevertheless, some researchers have suggested that different etiological factors may be associated with problems women encounter in each of these periods.[49] The findings of my own research indicate a relationship between response to the unborn child during pregnancy and to the infant at postpartum, but only a limited relationship between reactions to pregnancy and to motherhood itself.[50]

Ann Oakley has criticized much of this research for focusing on "adjustment" or "adaptation" and thereby reducing maternity to a symbol of conformity to cultural definitions of femininity.[51] In some studies, the presence of somatic symptoms during pregnancy has been viewed as a rejection of pregnancy, although little evidence supports this assumption.[52] Moreover, researchers often dichotomize feelings about pregnancy as "acceptance-rejection," ignoring the range of complex and contradictory feelings that is an entirely normal response to pregnancy.

Generally women who respond favorably to pregnancy react more positively to their babies.[53] There is also evidence that the babies of women who were highly anxious or who had considerable life stress during pregnancy are more likely to show behavioral deviancy or developmental difficulties.[54] Despite the fact that these studies are merely

48. Gordon and Gordon (n. 33 above); for other studies, see Anthony Davids and Raymond Holden, "Consistency of Maternal Attitudes and Personality from Pregnancy to Eight Months following Childbirth," *Developmental Psychology* 2 (1970): 364–66; E. H. Klatskin and L. D. Eron, "Projective Test Content during Pregnancy and Postpartum Adjustment," *Psychosomatic Medicine* 32 (1970): 487–93; Maurice Zemlick and Robert Watson, "Maternal Attitudes of Acceptance and Rejection during and after Pregnancy," *American Journal of Orthopsychiatry* 25 (1953): 570–84.

49. For studies not finding this association, see Virginia Larsen, "Stresses of the Childbearing Years," *American Journal of Public Health* 56 (1966): 32–36; Ake Nilsson and P. A. Almgren, "Paranatal Emotional Adjustment," *Acta Psychiatrica* 220 (1970): 1–141.

50. Leifer (n. 22 above).

51. Ann Oakley, "A Case of Maternity: Paradigms of Women as Maternity Cases," *Signs: Journal of Women in Culture and Society* 4, no. 4 (Summer 1979): 44–61.

52. See, for example, Nilsson and Almgren (n. 49 above) who regard both "excessive" vomiting and lack of vomiting as indications of poor adaptation to pregnancy.

53. Anthony Davids, Raymond Holden, and Gloria Gray, "Maternal Anxiety during Pregnancy and Adequacy of Mother and Child Adjustment Eight Months following Childbirth," *Child Development* 34 (1963): 993–1002; Zemlick and Watson.

54. Davids et al.; Antonio Ferreira, "Emotional Factors in Prenatal Environment: A Review," *Journal of Nervous and Mental Diseases* 141 (1965): 108–18; Richard Gorsuch and Martha Key, "Abnormalities of Pregnancy as a Function of Anxiety and Life Stress," *Psychosomatic Medicine* 36 (1974): 352–62; D. H. Stott, "Follow-up Study from Birth of the

correlational, researchers infer that the attitudes of the mother determine the behavior of the infant. However, recent studies suggest that a range of variables, including characteristics of the infant such as sex, temperament, and alertness (especially as influenced by the amount of medication received at delivery, amount of contact a mother has with her infant immediately following birth, the quality of the marital relationship, and the extent to which the husband or secondary parent provides help in caring for the infant) all significantly affect the development of maternal feelings and/or the developmental status of the infant.[55]

Theoretical Perspectives on Pregnancy

Most recently, a view of pregnancy as a normal developmental stage of the life cycle has dominated the psychological literature.[56] Although this perspective has usefully counterbalanced the stereotype of pregnancy as passive and focused attention on a uniquely feminine developmental experience, its grounding in psychoanalytic ideology makes the optimal outcome of pregnancy "adjustment" or "adaptation" to a traditionally defined feminine role. Failure to achieve this maturational step is attributed to the individual woman's failure to resolve intrapsychic conflicts. Moreover, the view of pregnancy as a normal crisis implies that stress is inherent in maternity; most theorists have not

---

Effects of Prenatal Stress," *Developmental Medicine and Child Neurology* 15 (1973): 770–87; Kay Standley, "Prenatal and Perinatal Correlates of Neonatal Behaviors" (paper presented at the Annual Convention of the American Psychological Association, New Orleans, August 29, 1974).

55. For studies relating infant characteristics to maternal behavior, see Shereshefsky and Yarrow (n. 18 above); Kenneth Robson and Howard Moss, "Patterns and Determinants of Maternal Attachment," *Journal of Pediatrics* 77 (1970): 976–85; Michael E. Lamb, "Influence of the Child on Marital Quality and Family Interaction during the Prenatal, Parinatal and Infancy Periods," in *Child Influences in Marital and Family Interaction: A Life-Cycle Perspective,* ed. R. M. Lerner and G. D. Spanier (New York: Academic Press, 1979). For studies relating delivery medication to infant characteristics, see Standley; Ross Parke, Susan O'Leary, and Stephen West, "Mother-Father-Newborn Interaction: Effect of Maternal Medication, Labor and Sex of Infant," *Proceedings of the 80th Annual Convention of the American Psychological Association* 7 (1972): 85–86. See Marshall Klaus and John Kennell, *Maternal-Infant Bonding* (St. Louis: C. V. Mosby Co., 1976) for a review of studies of the effects of early mother-infant contact. For studies assessing the impact of the husband or secondary parent on maternal behavior, see Candace Feiring and Jerome Taylor, "The Influence of the Infant and Secondary Parent on Maternal Behavior: Toward a Social Systems View of Infant Attachment," unpublished manuscript (Pittsburgh: University of Pittsburgh, Psychology Department, 1976); Shereshefsky and Yarrow (n. 18 above).

56. See Rhona Rapoport, Robert Rapoport, and Ziona Streilitz, *Fathers, Mothers and Society* (New York: Basic Books, 1977), for a comprehensive review of developmental theories of pregnancy.

examined the way in which broad social forces shape a woman's response to pregnancy. Alice Rossi, in developing a sociological analysis of parenthood, deliberately replaces the term "crisis" with the more neutral word "transition," maintaining that the application of the concept of crisis to parenthood dichotomizes normality and pathology and does not provide a single framework for dealing with a range of outcomes.[57] Rossi's conceptualization of pregnancy has been significant in bringing into clearer view the social aspects of maternity, although her focus remains on motherhood rather than fatherhood or parenthood.

The ecological theory of human development recently formulated by Urie Bronfenbrenner promises a more comprehensive understanding of parenthood.[58] Bronfenbrenner underscores the importance of analyzing developmental shifts as changes in ecological systems rather than as occurring solely within individuals. He would have us examine the way a broad range of phenomena influence a woman's experience of pregnancy and the way pregnancy in turn influences the woman's ecological environment. Such a perspective is badly needed in a field dominated by studies of isolated variables. Moreover, most studies of normal pregnancy have been of middle-class married women pregnant for the first time. The meaning of pregnancy for the husband and family unit, the impact of the second or subsequent pregnancies, the influence of socioeconomic level and ethnicity on response to pregnancy are just a few of the many areas that could be illuminated by an ecological approach.

Department of Psychiatry
University of Chicago

57. Rossi, "Transition to Parenthood" (n. 6 above).
58. Urie Bronfenbrenner, *The Ecology of Human Development* (Cambridge, Mass.: Harvard University Press, 1979).

Review Essay

Maternal Sexuality and Asexual Motherhood

Susan Weisskopf Contratto

The excitation felt in the genitals can also disturb the joy of nursing. For the nursing mother can bear almost anything

This paper exists because of two recent, extraordinarily important books. Adrienne Rich, *Of Woman Born* (New York: Bantam Books, 1977), clearly demonstrates the impact of patriarchy on the institution of mothering. After Rich it is impossible to talk of women's "natural" role. Nancy Chodorow, *The Reproduction of Mothering* (Berkeley and Los Angeles: University of California Press, 1978), shows how patriarchy effects individual personality development. What these writers laboriously set out to prove, I am privileged to be able to take as given. Nancy Chodorow read an earlier draft of this paper and made insightful comments and suggestions. I am indebted to her for these, as well as for support and discussions throughout the process of writing. In addition, I have profited from careful comments by Karen E. Paige and Guy E. Swanson. Conceptual and factual errors, however, remain my responsibility. I am grateful for the support of NIMH training grant MH 15122-03, which I received during part of this project. The title of the paper requires additional definitions and discussion. Throughout, I will talk about mothering as a woman's experience with her infant. Cross-cultural evidence indicates that early caretaking responsibilities fall almost universally to mothers (Michelle Z. Rosaldo, "A Theoretical Overview," in *Women, Culture and Society,* ed. Michelle Z. Rosaldo and Louise Lamphere [Stanford, Calif.: Stanford University Press, 1974]). In spite of media talk of househusbands, a variety of recent articles on dual-career professional couples indicates that, even among these couples, caretaking of small children is the woman's domain (Jeff B. Bryson and Rebecca Bryson, *Dual-Career Couples,* a special issue of the *Psychology of Women Quarterly* [vol. 3, no. 1] [New York: Human Sciences Press, 1978], passim). I define maternal sexuality in the most general way, as a woman's sexual feelings or behaviors while she is involved in tasks normally associated with motherhood. This does not specify who arouses the feelings and to whom they are directed, nor does it narrow down the tasks to only those which involve direct interaction with children. I will discuss asexual motherhood as both

more easily than the confusion of conscious, sexual emotions with the tender, loving action of nursing.[1]

I sometimes felt that my son derived sexual pleasure from my touching him (say, while giving him a bath). He was about four or five then. It was very confusing and embarrassing to me; I also felt guilty—clearly if I'd been a better mother this wouldn't have happened.[2]

You're writing a paper on maternal sexuality? What in God's name is that?[3]

At three o'clock in the Autumn afternoon, the American-born mother opens the door. She says there is no subject that cannot be discussed with her because she was born in this up-to-date place, the U.S.A. We have just learned several words we believe are the true adult names of the hidden parts of our bodies, the parts that are unnameable. . . . The American-born mother says those are the worst words of all, never to use them or think of them, to always feel free to talk to her about anything else.
    The Russian-born mother has said on occasions that there are no such words in Russian.[4]

Maternal sexuality is a topic that makes virtually everyone anxious. As a result, there is little systematic, good work on it. The work of those who acknowledge its presence suffers not only from the problems inherent in any study of sex but, more particularly, from the embarrassment, guilt, disgust, and anger that accompany tabooed behaviors and feelings. The sparse research that does exist, often confusing and contradictory, usually raises questions instead of providing answers. The scarcity of research and theory both constrains and liberates this essay. I can provide neither a satisfying review of the subject nor highly confident statements. All of the previous work at some point addresses the question of what is or should be the relationship between maternity and sexuality. I am not

---

the cultural belief that mothers are not, and should not be, sexual persons and as a prescription for behavior and feelings that individual women hold about themselves as mothers. I will also talk about gender identity. I mean to distinguish this from biological sex, e.g., male, female, and hermaphroditic, which is biologically determined and relatively uninteresting. Avoiding the nature/nurture controversy, I will assert that gender identity is that sense of oneself, conscious or unconscious, as male, female, or androgynous, which has been formed in a cultural context and is therefore highly dependent on socialization.

    1. Helene Deutsch, *The Psychology of Women,* vol. 2, *Motherhood* (New York: Grune & Stratton, 1945), p. 290.
    2. Shere Hite, *The Hite Report* (New York: Dell Publishing Co., 1976), p. 564.
    3. The mother of two small children and a friend of the author's.
    4. Grace Paley, "Other Mothers," *Feminist Studies* 2 (June 1978): 166–69, quote on p. 167.

comfortable with the different answers but lack adequate information to propose my own definitive solution. On the other hand, writing about a barely touched topic allows me considerable latitude in shaping this essay. I will move between offering data, proposing hypotheses that fit the data, and speculation. I will have succeeded in my task if this essay moves readers to consider maternal sexuality an appropriate and pressing topic of inquiry.

After first laying out the theoretical frameworks about maternal sexuality, such as they are, I will focus on several areas of a woman's experience where there is some research with which to evaluate the theories and flesh out the concept. This essay will also confront the powerful and, I think, pervasive ideology of asexual motherhood. The belief is that good mothers do not have sexual feelings in relationship to children, that good mothers are generally asexual. The work of three social commentators, Talcott Parsons in the 1940s, Erik Erikson in the 1950s, and Phillip Slater in the early 1970s, attests to the existence of such a phenomenon.[5] Though there is little information on who holds this ideology, let me propose that it is widespread, at least in the middle class, and that both the lack of research on maternal sexuality and the fragmented quality of what is available attest to the ideology's impact on scholars.

Finally, I will argue that a substantial group of women have internalized this ideology and, as a result, experience considerable psychological pain. Statements of women themselves, as well as of clinicians who see them as patients, and certain maternal behaviors suggest that many women who are pregnant or who are in relationship with small children are intensely uncomfortable with their own sexuality, consciously or unconsciously. I will argue that these women are not deviant. Rather, they have successfully internalized the identity of asexual motherhood.

Theoretical Frameworks

The two groups who have worked on the problem of maternal sexuality, the psychoanalytic theorists and the biosocial theorists, share

5. Talcott Parsons, "Age and Sex in the Social Structure of the United States," in *Essays in Sociological Theory,* rev. ed. (New York: Free Press, 1964), see esp. pp. 95–99, "Kinship System of Contemporary United States," in ibid., see pp. 193–94; Erik Erikson, *Childhood and Society,* 2d ed. (New York: W. W. Norton Co., 1963), pp. 288–98; and Phillip Slater, *The Pursuit of Loneliness* (Boston: Beacon Press, 1970), pp. 69–80. Recent historical work suggests that this ideology is not new. See, for example, Nancy F. Cott, "Passionlessness: An Interpretation of Victorian Sexual Ideology, 1790–1850," *Signs: Journal of Women in Culture and Society* 4, no. 2 (Winter 1978): 219–36; Ruth H. Bloch, "American Feminine Ideal in Transition: The Rise of the Moral Mother, 1785–1815," *Feminist Studies* 2 (June 1978): 100–126, and "Untangling the Roots of Modern Sex Roles: A Survey of Four Centuries of Change," *Signs: Journal of Women in Culture and Society* 4, no. 2 (Winter 1978): 237–52.

some common ground but differ dramatically as to what they feel the proper relationship between maternity and sexuality should be. The former say that in mature women sexuality is harnessed for or split off from motherhood; the latter suggest that sexual gratification can and should be an important bonus of motherhood.

Psychoanalytic theorists argue that, through a variety of twists and turns, the transformation of sexual energy in a woman's developmental history will lead to both the motivation and the capacity for motherhood. They spend time accounting for this transformation; address themselves to the relationship in the adult woman between sexuality and motherliness; and, because of the importance for them of infantile sexuality, write about the effect of mothering on the sexual development of infants. I will briefly address these three issues.

Early writers, including Freud, proposed that the wish to have a baby arose from the little girl's wish for a penis. Psychic maneuvers to compensate for the lack of a phallus led to a variety of distinctly female personality characteristics. Immediately there arose a disagreement, still unresolved, among the psychoanalysts. Some felt that the focus should be on what the little girl had rather than on what she did not. These theorists have stressed the unique contribution of the vagina.[6] Helene Deutsch has written extensively about maternal sexuality. Motherhood is the inevitable outcome of her argument that passivity, masochism, and narcissism comprise the feminine core, the very characteristics that lead to good mothering. The vagina finally comes into its own as an active reproductive organ in the mature female. She proposes that orgasm lends a sucking action to the vagina that aids in the mobility of the sperm and posits an antimotherly orgasm which expels seminal fluid.[7] Heiman concurs with Deutsch about the action of the vagina and further adds that lubrication during intercourse facilitates fertility by providing a more congenial environment for the sperm.[8] Most important, Deutsch and Heiman suggest that the woman experiences a psychic equivalency between coitus and childbirth and between coitus and nursing.[9] Intercourse, for the mature woman, is the first mothering activity.

Therese Benedek argues that motherhood is the essence of the

6. Space limitations preclude listing all psychoanalytic references on this subject. A recent article and book, however, reassert the penis-envy theory: Edward D. Joseph, "An Aspect of Female Frigidity," *Journal of the American Psychoanalytic Association* 1 (1974): 116–22; Humberto Nagera, *Female Sexuality and the Oedipus Complex* (New York: Jason Aronson, Inc., 1975). Recent works that actively question this theory are: Roy Schafer, "Problems in Freud's Psychology of Women," *Journal of the American Psychoanalytic Association* 3 (1974): 459–85; and various articles in a supplement to the *Journal of the American Psychoanalytic Association* on female psychology (vol. 24, no. 5 [1976]).

7. Deutsch, pp. 89–91.

8. Marcel Heiman, "Sexual Response in Women: A Correlation of Physiological Findings with Psychoanalytic Concepts," *Journal of the American Psychoanalytic Association* 2 (1963): 360–85, esp. pp. 365–68, 370–71.

9. Deutsch, pp. 242–43; Heiman, pp. 373–78.

female's sexuality, the primary organizer of her sexual drive and personality and a manifestation of the instinct for survival in the child.[10] She proposes, from research she and Rubenstein carried out in the early forties, that there is a female sexual cycle with increased sexual desire at mid-cycle (in the preovulative state) and a decrease of sexual desire postovulation and a concentration of psychic energy on the woman's own body and welfare.[11]

   Paradoxically, though visible pregnancy is a warranty of a woman's sexual identity for the analyst,[12] sexual feelings somehow are at odds with, or conflict with, motherly feelings. Deutsch argues that there is a split between sexuality and motherliness but that these can be psychically integrated, a coexistence of opposing tendencies that can be normal "and only a marked preponderance of the one or the other leads to complications and neurotic difficulties."[13] During pregnancy, motherliness begins to predominate.[14] Benedek suggests that the mature woman's ego identity is more invested in her aspiration to bear and raise children than in orgasm.[15] In another place, she contrasts the motherliness of the mature woman with the erotic sexuality of other (nonmature?) women.[16] I assume from these statements that Benedek is suggesting that the mature woman is simply not as sexual as she is motherly. Kestenberg describes an intricately complicated process for balancing motherliness and sexuality. The little girl practices "switching genital excitement on and off" in childhood, which will enable her to "desexualize her genital feelings and externalize her impulses upon her baby" while caring for it and to "resexualize her genitals and give up externalization" while filling her role as a sexual partner.[17]

   Within the psychological literature, there is considerable agreement that the early mother-child relationship is and should be erotic for the

   10. Therese Benedek, "Untitled Discussion of Sherfey's Paper on Female Sexuality," *Journal of the American Psychoanalytic Association* 3 (1968): 424–48, esp. p. 438.
   11. Therese Benedek and B. B. Rubenstein, *The Sexual Cycle in Women,* Psychosomatic Medicine Monographs, vol. 3 (Washington, D.C.: National Research Council, 1942); Therese Benedek, "Psychobiological Aspects of Mothering," *American Journal of Orthopsychiatry* 26 (1956): 272–78, esp. p. 274; Benedek, "Untitled Discussion," p. 435, and "On the Psychobiology of Gender Identity," in *Annual of Psychoanalysis* (New York: International Universities Press, 1976), 4:144; Judith S. Kestenberg, "Outside and Inside, Male and Female," *Journal of the American Psychoanalytic Association* 3 (1968): 457–520, esp. p. 514, extends the argument by suggesting that contraception is psychically equivalent to infanticide because of the essential connection of women's sexual activity and motherhood.
   12. Dinora Pines, "Pregnancy and Motherhood: Interaction between Fantasy and Reality," *British Journal of Medical Psychology* 45 (1972): 333–43, esp. p. 334; Benedek, "On the Psychobiology of Gender Identity," p. 144.
   13. Deutsch, p. 25.
   14. Ibid., p. 153.
   15. Benedek, "Untitled Discussion," p. 444, and "On the Psychobiology of Gender Identity," p. 148.
   16. Benedek, "On the Psychobiology of Gender Identity," p. 157.
   17. Kestenberg, pp. 470, 463.

child. This view, outrageous when proposed by Freud seventy-five years ago, is now taken for granted. Nursing, touching, and diapering all stir erotic sensations in the infant. As Kestenberg describes it: "Under ordinary circumstances, maternal care brings about direct and indirect stimulation not only to the outside but to the inside genital as well (as, for instance, through bath water). *It is the task of the mother to stimulate and prime all bodily functions.*"[18] Sarlin, who suggests, more specifically, that the nursing relationship evolves into the capacity for adult genital love, is eloquent in his description: the "infant at the mother's breast was an active participant in an overtly erotic relationship."[19]

What of the other partner in this "overtly erotic relationship"—what of the stimulator and primer? None of the writers who carry on about the quality and importance of this relationship for the child perceive the mother as a maternal robot. She explicitly should be warm, loving, and responsive in her caretaking relationship. Most writers ignore the possibility that she might find the relationship sexual also.[20] Others acknowledge the reciprocity of the unconscious erotic attachment between mother and child but ignore the possibility that specific caretaking behaviors might feel erotic to the mother.[21] Still others apparently assume that the mother has successfully accomplished the tricky psychic maneuvers which desexualize motherhood. In general, the psychoanalytic accounts of maternal sexuality are inadequate. They are wrong in some specific respects, for example, the theories about sexual cycle and the action of the vagina. They are most wanting, however, in their explanations of the relationship between sexuality and motherhood.

Niles Newton and Alice Rossi are biosocial theorists who have done work on maternal sexuality. Newton, by training a psychologist, wrote an early monograph on maternal emotions and has done later work on breast-feeding that is truly ground breaking.[22] Alice Rossi, originally a sociologist, enters the discussion of maternal sexuality because of impor-

18. Ibid., p. 466 (italics added).

19. Charles Sarlin, "Feminine Identity," *Journal of the American Psychoanalytic Association* 4 (1963): 790–816, esp. p. 798.

20. Ashley Montague, *Touching: The Human Significance of the Skin* (New York: Columbia University Press, 1971), provides a good example of this problem. He mounts a good case for the importance of tactile sensation for healthy infant development and points out that, in humans, mothers should provide this stimulation with warmth. He further remarks that women, for whatever reason, tend to be more sexually responsive to tactile sensation than men (p. 181). He does not wonder, however, about whether the mother (a woman) who is stimulating her infant is herself being stimulated.

21. For example, Talcott Parsons, "The Incest Taboo in Relation to Social Structure and the Socialization of the Child," *British Journal of Sociology* 2 (June 1954): 101–17, looks at the function of the erotogenic tie between mother and child in the family. He does not consider the possibility that this tie is based on behaviors or fantasies that might feel explicitly and consciously sexual, though they do not involve genital intercourse.

22. Niles Newton, *Maternal Emotions*, A Psychosomatic Medicine Monograph (New York: Paul B. Hoeber, 1955); Niles Newton and Michael Newton, "Psychologic Aspects of Lactation," *New England Journal of Medicine* 22 (November 1967): 1179–88.

tant comments on, and extensions of, Newton's work.[23] Newton argues that women's three reproductive acts—coitus, labor, and lactation—are pleasurable, a necessity for species survival, and interrelated: "All three are interpersonal, psychophysical acts that are psychologically inter-twined with affectionate partnership formation and caretaking behavior."[24] They may be, she posits, "the biologic foundation upon which patterns of family life are built."[25] Neurohormonally related through the action of oxytocin, easily disrupted in the early stages, they trigger caretaking behavior.[26] Rossi sums up the implications of these inter-relationships: "Good sexual adjustment, positive enjoyment of preg-nancy, low profiles of nausea during pregnancy, easier and shorter labor, desire for and success at breastfeeding, preference for a natural or minimal-drug childbirth, all seem to form a coherent syndrome."[27]

Newton suggests a quite different relationship between sexuality and motherhood from that of the analysts. While they propose that normal development leads to a split between motherly acts and sexuality, she argues that nature intended just the opposite. For example, she finds that mothers often experience sensual pleasure through breast-feeding, and suggests that the survival of the race depends on its being pleasur-able for them.[28] Likewise, she argues that it is equally pleasurable for the baby, that male babies often experience erection during nursing, and that "after feeding, there is often a relaxation that is characteristic of the conclusion of satisfactory sexual response."[29] She also argues that since the Industrial Revolution there has been a sharp conflict between a woman's cultural femininity and her biological femininity. Women's cul-tural femininity requires them to be both dependent and inactive, whereas their biological femininity demands activity, aggression, and competence. This conflict leads to antimotherhood feelings against which Newton warns us.[30]

Rossi proposes that the split between maternity and sexuality is con-nected to male dominance in western society. She implies that it is in the best interest of mothers, children, and, I assume, the culture in which they live to bring sexuality and maternity together: "It is to men's sexual advantage to restrict women's sexual gratification to heterosexual coitus,

23. Alice S. Rossi, "Maternalism, Sexuality and the New Feminism," in *Contemporary Sexual Behavior,* ed. Joseph Zubin and John Money (Baltimore: Johns Hopkins University Press, 1973), pp. 145–73.

24. Niles Newton, "Interrelationships between Sexual Responsiveness, Birth and Breastfeeding," in ibid., p. 91.

25. Ibid., p. 92.

26. Ibid., pp. 81–93.

27. Rossi, p. 169.

28. Newton, *Maternal Emotions,* pp. 50–51, 82–92; Newton and Newton, p. 1180; Newton, in Zubin and Money, eds., p. 81.

29. Newton and Newton, p. 1182.

30. Newton, *Maternal Emotions,* pp. 98–99, 63–71.

though the price for the woman and child may be a less psychologically and physically rewarding relationship."[31]

In sum, then, all the theorists are concerned with presenting women's sexuality as an entity in the service of reproduction; aspects of their reproductive function are psychologically and neurohormonally intertwined. A woman is a partner in an erotic relationship with a child. She either (normally) does not feel sexual feelings in this relationship or (naturally) does.

The Sexual Cycle

The concept of a female sexual cycle appeared in several forms in the previous discussion. Benedek argues that there is a fluctuation of sexual desire and activity when the woman is maximally fertile. Deutsch, Heiman, and Newton propose physiological and psychological equivalences between intercourse, childbirth, and nursing. Rossi talks of "a coherent syndrome." In this section I will argue that such a cycle does not exist, at least by any criteria researchers can agree on. I will suggest that political and social bias may shore up its appeal more than facts.

Mary Brown Parlee, several years ago, and Doreen Asso, recently, reviewed studies since Benedek that try to connect hormone level (menstrual phase) with affect, autonomic responsiveness, and behavior.[32] No consistent picture emerges. Data on the fluctuation of sexual desire suggest that peak desire can occur at virtually any time in the menstrual cycle. Kinsey found that 90 percent of the American women in his sample said they experienced heightened sexual desire in the luteal (postovulation-premenstrual) phase of their cycles.[33] Ford and Beach report that, cross-culturally, many women have highest sexual desire just before or after menstruation and that a much smaller group experience intense desire mid-cycle.[34]

Masters and Johnson looked at the possible role of the vagina and uterus in reproduction. They concluded that there is no indication of any sucking response of the uterus during orgasm and, in fact, suggest that the action may be expulsive rather than ingestive.[35] They looked at spermatozoal longevity and directional motility in the vagina throughout

31. Rossi, p. 167 (italics added).
32. Mary Brown Parlee, "The Premenstrual Syndrome," *Psychological Bulletin* 6 (1973): 454–65; Doreen Asso, "Levels of Arousal in the Premenstrual Phase," *British Journal of Social and Clinical Psychology* 17 (1978): 47–55.
33. Reported in Mary Jane Sherfey, *The Nature and Evolution of Female Sexuality* (New York: Random House, 1972), p. 96.
34. Clellan S. Ford and Frank A. Beach, *Patterns of Sexual Behavior* (New York: Harper & Bros., 1951), pp. 208–13.
35. William H. Masters and Virginia E. Johnson, *Human Sexual Response* (Boston: Little, Brown & Co., 1966), pp. 122–24, 126.

the menstrual cycle and concluded that the particular phase has no impact on the sperm. They did, however, suggest that vaginal lubrication might have an effect on spermatozoal motility and longevity since the lubricant might raise the pH slightly, thereby providing a more hospitable environment for sperm. They added, though, that it takes thirty minutes of sexual excitation to achieve a recordable change on pH value.[36]

The most telling problem in arguing that there is a psychic and physiological equivalency between coitus, birth, and lactation is the presence of pain. Most women experience pain in undrugged childbirth, though the degree to which they suffer may be affected by fear.[37] Few healthy women experience pain in coitus. Though some women feel pain early on in nursing (from uterine contractions associated with the action of oxytocin and from sore nipples), this soon passes.[38] For Deutsch, the presence or not of consciously felt pain is not a logical problem in arguing the equation because of the role she assigns to masochism. However, starting with Horney and continuing to the present, other analysts have effectively challenged this.[39]

Newton, on the other hand, simply ignores the normal pain of childbirth; in her charts comparing the physiological response of coitus to uninhibited childbirth, she does not mention pain.[40] This is all the more striking because, at another point in her monograph, she describes the pain of childbirth as "the most extreme pain human beings are capable of feeling" and likens it to torture and third-degree burns.[41] Both the psychological and the physiological equation of these events become seriously unbalanced when one adds the factor of different normal degrees of pain associated with them.

The frequency with which the cycle concept appears, in spite of a lack of evidence to prove its existence,[42] speaks, I think, to a cultural wish

36. Ibid., pp. 91–95.

37. Sheila Kitzinger, *The Experience of Childbirth*, 3d ed. (London: Pelican Books, 1972), pp. 18, 20.

38. Emanuel A. Friedman, "The Physiological Aspects of Pregnancy," in *The Woman Patient: Medical and Psychological Interfaces*, vol. 1, ed. Carol C. Nadelson and Malkah T. Notman, Women in Context Series (New York: Plenum Press, 1978), see esp. pp. 67–68.

39. Karen Horney, "The Problem of Feminine Masochism," in *Feminine Psychology*, ed. Harold Kelman (New York: W. W. Norton & Co., 1967); Harold P. Blum, "Masochism, the Ego Ideal and the Psychology of Women," *Journal of the American Psychoanalytic Association* 5 (1976): 157–93; Natalie Shainess, "Vulnerability to Violence: Masochism as Process," *American Journal of Psychotherapy* 2 (April 1979): 174–89.

40. Newton, in Zubin and Money, pp. 78–81, and *Maternal Emotions*, pp. 87–88.

41. Newton, *Maternal Emotions*, p. 13.

42. Francis J. Kane, Morris A. Lipton, and John A. Ewing, "Hormonal Influence in Female Sexual Response," *Archives of General Psychiatry* (February 1969), pp. 202–9, is a good case in point. The authors conscientiously review the data, noting, among other things, that ovariectomy does not necessarily lead to a decrease in sexual desire, that some

that it should exist. The picture is clearly pronatalist, implicitly pro-family, and ignores the possibility of female recreative, as distinct from procreative, sex. Inherent in the procycle position are questions about the normalcy of women who do not have children; who make homosexual, as distinct from heterosexual, object choices; and who do not form families. In fact, looking at the material from another angle, all of these are widely held cultural definitions of deviance; in the folk psychology, there is something "odd" about the unmarried woman, something "peculiar" about the couple (the woman) who choose not to procreate, and certainly being a lesbian is being "queer." I would suggest that the die-hard proponents of the cycle-syndrome picture of normal female development are trying to scientifically prove cultural attitudes about appropriate female gender roles.

I have belabored this notion of women's sexual cycle because it is so prominent in the literature that also claims that normal development is development for motherhood, that coitus is the first act of motherhood, and that normal female sexuality is procreative. I will assume, alternatively, that some normal women will become mothers and some normal women will not. The rest of my discussion of maternal sexuality will focus on women who become mothers.

Pregnancy

For some women, being a mother-to-be and being sexual are internally conflictual. Supporting this theory is clinical evidence about women in relationships to their own bodies and in sexual relationships to husbands. Given the sociocultural context in which mothering is reproduced, it is likely that many women may experience these conflicts. Carol Nadelson, a psychiatrist, summarizes briefly, and without speculating as to the causes, some of the psychological problems which occur during pregnancy. She remarks that some women experience embarrassment over the exhibition of the active sexuality that pregnancy represents.[43] Such feelings in a woman who was previously comfortable with her sexuality might indicate conflict over the association of sexuality with motherhood; her active sexuality has led to her maternal state, and in her psychic experience the two do not mix.

---

women experience peak sexual desire at a time of falling hormones, and that the increased hormones in pregnancy do not increase desire. Their conclusion is classic: "The literature reviewed in this paper would seem to indicate that there is variation in level of sexual interest and capacity for orgasm during the menstrual cycle in both animals and man [*sic*]," p. 208.

43. Carol C. Nadelson, "'Normal' and 'Special' Aspects of Pregnancy: A Psychological Approach," in Nadelson and Notman, eds., p. 74.

Nadelson also reports that pregnancy sometimes brings out sexual problems in a marriage for the first time.[44] She does not elaborate as to what these might be. Pines, a therapist, reports on the sexual fantasies of some of her pregnant patients. She reports that at the time of quickening some of the women she sees experience a decrease in sexual desire; they associate men with intruders, capable of harming the baby.[45] From her perspective as a childbirth educator, Kitzinger reports that some women dislike intercourse throughout pregnancy; they feel as if they are "sacred vessels of new life and thus should not be 'contaminated' by sex."[46] Even more graphic is a woman quoted in *Ourselves and Our Children:* "Sexually I was completely turned off. I didn't want to be touched. Intercourse seemed almost barbaric. . . ."[47]

Empirical studies with nonpatient women provide additional data about women's sexuality during pregnancy. A number of studies concur that during the course of pregnancy there is a general picture of declining sexual interest and activity.[48] This decline is not inevitable. Ford and Beach point out that there is considerable variability cross-culturally, ranging from prohibition of sexual activity from the moment the pregnancy is obvious to requiring it throughout the pregnancy.[49]

Several carefully done studies look at desire and behavior and make distinctions between the experience of women in their first pregnancy (nulliparous) and women in a later pregnancy (multiparous). Masters and Johnson studied the erotic desire and sexual performance of 111 pregnant women by means of four intensive interviews at different times in their pregnancies.[50] Forty-three of these women were nulliparous, sixty-eight multiparous. In the first trimester, thirty-three of the forty-three nulliparous women reported a reduction in sexual tension and effectiveness; all experienced sleepiness and chronic fatigue. Twenty-six of the forty-three said they feared injury to the fetus. Of the remaining ten, six experienced no change and four experienced increased sexual desire. As a group, the multiparous women experienced little change

44. Ibid., p. 75.
45. Pines, p. 336.
46. Kitzinger, p. 70.
47. Boston Women's Health Book Collective, *Ourselves and Our Children* (New York: Random House, 1978), p. 38.
48. Johann H. Duenhoetter, "Sex and Pregnancy," *Medical Aspects of Human Sexuality* 5 (May 1978): 45–50, esp. pp. 46–47; Celia J. Falicov, "Sexual Adjustment during First Pregnancy and Post Partum," *American Journal of Obstetrics and Gynecology* 7 (December 1973): 991–1000, esp. pp. 994–96; Herant A. Katchadourian and Donald T. Lunde, *Fundamentals of Human Sexuality* (New York: Holt, Rinehart & Winston, 1972), pp. 112–20; Ralph Larossa, "Sex during Pregnancy: A Symbolic Interactionist Analysis," *Journal of Sex Research* 2 (May 1979): 119–28; Masters and Johnson, pp. 156–60; Newton, *Maternal Emotions,* p. 86; Maureen Finnerty Turner and Martha H. Izzi, "The COPE Story: A Service to Pregnant and Postpartum Women," in Notman and Nadelson, eds., p. 112.
49. Ford and Beach, pp. 215–17.
50. Masters and Johnson, pp. 141–68.

from the prepregnancy state in the first trimester. In the second trimester, there was a general increase in eroticism and sexual performance regardless of parity or age. In the third trimester, thirty-one of forty nulliparous women were told by a physician not to have coitus from four weeks to three months prior to the delivery date. Thirty-three of the forty said they lost interest in sex during this period. The figures for the multiparous group were similar.

Falicov's intensive study of nineteen women in their first pregnancy shows a similar pattern of decrease in eroticism and sexual performance in the first trimester.[51] Their stated reasons were physical complaints and, more interestingly, a concern over hurting the fetus. These women also showed increased eroticism in the second trimester relative to the first, but nine of the nineteen women were still concerned with hurting the fetus. Among her subjects, over half who had continued to feel a decrease of sexual desire in the second trimester found that their desire increased in the third. Nonetheless, by the eighth month of pregnancy most of her subjects had stopped engaging in intercourse, though only five of the nineteen had been directly instructed by their physicians to do so; the others stopped because they heard or had read that they should.

These data suggest that pregnancy, particularly the first pregnancy, has a profound effect on a woman's sexuality—her waxing and waning of sexual desire—and this shifting might well lead to the marital problems which Nadelson remarks on. If we assume that the fluctuations of desire and activity are not biologically based, and if we ignore those women who experience physical discomfort in intercourse during pregnancy, there remain a significant number of women, particularly nulliparous women, whose asexuality in pregnancy is unexplained. The internalization of asexual motherhood might explain their behavior and mood shift; women who are pregnant for the first time have to make their psychological peace with the cultural wedge that has been driven between sexuality and maternity. The fear of injury to the fetus which appears in Pines's patients' fantasies, and which comes up again in the larger-sample, nonpatient studies, graphically represents the conflict women feel. A good mother protects her baby from harm. Harm arises from her own sexual activities. It is not necessary only to see men as intruders doing the harm; it is equally likely that women feel that their own sexuality, rather than their husbands' or lovers', might lead to the injury.[52] Their participation as sexual beings is, therefore, the focus of the conflict.

This internal conflict would also explain the ease with which most women go along with the obstetrical dictum of abstinence, even when they themselves have not been told it was necessary. Masters and

51. Falicov.

52. An unmarried woman in Masters and Johnson's study became a prostitute in the hope that her sexual activity would lead to abortion.

Johnson point out that the obstetrical prohibitions are confusing, contradictory, and maybe unwarranted. Further, their data confirm the widely held belief that husbands may find other sexual partners during the period of pre- and postlabor abstinence.[53] Yet over half of the women in Falicov's study were not told to give up sexual intercourse in the last trimester but did so anyway, saying that they had heard or read that they should. "Hearing" abstinence recommended provides a good reason for giving up sexual intercourse, a highly ambivalent activity for these women, since it is at odds with their image of themselves as mothers.

Breast-Feeding

Breast-feeding is an area which, perhaps more than any other, can highlight the conflict over the internalization of asexual motherhood. In our culture the female breast reigns as woman's major sexual display. Mammary glands have an obvious function, however, beyond their use as erotogenic organs; they produce milk which, from the beginning of human experience, has been a major food source of infants. Motherhood and sexuality fuse around the breast.

Breast-feeding, in spite of the advice of pediatricians and the work of the La Leche League, continues to be strikingly unpopular in America.[54] Fewer than 25 percent of all newborns are nursed, even for the five days of the usual hospital stay.[55] While there are many reasons

53. Masters and Johnson, pp. 164–65; obstetrical research and subsequent advice about abstinence in pregnancy is in and of itself a good example of the problems with work on maternal sexuality. Richard L. Naeye published an article in *New England Journal of Medicine* 301, no. 22 (November 29, 1979): 1198–1200, in which he argues that coitus "may increase the frequency and severity of amniotic fluid infections and thus increase the fetal and neonatal mortality rate." He goes on to say that he cannot specify preventive mechanisms since the reasons for the association are unknown, but suggests that fastidious cleansing by coital partners or the use of condoms might be helpful. In the same journal, an editorial by Arthur L. Herbst (pp. 1235–36) raises several serious methodological questions about Naeye's study. Further, he questions Naeye's recommendation about the use of condoms, suggests that the "natural" decrease in sexual activity that occurs in late pregnancy might avoid the problem for some women, and recommends abstinence in the third trimester for women with certain clinical conditions. The results of the research are questionable, then, and the recommendations which spring from them contradictory.

54. Karen Pryor, *Nursing Your Baby* (New York: Pocket Books, 1973), suggests that primarily the apathy of medical personnel and secondarily the "neurotic" associations of nursing with sexuality accounts for the low incidence of breast-feeding in this country. Yet Benjamin Spock, *Baby and Child Care* (New York: Pocket Books, 1972), is clearly and strongly in favor of breast-feeding, and a note in *Briefs: Footnotes on Maternal Care* 2 (February 1979): 30, points out that both the American Academy of Pediatrics and the Canadian Pediatric Society are "strongly supportive of breastfeeding."

55. Pryor, p. 90.

why women choose not to nurse, noteworthy are those women who are uncomfortable with breast-feeding because of guilt and fear about sexual arousal. Masters and Johnson discuss the reasons why twenty-five women in their sample who could breast-feed decided not to. Of these women, almost one-fourth decided not to nurse because of the conscious erotic quality of the experience. Other stated reasons—for example, experiencing nursing as degrading—might also reflect masked concern over sexual arousal.[56]

Masters and Johnson also had a group of subjects, twenty-four in all, who chose to nurse their infants. As a group, these mothers expressed significantly higher levels of sexual tension than the nonnursing mothers. In addition, these women reported "sexual stimulation (frequently to plateau tension levels and, on three occasions, to orgasm) induced by suckling their infants." Masters and Johnson add that "there was a heavy overlay of guilt expressed by 6 of the 24 women who were stimulated sexually by the suckling process."[57] Since Masters and Johnson's laboratory could not have been more accepting of sexual arousal, this guilt is a particularly striking finding and speaks to the gut level at which these feelings lie.

Deutsch and Heiman also comment on maternal guilt over sexual feelings which emerge in the nursing relationship.[58] Though Deutsch argues that the motherly woman learns to accept these feelings of arousal and incorporates them into her motherly self-image, this process seems strikingly at odds with the naturally oppositional tendencies of motherliness and sexuality which Deutsch proposes. Heiman, likewise, urges women to accept these feelings.

A less direct indication of conflicted sexual feelings over nursing is that, as a group, nursing mothers return to marital sexual relations faster than nonnursing mothers.[59] Masters and Johnson interpret this speedy return: "They were anxious to relieve concepts or fears of perverted sexual interest by reconstituting their normal marital relationships as quickly as possible."[60] I would argue that these women have internalized a gender identity which includes images and experiences of erotic arousal associated with their breasts. The physiological and psychological experience of breast-feeding can lead to sexual arousal

56. Masters and Johnson, p. 162; Kitzinger comments on the erotic quality of breast-feeding: "Other women recognize the erotic element in breastfeeding and dislike it intensely. They do not wish to confuse what for them are two distinct levels of experience, the sexual and the maternal, and breastfeeding may be unpleasant for them for this reason" (p. 231). She adds that GPs often do not mention this and that midwives find it embarrassing or irrelevant.
57. Masters and Johnson, pp. 161–62.
58. Deutsch, p. 290; Heiman, pp. 378–79.
59. Katchadourian and Lunde, p. 125.
60. Masters and Johnson, p. 162.

which is antithetical to equally powerful and deeply held psychic representations of the maternal role. Guilt, shame, and concern about sexual
perversion are predictable outcomes in this clash.

Conclusions

Should we, can we, change this situation? As scholars, our own
acceptance of ideology has blinded us to the problem. Surely there must
now be a serious study of maternal asexuality. If we define maternal
sexuality as something that does not exist or that we would like to have
go away, or, conversely, if we view it as a set of glorious natural feelings
that lead to harmonious contact between mother and child, there is no
reason to consider it seriously. Surely, too, the ideology as ideology
needs to be challenged. Mindless perpetuation of the split between sex
and motherhood fragments women's experience. To be a mother by
choice and a sexual person should be a woman's right.

Unfortunately, though recent feminist work recognizes asexual
motherhood, there is as yet no coherent approach to help guide us fully
with such questions. Shulamith Firestone is an active proponent of the
split between reproduction and sexuality and urges women to opt for
sexuality.[61] The authors of *Our Bodies, Ourselves* remark that doctors are
uncomfortable with mixing sex and motherhood and, therefore, are
often unhelpful in discussing sex with their pregnant patients. They too
fail to recognize that women have also internalized the conflict.[62] Adrienne Rich, on the other hand, recognizes the confusion and pain that
women experience because of desexualized motherhood but fails, I
think, to appreciate or clarify the level at which this has been learned.[63]
The women I have described, who shun intercourse in pregnancy, are
embarrassed about their pregnant bodies, and experience disgust or
guilt over breast-feeding are not easily reassured. Reasonable, rational,
and political logic does not speak cogently to the prereasonable level
where these responses in the individual woman have their origins.

Though I do not know what "should" be the balance between sexuality and mothering, it seems that balance is appropriate; neither rigid
repression of sexuality while mothering nor embracing the erotic aspects
of the mothering relationship seems to be correct. There is certainly no
evidence that good mothering requires a person to inhibit all aspects of
her sexuality in relationship to other adults, though there is evidence
that some women do this. The psychoanalytic theories propose that

61. Shulamith Firestone, *The Dialectic of Sex* (New York: Bantam Books, 1971), pp.
192–242.
62. Boston Women's Health Book Collective, *Our Bodies, Ourselves,* 2d ed. (New York:
Simon & Schuster, 1975), p. 264.
63. Rich, pp. 158, 179–80.

either such a generalized repression is inevitable with motherhood or the individual woman performs psychic feats to keep sexual feelings out of her mothering tasks but in her properly erotic relationship with her lover. These theories are based on unproven assumptions about the psychological balancing of sexual impulses and their relationship to other functioning. Until we have more data about women's sexual functioning, I am more content with the assumption that it is within the realm of each woman's potential to be a good mother and a sexual person, within limits with the child, and certainly with others.[64]

There are very few data and considerable confusion as to what constitutes *harmful* erotic interaction between mothers and children. For example, if a woman is sexually aroused while breast-feeding, if the infant is also aroused, are they engaged in a damaging erotic relationship? Is the infant sensing the mother's arousal, and is he or she reacting to it or indifferent? Is the reaction good for the child, bad for the child, or meaningless in terms of the child's subsequent development? Until we begin to ask these questions and, I hope, find answers to them, the proper relationship between motherhood and sexuality will have to be vaguely defined.

There are also a host of unanswered questions about those women whom I have suggested are conflicted over being sexual and being mothers. I have described women who are ashamed of their pregnancy, who are sexually unresponsive during this time, and who eschew breast-feeding out of concern for sexual arousal. As there are no longitudinal data from any group of women on maternal sexuality, the idea that these women present a coherent syndrome is premature. Furthermore, it would be important to determine whether maternal sexuality and asexuality were connected with other aspects of a woman's sexual functioning; for example, is a woman who is ashamed of her pregnant body tense about sexual functioning in general, and, conversely, is the woman who is sexually aroused while breast-feeding easily aroused in other situations?

Nor would maternal sexuality be such a problematic topic if there were not exclusively mother-raised children and if the power of the mother in child rearing were not so exaggerated. Maternal sexuality

64. I have avoided the challenge of specifying how this ideology is internalized and have asserted that it happens at an early age. Recent observational studies of children (see, for example, Blum [n. 39]; Robert J. Stoller, "Primary Femininity," *Journal of the American Psychoanalytic Association* 5 [1976]: 51–70; Eleanor Galenson and Herman Roiphe, "Some Suggested Revisions concerning Early Female Development," ibid., pp. 29–58; Henri Parens et al., "On the Girl's Entry into the Oedipus Complex," ibid., pp. 79–108) show that important aspects of gender identity, including pieces of mothering behavior, develop before eighteen months of age. I think I am on firm ground in suggesting that it is during this time that the "gut" feelings associated with asexual motherhood are learned by the little girl (and perhaps by the little boy also). Given the state of the research, it is impossible to specify with confidence *how* it is learned.

becomes "unthinkable" in a sexually restrictive society such as ours when it conjoins the myth of the all-powerful mother; the "hothouse" environment around mothers and children suggests, at the same time, the child's fragility and the importance of the mother's task. In a society which was more realistic about the mother-child relationship and where parenting, rather than mothering, was practiced, rather than talked about, by large numbers of adults, neither scholars nor mothers would have such a problem with maternal sexuality.

Department of Psychiatry
University of Michigan

Review Essay

Toward a Biology of Menopause

Madeleine Goodman

Any investigation of the menopause is bedeviled by the absence of a universally accepted category under which to consider the phenomenon. Clinical investigators have often looked upon the menopause as analogous to a degenerative disease. Some have actually called it a disease, and the descriptions of its symptomology have been a canonical feature of medical literature.

Methodologically, the derivation of the clinical conspectus of the menopausal condition has been naive. Physicians, reporting cases of women in their middle years, amalgamated their symptoms into a clinical syndrome, whose objective reality they have rarely doubted. Now, however, with the use of more sophisticated techniques of sampling and statistical analysis, quite a different picture of the menopause is beginning to emerge. Newer techniques in and of themselves, however, could not have brought about a more workable understanding of the menopause without a prior commitment to perceiving it in the context of human aging and to defining it developmentally rather than pathologically.

One reason why physicians have persisted in treating menopause as a disease has been the availability of hormone supplements which modify some manifestations of the menopause. An analogy was made in the mid 1960s by Robert A. Wilson, a leading promoter of estrogen-replacement therapy, between diabetes, a disease of insulin insufficiency, and menopause, a disease of estrogen deficiency. "In the course of my work, spanning four decades and involving hundreds of carefully documented clinical cases, it became evident that menopause . . . is in fact a deficiency disease. . . . To cure diabetes, we supply the lacking substance in the form of insulin. A similar logic can be applied to menopause—the missing hormones can be replaced."[1] This pronouncement, and the thinking it represents, influenced medical attitudes toward menopause and the role of estrogen-replacement therapy for several years.

The Case-History Method and Its Problems

The research alluded to by Wilson was based on medical case history, the least powerful methodology for the investigation of the physical aspects of menopause. Medical case history is a useful method of describing relatively rare clinical conditions whose prevalence and incidence in the population are so low and whose general manifestations are so uniform that descriptions of individual cases may be said to be representative of the general affected group. With regard to menopause, these premises break down. First, all women who live long enough will eventually become menopausal, passing from a "nonaffected" to an "affected" classification. There are no nonmenopausal women beyond a certain age, as there might be nondiabetics whose blood sugar will never rise into the hyperglycemic range. Second, the collection of case histories by a given clinician cannot represent an unbiased estimate of all menopausal women in the general population. Only those women who seek medical help for menopausal complaints will be included in such a case-history sample. Women whose menopausal experience does not include overly distressing symptoms may not present themselves to the gynecologist for treatment, nor will women whose cultural background provides nonmedical strategies for dealing with menopause. Yet, information obtained from such a medical sample of biased ascertainment forms the basis of a portrayal of the menopausal woman which readily finds its way into medical textbooks and other media. Medical textbooks perpetuated an image of the menopausal *patient,* which new generations of physicians were free to presume was a scientific description of the menopausal *woman.* Wilson's descriptions of case histories of distraught women disintegrating in a "horror of living decay" before the eyes of anguished relatives and medical attendants went beyond impressionism to an expressionistic mode, employing poetic devices not merely to describe but to arouse an emotive response. These are the methods not of clinical description, but of advertising, promotion, and prescription. The clinical literature had already created visions of a pathological syndrome. In the work of Wilson and others that syndrome was blown up into the

1. Robert A. Wilson, *Feminine Forever* (New York: M. Evans & Co., 1966).

exaggerated proportions of a cultural stereotype. Invention had become the mother of necessity. Drug companies eager to market estrogens on a mass scale sought to create a market demand. Wilson and others supplied a condition, estrogen deficiency, which the hormonal preparations could alleviate or at least symptomatically relieve.

Evidence of the persistence of Wilson's legacy is found in a recent issue of the *Medical Journal of Australia*. Jean Hailes and Henry Burger state that physicians today regard menopause as an estrogen-deficiency disease and set out to "assess the frequency and nature of menopausal symptoms in Australian women." They describe the difficulties they encountered in assembling their sample of fifty menopausal women, difficulties they attribute to "unproved myths regarding this area . . . in the whole community. Both patients and doctors regard any symptoms as being typical of a natural and transitory situation which will soon adjust itself. Their mothers endured them without serious mishap, so why should they not." The study population presented a variety of symptoms the investigators attributed to their perimenopausal state, including 92 percent showing hot flashes, 48 percent energy lack, 40 percent altered temperament, 36 percent dyspareunia, and 30 percent headache. The authors go on report that all fifty women they recruited into their project, ranging from premenopausal to many years postmenopausal, were administered a regime of Premarin and that "the symptoms were relieved in all cases."[2]

Research attempts such as this one add little to our understanding of menopause or to an objective assessment of the effects of estrogen-replacement therapy in ameliorating menopausal symptoms. While they employ some of the furniture of modern statistical analysis, such studies lack random-sampling techniques, double-blind controls, quantitative measures of measurable variables, and the critical use of statistical measures of significance. Although they appear to be, the presumed findings are no better grounded in fact than the more casual assessments physicians have traditionally prepared on the basis of their clinical experience. Yet studies characterized by such naive methodology continue to be published.

The Need for a Workable Definition of Menopause

The definitional problem itself is a major stumbling block for most menopause research. Once one presumes that menopause is a disease with specific symptoms, then it is easy to collect individuals who complain of those symptoms and to exclude from the study sample all those who

2. Jean Hailes and Henry Burger, "Oestrogens and Menopausal and Postmenopausal Women," *Medical Journal of Australia* 1 (May 1977): 803–6.

find the proffered description of menopause as a disease inapposite or incorrect. If, on the other hand, one's object is to find out what menopause is, then one must employ a different procedure. If there is some objective distinction between premenopausal and postmenopausal women, then it will be possible to determine whether the two groups differ clinically. But if a sample population is selected on any basis which involves the presence of symptoms, then the examination of that population for the presence of those symptoms becomes of no significance in estimating the relative frequency or severity of those symptoms within the general populace.

Traditionally, the menopause was assimilated to the grand climacteric, as part of the schematization of stages of the life cycle in accordance with the mystical, astrological, numerological significance of the passing calendar years. Scientifically what is of moment is not the neatness of a procrustean scheme, but the physiological phases of the life cycle itself as indicated by observable changes in function. More valuable still, of course, would be a causal account, one that began from an examination of the hormonal changes in the maturing and aging female system. As a general pattern these changes are fairly well known and increasingly understood in detail.

With the aging of the ovary, the number of primordial follicles decreases and the production of estrogen falls off. Failure of good corpus luteum formation occurs, accompanied by reduced progesterone secretion, disrupting the formerly smooth workings of the menstrual cycle. When estrogen levels eventually fall below those needed to induce endometrial shedding, menstruation ceases. These events may occur rapidly leading to an abrupt cessation of menses or, more commonly, take place over several months or years of greater and greater menstrual irregularity until menstruation finally terminates.

The altered relationship between ovarian hormones and those of the pituitary and hypothalamus which normally regulate the ovarian cycle may lead to further disequilibrium between the hypothalamus and the autonomic nervous system and possibly result in vasomotor manifestations such as hot, tingling flashes and/or warm flushes followed by perspiration and chills.[3] But in assessing the impact of the menopause on individual women, more than the general physiological pattern of events needs to be known.

Using the fairly readily determined criterion of cessation of menses as a working definition of the menopause, it is possible to ask a nontrivial question: What health conditions if any are associated with the occurrence of menopause? To single out the cessation of menses from the

---

3. See H. P. G. Schneider, "Endocrine Diagnosis in the Climacteric Female," *Hormone Research* 9, no. 6 (1978): 365–78.

phenomena associated with the female climacteric may sound as arbitrary as to begin from the clinical symptoms. But given the possibility in this way of collecting health data about a population of women not self-identified through menopausal complaints, it should be possible to determine far more accurately what the relationship is between menopause (defined as the cessation of menses) and the symptoms which have been associated with it. This was the approach undertaken in the past few years by myself and other investigators. The findings have changed the scientifically acceptable view of the nature of the menopause.

Two Population-based Studies of Menopause

In a study of certain medical and physiological variables among menopausal women living in Hawaii, my colleagues and I ascertained our postmenopausal and premenopausal samples from a larger group of 1,708 Caucasian American women and 1,221 Japanese American women who underwent annual multiphasic health screening at the Straub Clinic and Hospital in Honolulu as part of an employment physical, annual physical examination regime, or in connection with other health-care needs not specifically associated with the menopausal state.[4] The women in our sample, upon statistical analysis, were found to be representative of their ethnic groups in the state of Hawaii in biomedical, socioeconomic, and demographic profiles. To this sample we applied the criterion of date of last menses to classify women into postmenopausal or premenopausal states. Postmenopausal women were classified by the date of last menses at least twelve months prior to the date of the medical examination. Premenopausal women were defined as having menstruated within the past two months. The transitional group, who had menstruated last between three and twelve months ago, we defined as menopausal, although in our sample this group was not sufficiently large to study statistically. This conventional classification, adopted in several current studies,[5] has the advantage of insuring to a considerable degree that premenopausal and postmenopausal women are identified as such despite the possibility of some vagueness in recall

4. Madeleine J. Goodman, Cynthia J. Stewart, and Fred Gilbert, Jr., "Patterns of Menopause: A Study of Certain Medical and Physiological Variables among Caucasion and Japanese Women Living in Hawaii," *Journal of Gerontology* 32, no. 3 (1977): 291–98.

5. Mirjam Furuhjelm and P. Fedor-Freyburgh, "The Influence of Estrogens on the Psyche in Climacteric and Post-menopausal Women," in *Concensus on Menopause Research*, ed. P. A. van Keep, R. B. Greenblatt, and M. Albeaux-Fernet (Lancaster: MTP Press, 1976); M. D. Rader et al., "Plasma Estrogens in Postmenopausal Women," *American Journal of Obstetrics and Gynecology* 16, no. 8 (1973): 1069–73; Barbara Thompson, Shirley A. Hart, and D. Durno, "Menopausal Age and Symptomology in a General Practice," *Journal of Biosocial Science* 5, no. 1 (1973: 71–82.

and some fluctuation in cyclicity among women in the transitional group. Only naturally menopausal women were included in the study, and data were further stratified by ethnic group.

Applying these criteria for menopause to our sample, we found that only 28 percent of 170 Caucasian postmenopausal women and only 24 percent of 159 similarly identified Japanese women reported traditional menopausal symptoms, such as hot flashes, sweats, etc., on the general medical history forms completed at the time of the multiphasic screening examination, while 16 percent of 162 Caucasian premenopausal women and 10 percent of 187 Japanese premenopausal women in our sample also reported these same symptoms. Thus about 75 percent of postmenopausal women in our sample appeared to be asymptomatic by their own self-reporting, ascertained in this manner. No significant differences were found between postmenopausal and premenopausal women with regard to frequency of headaches or nervous tension, two symptoms commonly associated with the menopausal state. Postmenopausal women were found, however, to have a significantly higher frequency of arthritis, surgery for female disorders, and use of medication.

Further investigation into medical history, reproductive history, anthropometric, and biochemical variables, using multiple-regression techniques, allowed us statistically to consider the discrimination of postmenopausal from premenopausal women by ethnic group on the basis of several factors simultaneously and to adjust for the age differential between older postmenopausal and younger premenopausal women. After adjusting for the linear and nonlinear effects of age, the only variable to be retained in the regression models in both ethnic groups was "surgery related to a female disorder." In Caucasians only, one additional variable, "medication," was significant at the 1 percent level. Over half of the Caucasian postmenopausal women in our sample underwent some gynecological surgery and nearly two-thirds were under some medication, a startling proportion when it is borne in mind that only 24 percent of the postmenopausal women reported symptoms of menopause on their medical history forms.

Thus, using a general population sample, not ascertained through menopausal symptoms, we find that a substantial proportion of menopausal women in Hawaii either do not experience or do not mention the constellation of symptoms long associated with menopause on their medical history forms. In this study, the only distinguishing characteristic of the postmenopausal group as correcting for age effects is the increased likelihood that therapeutic measures are being employed. Questions remain, however. How typical was our sample? How widespread are the symptoms which are reported in the general population? To what extent are these attributable to the general effects of aging, and to what extent to menopause itself? Some answers may be found in the work of other researchers using similar sampling techniques.

In a study of menopausal age and symptomology in a mixed rural-urban population outside Aberdeen, Barbara Thompson and colleagues attempted complete ascertainment of all menopausal women in their district through a mailed questionnaire to all women aged forty to sixty registered with the National Health system in that area, which meant virtually every female resident of the district in that age group.[6] A 92 percent response rate to the mailed survey gives strength to the assertion that this study population is representative of the targeted group.

The results of this investigation show a different pattern of menopausal symptomology than we observed in our population in Hawaii. Among the 112 women who terminated menses over twelve months prior to survey in the Aberdeen study, the frequency of flushing (74 percent) was nearly three times as great as in the Honolulu sample, while among ninety-eight premenopausal women, applying our common operational definition, the frequency of flushing is congruent with our findings in Japanese and somewhat lower than our findings in Caucasians.

Do the discordant results for flushing in the postmenopausal women mean that there are different patterns of menopausal symptomology in Aberdeen than in Honolulu? Not necessarily. In both studies, where a conscious effort has been made to assemble representative samples of the perimenopausal population, the frequency of flushing in premenopausal women is similar. Upon closer scrutiny it appears that the discrepancy in flushing frequencies in postmenopausal women may in fact be explained as an artifact of the survey instrument.

In the Aberdeen postal survey, which focused on menopausal symptomology, respondents were asked to categorize flushing occurrence as either "current," "stopped," or "never." While premenopausal women in Aberdeen recorded only current symptoms, postmenopausal women were given the opportunity to record current and past flushing. In the Honolulu sample, only current symptoms were recorded as part of a general checklist of current health complaints. When only current flushing is counted in postmenopausal women in the Aberdeen study, the frequency is 34 percent, only slightly higher than in the Honolulu study. Without the valuable breakdown of the flushing variable by time in the Aberdeen study, comparisons of findings from the two sources would have been impracticable or misleading. Yet despite our ability to make some comparisons between the two studies, there still remain quite substantial differences in sampling frames, scope and type of data collected, and methods of analysis. Variations in accuracy of measurement

6. Thompson et al.

and reproducibility in self-reported symptomology are inherent in both studies.

The Problems of Age Adjustment

An appreciation of the general problem of age adjustment in menopause research is rarely exhibited in the literature. As menopausal or postmenopausal women for the most part are older than pre-menopausal women, the confounding effect of age presents a substantial and ubiquitous source of bias in postmenopausal-premenopausal comparisons. Even in the event that researchers are aware of the importance of age adjustment, they are usually at a loss as to how to proceed statistically beyond a recognition of the problem.

In a study of the relationship between sleep disturbance and menopausal status in 539 women, C. Barbara Ballinger found a trend toward progressively more frequent sleep disturbance with advancing menopausal status.[7] But there was also a clear age trend: 44.1 years was the mean age for premenopausal women, 48.4 years for menopausal, and 52.2 years for postmenopausal women. Was the observed sleep disturbance a result of hormonal changes at menopause or other dimensions of the general aging process? Ballinger conceded: "It is possible that the observed changes in reported sleep disturbance with menopausal status is just a reflection of increasing age." However, without applying appropriate statistical tests for this possibility, we are left with no means of distinguishing the effects of menopause from those of age.

Superficially, it may seem that the age differential between postmenopausal and premenopausal subjects might be easily overcome by the standard epidemiological convention found in case-control studies of assembling age-matched data. Applying this method, however, will almost inevitably generate specious comparisons. For young postmenopausal women (who are in that respect atypical of their age group) will be paired with premenopausal young women (who are in that respect not atypical). And older premenopausal women will be paired with the more typical postmenopausal women in their age group. Pairing such atypical women with their more typical age-mates vitiates the basic principle of case-control studies, which is that individuals compared should be as like as possible in every respect but that of the variable studied. Moreover, case-control studies afford no information with regard to the impact of matched variables, since these are held constant in the case-control pairs. But it seems injudicious to omit systematically

7. Barbara C. Ballinger, "Subjective Sleep Disturbance at the Menopause," *Journal of Psychosomatic Research* 20, no. 5 (1976): 509–13.

from study a variable already known to have a crucial impact on the menopause and its associated symptoms.

Another approach might involve an age adjustment based on the assumption that age trends are linear and that a simple linear function would provide sufficient correction to allow valid comparisons between the two groups. But if the true relationship of age to some pertinent variable is nonlinear, then there is no simple function of age such that addition of, say, N years to the ages of premenopausal subjects would render their cases uniformly equivalent with those of postmenopausal women. In previous research on diabetes in Hawaii, for example, my colleagues and I have found that blood glucose levels and cholesterol levels increase with age in a nonlinear fashion in Japanese and Caucasians.[8] So a simple linear adjustment would not be adequate here or in describing the relationship between age and many other biomedical variables.

A more ambitious attempt to find a valid single nonlinear function which would accommodate age effects would be possible only where considerable overlap in age distribution existed between the premenopausal and postmenopausal groups. One cannot assume that the same underlying function describes the situations of premenopausal and menopausal women. An extreme case of the problem is represented in a situation where not only mean ages but the distribution of ages differs among the groups to be studied. In order to verify that any single mathematical function could describe the relationship between a variable Y and age in both postmenopausal and premenopausal groups, one would have to find the same relationship to age in each of the study groups and a large enough overlap of age distribution among the two groups to enable the investigator to extrapolate the function confidently over the entire age range.[9]

Then, too, there is the possibility that the difference by age between postmenopausal and premenopausal women for a condition measured in units Y may vary, converging during some age spans and diverging during others. In this case, age adjustment would not be possible because the difference between the two groups for variable Y changes with age, but the mean difference between the variables as applied to the two groups is zero. In such a case there is no simple function which describes the procedure necessary for a uniform age adjustment.

Another pitfall disrupting potential attempts to "adjust for" age is the problem of secular trend, that is, an overall change over time in the

8. Madeleine J. Goodman, Chin S. Chung, and Fred Gilbert, Jr., "Racial Variation in Diabetes Mellitus in Japanese and Caucasians Living in Hawaii," *Journal of Medical Genetics* 11, no. 4 (1974): 328–34.

9. In our Honolulu sample we were fortunate enough to have a sufficiently large population and enough overlap in age distribution between the pre- and postmenopausal groups to accomplish this type of statistical adjustment for the effects of age.

population studied with respect to one or more variables. In a retrospective study of age at first pregnancy among middle-aged women participating in a breast cancer screening program in Honolulu, my colleagues and I discovered pronounced secular trends in age at first pregnancy;[10] and in another study based on this same population, we observed the well-known secular trend in age at menarche.[11] While our studies of age at menopause and those of Treloar[12] do not reveal secular trends, other factors which may influence the onset and character of menopause may be subject to them. If so, a cross-sectional study based on such data might give the impression that age effects were being observed, when in fact what was being seen was the impact of a secular trend. Women born in a given year share not only their age but certain segments of life experience. They have lived through the same span of history and possibly experienced similar socioeconomic vicissitudes and life crises.

One appealing method of circumventing the pitfalls of age adjustment would seem to be the cohort-analysis approach. Women grouped according to their year of birth might be compared with respect to age at menopause and various dimensions of the menopause experience. Here, however, new difficulties present themselves. At first glance, since all members of the cohort are of uniform age, it would appear that the effects of aging would be constant across the group. However, problems may be posed by excessive uniformity or heterogeneity within a cohort.

Uniform chronological age is no guarantee of similarity of life experience. As the pattern of aging is thought to reflect genetic propensities as well as environmental assaults, diversity in life experience and diversity in genotype may contribute to the breakdown of the integrity of the cohort. A spread of socioeconomic levels, a diversity of cultural and ethnic background or of reproductive history, health condition, marital status, and various life crises may all influence the course of the menopausal experience. Unknown subgroupings generated by unappreciated factors may obscure important findings. In the conditions of relative environmental uniformity in which representatives of the various racial groupings of Hawaii live, my colleagues and I found no significant racial differences in the biological impact of menopause.[13] But

10. Madeleine J. Goodman, John S. Grove, and Fred Gilbert, Jr., "Age at First Pregnancy in Relation to Age at Menarche and Year of Birth in Caucasian, Japanese, Chinese and Part-Hawaiian Women Living in Hawaii," *Annals of Human Biology* (1980), in press.

11. Madeleine J. Goodman, John S. Grove, and Fred I. Gilbert, Jr., "Menopause and Life Cycle Variables: A Biostatistical Investigation," *Women's Studies Program Working Papers Series* 1, no. 3 (1978): 1–13.

12. Madeleine J. Goodman, John S. Grove, and Fred Gilbert, Jr., "Age at Menopause in Relation to Reproductive History in Japanese, Caucasian, Chinese and Hawaiian Women Living in Hawaii," *Journal of Gerontology* 33, no. 5 (1978): 688–94; Alan E. Treloar, "Menarche, Menopause, and Intervening Fecundability," *Human Biology* 46, no. 1 (1974): 89–107.

13. Goodman et al., "Aging at Menopause."

then even Caucasians in Hawaii tend to eat more rice than their mainland counterparts. Consider the following theoretical case: It may occur in a population that is the subject of some future study that diet is a significant variable, an environmental factor often ignored even in the most serious studies. It could easily happen that in such a case a difference between persons who "eat rice" and those who "eat potatoes" might be erroneously registered as a racial difference.

Lack of differentiation in a sample can also render evaluation of the causal impact of crucial variables next to impossible. There may not be sufficient variation within an excessively uniform cohort to allow important causal factors to appear as statistically significant variables in a model which assigns statistical significance on the basis of a variable's capacity for accounting for variation. Clearly the problems of analysis surrounding any endeavor to make meaningful comparisons between premenopausal and postmenopausal women are formidable. But little work as yet has been done which recognizes the centrality of these problems and their intractability.

Problems of Measurement

Despite the technology to process vast amounts of data using replicable computer programs of great sensitivity and analytic flexibility, we are still hampered by the impurity of our input material. Much of the relevant information for menopause research is heavily dependent on subjective input. Nearly all the data on reproductive history in studies of menopausal women are based on recall by the subject, recorded unverified by the investigator. This type of information, especially age at first menses (menarche) and age at first pregnancy, is vulnerable to directional bias in recall. Age at menarche is typically rounded off to the last birthday, so that menarche at twelve years eleven months is consistently recalled as twelve unless years and months are specified. With other variables, such as age at first pregnancy, a subject may not wish to reveal a first pregnancy which ended in an induced abortion or illegitimate birth and simply choose to omit some of her early reproductive history, thus distorting and underreporting her true fertility.[14]

Other subjective responses regarding menopausal symptoms are converted into pseudo-objective variables through the use of scaling techniques. When the differences between an assigned code of 1 and an assigned code of 2 are greater than the degree of difference between a code of 2 and a code of 3, the design variable improperly quantifies the subjective responses. Worse yet, a scheme may be developed to convert qualitatively different responses into a single pseudo-objective variable

14. Chin S. Chung, personal communication.

where such transformation of data is logically unjustified and factually inaccurate. An example is the Blatt Menopausal Index,[15] which aggregates into an arbitrarily weighted summed score "somatic symptoms" such as numbness and tingling and hot flushes, and "psychological symptoms" such as trouble sleeping or feeling blue and depressed. In the scale developed by Bernice Neugarten and Ruth Kraines,[16] symptoms are more logically divided into somatic, psychosomatic, and psycological categories. Frequency and severity of symptoms are recorded, yet the interrelationships among symptoms within the categories are not established. Furthermore, when this scale is applied to women of different ages, we find 29 percent of adolescent women (aged thirteen through eighteen) recording such classical menopausally related vasomotor manifestations as hot flashes and 19 percent cold sweats, but we are unable to distinguish via such a self-reporting system any underlying hormonal or other factors which may account for such reports.

When the data sought are a quantitative measure of a physical state, difficulties remain to be overcome. Menstrual cycle research has often rationalized women's cycles of varying lengths into a uniform theoretical standard of twenty-eight days.[17] Ovulation is often retrospectively dated by counting backward from the onset of menses, when hormonal assays would be preferred as indicators of menstrual cycle events. Similarly, blood hormone measures are likely to be more valuable than urinary hormone measures. With the development of radioimmunoassay techniques, the measurement of sex hormones in the blood has become technically feasible. However, even here variability in hormone levels within and between days and in different parts of the body may require more than a single sampling to establish a reliable hormone level for cycling or for menopausal women. Then, too, the ratio of one hormone to other gonadal and pituitary hormones which operate in a woman's hormone system may be of greater relevance to the study of some behavioral trait or symptom than merely the quantitative measure of a single sex hormone. Again, there is the question of which hormone(s) to monitor. The latest reported endocrinological research on the hot flash, for example,[18] implicates the gonadotropic hormone LH rather than consistent changes in estrogen level in the occurrence of this phenome-

15. M. H. G. Blatt, H. Wiesbader, and H. S. Kupperman, "Vitamin E and Climacteric Syndrome," *A.M.A. Archives of Internal Medicine* 91, no. 6 (1953): 792–99.

16. Bernice Neugarten and Ruth J. Kraines, "Menopausal Symptoms in Women of Various Ages," *Psychosomatic Medicine* 27, no. 3 (1965): 266–73.

17. K. Dalton, "Menstruation and Acute Psychiatric Illness," *British Medical Journal* 1, no. 5115 (1959): 148–49; N. E. Liskey, "Accidents—Rhythmic Threat to Females," *Accident Analysis and Prevention* 4, no. 1 (1972): 1–11.

18. D. R. Meldrum et al., "Hormonal Variables Associated with Objectively Documented Hot Flashes," *Proceedings of the 61st Annual Meeting of the Endocrine Society*, abstract 138 (1979); R. F. Casper, "Physical, Neuroendocrine and Neuropharmacologic Correlates during Menopausal Flushes," *Proceedings of the 61st Annual Meeting of the Endocrine Society*, abstract 210 (1979).

non. The ability to quantify and objectify some variables, however, does not necessarily impart adequate precision or analytic capability or guarantee adequate interpretive skill in understanding the menopause experience.

New Perspectives in Menopause Research

The demythologizing of the menopause—that is, its dissociation from the long-familiar congeries of coincidental or subjectively associated phenomena—leaves room for a new approach to inquiry, an approach which is at once more empirical, more sophisticated analytically, and more holistic than the long-standing variations on the traditional clinical approach. We are beginning to realize that we do not yet know the biology of the menopause in an integrated way. And our growing experience with statistical analysis as applied to epidemiology and with new techniques such as radioimmunoassay provides us with tools by which the menopause can be studied in a general population rather than a sample of patients, via precise measurements rather than subjective reports, and in quantitatively controlled correlations with numerous other variables rather than mere stereotypic or pragmatically spurred associations. A neutralized menopause concept may prove to be invaluable as a life-cycle marker or milestone in new research directed at improved understanding of health problems and the aging process. In this respect, fresh utility might indeed be found for longitudinal studies.

There is probably no better way of studying aging than the careful longitudinal study. For some diseases, such as osteoporosis, whose ascertainment and treatment begin in conjunction with or soon after the onset of menopause, it would be of interest to monitor changes in bone density in advance of menopause and follow any changes with age which occur during the premenopausal period, establishing an aging rate which could then be compared to the changes in skeletal mass and density which occur later during the postmenopausal years. This type of approach, applied to osteoporosis here, but equally applicable to other conditions, would enable us to pursue the answers to two important questions: (1) Does osteoporosis, for example, originate prior to menopause? (2) Does menopause accelerate the aging process in women? The work of Garn and colleagues and that of Aitken leads us to believe that thinning of the bone matrix begins well in advance of natural menopause and seems to be an age-related change in both men and women.[19] And a three-year study of the relationship of menopause per se to changes in bone tissue is currently being set up by myself and

19. S. M. Garn, C. G. Rohmann, and B. Wagner, "Bone Loss as a General Phenomenon in Man," *Federation Proceedings* 26, no. 6 (1967): 1729–36; J. M. Aitken, "Bone Metabolism in Post-menopausal Women," in *The Menopause*, ed. R. J. Beard (Lancaster: MTP Press, 1976).

colleagues in Honolulu. A longer-term study, however, which measures premenopausal and postmenopausal aging rates in a single group of women, would yield more valuable data on the course of normal aging but would also involve substantial commitments of resources and time before results could be obtained and disseminated.

A second valuable approach would be a cross-sectional study of menopause, using sisters as controls. Generally of similar cultural backgrounds, sisters could be assembled into sibship groups with adjustment made for age differences within sibships. The variation in menopausal experience among and between sibships might prove useful in looking at familial or genetic factors in relation to environmental factors which may influence the pattern of aging generally and menopause specifically.

A third method, perhaps of greater theoretic than practical interest for the present, would be a generational family study. Here, patterns of menopausal experience might be evaluated in mothers and daughters. However, in the sort of study likely to be conducted under this rubric given the present state of the art, the quality of data assembled from currently menopausal daughters and the subjective recall of their living mothers would seem incommensurate. The availability of such data would also depend on survivorship, proximity, and so many other factors that what was collected might represent only a special subgroup of the general population and thus be of limited value.

A fourth approach might be an ongoing comparative study of normal aging in females and males. In light of our newly refined techniques of measuring bone density, hormone levels, and other biochemical variables which are known to alter with age, it would be of great interest to describe and compare physiological profiles and rates for males and females by chronological age. A good grasp of the patterns of normal aging by sex would be very helpful in our appreciation of the total physiological and psychological impact of the menopause experience as well as in our research into the observed sexual differences in the characteristics of many diseases of adult onset.

Menopause itself can also be a useful biological marker in the study of some diseases whose risk of onset increases with age. In an investigation of factors associated with breast structure in breast cancer patients, my colleagues and I applied a classification of breast structure based on prominence of ducts and radiographic density, or dysplasia, as seen by mammography, to 108 breast cancer patients in Hawaii.[20] The proponent of the classification, J. N. Wolfe,[21] has previously found that extreme radiographic density tended to disappear by age forty or fifty, leaving ductal patterns in the breast more prominent. These age-related

20. John S. Grove et al., "Factors Associated with Breast Structure in Breast Cancer Patients," *Cancer* 43, no. 5 (1979): 327–31.
21. J. N. Wolfe, "Breast Parenchymal Patterns and Their Changes with Age," *Radiology* 121, no. 3 (1976): 545–52.

changes, Wolfe suggested, were related to increased risk of breast cancer, age being associated with both increased risk of breast cancer and change in breast structure. Upon analysis of breast structure changes in our data with the addition of a menopausal state variable, we were able to demonstrate that among women in our sample the post-menopausal state was associated with less radiographic density in breast tissue, while age per se seemed to be of little effect.

In this case we did find evidence of independent menopausally related physiological changes which influenced risk of breast cancer. In applying this new information to breast cancer screening and detection via mammography, which displays breast structure changes in a soft-tissue X-ray, we have learned to appreciate the physiological or menopausal age, instead of merely the chronological age, as the relevant measure of an age-related change in breast cancer risk.

The study of menopause, like the study of so many biological phenomena in humans, is difficult yet vital to a holistic understanding of our multifaceted humanness. Even so simple-seeming a phenomenon as the cessation of ovulation cannot be comprehended biologically without combining the intellectual resources of biochemistry, physiology, endocrinology, medicine, biostatistics, psychology, and the social sciences. We are very far from being able to reduce any dimension of human experience to its quantifiable physiological parameters, and, happily, I think, we have begun to move in the opposite direction.

Women's Studies Program
University of Hawaii at Manoa

Review Essay

Social and Behavioral
Constructions of Female Sexuality

Patricia Y. Miller and Martha R. Fowlkes

The twentieth century has occasioned a major revolution in Western conceptions of the sexual. Freud, of course, is most widely credited with the secularization of human sexuality, recasting superego and libido in the roles traditionally played by their predecessors, "good" and "evil." While the Freudian conceptualization is constructed on a solid foundation of Judeo-Christian values, these are manifest only in the kinds of disguised forms Freud himself, in his dream analysis, trained us to perceive and explore. More critical than the foundation of his thought, however, is the apparent opposition to theological constructions in the Freudian edifice. For it is the semblance of scientific neutrality that Freud brought to the consideration of sexuality rather than the content of his provocative ideas that anticipated the full-blown emergence of what Robinson has called "the modernization of sex."[1] The hallmark of "modernization" is detached neutrality or, at least, the appearance of neutrality as thinkers and researchers—guided by the precepts of the scientific method—struggle to reconcile their own culturally linked biases with the data at hand. A few have been particularly influential. Their work does not in all cases represent an ideal application of the tools of science to human conduct but, in most instances, it is the kind of large-scale, well-funded, controversial research that must necessarily be

This paper represents a joint effort. The order of authors was established by the toss of a coin.
1. P. Robinson, *The Modernization of Sex* (New York: Harper & Row, 1976), p. vii.

assimilated in the work of others and in the public consciousness. It is this research that is the subject of review in this paper.

"The modernization of sex" has advanced under the standard of democracy. Male and female sexuality have warranted equal time, if not equal thought, in the few serious major studies extant. In consequence, female sexuality may have received particular benefits since, compared to male sexuality, it has been substantially more shrouded in misconception. Attending this small flurry of research is a growing acceptance of female sexuality as a topic of discussion among the larger public as well as the publication of numerous popular treatises on, exhortations to, and celebrations of the sexuality of women.[2] While actual knowledge and understanding have not kept pace with the assertion of female sexuality, be it heterosexual or homosexual, the thesis of this paper is that research and thinking are moving, not incrementally but productively nonetheless, toward a more accurate, if fragmented, understanding.

The majority of women enact their sexuality in the world of men, and usually marriage. Yet a search of existing literature reveals scant attention to the sexuality of adult women in the context of their normative social roles and relationships. The behavioral paradigms that dominate much of the work in sex research have led to the abstraction of sexual behavior and response from the social and interactional setting. Ironically, though, the researchers' own social norms tend to make their way into interpretations of the behaviors and responses they have observed or collected. This has the effect of imbuing behavioral data with social meanings, but the meanings are those of researchers, not of the women they study.

Researchers whose orientation is sociological are typically less interested in the normative than the nonnormative. In the study of social class, for example, sociologists have devoted far more time and energy to studying the organization and life-styles of the lower and working classes and the upper class than to those of the middle class. Similarly, in the sociological study of female sexuality, literature abounds on adolescent or premarital sexuality, and studies of extramarital sex occur with some frequency. Literature (albeit of varying quality) on lesbian sexuality and relationships proliferates. Increasing attention is paid to the sexuality of the elderly as well. In all of this, the woman's married heterosexual experience serves as a boundary delineator: it is an outcome, a point of departure, a way station. The most conscientious of sociological discussions, which take care to emphasize the emergent and socially con-

2. Obvious examples are: D. Reuben, *Any Woman Can* (New York: Bantam Books, 1972); A. Comfort, ed., *The Joy of Sex* (New York: Crown Publishers, 1972); Boston Women's Health Collective, *Our Bodies, Ourselves* (New York: Simon & Schuster, 1971); D. Martin and P. Lyon, *Lesbian/Woman* (New York: Bantam Books, 1972); S. Abbott and B. Love, *Sappho Was a Right-on Woman* (New York: Stein & Day, 1972).

structed nature of female sexuality, tend to fall down or, perhaps more accurately, to fall away in their approach to the adult heterosexual female. She is assumed to have one role—married—and the meaning and experience of a woman's sexuality are inferred from taken-for-granted normative assumptions about that role. This argument is borne out by the dearth of recent material on sexuality in marriage in so pertinent a publication as the *Journal of Marriage and the Family.*

The most comprehensive and, in their day, controversial studies are Kinsey's of male and female sexual behavior,[3] which broke new ground in depicting the norms of sexual activity, not in terms of what people should do, but in terms of what they, in fact, do. The overriding argument of Kinsey's work is that ideas of what should be ought to be refashioned to be consonant with what people actually—and naturally—do. Yet insofar as what people actually do represents a departure from the expected conventions and mores of social behavior, Kinsey rests his case for tolerance of those departures on the grounds that they are in the service of socially desired norms, particularly those of heterosexual marriage. Thus, for men and women alike, all premarital erotic and sexual activity is seen as facilitating adjustment to marriage. Kinsey is critical of the double standard of male and female sexual behavior that works disproportionately to inhibit women's sexual activity outside of marriage.[4]

However, Kinsey's support for increased female sexual autonomy is rendered suspect by his own double standard. Although Kinsey is concerned that women are able to experience sexual satisfaction as it is manifest in orgasmic outlet, his advocacy of women's premarital sexual activity is prompted as much by his commitment to the satisfaction of male sexual needs and desires as to that of women's. Premarital sexual activity is seen as a useful socializing agent for women in their relationships with men, as it enables women to learn to adjust emotionally to various types of men.[5] Since Kinsey's own data show that coitus (both marital and premarital) is far less frequently a source of orgasmic release for women than for men, he is essentially encouraging women to seek premarital coitus in the service of male physiological release.

A similar bias is revealed in Kinsey's interpretation of his finding that female sexual unresponsiveness is a major factor in women's premarital coital reluctance. A man, of course, may reach orgasm through coitus without doing much at all to arouse or stimulate response in his female partner. Rather than portraying men as the victims of women's

3. A. C. Kinsey, W. B. Pomeroy, and C. E. Martin, *Sexual Behavior in the Human Male* (Philadelphia: W. B. Saunders Co., 1948); A. C. Kinsey et al., *Sexual Behavior in the Human Female* (Philadelphia: W. B. Saunders Co., 1953).
4. Kinsey et al., *Female,* pp. 307–30.
5. Ibid., pp. 259–66.

unresponsiveness, it would be fairer to suggest that women may be victimized by men's self-interest and failure to show the consideration necessary to incorporate female orgasm into the coital experience.

The female orgasm itself is emphasized by Kinsey as a source of satisfaction and reassurance to the male. He states that "orgasm cannot be taken as the sole criterion for determining the degree of satisfaction which a female may derive from sexual activity. . . . Whether or not she herself reaches orgasm, many a female finds satisfaction in knowing that her husband or other sexual partner has enjoyed the contact, and in realizing that she has contributed to the male's pleasure."[6] The assumption that women can do quite nicely without an orgasmic accompaniment to coitus may be correct. But it is supported by no data from the females themselves about the place and meaning of sexual satisfaction in their marriage relationships.

Overall, when compared to males, Kinsey's females show a greater uniformity in their sexual behavior with respect to the impact of selected social variables, and they also exhibit consistently less sexual responsiveness and lower frequencies of orgasm than men. The differences between the sexual responsiveness of men and women are attributed to the greater "psychologic conditionability" or flexibility of men.[7] Although Kinsey does acknowledge the essential likeness of the physiological experience of sexual arousal and orgasm for men and women (in anticipation of the work of Masters and Johnson a decade later), he also views women as having less well-developed sexual interests than men and as more willing than men to subordinate those interests to an overriding commitment to home and family.

What Kinsey overlooked, of course, was the powerful influence of sex role itself as a variable in conditioning sexual response and behavior. Men are expected and socialized to be autonomous in their activities, including their sexual activities. Whereas males are encouraged to give full expression to their sexuality as an indication and demonstration of their masculinity, female sexual response has traditionally been thought to be appropriately derived from relationships with men and their needs. It is unquestionably true that women's sexuality is affected by socialization into the female sex role and the subordinate status attached to it in common ways that both supersede and preclude the potential effect of other social variables (at least, the social variables selected by Kinsey).

Kinsey's determination that women are generally less capable of sexual autonomy by virtue of being less psychologically conditionable itself reinforces a double standard for male and female sexual behavior.

6. Ibid., p. 371.
7. Ibid., p. 684.

It also constitutes a license for the perpetuation of predatory male sexual activity. It is precisely this predatory context which renders a derivative, rather than an autonomous, female sexuality functional. If women are to be sexually autonomous in a fashion similar to men, they must also participate in the social, political, and economic autonomy that has been granted to men. To suggest otherwise is to suggest that women should simply become more readily available to men for sex on the terms that men determine as a consequence of their dominant social roles. This would have the effect, on the one hand, of enhancing women's vulnerability to exploitation by men as sex objects and, on the other, of removing their sexuality from marriage (or potential marriage), thereby weakening the major institutional source of security and social approval accessible to them in a patriarchal society.

In contrast to Kinsey, Masters and Johnson in *Human Sexual Response* addressed the question of women's sexual autonomy solely and specifically in terms of physiological functioning.[8] Their documentation of a specifically orgasmic physiology for the female, including her multiple orgasmic potential, is both testimony and tribute to women's innate sexual capacities. In what we can only hope is a final debunking of the Freudian distinction between the vaginal and clitoral orgasm, Masters and Johnson use the evidence of their laboratory observations to recognize the clitoris: "The clitoris is a unique organ in the total of human anatomy. Its express purpose is to serve both as a receptor and transformer of sensual stimuli. Thus the female has an organ system which is totally limited in physiologic function to initiating or elevating levels of sexual tension. No such organ exists within the anatomic structure of the human male."[9]

Thus Masters and Johnson established unequivocally the physiological ability of women to achieve orgasm and dispelled any doubts that females might in any way be possessed of a lesser sexuality than males. Their findings indicate that women's orgasmic capacities are a given, and that the key variable in the achievement of successful orgasmic outcome for women is the quality of sexual attention they receive. Gone are both Kinsey's nonresponsive woman and the woman who develops her sexual responses in order to be able to fulfill male needs. Ironically, however, Masters and Johnson's own data show clearly that the sexual autonomy of women is manifest not only in their physiological functioning but in the nature of their response to sexual stimulation as well. For women "the maximum physiologic intensity of orgasmic response subjectively reported or objectively recorded has been achieved by self-regulated mechanical or automanipulative techniques. The next highest level of

8. W. H. Masters and V. E. Johnson, *Human Sexual Response* (Boston: Little, Brown & Co., 1966).
9. Ibid., p. 45.

erotic intensity has resulted from partner manipulation, again with established or self-regulated methods, and the lowest intensity of target-organ response was achieved during coition."[10]

It is not difficult to read this statement as the ultimate testimony to the autonomy of female sexuality. The female orgasmic response is demonstrably not correlated with—or, more accurately, is negatively correlated with—conventional heterosexual coitus. However, if the clitoris is no respecter of heterosexual intercourse, Masters and Johnson find that the vagina is. While the clitoris behaves like a wanton child, female vaginal response and activity are portrayed by Masters and Johnson as staunch defenders of the wisdom of copulation and, therefore, presumably, of the conventional heterosexual relationship:

> The vaginal barrel performs a dual role, providing the primary physical means of heterosexual expression for the human female and serving simultaneously as an integral part of her conceptive mechanism. . . . *To appreciate vaginal anatomy and physiology is to comprehend the fundamentals of the human female's primary means of sexual expression* [emphasis added]. In essence, the vaginal barrel responds to effective sexual stimulation for penile penetration. Just as a penile erection is a direct physiologic expression of a psychologic demand to mount, so expansion and lubrication of the vaginal barrel provides direct physiologic indication of an obvious mounting invitation.[11]

Masters and Johnson's conceptualization of the vagina—preparing for and accommodating to copulation and facilitating in multiple and essential ways the conceptive process—is a powerful corrective to the autonomous functioning and responsiveness of the clitoris. Their discussion of the vagina must be read basically as a statement of women's intrinsic heterosexuality and as a rejection of sexual activity that does not involve the vagina. Women's sexuality has again been reined in to conform to traditional heterosexual expectations. To be sure, an autonomous female sexuality is ultimately a social construction rather than simply a physiological reality. However, Masters and Johnson must be faulted for overriding their physiological data in a way that maintains rather than challenges traditional social constructions of women's sexuality.

For all that the majority of women themselves may sympathize with Masters and Johnson's sympathies for the heterosexual alliance, their research tells us much more about how people *do* sex than about sexual relationships as such. While it is helpful to know something of the sexual techniques that are the precondition for bringing women to orgasm, it

10. Ibid., p. 133.
11. Ibid., p. 68.

seems more salient to have some understanding of the kinds of relationships and communications between partners that predispose them
to knowing or wanting to know those techniques.[12] The major variable
influencing the achievement of sexual fulfillment for women as well as
men is, undoubtedly, not merely technique but the quality of the relationship itself. Masters and Johnson offer no recognition that effective
and meaningful sexual activity is not defined solely by the achievement
of orgasm, but may involve a wide range of behaviors and contacts that
are expressive of caring and commitment between partners. Masters and
Johnson have followed Kinsey's behaviorist lead to its logical conclusion.
They have earned for women the right to have equal time and space with
men on the sexual production line.

Gagnon and Simon's book, *Sexual Conduct,* presents a social interactionist perspective on sexual behavior, a perspective which stands as a
welcome and important antidote to the narrowly focused work both of
Kinsey and of Masters and Johnson.[13] For Gagnon and Simon, sexual
actors are neither mere representatives of statistical constituencies nor
demonstrators of the mechanical operation of the sexual machine.
Rather, they view sexual behavior as social behavior, entered into and
endowed with meaning by social actors whose interpersonal relationships are bound together by common and shared understandings
and communications that are the product of their common and shared
social and cultural worlds. Sexual behavior is, above all, learned behavior; sexual conduct is "neither fixed by nature or [*sic*] by the organs
themselves."[14] Social scripts organize our understanding of the participation in sexual activity. A sexual situation exists when the actors involved are responding to a socially constructed definition of what is
sexual with strategies for doing the sexual. "The social meaning given to
the physical acts releases biological events."[15] In other words, it is the
meaning assigned to behaviors by the actors involved—not the behaviors
themselves—that determines whether a situation or activity is sexual or
not.

These ideas would seem to hold much promise for understanding
the many and complex ways in which the sexual takes its cues from and is
embedded in the social. It is reasonable to expect Gagnon and Simon to
offer both insights and information about the meaning and management of sexuality in the context of that most salient and normative of
institutions by which relationships between adult men and women are
arranged, marriage. Indeed, Gagnon and Simon themselves acknowl-

12. It is also possible that individual variations in male or female physiology (surprisingly, unexamined by these researchers) account for variability in orgasmic response.
13. J. H. Gagnon and W. Simon, *Sexual Conduct* (Chicago: Aldine Publishing Co.,
1973).
14. Ibid., p. 9.
15. Ibid., p. 22.

edge that "the management of sexual commitments within a marital relationship characterizes the largest part of postadolescent sexual experience in our society."[16]

Yet their treatment of adult sexuality in marriage is limited in scope and shallow in content. To be sure, they do acknowledge the paucity of data on the topic of marital sexuality. However, it is disappointing that they do not apply their sociological perspective to formulating constructive questions and issues about the ways in which marriage per se and the evolving marriage relationship over time lend particular and characteristic kinds of meaning to the sexual behavior of men and women. Instead we are simply told that sex declines in salience after the formation of the marital unit. Women are assigned considerable responsibility for this decline because of the extra (and presumably distracting) burdens placed on them in their maternal roles. This is surely another way of saying that men's sexual energy and enthusiasm are sustained at the price of their wives' fatigue. In the end, Gagnon and Simon are guilty of the very reductionism that their interactionist perspective was meant to alleviate. Sexual behavior in marriage is viewed as consisting of little more than a variety of available bodily positions. Marriage itself is presented as a kind of social-interactional plateau from which all roads lead downhill.

Reflecting an instrumental male bias, Simon and Gagnon do not consider the possibility that sexual activity in marriage might be more appropriately assessed in qualitative rather than quantitative terms. Whereas adolescent sexual behavior has been described as "behavior in search of meaning,"[17] in marriage or other adult committed relationships, it may well be that, where sexuality is concerned, meaning is in search of behavior. The more complex and comprehensive and settled the intimacy between partners, the wider the array of available behaviors—of which sex is only one—with which to express that intimacy. In this way eroticism may actually come to carry more rather than less meaning as the relationship endures and sexual activity comes to have a focused and shared meaning in the affective repertoire of the couple.

Gagnon and Simon's inability to see beyond the form of marriage to the processes and interactions contained within it is the consequence of their having superimposed a symbolic-interactionist perspective on a developmental model of sexual behavior. The linear-historical emphasis of developmental analysis eventually and inevitably cancels out the symbolic-interactionist emphasis on the situational construction of behavior. Marriage is seen less as an entry into adult social and sexual roles than as the end product of childhood and adolescent socialization. In-

16. Ibid., p. 82.
17. P. Y. Miller and W. Simon, "The Development of Sexuality in Adolescence," in *Handbook of Adolescence,* ed. Joseph Adelson (New York: John Wiley & Sons, 1980).

deed, Simon and Gagnon actually characterize marriage as "post adolescent sexual development." In this framework, adult heterosexual relationships are the dependent variables flowing from earlier developmental processes. The potential of marriage to function as an independent variable acting on adult life and as a powerful socializing influence in its own right is virtually overlooked. Despite the deficiencies in their analysis of adult heterosexual relationships, Gagnon and Simon must be credited with bringing the study of sex fully into the sociological domain and with an ambitious attempt to establish a paradigm for thinking about sexual behavior as social behavior. Recently they have both independently shown signs of shedding the cumbersome baggage of developmental theory in moving toward a more effective application of symbolic-interactionist theories to sexual socialization and careers.[18]

Certainly other sociologists who have addressed themselves to the topic of human sexuality, and female sexuality in particular, do not begin to approach Gagnon and Simon's level of theoretical sophistication. Laws and Schwartz, for example, purport to offer a feminist-interactionist perspective on female sexuality.[19] Yet their use of the "scripting" concept does not convey the richness and complexity of the interaction process, but consists more of stereotypic descriptions of the influence of social norms on women's sexual identity and sexual behavior. Their claim to present a dynamic view of sexuality is belied by their static "stage model" of sexual development. While they describe what the alternatives to normative sexual transactions and life-styles are for women, they offer no analysis of how, in terms of social process, women might find their way into those. And they maintain a questionable separation between women's reproductive functioning and women's sexuality. Female reproductive processes and potential are seen as incidental to or contingent upon sexuality rather than as interactive with a woman's sexual self-concept and responsiveness.

Love, Sex and Sex Roles, by Safilios-Rothschild, is best described as a sociologically informed ideological essay.[20] Taking nearly 150 pages to make the point that so long as marriage is organized on the basis of traditionally unequal sex roles for men and women, marriage will not be a partnership of equals, her work reads like a feminist marriage manual. We can hardly quarrel with Safilios-Rothschild's observations about the ways in which social distance between men and women generally is transferred into the marriage relationship. However, the same or similar

18. See the discussion of Simon's (and Miller's) as well as Gagnon's recent work in a review by R. W. Libby of *Human Sexuality: A Comparative and Developmental Perspective,* ed. H. A. Kathchadourian (Berkeley and Los Angeles: University of California Press, 1979) in the *Journal of Sex Research* (November 1979), pp. 325–26.

19. J. L. Laws and P. Schwartz, *Sexual Scripts: The Social Construction of Female Sexuality* (Hinsdale, Ill.: Dryden Press, 1977).

20. C. Safilios-Rothschild, *Love, Sex, and Sex Roles* (Englewood Cliffs, N.J.: Prentice-Hall, Inc., 1977).

observations were made with considerably more depth and eloquence by Simone de Beauvoir over twenty-five years ago.[21] It is also unfortunately true, as Hacker noted in her classic essay, that equality has never been shown to be a necessary precondition for love.[22]

In the case of behaviorists such as Kinsey and Masters and Johnson, the imposition of unexamined social values and stereotypes on their data is understandable. The failure of sociologists to correct those stereotypes is less understandable. Equally disappointing is the sociological failure to advance the level of thinking about the analysis of female sexuality to treat the common and distinctive features of women's sexual experience against the backdrop of the many and varied forms the female life course may take. Although marriage may be the modal adult relationship for women, there are no grounds for assuming homogeneity among marriages or the sexual relationships contained within them. The long and venerable tradition in sociology wherein the impact of social-class and status-group subcultures on all manner of life-styles and values is examined does not, for the most part, extend to the study of sexual life-styles and values. The few exceptions are studies within a given class;[23] comparative, cross-class studies are notably lacking. We also know very little about how the particular stresses and rhythms of work and leisure associated with various kinds of occupational commitments (on the part of both men and women) affect the importance and timing of marital sex. And it is certainly well worth asking whether or how patterns of change in women's political and economic roles and bargaining power are reflected in changes in their sexual roles and bargaining power.

Our culturally cherished notion of the sexually settled, mature, and nurturing adult woman may account for the persistent sociological bias that, once a woman is anchored in the socially approved heterosexual world of marriage, her sexuality speaks for itself and is not a subject for investigation. Yet there is every reason to believe that a woman's sexuality is emergent and takes on new meanings and qualities in the context of the emergent marriage relationship itself. Then, too, the proliferation and popularization of research on women's sexuality and orgasmic potential has led simultaneously to unprecedented expectations and self-consciousness with respect to marital sexual performance and satisfaction. We may well wonder for how many women the potential for enhanced orgasmic experience is outweighed by the pressure to achieve orgasm in the service of their men's sense of sexual adequacy. The overlap of the sexual and the maternal in women's experience has been

21. Simone de Beauvoir, *The Second Sex* (New York: Alfred A. Knopf, Inc., 1953).
22. Helen M. Hacker, "Women as a Minority Group," *Social Forces* (October 1951), pp. 60–69.
23. See, for example, M. Komarovsky, *Blue Collar Marriage* (New York: Vintage Books, 1962); L. Rubin, *Worlds of Pain* (New York: Basic Books, 1976).

almost entirely neglected as an area for study. Both Rossi and Rich have mentioned the highly charged sexual feelings that are often involved in giving birth to and nursing a child.[24] The mothering role itself draws women into new sets of routines, responsibilities, and relationships, which may affect patterns of sexual expression and interest in the marriage. Furthermore, at the risk of pointing out the obvious, many women do not marry, marry in young middle age, or leave their first or subsequent marriages to move into new living situations or relationships. Each one of these arrangements must surely involve a variety of sexual transactions and different kinds of meanings attached to the expression of sexuality in them.

Finally, of course, a substantial minority will experiment with lesbian activity, and for a minority of these such experimentation will occasion the initial sociosexual expression of what is to become a lesbian career.[25] The major (and minor) fixtures of sex research have produced a noteworthy, albeit controversial, record of the experience of these women. Kinsey et al. is unequivocally the major transitional work marking a reconceptualization of scholarly thought on lesbianism in the twentieth century. Insisting on an "objective" posture bereft of the kind of moral biases that distinguish psychoanalytic writing, Kinsey denied the equivalence of act and actor on empirical grounds: "It would clarify our thinking if the terms could be dropped completely out of our vocabulary, for then socio-sexual behavior could be described as activity between a female and a male, or between two females, or between two males and this would constitute a more objective record of the fact."[26] Kinsey countered the etiologists' conception of lesbian activity—as an unfortunate outcome predetermined by the vagaries of development—with the zoologists' recognition of interspecific continuities and their implications. Following the dictum of parsimony, he posited two factors as the primary causes of lesbianism: the universal physiological capacity for same-sex response and the contingencies of opportunity to engage in lesbian relations. The latter are influenced by the "conditioning effects" of the experience itself and, more critically, the positive and negative social evaluations of lesbian activity encountered by the individual. Ever the naturalist, Kinsey argued that "it is . . . difficult to explain why each and every individual is not involved in every type of sexual activity."[27] Conceptualizing *any* exclusive preference as a

24. A. S. Rossi, "A Biosocial Perspective in Parenting," *Daedalus* 106 (Spring 1977): 1–31; A. Rich, *Of Woman Born* (New York: Bantam Books, 1977).

25. Sexual behavior does not necessarily imply anything about sexual identity. There is no common formula by which individuals uniformly weigh and sum the history of sexual activity and feeling to arrive at a satisfactory identification of themselves or others. Our separate treatment of heterosexual and homosexual forms here is an expedient dictated by our sense that somewhat different intellectual issues are relevant in the two cases.

26. Kinsey et al., *Female*, p. 447.

27. Ibid., p. 451.

perversion of the natural, Kinsey extended and inverted the psychoanalytic construction of innate bisexuality.

Structural variables, of course, dominated all of the work produced by Kinsey and his associates. These are not particularly powerful determinants of women's sexual experience, although they are somewhat stronger predictors of lesbianism. Not surprisingly, education and religiosity are modestly associated with the prevalence of lesbian experience. Interpreting these associations, Kinsey argued that "moral restraints" on heterosexuality serve to encourage lesbianism. Thus, lesbian interests are fostered where devout women, deterred from premarital heterosexual expression by church precepts, turn to lesbianism and, in consequence, abandon the ritual observance of their faith.[28] Similarly, the greater lesbian experience of college graduates follows from the disapproval of premarital heterosexual contacts by parents and college administrators. The emergence of heterosexual commitments among such women is delayed in the interest of education; no longer viable contenders in the marriage market, they subsequently drift into "convenient" lesbian liaisons.[29] Observing that same-sex relations occur more often among single and previously married women, Kinsey concludes that heterosexuality must function to immunize women from such relations. He was apparently unable to recognize the role of lesbian interests in diverting or extruding women from marriage.

Kinsey's stance on lesbianism was certainly more neutral than the moral posturings of the developmentalists. But that he devalued lesbian interests is undeniable. Withholding even the possibility of autonomy from these, he invariably constructed lesbianism as derivative of heterosexual experience and its social meanings. Lesbian encounters emerged because the dominant institutions charged with the moral development of the young too effectively discouraged heterosexual relations, while the failure to achieve marriage pushed women toward the mysteries of lesbianism. And so it goes. Isolating heterosexual prudery from the panoply of conflicting social pressures that females experience with respect to their sexuality, Kinsey promulgated the usual distortions that follow from single-variable explanations of any behavior. More critically, Kinsey failed to understand that women who have chosen to live outside of the restrictions of a virtually monolithic gender role may experience lesbianism as not only a viable alternative but as the one viable alternative that provides cohesive institutional forms. And, of course, the sense of autonomy necessary for entertaining alternatives would be higher in just those populations—the better educated, the irreligious, and the unmarried—where the prevalence of lesbian experience is greatest. Lesbian experience may flow from the social meanings attached to hetero-

28. Ibid., p. 465.
29. Ibid., p. 460.

sexuality, but it undoubtedly flows from the social realities of heterosexuality as well.

The larger contradiction in Kinsey's thought—where he alternatively posed as the champion of sexual tolerance and as the defender of the superiority of heterosexuality for women—perhaps stems in part from his own conviction that female sexuality, unlike male sexuality, lacks any integrity of its own. In this, he confused the nature of sexuality with the overriding mandates of sex roles—an understandable lapse for a zoologist. But his commitment to heterosexuality is also rooted in social and moral convictions. Kinsey the zoologist told us that lesbianism was an attractive, adult alternative; Kinsey the moralist moved discussion to "moral restraints" and magical phalluses. Ideological warfare is, after all, a zero-sum game.

The ideological battle over the valuation of sexual alternatives has recently moved to a curious ground. With the publication of their book, *Homosexuality in Perspective,* Masters and Johnson argue that "more" is actually "less." The "more" in this case refers to their observation that "committed homosexual couples generally become more involved subjectively in the sexual interaction than married heterosexual couples."[30] This recalls, of course, Kinsey's findings of higher orgasmic achievement among committed lesbians compared to married women.[31] While Kinsey traced the apparent superiority of lesbian relations to the technical advantage accruing to the same-sex partner who necessarily shares similar psychological and physiological structures, Masters and Johnson cite the "free flow of both verbal and non-verbal communication."[32]

Masters and Johnson seize the day, imaginatively attributing such communication to "necessity"—a necessity derived from the "long-term disadvantages" of homosexuality. These are of two types: (1) Two basic techniques—partner stimulation and fellatio/cunnilingus—are commonly employed by homosexuals. Because there are *only* two, "these techniques of *necessity* must be constantly varied and refined to the utmost to avoid the loss of stimulative effectiveness through long-term familiarity."[33] (2) One or the other of these techniques is employed by each partner, usually in turn. The mutual stimulation that obviously follows from coitus is lacking in this sequential form of organization, and the level of sexual arousal is accordingly depressed. Masters and Johnson concede that where readily available modes of mutual stimulation are used, the second factor ceases to detract from the viability of the homosexual union. But in the general case this obvious expedient is overlooked, and instead, elaborated forms of communication emerge to

30. W. H. Masters and V. Johnson, *Homosexuality in Perspective* (Boston: Little, Brown & Co.), p. 212.
31. Kinsey et al., *Female,* p. 477.
32. Masters and Johnson, *Homosexuality,* p. 213.
33. Ibid., p. 214.

counter the inherent disadvantage, ultimately leading to the higher states of sexual arousal observed in homosexuals compared to heterosexuals.

This convoluted line of argument is of interest because it belies the gloss of neutrality Masters and Johnson bring to the study of homosexuality, and also because it contradicts informed thought with respect to coitus. Masters and Johnson themselves have repeatedly insisted that, whatever its tension-producing characteristics, coitus is a significantly less effective technique for achieving sexual release. (Note that with respect to their enthusiasm for coitus, Masters and Johnson are essentially arguing that "less" is "more.") Moreover, coitus does not commonly culminate in simultaneous orgasm but, rather, orgasm occurs *in seriatim.* Thus, overwhelmingly, coitus shares with other sexual techniques this long-term disadvantage.

Holding aside its authors' ideological biases, *Homsexuality in Perspective* reports the results of a project that violates the central canon of research methodology. No data are marshaled in response to their research question: "Is there a fundamental difference in sexual physiology if the respondents are homosexually rather than heterosexually oriented?"[34] This is a study, not of physiology, but of orgasm, presumably as an indicator of physiology. Masters and Johnson leave no stone unturned in their exhaustive demonstration of the comparability in orgasmic achievement among heterosexual and homosexual men and women. But all of the study subjects have been carefully screened for "a history of facility to respond at orgasmic levels to the sexual excitation in masturbation, partner manipulation and fellatio. . . ."[35] So theirs, in fact, is a study demonstrating that homosexual and heterosexual women and men who have secure histories of orgasmic achievement do, indeed, relentlessly achieve orgasm in the laboratory.

Etiology, of course, continues to lurk about on the scientific agenda. The notion that some factor—genetic, hormonal, physiological, or psychological—predisposes certain individuals to homosexuality is ever with us. Masters and Johnson believe their study effectively removes physiological factors from the list.

Their own preference is for a version of the learning model that assumes meaning flows from behavior. The individual who achieves competency in the techniques of sexual pleasuring will, when motivated, achieve comfort from them as well. Masters and Johnson obtain a qualified success in the application of their learning-based treatment programs to men and women suffering from homosexual dysfunction and "homosexual dissatisfaction," respectively. The political nature of the sources of "homosexual dissatisfaction" is undeniable; but for Masters

34. Ibid., p. 124.
35. Ibid., p. 7.

and Johnson, politics are at a considerable remove from the practitioner's commitment to service. In a spirit of sexual democracy, they
devalue a homosexual orientation but they are utterly prepared to defend the individual's right to effective homosexual (or heterosexual)
sociosexual functioning.

For Masters and Johnson, as for Kinsey, the sex act is *the* problem. It
is a problem for the remainder of contemporary research on lesbianism
as well, but here it is a problem because it is not a problem. In recent
scholarly work, there is widespread agreement that the sex act itself is
not a fruitful area for study, that research interest is more productively
focused elsewhere. Ironically, the present state of affairs is undoubtedly
a consequence of successful attempts by Kinsey's successors at the Institute for Sex Research to extend interest beyond the historic preoccupation with etiology to the exclusion of other concerns.

The impetus for this tradition is found in a modest article written by
Simon and Gagnon for their reader, *Sexual Deviance,* and subsequently
elaborated in *Sexual Conduct.*[36] Based on eight interviews and a solid
grounding in the Kinsey research, Simon and Gagnon bring an instant
of clarity to the study of lesbianism with their observation, "the female
homosexual follows conventional feminine patterns in developing her
commitment to sexuality and in conducting not only her sexual career
but her nonsexual career as well."[37] Echoing the Kinsey motif, Simon
and Gagnon argue that lesbian sexuality, like female sexuality in general,
is less "autonomous," that is to say, less impersonal than male. Lesbians
have fewer sexual partners than males and, among lesbians (as among
other women), "the body is not seen . . . as an instrument of self-
pleasure."[38]

But the sexual is less interesting to these researchers than modes of
social adaptation. They view the ties that bind the lesbian to dominant
institutions—family, work, and church—as preponderantly problematic
and exacerbated by her sexual orientation and its social meanings.
Moreover, there is little solace to be found in the private sector. Friendships with men and women (including other lesbians) are fraught with
ambivalence; acceptance of self never can be really complete.[39] Simon
and Gagnon recognize that their very small sample provides a poor basis
for generalization. Predominantly working class in origin, most of the
women they interviewed were no older than twenty-five. The kinds of
problems that describe their lives—problems in resolving relationships
of self to family, work, friends—are not exceptional for young, single

36. W. Simon and J. H. Gagnon, "The Lesbians: A Preliminary Overview," in *Sexual Deviance,* ed. J. H. Gagnon and W. Simon (New York: Harper & Row, 1967), pp. 247–82; and Gagnon and Simon, *Sexual Conduct,* pp. 176–216.

37. Gagnon and Simon, *Sexual Conduct,* p. 178.

38. Ibid., p. 182.

39. Ibid., p. 213.

women attempting to organize viable adulthoods. There are, of course, many ways of constructing a lesbian career. Social class and life-cycle stage constrain options, as do other factors. The kinds of sexual careers individuals forge not only reflect nonsexual sources of influence but afford varying degrees of potential, in themselves, for facilitating or disrupting the individual's interactions in other, nonsexual spheres of life. Simon and Gagnon understand this level of complexity, but the historical moment, biases in their sample, and biases in their mode of inquiry obscure it from them. They leave us with an image of the lesbian as a tortured creature with few sources of consolation. Occasionally they struggle to bring some balance to their image of overriding estrangement and loss, but the sexual and social rewards of being lesbian ultimately elude them.

Despite the authors' candid admission of the limitations in their work, this provisional study by Simon and Gagnon has substantially anticipated subsequent inquiry with respect to lesbians. A focus on continuity and modes of social adaptation is evident in several studies that have been published in recent years.[40] Principal among these is *Homosexualities* by Bell and Weinberg, researchers from Kinsey's old shop, the Institute for Sex Research.[41] At the behest of the funding agency, this study, the largest of its kind, is primarily a study of homosexual men. But a substantial number of lesbians were interviewed as part of the data collection effort. The usual comparisons with a control group of heterosexual women are reported—religion, marital histories, contacts with the mental health establishment, etc. The growing recognition that lesbianism is not monolithic gains expression in the typology Bell and Weinberg construct, and it is this that distinguishes the work. They designate women as "close-" and "open-coupled," "functionals," "dysfunctionals," and "asexuals," based on the sexual and social adjustment of those who are and are not in couples.

Unfortunately the typology, which frames the major thrust of their analysis, generally is of little utility in discriminating the experience of their lesbian respondents.[42] But this is not the case where mental health experience is concerned. The close-coupled, who constitute the modal category, were happier and more self-accepting than the lesbian sample as a whole. They were also less likely to report loneliness, depression, tension, or paranoia. Moreover, the mental health profile of the close-coupled women was indistinguishable from that of the heterosexual con-

40. See, for example, C. Wolff, *Love between Women* (New York: Harper Colophon, 1971); J. S. Chafetz et al., *Who's Queer?* (Sarasota, Fla.: Omni Press, 1976); D. Wolf, *The Lesbian Community* (Berkeley and Los Angeles: University of California Press, 1979).

41. A. P. Bell and M. S. Weinberg, *Homosexualities* (New York: Simon & Schuster, 1978).

42. Seventeen of the 280 tests (6.1 percent) reported for the five types of lesbians in tables 14.1–20.11 are statistically significant.

trols.[43] In contrast, the adjustments of the asexual lesbians were more precarious; these women were significantly more likely than lesbians in general to report loneliness and histories of suicide attempts. The mental health experience of the remaining groups was generally comparable to that of the sample as a whole.[44] Thus, where lesbian forms parallel those valued by the larger society and lesbian women are able to satisfy their sexual and social needs within those forms, substantial mental health benefits accrue. Or, alternatively, the well-adjusted lesbian with a sturdy sense of self may be predisposed to adopt socially valued forms and to find solace in them.

A critical question remains: What are the social and psychological experiences and attributes that move the individual toward one or the other career mode? A partial answer is suggested in an elegant little study designed by Peplau and her associates.[45] Well-reasoned and carefully executed, the study focuses on the relationship between values and the content of lesbian life-styles. Peplau identifies two, somewhat antithetical, constellations of values that appear to organize lesbian commitments. An emphasis on "dyadic attachment" is associated with both romanticism and traditional sex-role values. Lesbians commited to such values manifest them in behavior; their relationships with lovers are more likely to have a domestic base where loving and liking are central. The relationships these women have made are of longer duration, and their endurance in the face of obstacles is anticipated. The second constellation of values, "personal autonomy," is more characteristic of politically radical lesbians. Negatively associated with romanticism and traditional sex-role values, an emphasis on personal autonomy portends less durable sexual relationships and less contact between sexual partners. Consistent with the commitment to autonomy are the more frequent lapses in sexual exclusivity these women report.

Peplau's work should provide a model for further research in the area. The conceptualization evident in this work responds to the well-recognized complexity of human sexual behavior. "Lesbian" is a term that masks immense variability. Different kinds of women come to lesbianism for different kinds of reasons. Personal values are expressed in different kinds of relationships and structural arrangements which, in turn, have consequences of sexual conduct both within and outside of the primary relationship.

In our review of recent work on lesbianism, we have identified a glaring omission which is probably a consequence of the movement away from a central focus on the sexual per se. The slippage between lesbian

---

43. Numerous studies examine the mental health of those with devalued sexualities; see *Journal of Clinical Psychiatry,* vol. 39 (July 1978), for a nice review article by Hart et al.

44. Bell and Weinberg, tables 21.1–21.28.

45. L. A. Peplau et al., "Loving Women: Attachment and Autonomy in Lesbian Relationships," *Journal of Social Issues* 34 (Summer 1978): 7–27.

behavior and identity transformation has been considered,[46] and the ways women drift into lesbian behavior were described by Barnhart in her study of the Portland community.[47] But the absence of a comprehensive, sensitive study of the coming-out process as problematic for women—where both the "called" and the "chosen" are simultaneously examined or, better yet, discriminated—continues to constitute a major gap in the literature.

Clearly, there has yet to emerge anything that resembles a dominant paradigm organizing the study and interpretation of female sexuality. Paradigms themselves, of course, are emergent, socially constructed phenomena and, as such, require time to coalesce. However partial or narrowly focused the insights and information contained in the various works we have reviewed, each study has, in its way, made a significant contribution in reinforcing the legitimacy of the study of sexuality and in dispelling the Freudian myths that have obscured the understanding of female sexual behavior, thereby constraining its expression. Although we have been particularly critical of the models advanced by the behaviorists, their empirical work most dranatically breaks with traditional Freudian thought, making possible the development of more comprehensive, sociological alternatives to Freudian modes of thinking, inquiry, and explanation. It may be true, as Freud contends, that the sexual sits at the center of personality. But it sits there, nonetheless, as "the changer and the changed," both shaping and being shaped in its dynamic relationship to the self and the society.

Department of Sociology
Smith College (Miller)

Office of the Dean of the College
Smith College (Fowlkes)

46. P. Blumstein and P. Schwartz, "Bisexuality in Women," *Archives of Sexual Behaviors* (April 1976), pp 171–81.

47. E. Barnhart, "Friends and Lovers in a Lesbian Counterculture Community," in *Old Family, New Family*, ed. N. Glazer-Malbin (New York: Van Nostrand Reinhold Co., 1975).

REVIEW ESSAY

"The Love Crisis": Couples Advice Books of the Late 1970s

Ellen Ross

Being part of a heterosexual couple is viewed as a deadly necessity in the mass-audience marriage advice books of the late 1970s. As George Bach and Ronald Deutsch put it in *Pairing,* couple love is so important that even romance, once the cornerstone of courtship, becomes a "luxury": " . . . what men and women seek from love today is no longer a luxury; it is an essential of emotional survival. . . . More and more it is the hope of finding in intimate love something of personal validity, personal relevance, a confirmation of one's existence."[1] Older marital functions, like shared material survival or the reproduction of future generations, are increasingly subordinated to this emotional tie between spouses or "surrogate spouses." As divorce rates rise, fertility declines, and the courts blur the distinction between the married and unmarried, what has emerged as the one constant of American family life is "the couple."

None of the advice books is intellectually substantial enough to merit an in-depth critique, yet their sales success makes them sociologically significant. Nena and George O'Neill's *Open Marriage,* for example, has been a spectacular seller since its hardcover publication in 1972, selling 1,988,000 copies in at least a dozen Avon paperback printings over the last decade. *Pairing,* also reprinted frequently, sold 710,000

My thanks to Hal Benenson, Barbara Engel, Ros Petchesky, and Christine Stansell, who generously provided ideas and materials.
1. George R. Bach [Peter Wyden] and Ronald M. Deutsch, *Pairing* (New York: Avon Books, 1970), pp. 14–15.

paperbacks in the 1970s. *Passive Men and Wild Women,* by Pierre Mornell, had already sold 17,000 hardcover copies in its first summer, 1979, which makes it also "very popular," according to the publisher's sales department.[2] Examining this literature in its political and social context sheds light both on the current "love crisis" (as one of these authors has named it) and on what political capital has been, and might be, made of it. For, although much more could be said about the relationship between these books and their mass audience, it seems safe to say that transformations in couple relationships are generating deep worries for a large social group.

Recent demographic indicators speak eloquently of very rapid shifts in family and marriage patterns. There are more points in the life cycle when Americans are likely to be "single" and courting actively. Since 1960 the proportions of young people who are simply not marrying in their twenties have increased dramatically, so that by 1976, 43 percent of all twenty- to twenty-four-year-olds were single.[3] The proportion of people living alone doubled between 1950 and 1973, and today a fifth of households consist of just one person.[4] These "primary individuals," in census parlance, are mostly old people, especially widows, but this group increasingly includes young men and women who move away from their parents' homes long before they themselves marry.[5] Women living with their children, who comprised over 14 percent of American households in March 1979, are another fast-growing group of "singles."[6]

People are having fewer children than ever before in U.S. history, and this, too, accentuates the emotional centrality of the adult couple.[7] As important as the declining number of children is the way they fit into the family life cycle. The cohort of American women born in the 1920s

2. Nena O'Neill and George O'Neill, *Open Marriage: A New Life Style for Couples* (New York: Avon Books, 1973); Bach and Deutsch; Pierre Mornell, *Passive Men, Wild Women* (New York: Simon & Schuster, 1979). (My student, Karen Magenta, called this book to my attention.)

3. In 1976 18 percent of women and 28 percent of men in the twenty-five to twenty-nine age group also remained unmarried (Charles F. Westoff, "Some Speculations on the Future of Marriage and Fertility," *Family Planning Perspectives* 10, no. 2 [March/April 1978]: 79–83, esp. p. 80; U.S. Bureau of the Census, *Marital Status and Living Arrangements: March 1978,* Current Population Reports, ser. P-20 (Washington, D.C.: Government Printing Office 1979), as reported in "Census Finds Unmarried Couples Have Doubled from 1970 to 1978," *New York Times* (June 27, 1979).

4. "Census Finds Unmarried Couples Have Doubled"; Frances E. Kobrin, "The Fall in Household Size and the Rise of the Primary Individual in the United States," in *The American Family in Social-Historical Perspective,* ed. Michael Gordon, 2d ed. (New York: St. Martin's Press, 1978), pp. 69–81.

5. Kobrin, pp. 73–76.

6. National Commission on Working Women, "An Overview of Women in the Workforce," *National NOW Times* (March 1979).

7. Projected fertility rates are now 1.9 children per woman, and some predict that the rate will decline still further (Westoff, p. 79).

had finished childbearing by the time they were thirty, while the eighteenth-century Quaker women studied by historian Robert Wells continued to have children into their late thirties. Longer life expectancy has obvious consequences for marriages and couples. Twenty percent of the Quaker marriages ended with the death of one spouse before all the children were grown,[8] but today's married couples are usually in their forties when they lose their children to college or separate residences, and death does not split them up until an average age of 65.[9] Thus they have twenty years together no longer as "parents" but as "couples."

High divorce rates, especially since the 1960s, make marriage look less and less like a permanent structure for the support of wives and children. Modest projections are that for women born in the late 1940s, 38 percent of first marriages, and a still larger proportion of second marriages (44 percent), will end with divorce.[10] But this trend reflects no disillusionment with the couple.[11] Indeed, more women born in the late 1930s have been married, at least for a while, than in any previous generation of American women. Remarriage rates are also high.[12]

Why have divorces become so common? Census bureau demographer Paul Glick suggests that improper matching is the problem: "Marriage partners are typically joined through a process of chance, often involving compromise, and . . . there should be no great surprise if the marriage is eventually dissolved."[13] But even if all marriages were made in heaven, or by computer, as an institution marriage has built-in structural "weaknesses," both economic and ideological. The legal and cultural imperative of male support of dependents, for example, generates a whole group of marital stresses. The poor and unemployed have traditionally had higher rates of divorce, separation, and single par-

8. Robert Wells, "Demographic Change and the Life Cycle of American Families," in *The Family in History: Interdisciplinary Essays,* ed. Theodore K. Rabb and Robert I. Rotberg (New York: Harper Torchbooks, 1973), pp. 85–94, esp. pp. 88, 90.

9. Janet Zollinger Giele, *Women and the Future: Changing Sex Roles in America* (New York: Free Press, 1978), p. 147.

10. Between 1963 and 1973 divorces increased by 113.8 percent, although marriages increased by only 38.1 percent (U.S. Public Health Service, National Center for Health Statistics, *Divorces by Marriage Cohort,* Vital Statistics, ser. 21, no. 34. (Washington, D.C.: Public Health Service, 1979), pp. 4–5.

11. See, e.g., Edward Westermarck's comment: "Far from being [the] enemy [of marriage], divorce is rather its saviour . . . a means of preserving the dignity of marriage by putting an end to unions that are a disgrace to its name" (*The Future of Marriage in Western Civilization* [1936; reprint ed., Freeport, N.Y.: Books for Libraries Press, 1970], p. 152).

12. Paul C. Glick and Arthur J. Norton, "Perspectives on the Recent Upturn in Marriage and Divorce," *Demography* 10, no. 3 (August 1973): 301–14, esp. p. 305. About 4/5 of divorced people remarry eventually, though rates are higher for men than for women (Paul C. Glick, "A Demographer Looks at American Families," in *Family in Transition,* ed. Arlene S. Skolnick and Jerome H. Skolnick, 2d ed. [Boston: Little, Brown & Co., 1977], pp. 90–108, esp. p. 92; Hugh Carter and Paul C. Glick, *Marriage and Divorce: A Social and Economic Study,* rev. ed. [Cambridge, Mass.: Harvard University Press, 1976], p. 239).

13. Glick, p. 101.

enthood.[14] There is also evidence of a correlation between working wives and divorce,[15] suggesting that female dependency helped keep marriage "stable" in past decades when fewer wives had jobs.

A second contradiction, and the one I want to emphasize, seems to have intensified in the 1970s: Marriage has been saddled with unprecedented ideological burdens. It has become the framework for couple relationships supposedly based on perfect mutuality, intimacy, sexual ecstacy, and mutual growth. Most marriages fail to fit this prescription. For heterosexual couples consist of two people, a woman and a man, for whom the experiences of the relationship can be remarkably divergent. This platitude is recognized in most marriage commentary, but it is seldom, except by feminists, viewed as a genuine contradiction in marriage as an institution. Recently feminist psychologists have tried to analyze closely what Freud also acknowledged but could do little more than despair over: the "asymmetry" (to use Nancy Chodorow's term) in love and sex between men and women which results not only from differences in socialization but also from fundamentally disparate kinds of human bonds established in infant experiences with mothering.[16] Reviewing empirical studies of "marital happiness," Jessie Bernard speculates that marriage's contradictions are expressed in the nervous and somatic complaints of married women, whose mental health and sense of physical well-being seemed much inferior to those of married men.[17]

The seventies' focus on couples has sharpened this gender dichotomy by encouraging people, especially women, to expect more from couple relationships. Most of the recent marriage advice books, judging from their content, are written for middle-class females who fear that they lack the "skills" needed to meet today's high demands for marital fulfillment; the traditional burden of female responsibility for emotional nurturance has probably increased. In Judy Blume's recent novel, *Wifey*, for example, the heroine, an avid reader of advice literature, tries out sex techniques and methods of improving "communication" on an ut-

14. See Carol Stack, *All Our Kin: Strategies for Survival in a Black Community* (New York: Harper & Row, 1974), chap. 7.

15. Glick, pp. 96–97.

16. The main contributions are: Juliet Mitchell, *Psychoanalysis and Feminism: Freud, Reich, Laing, and Women* (New York: Pantheon Books, 1974); Nancy Chodorow, "Mothering, Object-Relations, and the Female Oedipal Configuration," *Feminist Studies* 4, no. 1 (February 1978): 137–58, and *The Reproduction of Mothering: Psychoanalysis and the Sociology of Gender* (Berkeley: University of California Press, 1978); Dorothy Dinnerstein, *The Mermaid and the Minotaur: Sexual Arrangements and Human Malaise* (New York: Harper Colophon Books, 1977); and Jane Flax, "The Conflict between Nurturance and Autonomy in Mother-Daughter Relationships and within Feminism," *Feminist Studies* 4, no. 2 (June 1978): 171–89.

17. Jessie Bernard, "The Paradox of the Happy Marriage," in *Woman in Sexist Society*, ed. Vivian Gornick and Barbara K. Moran (New York: New American Library, 1971), pp. 145–62.

terly cold and rigid husband whose only interest is his dry-cleaning business.[18] As Janet Kohen and Roslyn Feldberg put it, the usual sexual
division of labor "prescribes a role for males that makes them marginal
to the central function of the family, the emotional-nurturant one."[19]

Earlier cultures seldom associated love, marriage, and profound
intimacy. The experience of romantic love has been known and honored
from Plato's *Symposium* through the Romantic poets, but always outside
of and in conflict with marriage. Seventeenth-century Puritans in England and its American colonies viewed marital affection as most pleasant and desirable, and eighteenth-century gentry families in England
adopted some of these domestic values. But domesticity and family solidarity did not usually lead to expectations of total intimacy or personal
fulfillment through marriage, and throughout the nineteenth century it
seems clear that most sought emotional contact not with marriage
partners but with kinspeople, neighbors, or work companions of the
same sex.[20] Describing the typical marriage of his own generation in
England, John Stuart Mill wrote, "The one has as little admission into
the internal life of the other as if they were common acquaintances."[21]

On both sides of the Atlantic beginning in the 1820s or earlier, small
bands of socialists, freethinkers, and Unitarians began to experiment
with the possibility of combining love and intimacy with marriage.[22]
Given nineteenth-century assumptions about the predatory quality of
male sexuality and about the feebleness of women's, it is not surprising
that many marriage reformers, including Mill and Harriet Taylor, did
not include sexual "communion" among the kinds of marital intimacy

18. Judy Blume, *Wifey* (New York: G. P. Putnam's Sons, 1978).

19. Roslyn Feldberg and Janet Kohen, "Isolation and Invasion: The Conditions of
Marriage and Divorce," in *The Family: Functions, Conflicts, and Symbols,* ed. Peter J. Stein,
Judith Richman, and Natalie Hannon (Reading, Mass.: Addison-Wesley Publishing Co.,
1977), pp. 314–25, esp. p. 315.

20. Some of the nineteenth- and early twentieth-century sources on which this sketch
is based are: Louise Tilly, Joan Scott, and Miriam Cohen, "Women's Work and Fertility
Patterns," *Journal of Interdisciplinary History* 6, no. 3 (Winter, 1976): 446–76; John Gillis,
"Servants, Sexual Relations, and the Risks of Illegitimacy in London, 1801–1900," *Feminist
Studies* 5, no. 1 (Spring 1979): 142–73; Gareth Stedman-Jones, "Working-Class Culture
and Working-Class Politics in London, 1870–1900: Notes on the Remaking of a Working
Class," *Journal of Social History* 7, no. 4 (Summer 1974): 460–508; Ellen Ross, "Family and
Neighborhood in Bethnal Green, 1870–1914," in progress; see also Carroll Smith-
Rosenberg, "The Female World of Love and Ritual: Relations between Women in
Nineteenth-Century America," *Signs: Journal of Women in Culture and Society* 1, no. 1 (Au-
tumn 1975): 1–29.

21. John Stuart Mill, "The Subjection of Women," in *Essays on Sex Equality,* ed. Alice
Rossi (Chicago: University of Chicago Press, 1970), pp. 151–52.

22. Owenism, e.g., provided a climate in which feminist critiques of marriage
flourished (see Barbara Taylor, "'The Men Are as Bad as Their Masters . . .': Socialism,
Feminism, and Sexual Antagonism in the London Tailoring Trade in the Early 1830s,"
Feminist Studies 5, no. 1 [Spring 1979]: 7–40, and *Socialism and Feminism in Early Nineteenth-
Century England* [London: Virago Books, in press]).

that might be achieved.[23] In the 1910s and 1920s, however, "sexologists" expanded the concept of couple rapport to include sexual intimacy. For example, in *Married Love,* Marie Stopes wrote, "The complete act of union is a triple consummation. It symbolises, and at the same time actually enhances, the spiritual union . . . and it is a *mutual,* not a selfish pleasure and profit, more calculated than anything else to draw out an unspeakable tenderness and understanding in both partakers of this sacrament. . . . "[24]

In the "romantic culture" of the American 1920s, finding the right partner was presented as a gateway to lifelong happiness.[25] But it is possible that there was a substantial gap between the prescriptive literature and people's actual behavior. In England, a parallel literature emerged in the 1920s, but among the working classes, my research suggests, only courtship seems to have been conducted in the language and with the expectations of romance. Once married, or even engaged, women and men lived according to more traditional patterns. Marriage continued to be viewed, perhaps through the Second World War in many communities, as an exchange of male wages for female domestic services, with peace, harmony, and a steady income the desired climate.

In the United States today, many older forms of nonmarital conviviality have broken down. The separation between work and leisure, a gradual process that began with industrialization, meant that living, eating, and socializing with workmates became rarer and rarer. For large segments of the population, traditional religion has ceased to be a center of social life. Urban renewal has gutted many of the neighborhoods that older women remember vividly as the scenes of female or ethnic solidarity. The frequency with which Americans move (a five-year study completed in 1974 found that 35 percent of a sample of 5,000 families moved during the period)[26] also makes contacts difficult to maintain. As Nena O'Neill writes in *The Marriage Premise,* "We may or may not know our neighbors. We know that the friend we make today may be gone tomorrow—consider how large corporations routinely shift executives and their families from one side of the country to the other. . . . We have . . . continuing contact with fewer and fewer people. Today, as never before, our marriages are assuming more responsibility for fulfilling the need to be known, for providing the continuity in our lives."[27] It is

23. See Linda Gordon's discussion of this issue in an American context: "Voluntary Motherhood: The Beginnings of Feminist Birth Control Ideas in the United States," *Feminist Studies* 1, nos. 3–4 (Winter–Spring 1973): 5–22.

24. Marie C. Stopes, *Married Love* (1918; reprint ed., New York: Eugenics Publishing Co., 1931), pp. 75–76; emphasis in original.

25. See Stuart Ewen, *Captains of Consciousness: Advertising and the Social Roots of the Consumer Culture* (New York: McGraw-Hill Book Co., 1976), pt. 3.

26. Mary Jo Bane, *Here to Stay: American Families in the Twentieth Century* (New York: Basic Books, 1976), p. 60.

27. Nena O'Neill, *The Marriage Premise* (New York: M. Evans & Co., 1977), p. 66.

acknowledged that people outside the couple might be able to come through emotionally, but these others appear almost exclusively as sexual partners of the central couple—in relationships variously labeled "nonmarital," "comarital," or "satellite." The enormous range of potential human connections disappears into the emotional woodwork.

Most of these books are a nightmare for any serious reader. They contain slogans rather than developed ideas and are filled with gossipy "case studies" ("Janice is a school teacher, unmarried and thirty-three years old. For four years she has been seriously involved with Mike . . . ").[28] Another staple are self-rating quizzes like the "Sexuality Preference Scale" or "The New Husband Scale" ("Couples who score too far apart on the scale are in urgent need of some heavy dialogue," warns the author).[29] The usual tone is the cheery banality Russell Jacoby excoriates in *Social Amnesia,* his critique of the "post-Freudians" who supply much of this literature's theoretical underpinnings.[30] Nearly all of the authors of this group of advice books are professional psychotherapists who have few doubts about the necessity for psychologizing in everyday life. The teenage dating manuals we relied on in the 1950s advised us to "be natural," but in the late seventies psychotherapy, or at least weekend "training," is a better preparation for dating and marriage. For those needing cheaper help, it is available at the local paperback bookshop. No matter how "liberal" the self-help book, all are based on the assumption that the problems to which they are addressed—loneliness, insecurity, and the incompatibility between the sexes—can be solved by individuals or couples using the proper techniques. Self-help becomes, as Jacoby notes, a substitute for organized action to change the social arrangements that generate this suffering.[31]

The two most clearly drawn couple models in my sample of advice books are the "modern," originating in the late 1960s and developing throughout the seventies, and the "traditional," which has made a striking comeback in these days of profamily and antifeminist backlash. The modern group incorporates themes from humanistic psychology, feminism (usually badly distorted), and classical individualism from the world of Adam Smith. Some of the initial best-sellers in this genre, however thin and shallow, were at least critical of marriage and hopeful about possibilities for change in heterosexual relationships. Ronald Mazur's *The New Intimacy* (1973) advocates a loosening of marriage to encompass additional sexual or emotional ties and is enthusiastic about

28. Ronald Mazur, *The New Intimacy: Open-Ended Marriage and Alternative Lifestyles* (Boston: Beacon Press, 1973), p. 141.

29. Andrew J. DuBrin, *The New Husbands and How to Become One* (Chicago: Nelson-Hall, Inc., 1976), p. 28.

30. Russell Jacoby, *Social Amnesia: A Critique of Contemporary Psychology from Adler to Laing* (Boston: Beacon Press, 1975).

31. Ibid., p. 51.

at least a dozen alternative life-styles listed in chapter 5. Psychologist Lawrence Casler's *Is Marriage Necessary?* (1974) attacks marriage as incompatible with individual self-development and argues that there are many equally plausible ways to obtain security and sex and to raise children.[32] *Open Marriage* (1972), probably the best seller of the entire group, is a lively attempt to make traditional marriage compatible with female equality and individual growth. Sexual relationships with others are not the point of *Open Marriage* and, although not condemned, do not get much attention. "Sex-roles" and traditional "couple" assumptions keep marriages "closed," locking partners into boring, prescribed emotional and household activities.[33]

However, a closer look at these modern models, even the ones critical of marriage, reveals an inability to conceptualize social bonds in anything other than the language of the marketplace. *Contract Cohabitation,* published in 1974, is certainly the most blatant example of this perspective. Disillusioned with both marital and nonmarital relationships, the author, a well-heeled 52-year-old Los Angeles chemist, had a flash of insight: "For years I had hired various people to help me in each of my creative activities. . . . Now I needed help, not with my creative work, but with my physical sense of well-being. Why couldn't I hire someone to take care of the physical me, releasing the creative me to get on with the exciting projects that lay ahead?"[34] "Elaine" answered the author's advertisement in the *Los Angeles Free Press,* which offered $500 per month ("about what a secretary could earn in Orange County") plus room and board in exchange for companionship, sex at night, and thirty-days' notice. The fascination of *Contract Cohabitation* is the good-natured ease with which the author accepts the cash basis of the relationship's compartmentalized "loving care and companionship." "Money can serve as an instrument of emotional exchange. It enables us, for example, to keep our accounts in current balance. . . . Each time that I give Elaine her salary check, my emotional obligations are paid up in full" (p. 118). Not just the sexual contact, as in prostitution, but the entire relationship is quite literally commoditized.

"Contract cohabitation" is not likely to catch on, and admittedly the book was a poor seller for its paperback house (only 10,000 copies sold since 1975). But the ideal of an affective "fair deal" between couples is central in the modern advice books. *Marriage in Trouble* (1976), by a Chicago clinical psychologist, describes unhappy marriages as those in which "two people are not sufficiently meeting each other's needs."[35]

32. Lawrence Casler, *Is Marriage Necessary?* (New York: Human Sciences Press, 1974).

33. O'Neill and O'Neill (n. 2 above).

34. Edmund L. Van Deusen, *Contract Cohabitation: An Alternative to Marriage* (New York: Avon Books, 1974), p. 41.

35. Eleanor C. Haspel, *Marriage in Trouble: A Time of Decision* (Chicago: Nelson-Hall, Inc., 1976), p. 4.

When needs are mutually accommodated, on the other hand, relationships give "satisfaction" or are "gratifying." Thus "the first step in looking at a troubled relationship is to ask what the relationship provides and to determine if one's partner can realistically meet one's internal psychological needs" (p. 10). In *No-Fault Marriage* (also 1976) we learn that our happiness in marriage can be assessed by our asking, "How much of what you *need* are you getting? How much of what you *want* are you receiving? How much of what you *expect* actually comes to pass?"[36] Jean Bear, in *How to be an Assertive (Not Aggressive) Woman,* has worked the mutual satisfaction of needs into a formal science. "Marital decision contracts," are regularly renegotiated, and "promissory notes" are used to effect changes in the actions of couples so that "each gets something he/she wants."[37] "In the Behavior Exchange Contract [for example] you contract for a change in certain specific unsatisfying behaviors." Rules include: "a. Each partner gets something he/she wants from the other. For instance, you contract 'to wear a nice robe in the morning instead of that torn one.' He agrees to 'come home for dinner on time instead of drinking with the boys.' You start with simple behaviors and progress to more complex ('She should initiate more sex.' 'He should kiss me more.')" (p. 210).

Taken as a group, these chipper, upbeat books present a depressing picture. For one thing, most do not admit the weakness of the bargaining position women bring into the emotional marketplace. For another, they assume a static social world in which hypostatized men's and women's "needs" are always in at least some conflict as each tries to squeeze the most "satisfaction" out of the other's limited supply of need-satisfying paraphernalia. Accepting that women as well as men may rightfully demand satisfaction is an advance over earlier views of females as intrinsically "altruistic" or even "masochistic." But presented in the reified form they assume in most advice literature, needs lose their connection to the material of human relationships.[38] Most needs posited in the self-help books are fictions. All but a few of our simplest biological requirements are generated in social situations and are thus very fluid. What women need emotionally from men seems greater in the middle class than in many working-class and ethnic subcultures. Marriages in

36. Marcia Lasswell and Norma M. Lobsenz, *No-Fault Marriage: The New Technique of Self-Counseling and What It Can Help You Do* (Garden City, N.Y.: Doubleday & Co., 1976), p. 23; emphasis in original.

37. Jean Baer, *How to be an Assertive (Not Aggressive) Woman in Life, in Love, and on the Job* (New York: New American Library, 1976), p. 208.

38. The "businesslike" ambiance of couple relations as they appear in many advice books is no accident; many of the authors have business connections. Jean Baer, e.g., is a former public relations director of *Seventeen* (Barbara Ehrenreich and Deirdre English, *For Her Own Good: 150 Years of the Experts' Advice to Women* [Garden City, N.Y.: Anchor Press, 1978], p. 273, see esp. the excellent analysis of 1970s advice books on pp. 268–81).

which the spouses are religious are less likely to be ended by divorce than are others and are more likely to be defined as happy.[39] Though there are many possible explanations for this finding, among the most plausible is that the commitment to marriage as serving a transcendent purpose may supply satisfaction beyond what emanates directly from the spouse.

Two very recent (1979) books in the modern category focus on survival in this jungle of needs. Their strengths are that they are less rigid in positing an emotional "economy" and that they openly acknowledge conflict between women and men. Their main weakness is their failure to draw serious conclusions from their own "data." *The Love Crisis,* written by a journalist consulting with a clinical psychologist, is a guide for the 27 million American single women, who, it is presumed, are hunting for men: "Women realize we are in a Love Crisis in this country. Never has such suspicion and mutual distrust existed between the sexes. Women find men erratic, elusive, devious, skittish, self-centered, alienated, subtly (or not so subtly) hostile, sexually troubled, and unable to love in a rational, giving, ongoing way. And they want to know why."[40] The authors' answer lies partly in male neurosis (presumably the psychologist's contribution) and, more interestingly, partly in "the collapse of convention" in the world of sex and dating (p. 6). However, most of the book consists of categorizing kinds of men we women will find on the dating market: "Hit-and-Run Lovers," "Jugglers," "Sexually Stingy Lovers," "Unreliable Men," "The Bastards," and so on. Some relationships, of course, do work out, and some men are even willing to marry: "Healthy Normal Men [the last of the categories] are nice. Try to find one. . . . Use these five points to evaluate any prospects" (p. 243). But by the time we do get to "David," the "Normal Man," the point has been made too forcefully: There are close to insuperable barriers to intimacy.

Based on clinical work with Marin County couples, Pierre Mornell makes a similar diagnosis in *Passive Men, Wild Women:* "In our own homes, most of us 'men'—we would-be emperors—have no clothes. We are passive and that drives our women crazy."[41] Like most American women, Marin County wives esteem close relationships, and their sense of self-worth is related, in particular, to the quality of their marriages. The husbands, mostly successful businessmen and professionals, however, view their lovers, wives, and families as a backdrop for their work, which brings the rewards of prestige, money, and self-satisfaction. But,

39. Thomas Hoult, Lura Henze, and John Hudson, *Courtship and Marriage in America* (Boston: Little, Brown & Co., 1978), p. 245; Gerald R. Leslie and Elizabeth M. Leslie, *Marriage in a Changing World* (New York: John Wiley & Sons, 1977), p. 125.

40. Carol Botwin, with Jerome L. Fine, *The Love Crisis* (Garden City, N.Y.: Doubleday & Co., 1979), p. 2.

41. Mornell (n. 2 above), p. 15.

to paraphrase Marx, they do not really feel "at home" when at work, whereas home is defined as the place where they are "not working."[42] The following clinical encounter encapsulates the impasse at which many of Mornell's couples could be found:

> *The wife began:*   I want some togetherness.
> *He replied:*   I want some space.
> *Wife:*   I need you to work on our relationship.
> *Husband:*   I work all week. I don't want to work on weekends. Why can't you understand that? [P. 27]

Repeated confrontations of this kind drive women "wild" with frustration; they leave their husbands hoping that another male in a spouselike role will better meet their needs. As in *The Love Crisis,* the problem looks global, requiring a restructuring of work itself and of all our gender arrangements: child rearing, male and female socialization, probably heterosexuality itself, and certainly marriage. Mornell instead prescribes "ten percent more activity and effort on the husband's part . . ." (p. 173), and he supplies a list of fifty-two topics guaranteed to stimulate household discussion. If all of the above fail, there is a list of referral agencies for psychotherapy.

The second group of self-help books, the traditional or "romantic"[43] manuals, are mostly simple reaffirmations of the status quo ante 1960. Their special intellectual poverty makes it tempting to downgrade the importance of this branch of couples literature. But Marabel Morgan's *The Total Woman,* which cheerily repudiated all the changes in marriage and women's situation since 1950, was 1975's top-selling book in any genre[44] and the ninth nonfiction best-seller of the decade.[45] The incredible rhetorical power of this vision supplies at least part of the force behind the antifeminist and antigay backlash.

In *The New Husbands,* Andrew J. DuBrin, another psychologist, refers to feminism as a "fad" that is now happily passing away.[46] He explains to those men who want to try being "new husbands" how to maintain a reasonable amount of sex-role flexibility—in housework, child care, and sex—without going "overboard" and becoming a "totally liberated husband." This latter should be avoided, for "without some de-

42. Karl Marx, "Alienated Labor," in *Writings of the Young Marx on Philosophy and Society,* ed. and trans. Lloyd D. Easton and Kurt H. Guddat (Garden City, N.Y.: Anchor Books, 1967), pp. 292–93. I owe this reference to Nancy Cott, *The Bonds of Womanhood: Woman's Sphere in New England, 1780–1835* (New Haven, Conn.: Yale University Press, 1977), p. 68.

43. As English and Ehrenreich use the term (chap. 1).

44. Jeremy Rifkin with Ted Howard, "Another Nation under God," *In These Times* (December 19, 1979–January 8, 1980).

45. *New York Times Book Review* (December 20, 1979).

46. DuBrin (n. 29 above), p. 2.

lineation between male and female behavior the result can only be confusion about sex identification and the imposition of bisexuality upon
children" (p. 27). A more cynical restatement of traditional gender arrangements is Albert Ellis's *Intelligent Woman's Guide to Dating and Mating.*[47] In an excerpt from *Cosmopolitan* we find him backing away from his
early 1970s positions critical of sexual traditions:[48] "For both biological
and social reasons, there are definite differences between males and
females. And if you're going to get along well, or at least gracefully, with
men, you'd better accept these differences. *Accept* is the key word
here—nobody's asking you to wax highly enthusiastic about them. . . . "[49]

Nena O'Neill's *The Marriage Premise* (1977) is also a retreat from her
more optimistic position in *Open Marriage,* written five years earlier.[50]
Her son's divorce was the turning point for O'Neill, since divorce meant
that the younger O'Neill would no longer have "the enveloping warmth
[marriage] can provide. Where else can we feel so safe, not being out
there alone with the world's winds blowing at our unprotected backs?"
(p. 26). O'Neill's is not so much a reasoned defense of marriage as a
sentimental restatement of hopeful pieties. Especially significant is her
assertion that "the couple itself constitutes a family, consciously choosing
in marriage the security and traditions of family life" (p. 32). She insists
that the arrival of children need not challenge the centrality of the
husband-wife relationship. As one of her interviewees commented,
"Children come and children go, and your spouse is there forever . . ."
(p. 81). Traditional marriage has usually been at women's expense, as
O'Neill acknowledges; yet she dodges the issue of female subordination
in marriage. To preserve marriage with all its contemporary contradictions, she suggests restoring its "romance and ritual," that is, re-
mystifying the marriage relationship.

Bring Back Romance (1979) is Natalie Willner's attempt to muster the
apparatus of the sexual revolution in the service of traditional marriage.[51] Beginning with an adventure in which Willner's husband "Irv"
discovered her late one night painting the kitchen completely nude "except for a clear plastic apron," the author eventually developed a more
practical (and lucrative) formula for bringing sexual excitement to her
own and others' marriages. She established a commercial consulting service in which clients get advice and help in setting up situations that
make them feel sexy. "Five years of therapy and training in psychological
group leadership" (p. 13) presumably improved her effectiveness.

47. Albert Ellis, *Intelligent Woman's Guide to Dating and Mating* (New York: Lyle Stuart,
1979).
48. See his "Group Marriage: A Possible Alternative," in *The Family in Search of a
Future,* ed. H. Otto (New York: Appleton-Century-Crofts, 1970).
49. *Cosmopolitan* (December 1979).
50. O'Neill (n. 27 above).
51. Natalie Willner, *Bring Back Romance* (New York: Berkley Publishing Corp., 1979).

Among her romance-inducing discoveries: candlelight, country inns, perfume, "lacy lingerie," thick bedroom carpeting, and trails of roses leading to the bedroom. Quite incompatible with romance ("Resentment Ruins Romance," runs a section heading) is conflict between couple members: "Emotionally and physically, men and women are good for each other" (p. 113). To feel sexually desirable, women need men, and for Willner, "one appreciative whistle" is just what a woman needs to give her "confidence" (p. 114).

Both the popularity and the contents of late 1970s marriage advice books (and those reviewed here are just a small part of this genre) may well be evidence of a genuine love crisis: a transformation of social life, marriage included, and a failure of resources for interpreting it or coping with it materially. Christopher Lasch, who has been functioning as the Edmund Burke of this crisis, blames it on feminism: "Democracy and feminism have now stripped the veil of courtly convention from the subordination of women."[52] In his analysis: "Formerly sexual antagonism was tempered not only by chivalric, paternalist conventions but by a more relaxed acceptance of the limitations of the other sex. Men and women acknowledged each other's shortcomings without making them the basis of a comprehensive indictment" (p. 195). The new clarity that feminist analysis has brought to our understanding of couples has been utterly disastrous for the dominant sex, according to Lasch. "The specter of impotence haunts the contemporary imagination" (p. 204). In Lasch's vision of the love crisis, the liberation of women from families means that family units break down into their individual component parts, narcissistically pursuing the maximization of pleasures.

In this supposed era of individualism, the pull of marriage, or "surrogate" marriage, seems to be more urgent than ever. Yet readers of popular literature will find only two kinds of solutions to their own fallout from the crisis. For the open-minded there is the vision of a sexual and emotional marketplace where only the ablest get a "good deal." For the others, there is the fantasy of returning to more traditional marriage forms and gender relationships, whose appeal—in the face of the alternative—is quite understandable. Why have feminists not yet provided an equally compelling choice?

From the chapters on sexuality in *Sexual Politics,* to the demystification of romance in *The Dialectic of Sex,* to more recent psychoanalytic studies on the origins of male-female asymmetry, feminists have produced potent critiques of marriage and existing gender relations. Yet this theoretical work has had restricted impact on this popular marriage literature and limited concrete results. Practical feminist energies have gone into creating friendship and work networks, as well as political, cultural, and economic forms that are rich resources for all movement

52. Christopher Lasch, *The Culture of Narcissism: American Life in an Age of Diminishing Expectations* (New York: W. W. Norton & Co., 1978), p. 190.

women. Heterosexual feminists have not, however, constructed parallel male-female worlds, and have frequently left their ties with men "unreformed."

To reach the millions of women and men caught in the maze of the contemporary crisis, we need to allow ourselves creatively to dream about heterosexual as well as lesbian combinations that promise security, delight, and a framework for bringing up children. In the short run, we also probably need feminist advice books that acknowledge the chasm separating the social experience of women and men as well as the need for forms of sociability that transcend couples entirely. Our advice books must suggest ways that women singly and in groups can cope with today's mess of contradictions. They also have to provide ideas for smaller changes—in child-care provisions, work hours, housing arrangements—which women can fight for immediately as part of the same drive to improve their social lives that motivates them to read advice manuals in the first place.

The love crisis in marriage and couples is one part of a larger conflict being waged in the national arena over gender, sexuality, and the family.[53] Central in right-wing propaganda is the charge that "the family is dying." For the last two centuries, indeed, the family has "died" at regular intervals, as, for example, when feminists 100 years ago in many Western societies were accused of sapping its vitality. Fears about family decline have been easy to exploit and manipulate for political ends, often, but not always, reactionary ones. While Lasch's critique is meant as an indictment of both advanced capitalism and feminism, most of today's predictions of family decay serve undiluted right-wing purposes. American voters are being mobilized nationally not only against abortion, affirmative action, and the Equal Rights Amendment, but also for bigger defense budgets, massive cutbacks in social services, and removal of restraints on corporate profits—all in in the name of the "love, trust, and fulfillment" of traditional marriage and the family. So long as most people can find no meaningful alternative to this fantasized vision of the family, the right will find it possible to exploit, and create, nostalgia for a lost intimacy.

School of Metropolitan and Community Studies
Ramapo College

53. For some recent comments on this conflict, see Linda Gordon and Allen Hunter, "Sex, Family and the New Right: Anti-Feminism as a Political Force," *Radical America* 11, no. 6, and 12, no. 1 (November 1977–February 1978): 9–26; Rosalind Petchesky with Rayna Rapp, *Women under Attack: Abortion, Sterilization Abuse, and Reproductive Freedom* (New York: Committee for Abortion Rights and Against Sterilization Abuse [CARASA], 1979), chaps. 5 and 9; interview with Amber Hollibaugh, "Sexuality and the State: The Defeat of the Briggs Initiative and Beyond," *Socialist Review* 45 (May–June 1979): 55–72.

REVIEWS OF CURRENT LITERATURE

Homosexuality in Perspective. By William H. Masters and Virginia E. Johnson. Boston: Little, Brown & Co., 1979.

Dr. Arnold M. Cooper, New York Hospital–Cornell University Medical Center

Homosexuality in Perspective, the fourth volume by Masters and Johnson, might appropriately have been subtitled, "A little of what you already knew about homosexuality and very very little that you didn't." This 411-page text—filled with moralisms, banalities, and tables conveying extraordinarily little information—might usefully have been edited into a short paper that reported on a few interesting questions. Unfortunately, we have instead been presented with a highly inflated piece of pseudoscience which advertently and inadvertently takes homosexuality out of any kind of broad perspective and discusses it from the generally uninteresting point of view of laboratory sexual performance. The approach is shallow, the lack of psychiatric knowledge abysmal and glaring, and the methodology shoddy.

It is also hard to know for whom the book is intended. If it was written for a lay audience of sexually naive, small-town religious fundamentalists—an audience which I suspect has been extinct for at least thirty years—the book might have a significant function. It reports that homosexual men and women are basically just like heterosexual men and women: they have the same genital apparatus, the apparatus functions according to the same physiological rules, and the things they do to each other sexually are not really different from the things that nice people do; therefore, they are just folks, and one can be nice to them.

However, the book purports to be a scientific study. Here we can only assume that Masters and Johnson have either given up any interest in convincing a scientific audience, or they have been so enraptured by their own activities that they no longer feel themselves subject to ordinary scientific rules. For example, in table after table we are told that data are significant, but none of the data is treated to statistical analysis. There are many pages about the development of the population sample for the study, but we are never told exactly how the sample was recruited, what were the precise criteria for admission to the study, what proportion of a homosexual population the study group represents, or how it differs from other segments of the homosexual cohort. We are told repeatedly that people with significant psychopathology were not accepted into the study, but we are given precious little information to assess psychopathology usefully. Almost every time we are given a glimpse of a case history, however, it is an eye-opener. One brief history (p. 57) of a person "without significant psychopathology" goes:

> Woman Y was a Kinsey 5 in the 41–50 year age group who had been gang-raped as a virginal woman 20 years old. There had been a good deal of physical trauma, necessitating some surgical repair of the vaginal barrel and the perineum. The story of the rape was common knowledge in the small town in which she lived, and her male contemporaries had not only been vicious in their comments, but sexually demanding. There had been no psychotherapeutic support provided by her family, and her inability to cope with the situation had led to total rejection of the male sex.
>
> Rejecting all social and sexual experience with males, woman Y assumed a male role herself within 18 months after the rape episode. She moved to a bigger community, began supporting herself, dressed in a masculine fashion, cultivated a low voice, and deliberately selected a lesbian life. When seen in the laboratory, she had ruled in complete double-standard fashion a committed lesbian relationship of over four years' duration. This specific relationship has been deliberately sought by woman Y, who seduced her best friend into a lesbian relationship.
>
> Woman Y regularly initiated sexual interaction, relieving her partner either by manipulation or cunnilingus or both, but she always refused physical approach or sexual release from her partner. As the partner was aware, woman Y masturbated at night to relieve tension. She maintained both dressing and toilet privacy for herself, but insisted upon freedom to observe her partner in both situations. She did not object to masturbation in the laboratory, but she was one of the women who requested that her partner not be present during the episodes. She cooperated twice with masturbational activity and was multiorgasmic on both occasions.

Who did the study is a puzzle. References are made repeatedly to "the Institute," as if this constitutes a scientific credential. A number of names are mentioned in the acknowledgment but without their degrees or expertise. One is left with the impression that the study was conducted by a group that lacked the training in specific areas of study that would have been essential. The mere fact that the authors consider it unnecessary to cite any scientific background other than that of "the Institute" indicates an airy and smugly self-satisfied dismissal of ordinary demands for scientific credibility or methodology.

The book is divided into two parts: a Preclinical Study conducted between 1957 and 1970, and a Clinical Study conducted between 1968 and 1977. The former is intended to place homosexuality "in perspective," the latter to test the clinical efficiency of Masters and Johnson's techniques in curing homosexual problems or converting homosexuals to heterosexuals. The aim and the design of the study indicate some of the misconceptions that enter into the entire book:

1. An aim is to investigate "functional" efficacy for homosexuals, comparing them in a laboratory situation with a heterosexual population. What is it that one intends to learn from this? Which group is more exhibitionistic? Whether, in fact, homosexuals or heterosexuals have better physiological apparatus? The authors never state what it is they think they will learn, but they look for statistical differences which they hope will be interesting. The absence of any intelligent premises makes all the rumbling apparatus of "study" seem ludicrous.

2. Masters and Johnson promise us a study of fantasy because "the experience of the research team in the original heterosexual research project had indicated that study subjects participating in a laboratory investigation were, after becoming comfortable with the research team and secure in the research environment, willing to share subjective material with unusual freedom and spontaneity" (p. 5). What they mean by "unusual freedom or spontaneity" is mysterious, since thousands of psychiatrists have been collecting fantasy material about sex for a long time. The authors' lack of sophistication concerning the nature of fantasy and their inability to derive something meaningful from fantasy material is too apparent.

3. Masters and Johnson state that "any investigation of homosexual response patterns gains particular perspective when related to equivalent data reflecting heterosexual response patterns" (p. 6). What this means is totally murky. Do they think homosexuals are or are not different from heterosexuals? What perspective is gained? And what is significant about response patterns isolated from all other aspects of sexual activity?

4. Recruitment was conducted during the 1960s, allegedly on a national level, through word-of-mouth networks among stable couples, focusing on the academic community and insuring a largely middle-class population. With screening intended to exclude almost everybody who had erective or orgastic uncertainty, or instability of coupleship, the project begins to study functional efficacy, which means, simply, how successfully in the laboratory one can carry out a variety of sexual acts: for example, masturbation and coition, cunnilingus, and fellatio. Three-quarters of the younger-age homosexuals were ruled out of the study because their coupleship was unstable. The selection process has produced an unusual group of homosexuals. Masters and Johnson blandly tell us nothing about the relationship of the group they are studying to the general homosexual population.

5. The authors state that since "research interest is directed towards physiologic response to sexual stimulation," they want sexually more reponsive subjects to represent "the full range of homosexual preference." Abandoning logic, they then leap to the decision that to achieve this goal, "in order to evaluate sexual interaction patterns with greatest accuracy, the focus should be on couples in committed relationships of reasonably long standing" (p. 10). They have at a stroke ruled out of the study that portion of the homosexual population whose preferences are cruising, "T-room" sex, one-night stands, and so on. In fact, it is likely that if one counts orgasms per week, this "uncommitted" group is far more active sexually. Studying a highly skewed sample, they have done away with any attempt to explore homosexuality in its own right and have focused on a small group most concerned with maintaining the closest imitation of middle-class heterosexual morality. One can only think that this represents the biases of the authors, or their naivete about the gay life.

6. While Masters and Johnson claim they are interested in the full range of homosexual activity, rectal intercourse was a relatively rare event in their study and not part of their original plan. Analingus is not mentioned at all, nor is the use of amyl nitrite, "leather," and so forth.

7. Finally, the authors discuss "sexual confidence," by which they seem to mean the ability of persons to function in the laboratory. One might predict that laboratory performance should be best among those who have the most isolated, least object-related version of sex. Sexual performance for a couple with a genuine relationship is more likely to be a sensitive variable, reflecting multiple events of their emotional lives of which sex is a part. The homosexual cruiser who prefers anonymous sex is, by Masters and Johnson's criteria, the most sexually efficient. The fact that homosexuals adapt more easily to performing as couples in the laboratory is regarded as evidence of their "sexual confidence," rather than, perhaps, their exhibitionistic gratification. However, homosexuals have more trouble masturbating in the laboratory, but Masters and Johnson offer no explanation. Are homosexuals more "sexually confident" in groups and less "sexually confident" in private? And what is "sexual confidence"?

What emerges from all this mishmash? With the caveat that the significance of any of the data is highly suspect, it seems that homosexuals in the sample communicated more and better sexually than did heterosexuals and were more attentive to their partner's needs. Interesting, if true. Masters and Johnson tend to treat this, as they do all their findings, as an innate characteristic of homosexuality, as if it were basic physiology rather than exploring the sources of differences. It may well be that middle-class homosexuals, forced to step outside cultural norms, were, in the 1960s, far more practiced in thinking about and consciously planning sexual activities than their heterosexual counterparts.

They also believe they have discovered a new animal—the "ambisexual." "These men and women reported frequent sexual interaction with members of both sexes and also described the additional exceptional characteristic of an apparent complete neutrality in partner preference between the two genders." They then go on to state, "These individuals were living lifestyles in which commitment to a dyadic relationship had never played a part. Sexual experience was viewed as purely a matter of physical release, and gender was of no importance, in acquiring a partner for any sexual episode" (p. 145). One would think the interesting data about these people would concern, for example, the nature of their affective capacity, ability to maintain object-ties, and incidence of depression. However, Masters and Johnson, after asserting, without data, that these individuals are free of psychopathology, go through their usual routines of testing their ability to perform coitus, fellatio, and so forth, with different partners, producing the predictably meaningless data with which they fill a chapter. The authors, incidentally, warn sternly about the perils awaiting the uncommitted homosexual who will grow increasingly lonely, but we are given no information on the interesting topic of the aging homosexual.

They also describe their successful treatment of male and female homosexual sexual dysfunction. The methods, the now tried and true social learning techniques of Masters and Johnson, seem to work at least as well with homosexuals as they do with heterosexuals, hardly a surprise. More interesting, they claim a success rate of about two out of three in conversion or reversion from homosexuality to heterosexuality, using basically the same behavior treatment techniques. Allowing for a bit of statistical fudging, the rate may be closer to 50 percent or less, but that is still a finding of some import. To begin to understand it, one has to look carefully at their selection criteria and their criteria for change. The motivating factors that seemed to them the most significant include such items as powerful social coercion (e.g., threat of losing one's job), the amount of fear generated by such a threat, previous unfortunate homosexual experience, or availability of a heterosexual partner. We are told nothing of psychosocial motivation. Supplementing these external criteria is the statement that "there are a number of other criteria for defining motivation that cannot be openly published. Public identification of these criteria would prejudice the Institute's screening procedures that have been developed over the last 11 years." So we have secrets. Bizarre!

Several case histories are notable for the amount of psychological disturbance characterizing the early years of the patients, which is incidentally reported. A typical story is that after ten years of homosexual life, someone is threatened with discovery and loss of his or her job and decides to become heterosexual. After a brief search for a partner, this person, with little or no previous heterosexual experience, finds a heterosexual partner who is, within a few weeks or months, totally committed to spending his or her life with the previous homosexual and is happy to join in the Masters and Johnson program, which requires that there be a committed partner for the treatment. Who these people are who fall so instantly in love is a fascinating study in itself, about which Masters and Johnson do not inform us. Almost everyone succeeds in the short run of treatment in functioning heterosexuality. We are not, however, told anything about the fantasy life which accompanies this new achievement. Have these individuals given up homosexual fantasy? That would, indeed, be startling and significant. One cannot escape the conclusion, however, that one important element in the success rate is the selection for therapy of a group of "as if" characters, whose depth of affective attachment is so shallow that they can readily learn to do whatever expediency dictates.

The implication throughout the study is that sex is primarily a physiological performance that anyone can learn, and that human beings, in fact, are performers and behavers whose psychological life is exceedingly unimportant in understanding them sexually. This view, not to be laughed off, is probably truer than some of us might like to think, but that does not justify the almost total neglect of psychological functioning. Explicit throughout the work is the idea that people are homosexual because of heterosexual traumas consciously experienced, usually in adolescent or adult sexual life. Incestuous episodes are surprisingly common. Since undoubtedly 100 percent of the human population has had heterosexual trauma of one kind or another, they can always find something that looks like an etiological event.

The authors go to great pains to point out that they are free of prejudice, without moral judgment. However, they favor being couples over being single, commitment over cruising, and they place absolutely equal value on every variety of sexual outlet, a moral judgment in its own right. One has the impression that their minds have been numbed by the thousands of sexual episodes that they have observed in their laboratory, each one programmed in advance—today it will be cunnilingus, tomorrow fellatio, the next day free play, etc. Activity is all, and meaning is gone.

This reviewer was one of those who staunchly supported Masters and Johnson's early research. There seems little question that they added a great deal to our knowledge of sexuality, especially of its physiology, and most particularly of the female version of it. Their work contributed to the liberation of female sexual preference from male dominance, a process still underway. This reviewer was opposed to the antiscientific pseudohumanism of Farber ("I'm Sorry, Dear"), for example, who opposed the research itself as being dehumanizing. This volume may, however, indicate that Farber was in a certain respect correct. Masters and Johnson seem to have lost any sense of what human relationships are apart from their sexual functions. We are simply told of the progression of sexual events in the lives of their subjects. Masters and Johnson seem convinced that that is important, not just for the purpose of the study but because it is all that they know how to study. It is a pity that a valuable, but sharply limited, therapeutic method is being misused by its developers to provide false justification for their private biases and their views of human nature.

The Hosken Report: Genital and Sexual Mutilation of Females. By Fran P. Hosken. Lexington, Mass.: Women's International Network News, 1979. $12.00

Elizabeth Fee, Johns Hopkins University School of Hygiene and Public Health

This is not bedtime reading. *The Hosken Report* is an impassioned account of the genital and sexual mutilation of girl children in a wide geographical belt of the African continent running parallel to, and north of, the equator. The practices Fran Hosken describes rank with European witch-hunts, Indian suttee, and Chinese footbinding as dramatic examples of culturally sanctioned violence against women. These other examples belong to the past; the practice of genital mutilation, while probably thousands of years old, continues today.

As a journalist, Hosken has traveled extensively in Africa. Since 1973 she has been documenting the existence of several forms of female genital mutilation: Sunna circumcision, excision, and infibulation. Sunna circumcision means removal of the clitoral prepuce and the tip of the clitoris, while excision, or clitoridectomy, involves removal of the entire clitoris, sometimes with parts of the labia minora and labia majora (the outer lips of the vulva). Infibulation or Pharaonic circumcision is a more extensive operation in which the clitoris, labia minora and parts of the labia majora are cut out, the soft tissue of the vulva scraped raw, and the sides of the vulva sewn or clamped together. Infibulation is most frequently done on young girls before puberty; after the procedure, the legs of the girl are tied together and she is immobilized for several weeks until the sides of the vulva have grown together. A small opening is left for passage of urine and menstrual blood by insertion of a sliver of wood or bamboo into the wound. The virginity of the child is thereby guaranteed, and she is ready to be sold in marriage.

Clitoridectomy reduces or abolishes a woman's capacity for sexual pleasure and orgasm; it is defended as a method for controlling women's rampant sexuality. Excised women are said to be more manageable, better behaved, and less likely to be interested in extramarital sex. Female sexuality is considered a threat to male control and a danger to marital stability.

Infibulation, practiced primarily in the Sudan, Somalia, and Mali, is another, even more dramatic, form of control over women's bodies. A woman's worth lies in her reproductive capacity, and access to her body is purchased absolutely by a husband through the bride price he pays her family. The sealed wound must be cut open on the marriage night, and the scar tissue must be cut again during labor and childbirth. Since sexual intercourse is prohibited during weaning, the wound may be sealed after childbirth and then reopened when the husband again requires access. A divorced woman will be reclosed and then opened again when she is sold in a second marriage. The consequences of this extraordinary set of procedures in terms of pain, trauma, infections, obstructed childbirth, hemorrhage, and fistulae (ruptures in the vaginal and rectal walls) are detailed by Hosken with the aid of statements from midwives and medical personnel who have dealt firsthand with the complications and casualties. The excisions and infibulations are normally done by traditional practitioners with knives or razor blades, without anesthesia or aseptic conditions; however, wealthy families have sometimes been able to use hospital facilities for their daughters' operations.

What can be done about these practices? Fran Hosken has been conducting a one-woman campaign to get international agencies interested in the problem. She has contacted religious groups and missions, population planning programs, international health specialists, and women's organizations in an attempt to encourage resistance to these genital operations. In the main, international agencies have ignored her advances, and her work has often been regarded with embarrassment or distaste.

Why this resistance to recognizing and dealing with an obvious health problem? In part, because African nationalist movements, intent on rejecting cultural imperialism, have promoted such traditional "cultural practices." Jomo Kenyatta, for example, defended clitoridectomy as a tribal custom of the Kikuyu in his book, *Facing Mount Kenya*. As a male, he was forbidden to attend the ritual operation, but he still felt able to claim that girls undergoing clitoridectomy felt hardly any pain and that the traditional practitioner worked "with the dexterity of a Harley Street surgeon."[1]

In response to such nationalist cultural resistance, Western countries have adopted a "hands off" approach to traditional practices. Although these countries accept or promote the economic and political manipulation of African societies by international agencies and multinational corporations, they discourage overt criticism of indigenous cultures. As Fran Hosken points out, however, the nationalist movements have been led by a male elite, and the voices of women have been silent in the debate. The burdens of traditional culture are borne mainly by

---

1. Jomo Kenyatta, *Facing Mount Kenya* (New York: Vintage Books, 1965), pp. 140–41.

women, while the benefits of modernization are usually reserved for men. Hosken argues that it should be for women to decide whether to defend the polygamous, patriarchal family and those customs, such as clitoridectomy, which are its supporting institutions.

There are now new organizations of African women, such as the Sudanese Women's Union, and new voices of African feminism, such as Awa Thiam's *La Parole aux Negresses*,[2] which can begin to speak for women's interests. Discussions of the dangers of female sexual surgery have begun in the Nigerian *Drum* and the Kenyan *Nation* and are likely to continue as women examine critically their own cultural institutions.

Fran Hosken has now proposed a human rights/health action initiative to organize technical and financial assistance for African women's organizations requesting such support and to establish international cooperation and joint actions with women in the West. Anyone interested in further information, or anyone willing to assist in this effort, should write to Fran Hosken, 187 Grant Street, Lexington, Massachusetts. (Copies of *The Hosken Report* are available from the same address.) Fran Hosken's work is extremely important in bringing the issue of female genital mutilation to public attention. It would be useful if her book, suitably edited, could be republished by a commercial press and widely distributed.

As Hosken acknowledges, the issue of sexual surgery has to be linked to a wider social and political analysis and not isolated as a single reform. Far-reaching changes in social and economic relations are required to provide alternatives to the patriarchal family structure. An ongoing struggle will be needed to maintain and extend the work now underway. The critique of genital mutilation must be connected to the larger aims of the African women's movements and African liberation movements if it is to be ultimately successful in promoting the liberation of women.

Sexual Excitement. By Robert J. Stoller, M.D. New York: Pantheon Books,

Robert Michels, New York Hospital–Cornell University Medical College

Sexual Excitement is a microdot. Robert Stoller borrows the term from the Nazi system for creating "a photograph the size of a printed period that reproduced with perfect clarity a standard-sized typewritten letter." For Stoller, microdots are fantasies that condense masses of memories, scripts, themes, and affects into instantaneous experiences. Stoller believes that the experience of sexual excitement is a microdot. His book is also a microdot, combining his theory of sexual excitement, a dramatic

2. Awa Thiam, *La Parole aux Negresses* (Paris: Donoel/Gonthier, 1978).

case history of a chronically sexually excited woman, and an almost poetic essay on the themes of mind, mental life, behavior, and psychoanalysis.

The book does not always integrate these themes; they are sometimes dissonant, while at other times they interpenetrate so that the reader may not be certain whether Stoller is talking about sex, life, or everything at once. For example, we learn his central thesis in the first chapter: "It is hostility . . . that generates and enhances sexual excitement." However, more than 200 pages later, in the next to last paragraph of the book, he reveals his view that hatred "probably is the primary driving force in neuroses." The question is not whether this latter point is true but the relation of the two ideas. For Stoller, and most other psychoanalysts, sexuality is closely related to neurosis. For Stoller, hatred is the primary factor in one and, therefore, of course, the other. In contrast, most psychoanalysts would see hatred as only one of the many possible contributing themes.

Microdots are most noted for their connotations rather than their denotations, and this book is no exception. The style is exuberant—lists of abstract nouns suggesting ideas never quite articulated, clinical vignettes interspersed with theoretical essays, and a tendency to the rhetoric of the naive child questioning the emperor's new clothes, with the new clothes varying from Freudian metapsychology (which Stoller is against) to the equation of vaginal with clitoral orgasms (which Stoller denies). Stoller makes clear how he feels, but he does not always do justice to those who feel otherwise. Most of his complaints about metapsychology are valid, but its more scientific replacements have yet to generate important new ideas about the mind. Some women report two quite distinct experiences as orgasms, others do not, and the observers who measure and record physiologic responses cannot tell them apart. Issues as complex as these are not resolved by voting for or against them.

Stoller is most at home with case material, and a lengthy case report constitutes almost half of the book. Belle, a patient, is feminine, exhibitionistic, masochistic, and, above all else, sexual. Much of the case presentation, and apparently much of her analysis and much of her life, centers on elaborate sexual fantasies. These are not particularly exciting, and that is Stoller's point, for he argues that the fantasies that are essential components of an individual's sexual excitement are highly specific, detailed, personal solutions to problems embedded in the life history of the individual. If you do not happen to share that specific problem and that specific history, the fantasy is not likely to turn you on. As Stoller points out, the situation is so precarious that most of us not only need our own fantasy, but we require that it remain only a fantasy (and, although he does not emphasize the point, often an unconscious one). In this regard, he offers an interesting definition of perversion—the ability to remain excited while really doing what one is thinking about. I would agree, but I suggest at least one nonperverse situation in which the participants remain excited while doing what they are thinking about— "normal" sex!

Belle's fantasy, complete with Nazis, stallions, masturbation, dirty old men, Amazon Queens, and more, is carefully traced to its origins in Belle's early life and its transformations through her development. We learn more about Belle than about sex, which is in keeping with Stoller's view that the fantasies related to sexual excitement have more to do with the individual's deepest wishes, fears, and hurts, particularly hurts, than with current sexual desires. The exhibitionistic and sadomasochistic themes of Belle's sexual fantasies are linked to her unique developmental traumas, but unless one believes that her traumas are universal, we are left with a theory of Belle's life rather than a theory of sex.

What is sexual excitement? For Stoller, excitement implies rapidly alternating anticipation of danger and the avoidance of danger. Hostility is the central dynamic of sexual excitement, hostility that is an attempt to undo childhood threats to the development of masculinity or femininity. By fantasy, we convert these painful memories to pleasurable experiences, reversing trauma to triumph, and create the setting for excitement.

There are some problems with his argument. He offers a universal dynamic, but his specimen case is not persuasive as the prototype of every woman (or every person, for he explicitly ignores the differences between male and female eroticism). He describes Belle's childhood as severely traumatized, and if we join him in accepting her view of her past as a valid description of the reality of the past, rather than of the experience she registered during it, we see her early models of gender role as caricatures.

We are left with the question of whether Belle's concerns, centered on separation, abandonment, and what psychoanalysts would call "pregenital" issues, are the universal themes that Stoller believes them to be, or whether his very theory dictates that all we can discover in analyzing someone's sexual fantasies are the psychological prerequisites of sexual excitement for that person. Perhaps in those with greater anxiety about sexuality (and I would include Belle in that group) the fantasies we discover are required for the individual to feel sufficiently safe even to think about sex. Belle's almost total concentration on sexuality and sexual fantasies may be more revealing in this regard than the thematic content of her fantasies. They are designed to salve her narcissistic wounds, and she seems more concerned with her fantasies than with her sexual acts or her sexual partners. If Stoller's point is that no one can be lustful when preoccupied with traumas of childhood, and that one must first repair those wounds, either in reality or fantasy, before proceeding with lust, I would agree; but it is less obvious that preoccupation with the painful memories of childhood narcissistic traumas is the inevitable human condition.

Stoller is one of our major theorists about sexuality. His studies of gender role, transsexualism, and perversion are classics. In *Sexual Excitement* he turns his attention to the core of sexuality, that which gives the subject its overwhelming interest to most of us. He makes an important contribution by pointing out that sexual excitement is impossible unless certain prior issues are addressed, and that for some those prior issues may be so overwhelming that they seem to become the heart of the sexual experience itself. The question remaining is, What constitutes the psychological core of sexual excitement after one attends to the residual narcissistic wounds of childhood?

The History of Sexuality. Vol. 1: *An Introduction*. By Michel Foucault. Translated by Robert Hurley. New York: Pantheon Books, 1978.

Elinor Shaffer, University of East Anglia

"This book makes an appeal to and provides backing for all of us who have for so long been campaigning under various banners for one and the same cause, that of human history," wrote Lucien Febvre, the leading figure in the *Annales* school that has made such a signal contribution to giving a voice to the mute and inglorious Miltons of human experience.[1] Febvre was singing the praises, not of Foucault, but of Gabriel LeBras's *Introduction à l'histoire de la pratique religieuse en France* (Paris: Presses Universitaires de France, 1942). But Foucault's enterprise, nothing less than giving expression to the history of human sexuality, like several of his previous writings, owes much to the same school of thought.[2] Put in the most general terms, the attempt has been to get beyond "the pageant of history," written in terms of the succession of monarchs, popes, presidents, and pitched battles, to the obscure life of the people. The challenge to the "Great Man" school of history is at least as old as Tolstoy, but the present movement has paradoxically required the most minute scrutiny of forgotten records and archives and the use of the most sophisticated statistical and demographical analysis in order to unearth the very materials of the lost history of humanity.

1. Lucien Febvre, "Religious Practice and the History of France," in *A New Kind of History*, ed. Peter Burke (London: Routledge & Kegan Paul, 1973), p. 270.
2. See Michel Foucault, *Madness and Civilization: A History of Insanity in the Age of Reason* [original title, *Histoire de la folie*, 1961], trans. Richard Howard (New York: Random House, Vintage Books, 1973), *The Birth of the Clinic: An Archeology of Medical Perception* [original title, *Naissance de la clinique*, 1963] (New York: Random House, Vintage Books, 1974), *Discipline and Punish: The Birth of the Prison* [original title, *Surveiller et punir*, 1975], trans. Alan Sheridan (New York: Pantheon Books, 1977).

For some writers this has meant the history of the despised and condemned: the criminals, the desperate fringe of the politics of revolution, whether the hunted or—like the female firebrands of the commune of 1871—the hunters. Foucault's studies of the treatment of those defined as "mad" by their society in various hospitals and madhouses from the sixteenth century to the nineteenth, of modes of capital punishment, torture, and the practices of penal institutions, have already contributed to this attempt to understand the history of the "underbelly," the degraded and outcast. At one level, then, this is the history of institutions and their official records: the courts, the prisons, the police force, the hospitals, asylums, and the schools of correction. At another, it is the reconstruction of lost lives.

If religion has often been the object of investigation, research has been conducted through detailed inquiry into the statistics of churchgoing in the dioceses of France, the number of masses provided for by the wills of the dying, and the nature of the funerary monuments erected. These massive and detailed statistical studies have in some cases given rise to surprising conclusions rather than documenting what had appeared to be the obvious. Robert Darnton's massive study of the subscribers to the *Encyclopédie* and of the methods of clandestine printing and distribution of its volumes has shown that the subscribers were for the most part not the bourgeois class but the intellectual elite of the *ancien régime,* who (another surprise) succeeded in many cases in surviving the Revolution to man the new centralized institutions of the Napoleonic era.

Along with detailed studies of regions and mailing lists has come the freewheeling essay that brilliantly and riskily sums up the "significance" of all these minute inquiries for large areas of human concern: for example, Philippe Ariès's well-known studies of attitudes toward childhood and death. Some historians, like Le Roy Ladurie, have done both. Foucault belongs among those who have written brilliant and provocative essays on these matters, rather than those who have done the slogging work, year in, year out, in the parish registers. The English word "essay" is misleading, however; the book under review (originally titled *La Volonté de savoir* [The will to know], translated into English as *The History of Sexuality*) is in the nature of an introductory sketch to a projected series of six volumes on a massive and ambitious topic, and is itself 160 pages long.

Like all Foucault's work, it is short on overt documentation, although it alludes briefly and dazzlingly to a series of pregnant examples, taken from a wide variety of sources. To the characteristically enterprising search for information on obscure or concealed matters that carried the new historians to the priests' manuals used in the confessional, the pious tract intended for servants, the medical case history, and the mute monument, whether the shape of the gibbet or the ossified ornaments of the charnel house, Foucault has always added the telling use of literary examples. Sometimes his brief references are to his own more detailed work, as here to the story, already published in book form, of a simple-minded French farmhand who was reported by other children for molesting a twelve-year-old girl. Even when he refers to a "Rapport médico-légal sur l'état mental," though, Foucault tends to sum up the case in a pun on the name of the hapless farmhand, who "as history would have it" was named Jouy—a play on the past participle of *jouir,* meaning "to enjoy, to delight in (something), but also, to have an orgasm, to come." Foucault is concerned, not with the sexual pleasures of the mentally unfit, nor yet with the sexuality of little girls, but with the "whole machinery for speechifying, analyzing, and investigation" assembled around "these timeless gestures, these barely furtive pleasures between simple-minded adults and alert children" (p. 32; all direct quotations are taken from the British edition, entitled *The Will to Know: The History of Sexuality* [London: Tavistock, 1978]).

It is this "machinery for speechifying," elsewhere dignified with the term "discourse," that Foucault has made peculiarly his own. This "area" is not a geography but an archeology, not of the Mediterranean nor of Arras but of knowledge itself as expressed in language. In this Foucault is closer to the structuralists than to the *Annales* historians; but he has always denied being of their party. In a sense he has combined the two, in a dazzling oxymoron of the mind, and attempted to write the mute history of discourse itself. In one of the most interesting of his earlier books, *The Order of Things: An Archaeology of the Human Sciences* (original French title, *Les Mots et les choses,* 1966), he asked the question: What if "the history of nonformal knowledge had itself a system?" His answer in that work was to explore the prehistory of disciplines which came to maturity only in the nineteenth century, namely, biology, linguistics, and economics, and to discuss them in terms of a common episteme shared by the Enlightenment. He attempted in later works to push back the boundaries and to explore, not the scientific disciplines, with their connotations of totality, rationality, and historical progression, but "discourse," a more anthropological notion of the ritualized stories which entire societies have in common. In *The Archaeology of Knowledge (L'Archéologie du savoir,* 1976) he attempted to press still further away from the investigation of rational knowledge, even rejecting his own notion of episteme in favor of "a multiplicity of vertical systems" simultaneously present in any period.[3]

It is, then, an entirely logical step in his own thinking that has brought him to the history of sexuality, to the mute history of the human body itself, and to the discourses that form our awareness of it. Not the terminology and structure of specific disciplines, nor the prehistory of

3. Michel Foucault, *The Archaeology of Knowledge,* trans. A. M. Sheridan Smith (New York: Harper & Row, 1976). For further comment, see E. S. Shaffer, "The Archaeology of Michel Foucault," *Studies in the History and Philosophy of Science* 7, no. 3 (1976): 269–75.

those disciplines, but the discourses of the physical body present themselves for investigation. This is a paradox, an impossibility, for Foucault does not intend an inquiry into the language of gesture and signal, as in recent semiotic studies of animal behavior and communication. That he might take to be another scientific discipline, ethology. Instead, he remains well within the limits set by written sources, the manuals for use in the confessional, the pedagogical treatise, and the growing body of clinical and psychoanalytical case histories from the nineteenth century, the *scientia sexualis* of modern times.

As it turns out, the oxymoron of "mute discourse" is less complete, less paradoxical than it might have been. Foucault's main contention is that the history of sexuality is less mute, less suppressed than has been thought—that, on the contrary, there was a growing explicit commentary on sexuality, not a repression of discourse, from the onset of capitalism. We did not suffer a repression of sexuality in the aid of capitalist accumulation, as Weber and Freud argued from their differing standpoints—or at least, we did not suffer a repression of discourse about sexuality (and it is not Foucault's business in this book to distinguish between discourse and practice). Instead, sexuality was harnessed and converted into a new domain in which power could be displayed and technology employed. In short, Foucault denies "the repressive hypothesis." As he puts it, "What is peculiar to modern societies, in fact, is not that they consigned sex to a shadowy existence, but that they dedicated themselves to speaking of it *ad infinitum,* while exploiting it as *the* secret" (p. 35).

Foucault retains the economic analysis of the repressive hypothesis but maintains that garrulity was more effective than silence for the control of sexuality. It may well be that during the whole period from the beginning of the seventeenth century until the present day the emphasis on genital sexuality had but one set of aims: to "ensure population, to reproduce labor capacity, to perpetuate the form of social relations: in short, to constitute a sexuality that is economically useful and politically conservative" (pp. 35–36). The means, however, consisted not in reduction but in multiplication of discourse. Foucault thus carries on an implicit critique of the liberal Millian doctrines of "the marketplace of ideas": discourse is not of itself linked with liberty. By the same token—and this is the conclusion of his essay—we are fools if we imagine that we are now "liberated."

The three major explicit codes that governed sexual practices until the end of the eighteenth century were the canon law, pastoral instruction, and civil law. These centered on matrimonial relations, which were under constant surveillance and beset by rules and recommendations. Later, the "peripheral sexualities" came under scrutiny, those of children, the mad, the criminal, as well as all the minor perversions entomologized by the nineteenth-century psychiatrists; thus scrutiny served to "strengthen the disparate forms of sexuality."

There is a kind of break in the story at the point where the church's authority begins to recede and the medical profession steps in. But for Foucault that break is ostensible rather than real. This is so partly because of the nature of the science of sexuality in the nineteenth century: "It became associated with an insistent and indiscreet medical practice, glibly proclaiming its aversions, quick to run to the rescue of law and public opinion, more servile with respect to the powers of order than amenable to the requirements of truth. Involuntarily naive in the best of cases, more often intentionally mendacious, in complicity with what it denounced, haughty and coquettish, it established an entire pornography of the morbid, which was characteristic of the *fin de siècle* society" (p. 54). It was strongly in the service of racism, social Darwinism, and imperial expansion. If after all Foucault is still writing the early history of disciplines, he has returned to his old subject, the history of psychiatric medicine. But, more profoundly, the break was only ostensible because in fact it has been a constant throughout Western history that sex has been placed within "an unrelenting system of confession," whether Christian or psychiatric.

In either case, the contrast is stark between Western Christian discourse and the *ars erotica* that is the essential discourse on sex in some other societies. "In Greece, truth and sex were linked, in the form of pedagogy, by the transmission of a precious knowledge from one body to another; sex served as a medium for initiations into learning. For us, it is in the confession that truth and sex are joined, through the obligatory and exhaustive expression of an individual secret. But this time it is truth that serves as a medium for sex and its manifestations" (p. 61). In our society, "the confession was, and still remains, the general standard governing the production of the true discourse on sex" (p. 63).

To be sure, "penance" has ceased to be the aim of confession. But the power relations remain unchanged. "By virtue of the power structure immanent in it, the confessional discourse cannot come from above, as in the *ars erotica* . . . but rather from below, as an obligatory act of speech. . . . The agency of domination does not reside in the one who speaks (for it is he who is constrained), but in the one who listens and says nothing; not in the one who knows and answers, but in the one who questions and is not supposed to know. This discourse of truth finally takes effect, not in the one who receives it, but in the one from whom it is wrested. With these confessed truths, we are a long way from the learned initiations into pleasure, with their technique and their mystery" (p. 62). We are closer to the familiar Kafka tale, "In the Penal Colony," in which capital punishment is carried out by a machine that slowly incises the words of the sentence into the body of the criminal until, finally understanding their transcendental import, he dies. Given the "internal ruse of confession," one has to have "an inverted image of power in order to believe that all these voices which have spoken so long in our civilization—repeating the formidable injunction to tell what one is and what one does, what one recollects and what one has forgotten, what one is thinking and what one thinks he is not thinking—are speaking to us of freedom." On the contrary, confession is "an immense labour to which the West has submitted generations in order to produce—while other forms of work ensured the accumulation of capital—men's subjection: their constitution as subjects in both senses of the word" (p. 60). Priest and psychoanalyst are administrators of confession, a chief instrument of the "disciplinary society," to borrow a key phrase from Foucault's earlier book, *Discipline and Punish*. This has had profound consequences for literature, reaching far beyond the genre of "confession" proper, as well as for the social sciences.

During the course of the first half of his book, then, Foucault has reconstituted his subject as "the 'political economy' of a will to knowledge" (p. 73). How, he asks in the second half, is sexuality deployed in our society? In order to understand the new technology that has governed sexuality, "we must construct an analytics of power that no longer takes law as a model and a code." In short, nothing less than a new theory of power is required, and nothing less, he claims, will emerge from this series of studies on sexuality. Power is "not an institution, and not a structure; neither is it a certain strength we are endowed with; it is the name that one attributes to a complex strategical situation in a particular society" (p. 93). Foucault's stated aim is to rewrite Machiavelli's *Prince* without the persona of the Prince, that is, to replace the privilege of sovereignty with the analysis of a "multiple and mobile field of force relations, where far-reaching, but never completely stable, effects of domination are produced" (p. 102). Seen from this vantage point, sexuality is not to be described in the Freudian manner as a stubborn drive, of necessity disobedient to a power which can never wholly control it. Far from being the most intractable element in society, it is endowed with the greatest instrumentality and is amenable to the most varied strategies. "We must not make the mistake of thinking that sex is an autonomous agency which secondarily produces manifold effects of sexuality over the entire length of its surface of contact with power. On the contrary, sex is the most speculative, most ideal, and most internal element in a deployment of sexuality organized by power in its grip on bodies and their materiality, their forces, energies, sensations, and pleasures" (p. 155). Of his "theory of power" there is here only the merest adumbration and promise, but his paradoxical stress on the malleability of sex in the interests of other ends provides a striking insight not only into the variety of sexual experience (all of which Foucault appears to consider legitimate in itself) but also into the sense in which it is created by and harnessed to the techniques of repression in "the disciplinary society."

Behind this whole argument lies the thesis Foucault worked out more explicitly and with more extensive documentation in his book *Discipline and Punish,* perhaps his best book to date apart from *The Order of*

Things. For him, the modes of execution, torture, and confession practiced until the end of the eighteenth century, which he illustrates in graphic detail (whereas in the present book the reader accustomed to Steven Marcus's practice in *The Other Victorians* of quoting large chunks from Dr. Acton or Frank Harris is deprived of what he may feel is his due portion of scholarly "porn"), gave way to new modes of social control which only appear to be more liberal. He investigated in considerable detail the arguments relating to prison reform and the new organization of the punishment of criminals. If the old methods literally carried out the sentence on the body of the prisoner even after he was already dead, in order to engrave a menacing message in the minds of the spectators, the new methods established a subtler and more thoroughgoing mesh of observation and control of the entire society. Foucault takes as emblem of this change the Panopticon of the liberal reformer Jeremy Bentham, that ideal prison house of the Enlightenment in which the central tower was designed so that the observer could keep each cell, each prisoner, under constant surveillance. In bringing to our notice the subtle forms of the control of sexuality through "discourse," Foucault is only continuing his argument: it is not only that information about every member of society from birth to death may be stored on microchips—a miniaturized and ubiquitous Panopticon—but "the clinical eye" of which he spoke in *The Birth of the Clinic* extends its gaze and its determining presence into the very bed of pleasure, whether marriage bed, hotel "quickie," or haystack.

Foucault does not single out any group, economic ("workers"), biological ("women"), or sexual ("gays"), for extended discussion. Although children's sexuality has seven entries in his index, "women" appear only under the heading "women's bodies, hysterization of." Foucault wishes to make a general case for the continued subjection of all groups to the disciplinary deployment of sexual power relations, rather than to single out any particular objects or "victims." In the volumes to follow, however, he promises to study the deployment of sexuality through the four great strategies of the nineteenth century: "the sexualization of children, the hysterization of women, the specification of the perverted, and the regulation of populations" (p. 114). He offers some hints of what his further explorations of the special forms of subjugation through analysis will offer. Four privileged objects of knowledge emerged from the preoccupation with sex which mounted throughout the nineteenth century: the hysterical woman, the masturbating child, the Malthusian couple, and the perverse adult. Foucault is even-handed here, too: the disciplinary society created and made use of the sexuality of "women, children, and men."

According to him, it was in the "bourgeois" or "aristocratic" family (we may feel he is intolerably vague here) that the sexuality of children and adolescents was first made problematic and feminine sexuality medicalized; it was the first to be alerted to the potential pathology of sex, the urgent need to keep it under close watch and to devise a rational technology for its correction. The first figure to be "sexualized" was the "idle" woman, on the fringe of the world of work, where she was obliged to figure only as a "value." As other writers have shown in convincing detail (see, for example, the work of Louise A. Tilly), women have for the most part been part of the world of work, and it is a phenomenon of the eighteenth and nineteenth centuries that women should temporarily have appeared as "the angel in the house."[4] It is this moment Foucault singles out: the moment at which the "nervous" woman appears, the woman afflicted with "the vapors." In this figure, the hysterization of woman found its anchorage point. From this vantage point, the "Women's Movement" might be viewed as the latest stratagem in the hysterization of the idle *bourgeoise*.

Equally, the masturbating child or the onanistic adolescent was not the future worker, but rather the well-to-do schoolboy, the child surrounded by domestic servents, tutors, and governesses. Indeed, as Foucault argues, the working classes evaded the deployment of sexuality for some time, partly because the Christian technology of the flesh never had much reality for them. Here Foucault is drawing on the debates about the early secularization of the masses, which have sometimes gone so far as to advance the claim that popular culture was permanently heathen and hedonistic and everywhere succeeded in resisting the Christian call to self-sacrifice. Foucault argues that only in the 1830s did the organization of the conventional family come to be regarded not only as an instrument through which ecclesiastical authority could be exercised but as an indispensable instrument of political control and economic subjugation of the proletariat. The renewed campaign for "moralization" of the poorer classes served this end.

Sex was defined in three ways in the process of hysterization of women: as that which belongs, par excellence, to men; and hence that which is lacking in women; but, at the same time, as that which by itself constitutes woman's body, ordering it wholly in terms of the functions of reproduction and keeping it in constant agitation through the effects of that very function. Hysteria was interpreted in this strategy as the movement of sex insofar as it was "the one and the other," "whole and part," "principle and lack" (p. 153). In the sexualization of childhood, it was argued by eighteenth- and nineteenth-century medicine that precocious sex would nullify the sexuality of the adult through sterility, impotence, frigidity, or the deadening of the senses, and must therefore be prevented from coming to expression. In the psychiatrization of perversion, "fetishism" served as the model perversion, in which one could

4. For a succinct summary of this argument, see Joan W. Scott and Louise A. Tilly, "Women's Work and the Family in Nineteenth Century Europe," in *The Family in History*, ed. Charles E. Rosenberg (Philadelphia: University of Pennsylvania Press, 1975).

clearly perceive the way in which the instinct became fastened to an object in accordance with the individual's history and his biological inadequacy. Finally, in the socialization of procreative behavior, sex was placed between a so-called law of reality (economic necessity being only its most pressing form) and an economy of pleasure which was always attempting to circumvent that law. This strategy is summed up in "the most notorious of frauds," *coitus interruptus,* representing "the point where the insistence of the real forced an end to the pleasure and pleasure found a way to express itself despite the economy dictated by the real" (p. 154).

There is clearly much in Foucault's enterprise that is controversial, much that is questionable, much that is merely sketeched in or even fanciful—he is nothing if not a Parisian *enfant terrible.* Yet even this prelude to the fuller studies he promises is a provocative challenge to a number of received ideas. Let us hope that he will not find, in the ensuing volumes, that sexuality is an intractable element after all, and not wholly to be subjugated to the discourse of Foucault.

ARCHIVES

"I Am Not Contented": Female Masochism and Lesbianism in Early Twentieth-Century New England

Martin Bauml Duberman

The documents which follow have been excerpted from a considerably larger packet of material, the L. Eugene Emerson Papers on deposit at the Countway Library of Medicine in Boston. The material divides itself naturally into two parts. The first consists of the handwritten, penciled notes Dr. Emerson jotted down in 1912–13 during his therapy sessions with Honora Downey, a twenty-three-year-old patient at the Psychopathic Hospital in Boston at which Emerson was a staff member. The second part consists of excerpts from letters Downey wrote Emerson after she had been discharged from the hospital. The first—Emerson's notes—focuses on Downey's masochism; the second—excerpts from Downey's letters—is of unique interest for its information on lesbianism among working-class women.

Beyond the scant biographical details contained within these documents themselves, we know nothing of Honora Downey's life, and of Dr. Emerson we know little more than his dates (1873–1939) and the fact that he was among the earliest followers of Freud in America.[1] By contrast, the literature on the two main subjects of these documents—female masochism and lesbianism—is in the former case vast (and currently in

I am grateful to Richard J. Wolfe, chief archivist at the Countway when I worked there in 1976, for granting me permission to research and publish excerpts from the Emerson Papers.

1. For some slight additional information on Emerson, see the pioneering work of Nathan Hale, Jr., *Freud and the Americans* (New York: Oxford University Press, 1971); and Martin Duberman, "The Therapy of C. M. Otis: 1911," *Christopher Street* 2, no. 5 (November 1977): 33–37.

theoretical disarray) and in the latter case recent (and to date still slight). Given the state of the literature—controversial and/or sparse—it is not possible to generalize with any confidence about the "significance" of Honora Downey's history. Dr. Emerson's notes about her and the letters written by her are immensely suggestive, but it may well take a generation or more of scholarship before there can be informed debate about how "representative" Downey's attitudes and experiences were, before we can place them in any assured context. For now, only the most tentative estimates are possible. I have tried to offer some of these preliminary interpretations in footnote queries and commentary.

Department of History
Lehman College, City University of New York

*   *   *

Part 1

[August 12, 1912; Lynn (Mass.) Psychopathic Hospital]
A relative began masturbating her when she was abt. 8. He threatened to tell her fa.[ther] abt. some childish error if she wouldn't let him do as he pleased & she was afraid of her fa. He used to tie the boys in bed thrash them & she was afraid of that. This relative tried to have connection w. her when she was abt. [about] 12 but was not successful.
A Dr. in Lynn told her she should have connections [sexual intercourse] that it would cure her desire to cut herself.
The reason she cut herself first was to scare a cousin who was trying to have connection with her. He was afraid of blood. She wanted connection last night & that was why she cut herself . . .
Mother never washes; father seldom.
Hates her family.
All but youngest brother asked for "connections" . . .
Stuck a german silver wire in her hand so the surgeons would have to cut her open . . .
The man she went with at dr.'s advice 3rd night wanted her to take it in her mouth so she got up, dressed, & refused to have anything more to do w. him . . .

[August 13, 1912]
Has cut herself 28 or 30 times.
Arthur [brother?] called her a "whore" when she told him abt. herself & she went upstairs, drank a glass of bro's [brother's] whiskey, took his razor & cut a "W" on her right leg . . .
Believes in neither god, devil, heaven, nor hell . . .
Cuts herself slowly to bring out the pain.
Fa. tied her bro. to a post in the cellar and whipped him.

Mother whipped her with horsewhip. Shows mark on cheek.
Family would think it a disgrace if they knew she was in Psy. Hos.
Wants to hug and kiss somebody, doesn't know whom . . .
"I don't think anyone could despise anyone as much as I despise myself."
She almost cried.

[August 15, 1912]
Father loved her much till 5 when other girls began to come. Sec. time
she cut herself abt. 3 wks. after 1st. Bad feeling in head. She had had a
bad headache & bad feeling 3 days when cousin attempted assault. While
she cut to scare him she noticed her headache stopped & thought of it as
a cure. Never felt that life was worth living till yesterday.
Always had these bad feelings in her head. During the worst periods
would sit morose & sullen & noone dared to speak to her.
Hates being fat. Fat girls never flow regularly.
Stuck a pen-knife in her Vagina once, to make herself flow.
Thought bleeding would reduce fat.
Girls in shop used to say fat girls will go it forty diff. ways. Hated it . . .
Mother wouldn't let her wear corsets—became so fat, girls said she was
"up" [pregnant]. Heard of this when she was 16 or 17 . . .
Sometimes she would plan to cut, & sometimes impulsively do it . . .
Never wanted to kill herself; but sometimes didn't care. Once, "didn't
care" so much she almost cut an artery, but the feeling passed before she
had cut deep enough . . .
Yesterday was the first time she thought life endurable, the first day she
was willing to live.
Never flowed regularly, always wanted to.
Father used to beat the boys till they couldn't stand up. Then one of her
brothers told the Police & showed his bruises. The Police came &
told Fa. if he did it again he would be arrested. He took him upstairs &
beat him worse then he had ever done before and said if he told he'd
give him a still worse one.
She used to hide her head in the pillow to keep from hearing her
brothers scream.
Fa. used to kick her, but he never whipped her as he did her bros.
She used to hug and kiss the boarders who used to bring her candy etc
. . .
Says she *knows* she will never cut herself again . . .

[August 20, 1912]
. . . Said she had made up her mind this afternoon never to have re-
lations w. a man again . . .
It was a common belief among the girls where she worked that if a girl
did not flow regularly she would either have consumption or go insane.
When she began to cut herself she thought she was insane.

When the story was abt. the shop that she was pregnant, the girls asked her best friend if it were true. She said it was. Luckily, she never lost a day at work, that year. If she had, they would say she had gotten rid of a baby . . .

This relative began, after a while, to masturbate her sister. This she could not stand & she told him if he didn't stop she would tell her father. From this she discovered he wasn't going to tell on her & so she never went with him anymore.

She has a strong feeling against her mother continuing marital relations with her father.

[August 21, 1912]
Not feeling so well today. Has the queer feeling.
Has a slight discharge, whitish, evil smelling, & staining her clothes. This has previously always preceded cutting . . .
Denied there was anything on her mind but finally I got her to close her eyes. She said she always saw babies when closed her eyes . . .
She told me her *Uncle* was the man who masturbated her.

[August 22, 1912]
Had a good afternoon. No dreams. All right this morning. In probing for the specific reason as to why she cut herself last—it brought back the bad feeling she had & and in the mood wh.[ich] persisted she told the following.
Abt. 3—in highchair at table—wasn't feeling very well & didn't want oatmeal—pushed it away. God-mother pushed it back & hit her over the hand. Caused blood.
When she was abt. 20 bro.[ther] came to her room, made suggestive movements with his fingers. Offered her some money—threw it in his face. "Say you needn't mention this."
Fa. had habit of coming into her room. Broke in the door. Uncle 15.
Bro. pushed her down the stairs onto boards with nails . . .
Blacksmith bro. punched her in side . . .
Time she cut her vagina 3 A.M. Half asleep . . .
Didn't go to doctor because girls said they would handle her and have intercourse w.[ith] her . . .

[August 26, 1912]
Dr. Briggs stroked her arms & breast, an hour or so. First time she ever remembered being sexually excited . . .
Feels terrible—especially at the loss of respect for Dr. Briggs whom she regards as having experimented on her.
"Let sleeping dogs lie."
She thought this all out from my having said stroking arms was a kind of masturbation.

[August 27, 1912]
Dr. Briggs got a "hard-on." Took her hand & put it on his penis, wanted her to "jet" him. Did not have connection, at this time at any rate, though she has done something she has promised not to tell of.
After she left Dr. B. that night was offered $20. to spend the night w. a man.
What Dr. B. did was repulsive to her, but if she had thought he *really* wanted it she would have done anything to please him.
She felt he had forgotten himself for a moment.
With his defection she felt there were *no* good men in the world . . .
Has felt like cutting herself all day, but won't.
It is to drive away a big pain by a little one. She feels so badly over what Dr. Briggs did she wants to take her mind off it.
A doctor in Lynn masturbated her over an hour without its producing the slightest effect. He caressed her breasts & manipulated her genitals & said he never saw such a girl . . .

[August 29, 1912]
The sec.[ond] time Dr. Briggs saw pt.[patient] he examined her heart & lungs. Then he masturbated her breasts & genitals over an hour. It had no effect on her but did on him . . .

[August 30, 1912]
. . . Hated fa. Hurt self. Tried to cut him once—cut self. He said she was out on a pick up. Told mo.[ther] better keep girls in or they'd be coming home w. a big belly.
Beat mother & dragged her around by the hair . . .

[September 2, 1912]
Looks very stern and decided.
Saturday decided never to have children.
Intends to work, study psychology, write, & do social service. Gives herself 10 yrs to become the equal of Dr. Briggs. Regards the wrong he did her greater than that of her father . . .
One of the reasons she gave for not bringing children into the world was her heredity. With her family she felt she had no right to bring children into the world.

[September 10, 1912]
Dreamed she killed her Uncle & was being tried for murder.
Dreamed she had a baby . . .

[September 12, 1912]
She is going to Miss Hitchcock, Welcome House, tomorrow.

[September 13, 1912]
At Welcome House—1 hour & made good so far—Miss Hitchcock likes her—
Said yesterday she was sorry, in a way, to leave hospital.
Is to have a lot of tutoring.

[November 11, 1912]
Wanted to go w. a man last week but wouldn't till she had seen me. Now isn't. Has decided to stay at Welcome House for the present . . .

[November 25, 1912]
Lying awake nights thinking how she could assist girls in the wickednesses.
Never had such temptations till lived in Welcome House . . .

[December 23, 1912]
Sitting in window ledge. Thought of going out & then thought of my saying she hurt herself as a sort of club over people, etc. It frightened her.
Sister Alice probably pregnant: mother asked her to get something to bring on a miscarriage.

[January 20, 1913]
Sister is pregnant.
Much disturbed because she told Miss Hitchcock abt. Dr. Briggs.

[January 27, 1913]
Took sister for operation. Won't come back to see me.[2]

[March 28, 1913]
Remembers once when Uncle had stopped she wanted him terribly at night, to hurt her. He often used to hurt her horribly when he masturbated her. Sometimes when she had terrible headaches, Uncle could stop them by knocking his two fists against her head . . .

[March 16, 1914]
Met her at Pub. Library . . . Had to tell truth to me . . . things that were not true were that she had ever had intercourse, or done the things she wrote in her diary. They were stories she had heard at the factory & had told Dr. Briggs thought she must tell me to be consistent.

2. Excerpt from letter, Downey to Emerson, January 27, 1913: "Do not tell me that you don't want to influence me, that you want me to depend upon myself, and that I must decide things myself. Wait until I have got something in myself to depend upon."

[December 1, 1914]
Said she hadn't been feeling very well. Sexual conflicts. Said it was her difficulty in controling [*sic*] her sexual cravings. Had been going out w. a man & felt she might give in if she went tonight so came suddenly to Boston & wasn't going to get back till too late . . .
Planning on Waltham Training Sch. for Nurses.
Looked remarkably well.

[December 6, 1914]
Still doing well.
Discussed sister. Gives up trying to control.
Feels a little bad when colleagues question abt. cuts on arm, but is able to put 'em off, & knows she must bear it, so forgets.

[July 29, 1916; last entry made by Emerson in his notes]
Has seen that she has excited herself sexually by her own attitudes & thoughts—(Narcissism) . . . [3]
Sees her own bisexual nature & tendencies [see the letters in part 2, which follows]. Speaks of a "sexual attraction" quite distinct from looks. Thinks she herself looks best in a sheet, like toga, but as she can't sleep so, makes herself beautiful night-gowns.

Part 2[4]

[Downey to Emerson, July 25, 1917]
    I am writing to you about this crush business I am getting mixed up in.
    A crush means that one girl arouses a desire in another girl for sex satisfaction.[5] This is,—I don't know just how to make it plain—She acts

3. Excerpt from letter, Downey to Emerson, July 24, 1916: "I feel that somehow I must manage to cure myself. . . . but I hardly feel as if I wanted to take the cure—for it is too strenuous a one—I know now that I myself have been unconsciously exerting a sexual appeal to my sexual self—I wonder if that is plain enough for you to understand, it sounds rather complicated to me—and it is complicated—it took me a long time to comprehend[?] what kept my emotions on the go so much—"
    4. These excerpts are from Downey's letters to Emerson after her discharge from the Psychopathic Hospital. The location of Emerson's side of the correspondence is not known, if it ever existed. In a postscript to one of her letters not excerpted here (May 25, 1917), Downey wrote, "I think that I want you to answer this for I do want to know just what to do. Perhaps you do not know, but at least you can advise me what to do." Though open to interpretation, that postscript does suggest Emerson was not in the habit of replying to Downey's letters regularly and may never have done so at all.
    5. For more on the phenomenon of the "crush," see Carroll Smith-Rosenberg's brilliant, path-breaking article, "The Female World of Love and Ritual: Relations between Women in Nineteenth-Century America," *Signs: Journal of Women in Culture and Society* 1,

like a man would if he wanted to seduce a girl. The girls in the majority of cases do not understand what has happened, or how it has happened that they are crazy over this girl who has played the part of a man. For a time the crushes are practically nuts, they spend every cent they can get on their crush—At first they buy her candy and flowers. They idealize their crush so much, that they do not dare offer her things more useful,[6] but the crush soon intimates to them what she would rather have and gets it, and when her gifts are to her liking seems to be about the time she gets her solid work in on the girls, that is about the time they begin to spend all their time together, even sleeping together if they can manage it. Of course the crushes outgrow this phase and cool off, but it leaves them hardened—and they are not quite such nice girls, as they were before they were hurt.

I was shocked when I realized just what a crush was—I could not see any difference between a prostitute and a crush—they both work in the same manner (practically) for what they can get—

For a few days I said nothing, then I went for the nurse who is the worse at the business. First I mentally dissected her from the crown of her head to the soles of her feet—There was nothing extraordinary

---

no. 1 (Autumn 1975): 1–29; and Nancy Sahli's important article, "Smashing: Women's Relationships before the Fall," *Chrysalis* 8:17–27. I have never been entirely convinced that *all* the relationships Smith-Rosenberg describes in her article were, as she insists, sensual without being sexual—that is, intensely emotional (and to some extent physical) but never genital. Some of the internal evidence Smith-Rosenberg herself presents does, I think, allow for a contrary view, just as certain shifts and ambiguities in her use of key words (e.g., "sensual" and "physical") additionally suggest that more debate on her conclusions is needed. That debate cannot appropriately be inaugurated or detailed here. But it should be noted that some of the material in Honora Downey's letters—such as her direct references to "sex satisfaction"—provide significant data for such a debate. Downey's descriptions of "this crush business," moreover are the first evidence (of which I am aware) that the phenomenon was not confined to the middle- and upper-class women Smith-Rosenberg and Sahli studied. It remains to be seen whether this is a case of cultural "filtering down" ("crushing" affecting lower-class women like Downey later in time than it did their upper-class sisters), and also whether direct references to "sex satisfaction" reflect a difference between the classes in actual experience or only a difference in the less squeamish language lower-class women used to describe what was essentially the same experience. Further valuable additional data for debating these issues can be found in Lillian Faderman, "Female Same-Sex Relationships in Novels by Longfellow, Holmes and James," *New England Quarterly* (September 1978); William G. Shade, "'A Mental Passion': Female Sexuality in Victorian America," *International Journal of Women's Studies* 1, no. 1 (1978): 13–29; Carl N. Degler, "What Ought to Be and What Was: Women's Sexuality in the Nineteenth Century," *American Historical Review* (December 1974), pp. 1467–90; Catharine R. Stimpson, "The Mind, the Body, and Gertrude Stein," *Critical Inquiry* 3, no. 3 (Spring 1977): 489–506; and Blanche Wiesen-Cook, "Female Support Networks and Political Activism: Lillian Wald, Crystal Eastman, Emma Goldman," *Chrysalis* 3:43–61.

6. This suggests an association of caring with the nonmaterial, even the nonfunctional; it ought not to be confused with (contaminated by?) the mundane associations of the male world.

about her & I was puzzled as to why the girls should fall for her so easily—I watched her and analysed everything she did every oppurtunity [*sic*] I got.

I no longer wonder why Faculty disapproves of this crush business. This nurse in particular who gets a crush on two or three girls in every new class that comes in—always the girls who have plenty of money—I went for hot and heavy—I intimated to her what I thought about them. She immediately intimated that there was nothing wrong in them that she and her girls simply liked each other pretty well—I spoke very plainly telling her that I knew just what a crush was & what I was talking about—She insinuated that it was none of my business, but I have made it my business & for quite a while now I have bombarded her with sarcasm & contemptuous remarks—always in public—remarks to which she could make no answer but to laugh and try to pass it off. Then to shut me up she conceived the idea of making me have a crush on her—At first I felt puzzled as to why I was trying to think her nicer than I thought her—then one day when I had made an especially cutting remark I saw something flash in her eyes—You may laugh—but I knew that she was falling for me in earnest and I knew why and also the secret of her success with her crushes—It is simply that she excites them sexually, consciously, but she would do it unconciously [*sic*] anyway unless she controlled it for she would not be able to help it—and unconsciously I exerted the same influence over her—now I do it consciously for I want to make her look rediculous [*sic*] and I can do it—that is why I am afraid—I am afraid that I may carry it too far—but I despise her so that nothing that can happen to her seems bad enough to suit me—She cannot help haveing [*sic*] that sex influence but she can help prostituting[7]—I really can not explain all I am afraid of when I think it over—It is all disgusting and I feel disgusted with myself that is why I know I must be doing wrong although it does seem as if the end I have in view will justify the means.[8]

7. Does this mean "exploiting her attractiveness"? The particular association Downey makes between strange, unconscious powers and prostitution is unclear but is perhaps partly related to the "white-slavery" scare then endemic in the culture. See, e.g., the contemporaneous debate in Congress, "Importation and Harboring of Women for Immoral Purposes," Senate Document 196, 1909–10, which details the widespread belief in the existence of a Svengali-like ring for the procurement of young girls (a belief which in turn reflects the assumption that same-sex attraction, and perhaps all sexual appetite, is demonic in origin).

8. Why the self-disgust? Solely at humiliating publicly another person? Or because Downey sensed that she was negating her own "bisexual nature," as discussed with Emerson (see her letter to him of July 29, 1916)? Even Downey's apparent confidence that the end justifies the means raises questions. Did she feel it "right" and necessary—à la Freud, via Emerson—to exercise control over "natural" bisexual feelings (over all sexuality?) in the name of "civilization"? That Downey housed a double, warring sense of the naturalness of same-sex attraction *and* the need to restrain it seems confirmed in a passage from a letter Downey wrote to Emerson the following month, August 14, 1917): "That girl I told you

This my fourth week housekeeping. I like it very much—but at times it is almost impossible to realize that it is I who have control of everything that the hospital & nurses need—

[April 22, 1913]
I have come to realize that great as you are you are only a man after all, and therefore incapable of understanding some things.

[November 6, 1915; Waltham Hospital]
P.S. In fact I am in such a mixup with my thoughts of the past & present that at times I am very unhappy—at others scornful & skeptical of everything good. . . . Perhaps you will understand the mental condition I am in at present. I hardly do myself I only know that I am struggling to rise over obstructions that threaten to submerge me. I am very glad that I am here and that they placed me in the men's ward. I like the work very much, much better than I had any right to expect I would, and what is best I have very little time to think about anything but my work excepting when I am in bed, then my bones are so stiff & sore that I could not go wandering around even if I were at liberty to do so; which I am not. I would not be able to write this letter today at all only that I happen to have what is called "morning time" off, and there are no other nurses to bother me by coming into my room to talk. Perhaps you will understand—I do not know but I hope you will, and please don't praise me very much until I tell you I deserve it, and when I think I deserve it you will probably think I won't, which will be true—
H. A. Downey

[n.d.; Cutler House, Waltham]
After telephoning to you last night I felt much more contented except for that feeling of having left something untold that I wanted to tell you. I . . . called up someone in Boston I told him I was lonesome. He understood, and said he would meet me in Newton, so I went to Boston by way of Newton. He suggested several things to do for amusement, but I was tired and said so. I said I would rather talk, so we went to his rooms. I knew when I got there that I had come with a definite purpose, yet I stayed. I used whatever sex influence I had. I deliberately tried to arouse a sexual desire in him, by willing him to want me, and by using what sex influence I had. He yielded to it. I knew he would before I went there only I hadn't been concious of knowing it or of just what I had come for.

---

about 'Farrar' does contrive to make me think about her. I have grown to like having her come up to the stock-room after something or other. I do so like the aggressive tilt of her chin when she enters on an argument. (We had one today—I did not give her what she wanted—but after she went I did wish I could have done so)." Maybe Farrar only wanted a jar of jelly, but in my reading the overtones are sexual.

He wanted to touch me, but I would not let him because of a certain bodily exclusiveness I have acquired somehow. I willed him to continue and break down my resistance and he did. He was rough and brutal yet I liked it. If he had hurt me much more than he did I would have liked it. Then I realized suddenly that he was about as hot as I had started out to make him and I thought it was time to stop—so I tried to stop him but couldn't and before I knew what was happening I was quite as hot as he and was wanting him to be as passionate as he could. I loved him because he was so strong. The more he hurt me better I liked it. My arms are bruised, but I love the bruises and the strength that caused them. I relaxed unconsciously, quite willing to give in—suddenly understanding what was the cause of all my restlessness—although of course I had always known it subconciously—I must have—I decided I would take what I wanted so badly and that every time the restlessness attacked me I would come to Boston to him and have him give me what I wanted and what I felt I needed. He was murmuring to me of his desires—What he said doesn't matter—it vaguely displeases me, yet it was what I wanted to hear—He was sure of me because he could see that I was quite as passionate as he if not more so. I at least loved his strength if not him—but I did like him—so I forgot what he was saying. It seemed to me as if I were on fire I was so hot—and I wished him to hurry. My whole body was one leaping pulse and I was in such agony, yet the pain was exquisite. I was mad with desire and could have begged him to give it to me. When he did try to do so all the heat left me, I became as cold as ice & felt absolutely stony. Then I was compelled to fight to get away from him. When he saw I meant it he let me go, but he argued, coaxed & threatened—I don't know what did happen—but when he touched me to do that, such a feeling of repulsion swept me that it wiped out all passion and left me cold. If he had gone any further I would have killed him when he finished and thought me complacent. He could have gone further if he had dared—for I would not have made an outcry and he was much stronger than I, but if he had I would have killed him just as surely as I am writing to tell you about it, and I am sure to tell you everything eventually. He accused me of everything I had done and I admitted the justness of his accusations, but yet could not tell him why I would not be a good sport and go all the way. Why couldn't I Dr. Emerson? and why should I have gone to him last night when I had not thought of it even before I telephoned to you?

After coming back here it seemed as if I could not go to sleep for hours. When I finally did I dreamt such awful dreams. One was that I saw a man I knew coming right through the door of my room, and on his face was such an expression of leering triumph I shrunk from him, but he came straight on right to my bed. I was mad with anger and waited for him, waiting to spring. The next dream I remember was that there was a car in Central Sq. without a motorman and Margaret Wright was going to run it. I saw her in the vestibule of the car and was horrified to think of her even trying to run the car, for she was not strong and has had to wear a brace for spinal trouble ever since she was a child. I said, no she could not, for she was not strong enough. If there was no one else I would run it. The interior of the Car held about nine people. I knew none of them nor could I see them distinctly. I started the car. It was an awful night and the rain pelted down like fury, and in places along the route the tracks were entirely obliterated by mud. I had to go so carefully, practically feel my way along. Sometimes it seemed as if I had lost the track and that we were way off our course but always we hit the track a little further on. Finally we arrived at the end of the route, and everyone got out. I also got out and took care of a patient all night. In the morning I drove the car back to Central Sq. with practically the same experience with the track. I drove the car every evening for six evenings in succession also took it back to Central Sq. six mornings in succession, always with the same trouble with the track and at night and in the morning it rained and rained and there were mud holes everywhere. Always there was that awful fear of losing the track, and of feeling my way through gallons of mud.

I am so tired today, exhausted mentally and physically, yet there is an haunting feeling of dissatisfaction and an incipient restlessness. I won't have to go through the experience of last night for at least another month will I? I cannot do a thing like that very often for I would soon use up the few men friends I have, for of course I can't expect a man to want to see me again who got fooled the way that one did last night.

I know now that I do not need overdoses of migraine when those fits of restlessness attack me. You will say control them. Impossible! You don't know at all what they are like. You may have some idea, but you don't know. I do—and I am so afraid of the next one.[9]

I use [*sic*] to hope that the maternal feeling was stronger than the restlessness, and sometimes I thought it was. Lately I don't feel in the least like mothering anybody or thing. I don't even want a baby. Yet when I think I will never have one it makes me frantic and I try to forget it. Sometimes I succeed—[10]

[June 5, 1916; Waltham Hospital]
    . . . I am in the Diptheria Ward and have two patients one a Graduate Nurse and the other a baby boy 22 months old he has been intubed and extubed nine times today was the ninth—the more I see of

9. Downey is able—in some moods—to face her strength directly and defy Emerson, just as she faces her strength indirectly in the heroic self-images she creates in dreams: running the car *and* taking care of a patient all night.
10. She even has the strength to declare that her "maternal instinct" fluctuates—and is sometimes no match for the instinct of lust. Given the values of her day, this was strength indeed.

him the more I love him and the more I want a baby of my own—This morning I woke up with a positive feeling that I would never have any children of my own—You will laugh and think it nonsense, but I have a great deal of faith in my feelings and prophecies. I felt very badly and still do for as yet I have not seen a child whom I could think would be as good as one of my own would be—I am so sorry that I must wait until I am thirty-five before I can marry for it does seem such an awful long time to wait.

Three more girls have left in my class. So that leaves only five out of a class of sixteen. Rather discouraging, isn't it? I am very doubtful as to whether I will finish the course—not because I don't like it, but just because I am always afraid that I will do something that will get me in wrong with the head ones—and really I am quite apt to do something wrong . . . but not deliberately—

Often I wish it was not so easy for me to learn how to do things. I observe & memorize almost unconciously [*sic*]—and it spoils my trying hard to do things exceptionally well.

My graduate nurse [patient] is a person who has no control over her sexual impulses—and the other night she showed it very plainly—She suffered very much, and begged me to give her some sort of dope which of course I couldn't do without an order and I had to wait about an hour before I could get one. . . . the next day . . . the Matron . . . laughed at me because I didn't know what was the matter with her and the Doctor in service laughed when he read her chart which I don't think was at all nice—if she was suffering from thwarted sex feeling—She had my sympathy tho I was disgusted with her to think of her absolute want of self control when she knew she could not get any satisfaction here—She threatened to get up and get the dope herself if I wouldn't give it to her, and I actually had to pick her up and put her back in bed once because she started to do it. I didn't put her back any too gently either—I am telling you about her for she has my imagination working over time because of a remark the matron made—She said that my patient acted toward girls "as men would like to act towards them if they could"—and she said that if Miss F. had a girl here who was under her thumb she would be perfectly happy—so of course right away I must needs try to figure out why Miss F. prefers a girl to having a man for relieving her passion—It isn't nice to write this, but it is so much better for me to write it then to be stewing over it continually because I do not know the why of it—

[July 19, 1916; Elmwood, Conn.]

So far I have been fairly contented here. I really have not done very much sightseeing . . .

That which I told you seemed so simple to me, does it not seem at all simple now—and I am sorry that it should be so, for if one must sin, it is so much easier to sin when you think you are really not sinning—I cannot think it simple to do as I want, after being here with Lulu for a week and also I remember everything you said to me the last time I saw you—I resented some of the things you said then, but I don't think I resent them now—I know that everything you said is quite true although I do not like to admit it.

Just the same knowing that you are right and that my doing what I wanted to do was not so simple as I thought—does not cure me of what I want so much.[11]

I do wish so very much that I could have gone away as a war-nurse and if ever there is a chance of my going I will most certainly nab it on the first opportunity—I do want excitement and to feel that I am really living—I don't feel as if I were living now at all. . . . I do a little (a very little) housework, sew and read a great deal—I hate Dickens' work and yet I read them—I have gone out on a few after calls—It seems to be that all anyone here in Elmwood does is accumulate babies and that is all they talk about.[12]

The only single man Lulu has introduced me to talked about nothing but his sister, her husband and her children. Very interesting? Not. He ended up by saying that every woman who was married should have at least twelve children and more if possible, for the more children they had the less they were apt to get into mischief. I was so angry I could have slapped him good. He made me feel like a suffragette and I don't like to feel like a suffragette for I have no desire to be one.[13] I was all the angrier for I recognized a tiny grain of truth in what he said. When he was leaving he asked me if I would go to Hartford to the Theatre with him, but I slammed him good—Perhaps you don't know what slammed means—It means to snub some one hard and yet do it politely—What the dickens do people want twelve children for I wonder? I am sure I don't know, but it seems to be the ambition of Elmwood . . .

Perhaps when it is time for me to leave here I will be all over those wretched feelings and I won't want to do what is not right. I do know that just now I am not quite as stubborn about wanting it as I was at first.

[July 13, 1916; Elmwood]
. . . Elmwood is full of Children and Babies. Everybody seems to have at

11. An early example of what many have only recently come to feel about the limitations of the "talking cure": that intellectual understanding of the causes, contours, and consequences of one's behavior often brings only minimal, if any, change in that behavior, and even fails to solidify the will to change.

12. This is another sample of Downey's "advanced thinking," her independence from standard norms—though the independence is unsteady, alternating with childlike deference to Dr. Emerson and with yearnings for stereotypic female roles.

13. It seems more likely, given her unorthodoxy and strength, that Downey did not feel entitled to be one, perhaps because Dr. Emerson (and/or others she respected) had denigrated the suffrage movement.

least two of them and everybody talks about themselves and their babies—and a few think it queer that I should prefer Nursing as a profession, to getting married & having babies—They amuse and interest me very much . . .

I am trying hard to control my sexual feelings and during the daytime I succeed very well, but I cannot control my thoughts and feelings at night. I try hard during the day to become so tired by night that I will feel sleepy & I do not go to bed until 12 but even then I stay awake several hours. I seem bound to have these spells every once in awhile, but never before has it seemed so simply all right for me to do what I want to do and I feel thwarted because I do not do as I wish now—[14]

Lulu is so good and she thinks me so wonderful that I feel ashamed, for I know that she never has had feelings similar to mine. . . . she would be horrified if she knew just how I think about some things.

I am keeping busy and I try to be interested in everything and everybody and I do try to help everybody whenever I can, but at night I am very conscious of myself—and what I want—

[July 28, 1916]
I do want to get to the top & be really cultured, but it does seem impossible for me to accomplish. . . . I do think that all that sexual excitement has held me back and made me see things crooked—I do so want to be all that you & the others think I can be . . .

[May 8, 1917]
. . . I am asking you why you did not recognize me when you saw me last evening in Harvard Sq. . . . Do I not look sufficiently dowdy or respectable, even yet? Do I look like a prostitute even if I am not actually one?

[May 9, 1917]
I don't want joy-rides, booze, smutty stories or to be pawed over by irresponsible men. I am afraid I gave you that impression I did Monday. I do want a husband like you or Dr. Fuller sometime when I am around thirty-five & at present I do want sexual intercourse with a certain person whom you would not approve of.

[August 14, 1917; Waltham Hospital]
. . . I never am as confident about some things as I often look to be. . . . When I went down to School, Faculty there praised me very much for what I had done—which was a sin as my head enlarges so easily . . .

I like to write to Esther Bocher and to have her write to me—To

14. While this suggests a growing confidence in the rightness of her own feelings and values, it is not a consistent enough confidence to allow her to act on them; Downey remains caught between two worlds—between two sets of views about what is or is not appropriate behavior for a woman.

think of her gives me pleasure and lately I have a suspicion that I like her as much as I think she does me.[15]

This letter is full of I's but that cannot be helped at present for as yet I am the most important person to myself—I wish I was graduating next month and could go to the war—I want to go so much I find myself feeling afraid that the war will be over before I will be able to go and that is wicked—for of course I ought to hope that the war will end very soon.

[August 15, 1917]

. . . I have become reconciled to the knowledge that I will do the same things over & over again, if I want to and feel that I must. So of course I don't deserve sympathy—Truly I am sorry that I have ended up so badly and that I could not have managed to stay at least fairly decent—

I am not contented and find no pleasure in anything but the power of being able to do things.[16]

[June 8, 1918; Waltham Training School]

. . . I know I shall never be married until I can feel that I am willing to shoulder every obligation that marriage entails and the decision makes me so lonesome and rebellious. I fight against myself continually—that was why the thought of not being able to reason at all seemed so enticing to me. If I could not think or reason I would be but a spineless creature. That reminds me—Last night the House Doctor came into the Office and as I thought he spoke I said, "What did you say Dr. Brown?" He said, "I said nothing—I was thinking." I said "Oh! was it painful?" He was so mad and I was pleased for he and I are on the war path—because the night before last he told me not to irrigate my patient, and I told him my patient wasn't draining properly and went ahead and irrigated any-way. He was so peeved and I was a little bit scary myself, for of course if it wasn't the right thing to do I would catch Hail Columbia, but I knew I was right. . . . You mustn't think that we nurses have a habit of disregard-ing the Doctors orders for we would not dare, but a House Doctor is different and they do not very often know much so occasionally they have to be squelched. . . . It would be nice if one could always shift responsibilities, but then it isn't always right to shift them. I expect to finish Specializing tonight and that means that I leave the School for a [two illegible words] at least and possible long. . . . for as long as I feel as if I were caged in and tied with invisible ropes it is wiser to get away where there will be more freedom.

15. Is sexual attraction implied? That interpretation seems at least plausible, given such comments in Emerson's notes or that of July 29, 1916: "sees her own bisexual nature and tendencies."

16. A pleasure that continues to abide uneasily, it appears, with a sense that she is unworthy of sympathy, with the self-image that she is somehow less than "decent."

. . . It does seem rather nervy to expect you to waste your time reading my letters, but perhaps some of them will be worth reading—I hope so at least—

[July 6, 1918; Waltham Hospital]
I am miserable—and to make matters worse that craving for sexual intercourse has come back stronger than ever—I don't have to try to resist it, for there is no temptation here, but it wears me out trying to endure it. What [*sic*] do I have to endure it when I must always refuse to gratify it? Sometimes I feel like an abortion—just what I mean I cannot explain.

ARCHIVES

Female Sexuality and the Catholic Confessional

Eli Zaretsky

The document excerpted below was written by an anonymous Galician priest, probably around 1910, at the behest of William I. Thomas, the University of Chicago sociologist, and Florian Znaniecki, the Polish philosopher, for inclusion in their now-classic work, *The Polish Peasant in Europe and America.*[1] It is a description of the use of the confessional in maintaining social control by regulating sexual life, especially female sexual life, and, in material not presented here, by encouraging respect for property. Thomas and Znaniecki present the document as an example of "the methods applied by the clergy to individual members of the peasant community in struggling against the disorganization of the traditional system."[2] The excerpts reprinted here should be read for the light they shed on two different but related subjects: first, the sexual and familial problems which the penitents, mostly women, bring to the confessional, and second, the stance and outlook of the priest.

Although the document contributes to our knowledge of traditional or premodern sexual and familial relations, its greater significance lies in showing the sexual discontent among women in a society undergoing

1. William I. Thomas and Florian Znaniecki, *The Polish Peasant in Europe and America* (Chicago: University of Chicago Press, 1918) (vols. 1 and 2) (Boston: Badger Press, 1920) (vols. 3–5). An abridged edition by Eli Zaretsky is forthcoming in the University of Illinois Press's series on The Working Class in American History. The document excerpted below is found in 4:103–20. (All italics, brackets, and parentheses that appear in the excerpt are in the original.)

2. Ibid., 4:103.

disruption and modernization. Poland, which had been partitioned among Russia, Germany, and Austria at the Congress of Vienna in 1815, underwent a revival of nationalism in the years between 1890 and 1910 (to which this undated document roughly applies). Women's organizations played a major role in a contemporary movement toward modernization, largely directed toward the peasantry, which sponsored agricultural reeducation and the formation of cooperatives; literacy, reading, and peasant newspapers; the use of the Polish language and support for Polish institutions; the spread of kindergartens; and the prevention of the swathing of children. It also campaigned against the use of alcohol and tobacco.[3] The document below demonstrates that other concerns had simultaneously arisen among women. "Sexual questions," writes the priest, "are indisputably those most frequently raised during confession. . . . the priest must more and more frequently answer the questions of women." These questions included birth control, lesbianism, masturbation, and the double standard in sexual and familial relations.

That the document should be interpreted in this way is also indicated by the priest's explicit perspective on the importance of regulating sexual mores as part of the general task of maintaining social order. A key problem raised in the confessional was that of "avoiding a new increase of the family," and from the priest's point of view "sexual abuses (lack of continence)" between husband and wife are only venial sins as long as "the possibility of fecundation is not excluded." Another indication that we are probably dealing here with changes in family life are the cases in which the priest is called upon to intervene between husbands and wives. It is noteworthy how often, and in what ways, his intervention moderates the husband's direct control. A final point concerns the relation of racial thought, in this case anti-Semitism, to the regulation of female sexuality. The Jews are blamed for both the material enslavement of Polish women and for introducing them to an eroticism previously "unknown." Sexuality, from the Polish church's point of view, was spiritually sanctified not only through marriage but through the blood relations of the Polish kindred.

The central theme of *The Polish Peasant in Europe and America* is the importance of subjective values and attitudes to social change. In its own time it argued against the Americanization movement, which did not respect the immigrant's particular culture, and against those progressive reformers who ascribed an "exaggerated importance . . . to changes of material environment [and who] assumed that good housing conditions will create a good family life [or] that the abolition of saloons will stop drinking."[4] In the context of their book, it is clear that Thomas and Znaniecki viewed the priest as excessively conservative, but the extent to which he shares their sophisticated viewpoint is striking. The church, he writes, must regulate "the pettiest questions of everyday life," for all

3. Ibid., pp. 261, 319.
4. Ibid., 1:13.

social action will be inadequate without the individual, psychological transformation which the confessional affords.

Center for the Study of the Family and the State
Duke University

*   *   *

The Catholic confession, according to the intention of the Church, is not only a disclosure of sins for the sake of remittance, but also a means of directing the believers, regulating their everyday life according to the Christian principles as they are exposed by the Catholic Church. . . . The activity of the confessor concerns: *sensual life, family [and community] life* (relation of husband and wife, education of children), [relation between members of the large family and the community], *economic life* (questions of expenses, wages paid to servants, conditions of work, etc.), *social life* (life in the state—question of taxes, of fulfilling duties; class-relations; relation to Jews, etc.), *national life* (Polish language, national feeling, relation to national enemies), *church life* (fulfilling religious duties). . . .

Sensual life. Sexual questions are indubitably those most frequently raised during confession. . . . The regulation of sexual relations between husband and wife is a field of enormous influence of the priest. . . . The problem of avoiding a new increase of the family steps more and more frequently over the peasants' thresholds. And the priest must more and more frequently answer the questions of women, more scrupulous than men, whether washing the vagina after the coitus or using medicines is a sin or not. He must teach that conjugal onanism, use of pills, condoms, washing of the vagina are immoral, sinful, contrary to nature. In more serious cases, he must teach further what can be done with pure conscience (have relations only at a determined time).

Let us take some examples (I take them here merely from the standpoint of the church).

1. A woman complains that children emaciate her and that a physician told her that one more childbirth will kill her. But the husband does not even want to listen about stopping the sexual relation and orders her to take some pills into the vagina before the coitus. She had doubts for a long time and finally went to the priest for advice. . . . She does not want to die, but she neither can nor will refuse her husband. The priest stands before an alternative. If he says that it is a sin, the woman in spite of all will continue to act this way, and if he says that it is not a sin, he will act against the moral law and his duties.

First of all, the priest should question the decision of the physician and send her to another. . . . Then—whether her husband considers it sinless. If he does, then the priest must tell the woman not to touch this question with her husband from the moral viewpoint, but to try to influence him so as to make him perform their relation in a natural way. ... Then he must tell the woman to reject all fears, to try to strengthen herself as much as possible and to have the conjugal relation only at the time when the possibility of fecundation is the smallest (that is, during the period of 10–14 days between one menstruation and another, avoiding sexual relation a week before and a week after the menses), although even this is not an absolute security. ... The result is a normal life of husband and wife and more children. The physicians exaggerate very frequently or follow the wish of the woman in their decisions. The influence of religion, the belief in Providence often plays a great role in dispelling the fear of childbirth. ...

Sometimes the man has scruples as to whether he can have relations during pregnancy. Particularly among the peasants there is a very strong sexual respect for a pregnant woman. The priest must teach him that it is better to abstain, particularly during the first two months, but if for the man there is *periculum incontinentiae*[5] he can, but carefully . . . .

Very frequently people come with questions concerning the quantity of sexual life. How often, whether it is a sin to do it while completely nude; whether certain kisses and touches are a sin and when. The rule is that between husband and wife some sexual abuses (lack of continence) can be only a venial sin if . . . the possibility of fecundation is not excluded. . . .

System of treatment of sexual deviations. . . . As far as my personal experience in the confessional has taught me, masturbation is a very rare kind of sexual deviation among peasants, particularly in the country. In towns it happens more frequently. . . . There is a greater tendency to a normal satisfaction of the sexual instinct, particularly among boys, or to bestialism. The sexual intercourse of animals is usually a stimulus to analogous play of boys in the period of puberty with girls below ten years of age. These offences are habitual in the poorer class of peasants, daily workers, servants, shepherds (mainly), youth as well as older people. Bestialism is relatively rather frequent among the country population. . . . Bestialism happens more frequently in the period of puberty (2%–3%) and then again toward the end of sexual life (1%) than in the period of maturity and happens almost exclusively among men, very seldom among women. . . . Pederasty is very rare among our peasants; it happens almost only among young people of small towns and only in the form of experiments. At least I have never observed it as a habitual vice. Relatively more frequent is Lesbian love among girls, but also only in towns and between servants living together. This manifestation is con-

5. Danger of incontinence.

nected very frequently with a false devotion . . . and limits itself to very unelaborate means.

Intentional abortion . . . happens more frequently in towns than in villages. As far as I was able to observe the causes of this difference, these are: a greater dissoluteness, a looser idea of morality, the question of supporting children, which is more difficult in a town, and finally a greater facility for concealing the offense. . . . Abortion in towns happens more frequently among married women, in the country among girls. . . . On the other hand, there are in the country many vain endeavors to provoke abortion, such as charms, medicines, etc.

The large proportion of illegal children in the country is caused by the greater liberty of intercourse among youth of both sexes, a greater facility of hiding during the sexual relation, a greater intimacy between the master and the servants . . . lack of other distractions. The largest number of illegitimate children is furnished by daily workers and girls serving in manors or with rich peasants, in houses of officials, etc. . . .

Examples: *Masturbation.* A boy, son of a poor farmer, 14 years old, low mental and physical development, father a drunkard. The boy pastures the cattle of the priest. He masturbates when he is in the forest or the field, also in the stables, sometimes as much as three times a day. He thinks continually about it; it is his only amusement and distraction during the long hours of solitude. The priest wants to save him, for this state is even physically dangerous. He orders him to search for other work to learn a handicraft, and helps him to get an apprenticeship with a carpenter, in order . . . to take him from the sphere of dreams into that of activity. The boy scarcely knows how to read, so the priest teaches him, gives him books with descriptions of the world. He recommends also frequent confession with the same priest, the rosary, and company of strong and merry boys. The boy had a weak will but was easily influenced. He was frightened by the physical consequences of his vice and reformed. In the beginning he relapsed, but more and more seldom. Gradually there began to awaken in him some interest in nature, astronomy, finally in girls, which was at first rather ideal. Within two years the boy was reformed thanks to the continual ethical and intellectual leadership of the priest. He began to grow to be a healthy and strong boy. . . .

A woman, married, over 40 years old. Her husband travelled, trading in pigs, and she could not hold out and satisfied herself, sometimes more than once during the night. She knew that it was bad but could not control herself. The priest ordered her to take her grown-up daughter to bed with her these nights to make her control herself. This helped *almost* always.

Lesbian love. A girl about 35 years old lives with her younger sister, a widow who cannot cease mourning about her dead husband. Both are very religious, belong to church-fraternities and do much good, although they are poor themselves (they have a shop in the village and 2 morgs); they sew dresses for poorer people and for children, etc. The sisters love each other very much and for nothing in the world would they part. They have lived so together for four years. There is only one "but"; they love each other so much that they kiss each other and touch each other everywhere, from time to time even very much, "as it ought not to be." A severe reprimand by the confessor and an explanation provoke only spasmodic crying. . . . When one tries to keep far, the other approaches. Formerly they did not think that it was a sin. One of them scarcely knows how to write and count, the other [the widow] has not even this learning. They are a farmer's [peasant's] daughters. Later, the maid went to a convent, the widow married for the second time and their relation was interrupted. . . .

Abortion. [Cases of abortion with disastrous results quoted.] In some cases priests succeed in saving the girls from shame and death and direct them on the normal way. For example: A girl served in the manor and yielded to the teacher "of the lord's children." She became pregnant and came to confession. The priest instead of abusing her (as frequently happens), calmed her, explained that everything could be repaired and asked her permission to use this news outside the confessional and then he would settle it with the manor-owner. And thus it happened. The girl was sent to the town to the hospital, under the pretext of work; there she bore a child which was given to an asylum. She came back and married a driver, "with the lord's favor" [probably a dowry]. After a year, with the consent of her husband, she took the child home and there was no scandal. "People talked a little" but did not annoy her, and the girl remained a good wife and mother and always thanked the priest for having saved her, "for she already wanted to go to a woman in order to lose it."

Many girls in analogous situations come to confession, but the priests do not always behave to the point and frequently by sharp criticism push the poor girl to a desperate step. The social ostracism is pitiless enough in such cases, and if the last refuge—religion—also condemns her, it is not strange if the girl loses courage and has decided to do anything. . . .

Family [and community] life. . . . People usually confess matters concerning conjugal life or bad example given children, but seldom (almost never) confess negligence in the education of children. For example, a peasant confessed that he beat his wife for not keeping the house and the children clean and not caring for the cattle. . . . The priest teaches him how to handle his wife to teach her order in a friendly way. Evidently the means are various according to the economical conditions. Sometimes advice to bequeath a morg to the wife if she is clean about the house and cares for the stock or to buy a pretty dress, and to give a good example first of all and not leave everything upon the shoulders of the woman, has an excellent effect.

A peasant confesses that he quarrels with his wife. It proves that the man likes to drop into the tavern, and that his wife does not like it for she likes money. But he wants to have some distraction "and when one is continually with the women, sometimes an ugly word falls out." And when he returns from the tavern she curses him and he curses her, and she does not want to have anything to do with him and drives him out "to clean his mouth from the smell of liquor and then to come back to her." From anger he goes to a kuma, whose husband is night-watchman, and sleeps with her sometimes once, sometimes twice a week. Then when he returns home his wife sometimes tries to please him, but then he pushes her away, sometimes striking her, etc.

The ecclesiastical law says that a husband (or wife) who has committed adultery loses the right to demand coitus and only a priest can give him this right back. . . . The priest has to find a *modus vivendi* for them in order to avoid quarrels and to introduce normal relations; he must force the peasant to stop visiting the tavern (pledge not to drink) and try to make each party yield a little. . . .

Christianity requires necessarily interference with the pettiest questions of everyday life in conformity with the principle that it is a doctrine which should not only be recognized but also put into action. . . . The task of the priest in general is to maintain in the mind of the peasant the idea of order in the universe (ascribed to Divine Providence) and adjust to this idea the performance of all the familial or economical activities. A suitable treatment of the wife, children, parents, servants if there are any at home, must be based upon this great harmony of the universe, be connected into one whole, one accord in this harmony, so that everything shall be to the benefit of the family itself (of the head of the family and his wife in first instance) and to the glory of God. The glory of God in the conception of the priest and also of the peasant lies precisely in preserving and developing the order which is one of the manifestations of God's thought in the world. . . . Such teaching . . . sows in a mind that has perhaps never before analyzed its social duties . . . a critical sense and view of functions of life as eating, dressing, spending of money, all kinds of economic transactions, the whole system of private economy, the theory of property, and so on. . . .

The relation of the peasant to the Jew. . . . The priests even today maintain, with a few exceptions, the mediaeval exemptions against the Jews, trying on the other hand to inculcate the Christian spirit of charity with regard to them also. But in this they have much less success. The peasant cannot be persuaded by any means that the Jew is a man like himself. And even if sometimes theoretically he acknowledges his equality "before God," he never introduces this theory into practice in his relations with the Jews. But poverty or the need of earning make him often a real

Jewish slave. From this precisely, from this material slavery, moral depravation and social degradation, the Church wants to save and to preserve its members.

Again a few examples. The penitent comes from a poor family of kormorniks.[6] She was obliged to go to serve. She went to the Jewish tenant of a farm. One of the young Jews often accosted her but she felt a disgust toward him: "Though a handsome boy, still he is a Jew." Once in winter she got very cold. The housekeeper, formerly a nurse in Jewish houses, gave her tea with arrack[7] and told her to stay in the kitchen near the stove for the night. The housekeeper herself slept in a room near the kitchen. The girl was dizzy after the arrack and she fell asleep "like a log." At night she woke in the embrace of the young Jew, already too late. For some time afterwards he was good to her and she even liked him, "and they slept frequently together." But when the consequences of this love were too marked, he dismissed her and gave her only horses to carry her to the town. Then the fault was put upon parobeks[8] and it was said that the girl "frolicked" with everybody in the stable. The child was a typical little Jew; I baptized it myself. But the girl became an ordinary prostitute. She was for a time a Jewish wet-nurse, and then "she went with everybody," even without money, more than once in a pit near the road. Sometimes she came to confession but she made the impression of being hysterical and she considered dissolute sexual acts something unavoidable. Sometimes she felt that she was behaving badly, but she always was persuaded that "something [inside] was pushing her." Frequently at night she left her house and wandered about the road giving herself to everybody who accosted her. Aside from this she was normal. . . .

Another girl allowed heself to be tempted by a richer Jew, a bachelor, who rented a room from the Jewish family with whom she served. The girl had a weak point; she liked to dress herself. He promised her a dress and also to give her medicine to avoid a child. She received the dress all right, but when he got tired of her he moved away and sent her to his friend. The latter promised to marry her (though he also was a Jew), lived with her for about two months and left her. The girl was very good by nature, she was pained that she had fallen but already it was difficult for her to withstand or to refuse anybody. The Jews have this peculiarity that they teach the appreciation of the body and of sexual relations. They bring into the mental horizon of the Polish peasant girls the erotic element (in spite of the brutality and coarseness with which they treat her) which is unknown to the soul of the Polish peasant and so different from the severe Christian view upon the body and sexual functions. She did not see in her actions the "moral ugliness"

6. Tenant farmers.
7. Alcoholic beverage.
8. Farmhands.

which the Christians usually feel, but only the transgression of a law, of a cruel law that forbids her such a good thing and moreover brands her, particularly for the relation with a Jew. (The sexual relation with a Jew is in the eyes of the church a particularly aggravating circumstance in view of the familial connection established by the coitus, the danger of the child being educated in the Jewish religion, and the "mixing" of Christian and Jewish blood.) . . .

Reformatory character of the confessor's influence. . . . Confession is in many cases a powerful reformatory factor in social evils such as alcoholism, theft, immoral behavior, etc. [There is marked improvement throughout Poland, particularly as regards alcoholism.] . . . Certainly other social factors play also a certain part such as more enlightenment, social organization and social action against liquor-shops. But these factors have only a preventive value. Where the problem is how to eradicate an inveterate evil, confession—the force of religious beliefs—must be added to a common social activity if positive results are to be obtained.

The influence of confession is strengthened by suitable sermons and teachings. They prepare also the way for breaking and converting the obstinate. But confession is always the moment of crisis and even if in individual cases it does not bring a definite victory, in any case it undermines the force of the bad habit. This extraordinary influence of confession lies (1) in its ordinary psychological action, (2) in its supernatural, magical "charm," connected with the fear of the judgment of God, the feeling of the unworthiness of the vice and the hope of pardon through confession. The personal force of the confessor's action is also based upon two types of factors—his natural cleverness and ability to influence others, and upon the magical powers which the faith of the penitent ascribes to him. The method of action depends on the individual, on his disposition and on the force of the habit . . . it must be different in almost every particular case. . . .

Index

Abortion, and the Catholic Church, 329, 330; claims of feminist writers on, 100; as class issue, 99, 106, 109; court cases involving, 33, 96, 97; cutbacks in funding of, 99; feelings of women on, 26, 92–93; liberal laws on, in Communist countries, 110n; moral and social values in making choice on, 93, 101, 103; as universal phenomenon, 93

Abortion speak-outs, 26

Abstention, as issue of female sexuality, 55

Adams, D. B., 200–201

Adam's Rib (Herschberger), 22

Adjacent Lives (Schwamm), 165–66

Adolescence, behavioral manifestations of sexuality in, 54–55, 76–77, 257, 263

Advertising, role of sex exploitation in, 22; *see also* Media

Age adjustment, problems of, in menopause research, 248–51, 254–55

Aitken, J. M., 253

Androgen, effect of, on genetic development, 176, 177, 178–81, 185; insensitivity, 177, 180–81; role of, in sexual cycle, 1, 202

Anorgasmia, female sexuality as issue in, 54, 55, 56

Antifeminism movements, 33

Antilesbianism, 20

Antinatalist policies, 113

Anton, Kate Scott, 82

Anukite Ihanblapi (Double woman cult), 118, 124–25

Appetites (Schor), 172–73

Appetitional theory of sexual motivation, 38, 42–44

Archaeology of Knowledge, The (Foucault), 301

Ariès, Philippe, 300

Aronoff, Michael S., 192–211

Artificial uteruses, 108n

Asexual motherhood, definition of, 224–25n; ideology of, 226, 238–40; and maternal sexuality, 224–40

Asso, Doreen, 231

Atkinson, Ti-Grace, 29

Atwood, Margaret, 170, 174

Autosexual activity, increase in, in midcycle menstrual phase, 201

Awakening, The (Chopin), 88

Bacdayan, A. A., 119

Bach, George, 274

Bachy, Victory, 140

Baker, Susan W., 175–91

Ballinger, C. Barbara, 248

Balzac, Honoré de, 150

Bardwick, J., 194–95

Barnhart, E., 273

Barry, Kathleen, 66, 71, 74–75, 76, 77

Beach, Frank A., 38, 42

Bear, Jean, 282

Beguines, 82

Behavior, and the menstrual cycle, 192–211

Behavior Exchange Contract, 282

Bell, A. P., 271

Bellow, Saul, 162

Benedek, Therese, 203–4, 205, 206, 207, 212, 227–28, 231

Benjamin, Ira, 156

Bentham, Jeremy, 305

Bernard, Jessie, 277

Bestialism, 328

Bethel, Lorraine, 88

Beuchel, Eugene, 126

Beumont, P. J. V., 198

Bibring, Grete, 212

Bildungsroman, 161

Biological determinism, 184

Biological sex, 36–37

Birth control, advocates of, 97; and the Catholic Church, 326, 327–28; as class